D1573200

Intelligent User Interfaces

ACM PRESS

Editor-in-Chief:

Peter Wegner, *Brown University*

ACM Press books represent a collaboration between the Association for Computing Machinery (ACM) and Addison-Wesley Publishing Company to develop and publish a broad range of new works. These works generally fall into one of four series.

Frontier Series. Books focused on novel and exploratory material at the leading edge of computer science and practice.

Anthology Series. Collected works of general interest to computer professionals and/or society at large.

Tutorial Series. Introductory books to help nonspecialists quickly grasp either the general concepts or the needed details of some specific topic.

History Series. Books documenting past developments in the field and linking them to the present.

In addition, ACM Press books include selected conference and workshop proceedings.

Intelligent User Interfaces

Edited by
Joseph W. Sullivan
Sherman W. Tyler

Artificial Intelligence Center
Research and Development Division
Lockheed Missiles and Space Company, Inc.

ACM Press
New York, New York

Addison-Wesley Publishing Company

Reading, Massachusetts • Menlo Park, California • New York
Don Mills, Ontario • Wokingham, England • Amsterdam • Bonn
Sydney • Singapore • Tokyo • Madrid • San Juan • Milan • Paris

ACM Press Frontier Series

The programs and applications presented in this book have been included for their instructional value. They have been tested with care, but are not guaranteed for any particular purpose. The publisher does not offer any warranties or representations nor does it accept any liabilities with respect to the programs or applications.

Many of the designations used by manufacturers and sellers to distinguish their products are claimed as trademarks. Where those designations appear in this book, and Addison-Wesley was aware of a trademark claim, the designations have been printed in caps or initial caps.

Library of Congress Cataloging-in-Publication Data

Intelligent user interfaces / [edited by] Joseph W.
  Sullivan and Sherman W. Tyler.
      p.   cm.—(ACM Press frontier series)
    Papers from a workshop held Mar. 1988 in Monterey, Calif.
    Includes bibliographical references and index.
    ISBN 0-201-50305-0
    1. Human–computer interaction—Congresses.   2. Artificial
  intelligence—Congresses.   I. Sullivan, Joseph W. (Joseph William).
  1947–   . II. Tyler, Sherman W.   III. Series.
  QA76.9.H85A73   1991
  004′ .01′9—dc20   90-48188
                                                                CIP

1 2 3 4 5 6 7 8 9 10-MA-9594939291

CONTENTS

FOREWORD

The great thing about the title *Intelligent User Interfaces* is that it is ambiguous: is the book about interfaces for intelligent users, or intelligent interfaces for any users? I think the answer isn't simple.

From the very beginning, user interfaces have been designed to enable users to act intelligently in the foreign (and sometimes hostile) world of application software. Human beings learn quickly, remember well, behave resourcefully, and exhibit extraordinary patience if they believe they are being treated fairly. There is nothing wrong with designing an interface to rely on these characteristics. In fact, there is no point in designing an interface that does *not* rely on them—if an interface does not require human skills to operate it, the application is some sort of automatic problem solver that does not need a user interface in the usual sense of the word.

User interface technology has been getting better and better at placing appropriate reliance on human capabilities, and computer software has become dramatically more usable. But as software applications become more complex, it becomes extremely difficult to design an interface environment that allows users to act intelligently. In a complex environment, it is very difficult to distill out a set of interface controls that deliver the application's power, but that human beings can learn and remember; it is very difficult to define interface behavior that treats users fairly—does not hector them, mislead them, punish them for experimentation, and so on.

This book argues that though conventional techniques have worked well for the relatively small application domains that make up the bulk of computer software today, they cannot be extended to the more complex software environments that are starting to become available. A new approach is required.

The new approach put forward here is based on the observation that in complex environments people often work in teams, coping with complexity by sharing the burden. People expect their teammates to take responsibility for doing part of the job. If this expectation is consistently satisfied, they learn to rely on it, and some piece of the complexity falls out of their purview. The more responsibility they can reliably delegate, the more the complexity is reduced.

The goal of the technology presented in this book is to promote the interface to "team member," in particular, the team member in charge of getting things done on the system. The goal is no longer to design a user interface that has a complete set of usable controls and understandable behavior. The new challenge is to give the interface some understanding about what the users are trying to do and how they need to go about doing it. The chapters discuss various aspects of this challenge and propose some solutions. The interface must be given enough knowledge of the problem to allow it to take on significant responsibility. The interface must be able to communicate with the user at the level of taking direction and giving advice *about* tasks—if the user has to communicate at the level of detail within tasks, no significant delegation has taken place. The interface must be able to explain its activities in order to allow the user to build up confidence that it is to be relied upon.

Whether any of this makes the interface "intelligent" is problematic: seeing intelligence in someone (or something) else is a matter of expectation and perception. A user who sees an interface perform an automatic spelling correction may view this as an act of intelligence; if the correction includes a passive verification, the user may view the system as a modest and well-mannered comrade.

I think that it is fair to say that it is the user who makes the interface intelligent. But more and more, it will also be the interface that makes the user intelligent. It comes back to expectations: mutual expectations. Users will expect interfaces to know about the system, and to help them perform their tasks; and interfaces will expect users to give them responsibility and to value their suggestions and guidance.

WILLIAM MARK
Chief Scientist
Lockheed AI Center

PREFACE

This book explores the state of the art in intelligent user interfaces research. It has been prompted, in large part, by a compelling practical need. As the computer systems we build become more complex and begin to achieve the ability to reason and make decisions on their own (through the use of artificial intelligence technology), the role of the computer-human interface (CHI) is increasingly move critical to overall system performance. Concomitant with this growing complexity, the interface is becoming more difficult and time-consuming to build. Much of CHI research to date has dealt with interfaces to computer applications such as spreadsheets, text editors, and the like because these represented the typical target systems of users through the early 1980s. These types of interfaces are characterized by a fairly small command set and narrow scope of system functionality.

The research literature amply supports the contention that, even for these apparently straightforward applications, the interfaces must be well thought out if they are to be easy to use and understand. The systems currently being built for aerospace and military applications (e.g., the NASA Space Station and the DARPA Pilot's Associate Program) exemplify a whole new set of interface issues that will need to be addressed if humans are going to be effective and efficient users of such systems. These systems are characterized by large amounts of information to be conveyed and understood, complex task structures, real-time performance characteristics, and incorporation of autonomous or semiautonomous agents. Interfaces to such systems are going to exceed the capabilities currently provided by, for example, the

Macintosh direct manipulation type interface. It is in these situations that we believe intelligent interfaces will serve an important and necessary role.

In the fall of 1983, Edwina Rissland hosted a small conference entitled *Intelligent User Interfaces*. At this conference the participants discussed a number of issues concerning the necessary features of an intelligent interface. Several implemented systems discussed at the conference (e.g., ZOG, RABBIT, TINKER, POISE, and BALSA) contained some of the features of an intelligent interface but would not themselves be characterized as intelligent interfaces.

Nearly five years later, in March 1988, another group of researchers met in Monterey, California to participate in the workshop entitled *Architectures for Intelligent Interfaces: Elements and Prototypes*. An important criterion for participation in this workshop was that the attendees be prepared to discuss demonstrable implementations of their theoretical and empirical work on intelligent interfaces. It was our belief that if this area of joint artificial intelligence and cognitive science research is to be taken seriously, it was imperative to show substantive progress since 1983. In this regard we believe the workshop was a major success.

In order to make the results of this workshop available to the broader research community (both AI and CHI) we decided to select, through a peer review process, a subset of those conference papers to be revised and expanded for publication in a book that would capture the current state of research in intelligent user interfaces. The chapters in this book incorporate the authors' latest results and provide a more detailed description of their work. As attested to by the collection of chapters contained in this volume, we feel there has been great progress in making intelligent interfaces a demonstrable technology. The sections of the book present implementations of interfaces that adapt to individual users, recognize user plans, provide multimodal communication capability, dynamically generate presentations of information, and provide a number of tools to facilitate the construction of intelligent interfaces. Intelligent interfaces research is maturing from a purely academic pursuit to an implementable reality. This should not be taken as an indication that the technology is fully mature and ready for widespread application. Rather, it means that it is now possible to further test the concepts by incorporating them within the framework of existing computational intelligent interface environments and to begin empirically evaluating the effectiveness of such systems.

In the future, we look for the beginning of more interaction and cross-fertilization between the growing intelligent interface researcher community and intelligent training researcher community. They share many underlying technologies (e.g., user models, domain models). The combination of these two areas offers a powerful capability in which one system could both support the use of a complex system as well as provide training to new users and retraining to experienced users when upgrades are made to the system. Much exciting interaction and research lies ahead.

ACKNOWLEDGMENTS

We would like to thank the ACM Special Interest Group in Computer-Human Interaction (SigCHI), the American Association for Artificial Intelligence (AAAI), and Lockheed Corporation for their support and cooperation, making possible the workshop on *Architectures for Intelligent Interfaces: Elements and Prototypes*. We would also like to thank the reviewers, Anthony Norcio, University of Maryland, Raymond Kirsch, LaSalle University, and Philip Hayes, Carnegie Group, Inc. for the many insightful suggestions they had for improving and focusing the chapters. Special thanks to Peter Gordon and Helen Goldstein of Addison-Wesley for making our journey through the publication process an enjoyable one. Peter began the journey with us from the beginning stages of planning the workshop. We think his early involvement greatly enhanced the quality of the final product—this book. Finally, we owe a great deal of gratitude and appreciation to Jon Schlossberg, who did a tremendous job managing the electronic collection of the chapters submitted by the authors via e-mail and other electronic media, messaging of the chapters (e.g., putting them in LAT$_{E}$X format), and finally sending them on to Addison-Wesley via magnetic tape—a truly paperless process!

Joseph W. Sullivan
Sherman W. Tyler

CONTRIBUTORS

Peter Aberg
Information Sciences Institute
University of Southern California
Marina Del Rey, California

Yigal Arens
Information Sciences Institute
University of Southern California
Marina Del Rey, California

Jeffrey G. Bonar
Guidance Technology
Pittsburgh, Pennsylvania

David N. Chin
Department of Information and
  Computer Sciences
University of Hawaii at Manoa
Honolulu, Hawaii

Phillip R. Cohen
SRI International
Menlo Park, California

Linda K. Cook
Lockheed AI Center
Palo Alto, California

Allen Cypher
Intelligent Applications
Apple Computer, Inc.
Cupertino, California

Michael DeBellis
Information Sciences Institute
University of Southern California
Marina Del Rey, California

Steven Feiner
Department of Computer
  Science
Columbia University
New York, New York

Tim Finin
Paoli Research Center
Unisys Corporation
Paoli, Pennsylvania

James D. Foley
Department of EE & Computer
  Science
George Washington University
Washington, DC

Robert A. Gargan, Jr.
Lockheed AI Center
Palo Alto, California

Jonathan Grudin
Microelectroiinics & Computer
  Technology Corporation
Austin, Texas

William Hill
Bell Communications Research
Morristown, New Jersey

James Hollan
Bell Communications Research
Morristown, New Jersey

Robert Kass
Center for Machine Intelligence
Ann Arbor, Michigan

Won Chul Kim
*Department of EE & Computer
  Science
George Washington University
Washington, DC*

Srdjan Kovacevic
*Department of EE & Computer
  Science
George Washington University
Washington, DC*

Blaise W. Liffick
*Department of Computer Science
Millersville University
Millersville, Pennsylvania*

Jock D. Mackinlay
*Xerox PARC
Palo Alto, California*

William Mark
*Lockheed AI Center
Palo Alto, California*

Joe Mattis
*Intelligent Systems Laboratory
Robotic Institute
Cargnegie Mellon University
Pittsburgh, Pennsylvania*

Xavier Mesnard
*Intelligent Systems Laboratory
Robotic Institute\par Carnegie Mellon
  University
Pittsburgh, Pennsylvania*

James R. Miller
*Hewlett Packard (MSIU)
Palo Alto, California*

Lawrence Miller
*The Aerospace Corporation
Los Angeles, California*

Kevin Murray
*Department of EE & Computer
  Science
George Washington University
Washington, DC*

Brad A. Meyers
*Computer Science Department
Carnegie Mellon University
Pittsburgh, Pennsylvania*

Jeannette G. Neal
*Calspan-UB Research Center
Buffalo, New York*

Robert Neches
*Information Sciences Institute
University of Southern California
Marina Del Rey, California*

Sharon L. Oviatt
*SRI International
Menlo Park, California*

Elaine Rich
*Microelectronics & Computer
  Technology Corporation
Austin, Texas*

Steven F. Roth
*Intelligent Systems Laboratory
Robotic Institute
Carnegie Mellon University
Pittsburgh, Pennsylvania*

Jon L. Schlossberg
*Lockheed AI Center
Palo Alto, California*

Stuart C. Shapiro
*Department of Computer Science
State University of New York at
  Buffalo
Buffalo, New York*

Norman Sondheimer
*GE Corporation
Schenectady, New York*

Marilyn Stelzner
*IntelliCorp
Mountain View, California*

Joseph W. Sullivan
*Lockheed AI Center
Palo Alto, California*

Pedro Szekely
Information Sciences Institute
University of Southern
  California
Marina Del Ray, California

Sherman W. Tyler
Lockheed AI Center
Palo Alto, California

Wolfgang Wahlster
AI Lab, Department of Computer
  Science
University Des Saarlandes
Saarbruecken, Germany

Wayne T. Wilner
Bell Communications Research
Morristown, New Jersey

Kent Wittenburg
Microelectronics & Computer
  Technology Corporation
Austin, Texas

David Wroblewski
Microelectronics & Computer
  Technology Corporation
Austin, Texas

John Yen
Department of Computer Science
Texas A&M University
College Station, Texas

Robert L. Young
Schlumberger Laboratory for
  Computer Science
Austin, Texas

CHAPTER 1

INTRODUCTION

JAMES R. MILLER
Hewlett Packard Laboratories

JOSEPH W. SULLIVAN *and* **SHERMAN W. TYLER**
Lockheed AI Center, Research and Development Division

Intelligent interface research offers a particular perspective on human-computer interaction (HCI). To some extent, that perspective is no different than that of any other part of HCI—it addresses the same questions that have driven research in the general area of user interfaces for the past ten years:

- How can interaction be made clearer and more efficient?
- How can interfaces offer better support for their users' tasks, plans, and goals?
- How can information be presented more effectively?
- How can the design and implementation of good interfaces be made easier?

Explaining why a particular interface should be called an "intelligent interface" is as difficult as describing "where the AI is" in an expert system. However, one thing that makes research on intelligent interfaces stand out is its belief that artificial intelligence (AI) techniques offer significant leverage on the user interface problems described above. This belief is founded on a set of techniques that ease the solution of large, complex problems that challenge solution through algorithmic techniques. The utility of these techniques can come from a number of sources. It may be a matter of efficiency—a solution might be computable through traditional algorithms, but the size of the search space makes this approach impractical and requires knowledge, and reasoning techniques utilizing that knowledge, to prune the search space to a manageable size. It may also be a matter of effectiveness—a knowledge-representation language may be the clearest way to capture the information relevant to the problem and may increase the modularity and enhance the extensibility of the system. Finally, it may be a matter of generality—being able to factor out the knowledge about a particular problem from the problem-solving techniques that produce a solution and to create other systems for other similar problems by adding the knowledge relevant to this problem to the general reasoning component. Intelligent interface research starts with this technological basis, and looks toward the question of how interfaces can be improved, for both users and developers, by the use of these techniques.

1.1 WHAT'S NEW?

The general idea of an intelligent interface is certainly nothing new. Some of the oldest work in AI, including most of that on natural language and much of the work on problem solving as well, amounts to research on intelligent interfaces: how might people interact with systems capable of solving large, complex problems?

So how has this field evolved in the past thirty years? One set of changes has been gradual, a matter of evolutionary improvements. There has been steady progress on knowledge representation and reasoning, and the field of human-computer interaction has developed as both a scientific discipline and a source of solutions to practical user interface problems. And, of course, this area has benefited from advances in basic computer infrastructure—speed, memory, networking, and the like.

However, another set of changes has been more profound. From an interface perspective, the early work on intelligent interfaces was dominated by the metaphor of natural language-like discourse: the user asks questions, and the computer replies. This vision was strongly reinforced by the interface technology of the times, the teletype. If all you have is a teletype, it's difficult to think of any metaphor for interaction except one of conversation. The natural-language metaphor was further reinforced by the interest in and research on natural-language understanding. The initial successes in that area promoted a compelling, almost romantic vision of how people might interact with the systems they were building—people would work with the humanlike agent behind the natural-language system just as they interacted with other people, through query and response.

This vision has shifted considerably in recent years. In particular, the development of graphical interfaces has changed everything, especially in coming at a time when natural-language understanding has remained a challenging area of research rather than a source of easily applicable interface technology. The availability of inexpensive graphics has meant that interfaces need no longer be bound to a linguistic style of interaction, in which task and domain concepts can be referred to only by name or description. Instead, the the domain of the interface can be depicted graphically, with the important concepts explicitly presented and directly manipulable [Hutchins86]. This benefits users by providing them with clear and powerful means of interaction. In addition, graphical interfaces can make it easier for intelligent systems to determine the meaning underlying users' actions: instead of having to search for the meaning in a natural-language statement, a graphical interface can be built around the important concepts in the task and domain at hand, making the intent of a user's actions immediately accessible to an underlying reasoning system. This is not to say that direct manipulation interfaces are always better than natural language or other agent-oriented interfaces: one of the central intelligent interface research topics is to understand the relative strengths of these metaphors and to learn how linguistic notions of conversation and dialogue can be incorporated into graphical interfaces [Cohen89]. The creative tension between these two approaches is an important and ultimately positive aspect of intelligent interface research and follows from a basic set of propositions about the nature of HCI and how progress in that field will be made.

1.2 UNDERLYING PROPOSITIONS OF INTELLIGENT INTERFACE RESEARCH

The first proposition is that *serious interface problems are ultimately semantic problems*. By now, enough progress in HCI has been made that there is no longer any reason for interfaces to be flawed by such problems as inadequate menu selection techniques—remember having to select an item from a menu by typing a seemingly random letter instead of clicking a mouse on the item?— or inconsistent and confusing command languages. The problems that continue to challenge interface designers are matters of how well an interface addresses the semantics of its task and problem domain and addresses its users' knowledge and abilities. Basic guidelines of good interface design are known: provide direct access to the concepts that users associate with work in the domain, and provide appropriate feedback to users' actions [Norman86]. The current challenge is how to find the best way to incorporate the semantics of the task and the domain into the interface. Modern interfaces may still have problems with menus and messages, but these problems are centered on the content, not the mechanics, of the interaction.

The second proposition is that *these semantic problems cannot be solved through good interface techniques alone*. The use of the best available interface techniques does not assure the production of a good interface; a good menu system cannot make up for a poor task analysis. Success in interface design comes when an interface properly addresses the semantics of its users' tasks

and domains. If the interface fails to reflect these semantics, a variety of interaction problems can occur. Users may be barraged with interaction options,
many of which may be irrelevant to their particular tasks, and the interface may produce vague messages that fail to address the users' exact needs.
What is needed to avoid these problems is knowledge about the context of
actions—what meaning a particular sequence of actions might have—as well
as knowledge about the context of interface objects—what might be inferred
from the fact that a user is manipulating a certain collection of objects, each
of which has its own semantics and its own semantic relations to the other
objects in the interface.

Of course, this is not to say that any interface that offers a good match to
task and domain semantics falls into the category of intelligent interfaces, nor
that these goals cannot be achieved without the explicit use of AI techniques.
For limited tasks and domains, a good designer can identify this contextual
information and its implications and can build an interface around it. What
the intelligent interface approach offers is a more general set of techniques
for capturing and applying this information to interfaces, especially for those
tasks and domains that are so large or complex that it is not feasible to enumerate all the ways in which task and domain semantics will affect the users'
interaction, and to hard-code them into a traditional interface.

Third, *these problems cannot be solved by AI alone*. If we view AI as a technology to be exploited to build better interfaces rather than as a field of
basic research, then good work on intelligent interfaces has all the strengths
of good AI work. A good representation of the domain knowledge is critical, as is picking the right level of representational granularity for reasoning
about the problem. Consider the problem of an intelligent advisory system
that helps users plan their use of a statistical package. If the representation
of knowledge about the package and users' interaction with it is too finely
grained, then the system will have to do extra, and ultimately unnecessary,
work to produce its advice [McKendree88]. The development of the system
will be slow and difficult, due to the increased complexity of the knowledge
representation stage; in addition, more opportunities for error will be introduced into the process, and run-time performance will be poor. Conversely,
if the grain size is too large, the system's reasoning will be shallow and inflexible [Lenat86]. This is an especially serious problem for intelligent interfaces, because the users of such a system are likely to challenge the system's
basic reasoning. These systems will not be infallible: queries will be ambiguous or misinterpreted, and follow-up questions to inadequate answers can be
expected.

However, even if all of these problems are addressed, the most clever
computational system will fail if it does not match the full range of its users'
needs. Computing the right answer to a problem is useless if that answer
is not communicated to users properly. This is largely a matter of interface
design, as discussed earlier. However, it is also clear that the personal and
organizational needs of users must be considered in the design and delivery of intelligent systems. Inadequate attention to these details had a great

deal to do with the lack of user acceptance of some early medical expert systems [Shortliffe87]: they were computationally superb, but their designers failed to address how doctors function as members of an organization, and what kinds of computational services would satisfy the resulting social and organizational requirements. This often recommends a strategy of augmentation, rather than replacement. It means augmenting people and their skills, through a better understanding of the relative strengths and weaknesses of people and computers, and targeting the technology to those weaknesses. It also means augmenting existing systems rather than replacing them and disrupting the social and organizational structures that have grown up around them. This does not mean that software systems—intelligent or otherwise—cannot trigger revolutionary changes in how people and organizations work. It does mean, however, that unless the value offered by the technology is so great that people will reconfigure themselves and their work to take advantage of it, the social implications of such technology must be understood and anticipated in the design of the system.

The final proposition of intelligent interface research is that *what is needed to address these problems is a synthesis of the two perspectives*. Such a synthesis presupposes a creative tension between conflicting perspectives, and much of what makes work in intelligent interfaces exciting is the existence of that tension. The hope is that the field can merge the strengths of AI—a broad, powerful set of representational and reasoning techniques for computing about complex domains and tasks—with the strengths of good user interaction techniques—a means of direct user access to these concepts, providing a broad communications channel between the users and the computational engine. The goal—and what makes research in this area especially valuable—is the resulting synergy between these two collections of perspectives and techniques.

1.3 ADDRESSING THE OPPORTUNITIES: AN OVERVIEW OF THE CHAPTERS

At this point, it is worth reviewing our original set of questions about HCI: they capture the issues discussed by the chapters in this volume, and they offer some insights into how the projects relate to each other.

How can interaction be made clearer and more efficient?

The chapters in Part I address a particular aspect of how human-computer interaction can be enhanced: by providing a richer set of channels through which the user and the computer system can communicate. Extending the realm of interaction from simple textual and graphical techniques to include such techniques as natural language, voice, three-dimensional graphics, and video may allow future systems to approximate more closely the richness of human communication. Especially valuable is the *integration* of these modalities: allowing all of a conversation's modalities to refer to and depend upon each other is a key to the richness of human communication.

Supporting this richness leads to many challenges, both computational and interactional. In particular, the system must understand what sequences of user actions within and between modalities have meaning, in much the same way that certain sequences of words have meaning. This is not a problem in present-day interfaces, because their designs and their demands upon the user are so restrictive that the intent of a sequence of actions can be easily determined. These restrictions might be loosened in future interfaces, allowing more flexible and expressive interaction, but only if techniques are available for resolving the meanings of potentially ambiguous events (e.g., "was that click intended for the icon or the window?"; see Wahlster, this volume). Knowledge-based techniques may be valuable here, in using task and domain semantics to resolve the ambiguities in a sequence of events.

Such a system must also possess basic knowledge about the objects in the interface, the domain, and the user tasks. As in any knowledge-based system, this knowledge is used to interpret these raw events as meaningful actions applied to meaningful objects. However, multimodal interaction may extend the knowledge-representation requirements beyond systems with more limited interaction techniques. One of the important research issues in this area is to understand the extent to which this is the case and to characterize the new kinds of knowledge that are required. Finally, progress in this area is dependent upon understanding more about the nature of multimodal dialogues between people and computers: how do people make use of them, and how do these usage patterns determine the optimal design of the techniques?

These challenges are highlighted by the papers in this section. Neal and Shapiro describe an interface that supports coordinated graphics, natural language, and gestural input by the user, and the generation of multimedia output by the interface. Although the papers in this section primarily address input techniques, the generation capabilities of their work are also relevant to the automatic presentation design work discussed in Part III. Wahlster focuses on the integration of deictic gestures (such as pointing) and natural-language communication, and the use by the interface of discourse and user models to support multimodal communication. The final chapter by Oviatt and Cohen presents an empirical study of the effects of mode (i.e., speech versus keyboard) and degree of interactivity on the structure of the natural-language discourse and offers insights into the design of predictive models able to characterize the effects of differing communication modes on user-computer dialogues.

How can interfaces offer better support for their users' plans and goals?

The chapters in Part II address various aspects of the use of plans, goals, and models by an intelligent interface. There are two general ways of raising the level of interaction to address a user's goals and plans directly. The more traditional AI approach is based around the notion of *agents* [Laurel86]: an active inferential component that examines basic user actions and, through the use of task and domain knowledge, infers from these actions the plans and goals of the user. These plans can then be used to modify the appearance or behavior of the interface to meet the inferred needs of the user, detect and avert potential errors, or carry out certain actions for the user. In this way, users are able to interact with the system on their own terms. They can rely upon the system to identify the plans underlying their actions and act on them.

This general position is taken by several chapters in this volume. Tyler, Schlossberg, Gargan, Cook, and Sullivan describe the potential of user and domain models for supporting adaptability, task support, system understanding, information presentation, and intelligent tutoring. Kass and Finin describe an infrastructure designed to provide general user modeling capabilities to a variety of applications. Chin, like those researchers building intelligent tutoring systems, is concerned with giving an interface the ability to take the initiative when it believes the user has a misconception or could benefit from receiving additional information.

In contrast, the *model world* approach is based on the use of direct manipulation techniques and provides an explicit, graphically manipulable representation of domain concepts and user goals, as well as a representation of the actions that can be achieved by the the system. This enables the user to communicate directly with the system concerning concepts, goals, and plans; it leaves the system with the responsibility to implement low-level actions necessary to achieve these goals. Supporting goal-directed dialogue also lessens the computational burden on the interface by not requiring it to infer user goals and intentions from lower-level actions. The chapters by Bonar and Liffick and by Young both describe work of this style; Bonar and Liffick take this approach a step further by supporting the user in modifying and creating new plans.

This is an area of much controversy; the approaches make very different assumptions about users, technology, and the interface development process. The model world approach has evolved out of a skepticism surrounding whether the goal recognition process at the heart of agency is tractable: as noted earlier, inferring plans and goals from low-level actions is very difficult, both in terms of the knowledge that such techniques require and the inferential processes themselves. The properties of a domain and task repertoire addressed by an interface will have a great deal to say about the ultimate success of such a system. There is mixed empirical evidence surrounding the utility of interfaces that modify themselves to adapt to inferred user wishes, and it is difficult to identify good strategies for deciding when and how to interrupt users who may (or may not) have taken a wrong step down a plan inferred by the system [Miller90]. On the other hand, the model world approach assumes that users will benefit from having to adopt a single way of approaching a problem—that specified by the model world interface. It also assumes that the design of interfaces that reflect the underlying user goals is feasible, and that the implementation of these interfaces can be made simple enough that developers will be able to build the multitude of graphical interfaces that is needed to cover all the user tasks for which interfaces are needed (see also Part IV). This is the tension between "intelligence" and "interface" again; these chapters offer insights into the sources of this tension and the advantages of the different approaches.

How can information be presented more clearly and effectively?

Much of the effort in the design of a good interface is typically devoted to good information presentation. Currently, through a combination of design knowledge, experience, and task analysis, an interface designer determines what information should be presented to the user, organizes the information into displays that illustrate the important aspects of the information, and designs the presentation format of each display. This is a process that takes place once, during the design of the interface, and that is fixed (ignoring for the moment the relatively minor customizations that some systems allow) once the interface is completed. The problems with this approach are clear. First, designers with the knowledge and skills to create good interfaces are hard to find. Second, even if a good interface is produced, that one interface must be used in all circumstances, regardless of the needs of the particular user, that user's particular set of tasks, or the circumstances under which the interface is used (e.g., sometimes it might be more important to bring up a display quickly; other times it might be more important to render it in high resolution). The number of potential choices can easily become so large that it is not feasible to rely completely upon the user.

The research presented in Part III concerns the most effective methods for determining the information that should be displayed and the best ways to present it to users, based on the current state of the interaction. In order to adapt the presentation to the current task, domain, and user, the system must contain knowledge about the task and domain, and about how to present information relevant to that task. Several of the papers address how to make use of different presentation modalities, to insure, for instance, that information will be presented in the modality in which it will be best perceived and processed. This may be especially useful when large amounts of information must be viewed, or when a particular modality offers an especially good match to certain kinds of information (e.g., presenting spatial information graphically). It may also be helpful to present information in several modalities at once, when it is important that the information be quickly understood (e.g., emergency messages).

These papers describe several approaches to information presentation. Arens, Miller, and Sondheimer focus on a presentation design system that contains models of the application domain, the structure of the display and its graphical features, the underlying functional modules of the application, and the interface functions. The system then uses these models to decide, at run time, what output mode or combinations of modes (including natural language, graphics, menus, and forms) should be used to present each piece of information. Roth, Mattis, and Mesnard consider the types of knowledge and planning that are required to generate cogent multi-media explanations. Feiner's paper is concerned with similar issues, but is primarily concerned with the generation of graphical interfaces. Finally, Mackinlay discusses the theoretical and technical underpinnings of the automatic design of graphical interfaces, and what a system that intends to offer these capabilities must provide.

How can the design and implementation of good interfaces be made easier?

The scarcity of designers with good interface design skills has already been noted, as have the problems this scarcity causes during application development. At such times, the right design is not always clear, and the resources that might produce a critical task analysis or one more iteration through the interface's test-and-redesign cycle are in great demand. One of the most significant opportunities in the work on intelligent interfaces is to carry the ideas underlying the work on intelligent presentation techniques one step forward and produce development environments and tools that contain knowledge about good interface design and development techniques.

Part IV contains six papers that address interface-building tools, each of which uses a different method to prove traditional user interface management systems in a different way. Some of these tools apply AI technology to support the development of conventional interfaces, while others support the development of interfaces that apply knowledge about their problem domains to the ongoing benefit of their users. The chapter by Hollan, Rich, Hill, Wroblewski, Wilner, Wittenburg, and Grudin describes an effort to support all stages of the interface development process: design, implementation, run-time execution, and evaluation. Foley, Kim, Kovacevic, Murray describe a knowledge-based assistant for interface design that can generate multiple design alternatives, all of which adhere to the specifications of the interface, and which can then be evaluated in order to select the one that best achieves the design goals. Myers presents a system that uses programming-by-example techniques to enable nonprogrammers to construct complex interface objects. Cypher and Stelzner address a tool for developing direct manipulation interfaces to intelligent knowledge-based systems. Yen, DeBellis, Szekeley, and Aberg demonstrate how the retrieval by reformulation paradigm can be generalized to create a shell for the development of a broad class of applications. The underlying structure of the shell also provides coherence and integration when multiple, interacting applications are involved. Finally, Szekely describes an application-independent language for defining the communication between the application software and the user interface, one that captures both the information that must be supplied by the application and how that information should be presented to users for interaction.

1.4 SUMMARY

The work in this volume brings the field of intelligent interfaces a new focus and brings a new direction for the relationship between AI and human-computer interaction. Much of this focus comes from the strategy of enhancing interfaces to carefully constrained domains and tasks. Intelligent interfaces can complement human capabilities by identifying and augmenting shortcomings in what people can do; they can also be integrated into the tools that people and organizations already use to structure and carry out their work. Both of these directions suggest a broader notion of "intelligent interface" than we have known in the past, but the work in this volume is evidence that using this broader definition is paying off. We now have examples of how intelligence can be added to interfaces in ways that are both significant and practical, giving us not only a foundation for future work, but also the opportunity to observe these systems in use and to refine our notions of how intelligence can best be employed in user interfaces.

REFERENCES

[Cohen89] Cohen, P. R., Sullivan, J. W., Darymple, M., Gargan, R. A., Moran, D. B., Schlossberg, J. L., Pereira, F. C. N., and Tyler, S. W. 1989. Synergistic use of direct manipulation and natural language. *Proceedings of CHI '89*, Austin, TX: ACM Press, pp. 227–233.

[Hutchins86] Hutchins, E. L., Hollan, J. D., and Norman, D. A. 1986. Direct manipulation interfaces. In Norman, D. A. and Draper, S. W. (Eds.), *User centered system design*. Hillsdale, NJ: Erlbaum, pp. 87–124.

[Lenat86] Lenat, D. B., Prakash, M., and Shepherd, M. 1986. Cyc: Using common sense knowledge to overcome brittleness and knowledge-acquisition bottlenecks. *AI Magazine*, 6, pp.65–85.

[Laurel86] Laurel, B. K. 1986. Interface as mimesis. In Norman, D. A. and Draper, S. W. (Eds.), *User centered system design*. Hillsdale, NJ: Erlbaum, pp. 67–86.

[McKendree88] McKendree, J., and Zaback, J. 1988. Planning for advising. *Proceedings of CHI' 88*, Washington: ACM Press. pp. 179–184.

[Miller90] Miller, J. R., Hill, W. C., McKendree, J., McCandless, T. P., and Zaback, J. 1990. IDEA: From advising to collaboration. *SIGCHI Bulletin*, 21(3), pp. 53–59.

[Norman86] Norman, D. A. 1986. Cognitive engineering. In Norman, D. A. and Draper, S. W. (Eds.), *User centered system design*. Hillsdale, NJ: Erlbaum, pp. 31–61.

[Shortliffe87] Shortliffe, E. H. 1987. Computer programs to support clinical decision making. *Journal of the American Medical Association*, 258(61), pp. 61–66.

ACKNOWLEDGMENTS

Thanks to Mark Miller, Bonnie Nardi, and Jasmina Pavlin for helpful comments on this chapter.

PART I

MULTIMODAL
COMMUNICATION

CHAPTER 2

INTELLIGENT MULTI-MEDIA
INTERFACE TECHNOLOGY

JEANNETTE G. NEAL *and* **STUART C. SHAPIRO**
Calspan-UB Research Center (CUBRC)

ABSTRACT

The Intelligent Multi-Media Interfaces project is devoted to the application of artificial intelligence methodology to the development of human-computer interface technology that will integrate speech input, speech output, natural-language text, graphics, and pointing gestures for interactive dialogues between human and computer. These dialogues are modeled on the manner in which two people naturally communicate in coordinated multiple modalities when working at a graphics device. The objective is to simplify operator communication with sophisticated computer systems. As part of this project, a knowledge-based interface system, called CUBRICON (the CUBRC Intelligent CONversationalist), is being developed as a proof-of-concept prototype.

This research is supported by the Defense Advanced Research Projects Agency and monitored by the Rome Air Development Center under contract no. F30603-87-C-0136.

CUBRICON possesses the following critical functionality.

1. CUBRICON accepts and understands multi-media input such that references to entities in a natural-language sentence can be accompanied by coordinated simultaneous pointing to the respective entities on a graphics display.
    a. It is able to use a simultaneous pointing reference and natural-language reference to disambiguate one another when appropriate.
    b. It infers the intended referent of a point gesture that is inconsistent with the accompanying natural-language.
2. CUBRICON automatically composes and generates relevant output to the user in coordinated multi-media.
    a. It automatically selects appropriate output media/modalities for expressing information to the user, with the selection based on the nature of the information, discourse context, and the importance of the information to the user's task.
    b. It uses its media/modalities in a highly integrated manner.
    c. It judges the relevance of information with respect to the discourse context and user task and responds in a context-sensitive manner.
    d. It adheres to respected human factor guidelines for human-computer interaction and information presentation, including:
        i. maintaining the context of the user/computer dialogue,
        ii. maintaining consistency throughout a display, and
        iii. maintaining consistency across displays.

2.1 INTRODUCTION

The introduction of improved and advanced processing capabilities into Air Force Command and Control (C2) systems is proceeding at an ever-increasing rate. It is essential that the human-machine interfaces resulting from these developments not be limiting factors that degrade the performance of the system. Many times this issue is either overlooked or handled much like a retrofit after the fact. Much of the general guidance for the introduction of decision support capabilities has been based on the simplified statement that the overall goal is to allocate information processing and decision functions between human and machine in a way that optimizes the use of their respective strengths and compensates for their respective weaknesses. Many aspects of C2 operations are mandated to be human decision processes (e.g., nuclear enablement, fire control, target designation). In many cases, the processes involved and the mechanization of the interface have resulted in performance that is far less than optimal. Considerable R&D has been initiated to support elements of this critical human-machine interface, but attention has only recently been focused on the development of intelligent multi-media interface technology.

This paper discusses an intelligent multi-media interface system called CUBRICON (the CUBRC Intelligent CONversationalist), being developed as part of the Intelligent Multi-Media Interfaces (IMMI) project. The IMMI project is devoted to the application of artificial intelligence methodology to the development of human-computer interface technology that integrates speech input, speech output, natural-language text, graphics, and pointing gestures for interactive dialogues between human and computer. These dialogues are modeled on the manner in which two people naturally communicate in coordinated multiple modalities when working at a graphics device. The objective is to simplify operator communication with sophisticated computer systems. The interface system accepts coordinated graphic/verbal input and composes multi-media output to best convey information to the user.

The critical functionality of CUBRICON is itemized in the next section. Section 2.3 presents related research. Section 2.4 presents the main components of the software system, the I/O devices, and the development environment. Section 2.5 discusses the CUBRICON knowledge sources. Section 2.6 discusses the multi-media language understanding process, and Section 2.7 the multi-media output composition process. An example of a dialogue is presented and discussed in Section 2.8. Section 2.9 presents some future directions for this research, and Section 2.10 summarizes the paper.

2.2 SYSTEM DESIGN

The CUBRICON system design is based on a *unified view of language*. Language is a means of communication, whether verbal, visual, tactile, or gestural. Human beings communicate with each other via written and spoken natural language, frequently supplemented by pictures, diagrams, pointing to objects, and other gestures. The CUBRICON system design provides for the use of a unified multi-media language, defined by an integrated grammar, consisting of textual, graphic, and combined text/graphic symbols. Input and output streams are treated as compound streams, with components corresponding to different media. This approach is intended to imitate, to a certain extent, the ability of humans to simultaneously accept input from different sensory devices (such as eyes and ears), and to simultaneously produce output in different media (such as voice, pointing motions, and drawings). The CUBRICON system includes (1) language parsing and generation to accommodate the compound streams, (2) knowledge representation and inference to provide reasoning ability, (3) knowledge bases and models to provide a basis for its decision-making ability, and (4) automated knowledge-based medium selection and formulation of responses.

The system's critical functionality is as follows. CUBRICON:

- Accepts and understands multi-media input such that references to entities in a natural-language sentence can be accompanied by coordinated simultaneous pointing to the respective entities on a graphics display

   Is able to use a simultaneous pointing reference and natural-language reference to disambiguate one another when appropriate

   Infers the intended referent of a point gesture that is inconsistent with the accompanying natural-language

- Automatically composes and generates relevant output to the user in coordinated multi-media

   Automatically selects appropriate output media/modalities for expressing information to the user, with the selection based on the nature of the information, discourse context, and the importance of the information to the user's task

   Uses its media/modalities in a highly integrated manner, including simulated parallelism

   Judges the relevance of information with respect to the discourse context and user task and responds in a context-sensitive manner

   Adheres to respected human factor guidelines for human-computer interaction and information presentation, including (a) maintaining the context of the user/computer dialogue, (b) maintaining consistency throughout a display, and (c) maintaining consistency across displays

2.3 RELATED RESEARCH

Research and development of artificial intelligence (AI) systems for human-machine interfaces have focused on natural language (NL) text, speech, and graphics primarily in isolation, rather than in integrated interfaces. With the increased functionality and reliability provided by new developments in interface devices such as speech recognition and production systems, high-resolution color and monochrome graphic displays, and pointing devices, as well as the availability of increasingly powerful workstation environments, it is a natural and timely step in the evolution of human-computer interfaces that the media be integrated to meet the information processing needs of the user community.

Computer-based multi-media communication between people has received support via the development of multi-media electronic document systems and mail systems. This research and development includes the electronic document systems at Brown University [Feiner82], an experimental multi-media mail system at ISI [Katz84], a multi-media message system at SRI [Aceves84], and the Diamond message system at BBN [Thomas85]. Hypertext [Conklin87; ACM88; Egan89; Shepard89] provides for multimodal, multidimensional document representation and access.

Intelligent interactive human-computer dialogue via multi-media language (e.g., simultaneous natural-language and graphics) has just begun to be developed. Work has begun on intelligence in interfaces [Neches86; Sullivan91] and, in particular, on the issue of the intelligent use of multiple media and/or modalities for human-computer communication [Arens88; Arens91; Hollan91; Kobsa86; Neal88a; Neal88b; Neal89; Reithinger87; Roth91].

For input, the CUBRICON project focuses on the understanding of natural language accompanied by simultaneous coordinated pointing gestures, particularly the problem of referent identification. Related work includes the development of the TEMPLAR system [Press86] at TRW and XTRA [Allgayer89; Kobsa86] at the University of Saarbrucken. The TEMPLAR system seems to provide only for a pointing gesture to *substitute* for a NL definite reference within a NL sentence, rather than allowing a pointing gesture also to be used *in combination with* a NL reference. In the TEMPLAR system, the NL phrase for the object selected by the point is inserted in the input string to allow the NL parser to complete its processing. Our approach is closer to that of Kobsa and colleagues with the XTRA system, in accepting dual-modality input and applying several knowledge sources for referent identification. Our systems differ in the types of objects that can be targets of pointing gestures, as well as in the knowledge sources that are used.

For output, the CUBRICON project is addressing the problem of having the system select the media/modalities for expressing information to the user, as well as composing the output in the selected media/modalities. Related work includes that of Reithinger [Reithinger87] in generating referring expressions and pointing gestures. The Integrated Interfaces project [Arens88; Arens91] uses a variety of output modalities but does not include speech production or deictic pointing gestures during output. The CUBRICON project and the work of Roth et al. [Roth91] are both concerned with the problems of selecting relevant information to present to the user, composing text and selecting and designing pictures to convey the information, and coordinating the two different modalities. Feiner and McKeown [Feiner89] are also working on the problem of coordinating text and graphics, both displayed on a computer screen, in the generation of explanations to accomplish communicative goals. The CUBRICON project is concerned with the appropriate selection, generation, and coordination of a wider variety of output modalities (e.g., speech, tables, and form output in addition to printed text and graphics).

The CUBRICON system includes several knowledge sources (e.g., application-specific knowledge base, discourse model, user model) to generate relevant helpful responses, maintain the discourse context when appropriate, manage its display resources, provide the user and system with the ability to reference the display objects, and use the modalities in coordinated combinations for output generation. Cheikes and Webber [Cheikes88] and Kaplan [Kaplan82] address the problem of generating relevant cooperative responses. The issue of models to support intelligent behavior of interface systems is also addressed by Wahlster [Wahlster91], Mason and Edwards [Mason88], Kass and Finin [Kass91], and Young [Young91].

2.4 SYSTEM OVERVIEW

The CUBRICON team has designed and implemented an integrated user interface system with the functionality described briefly in Section 2.2. Figure 2.1 provides an overview of the software system and hardware I/O devices.

CUBRICON accepts input from three input devices: speech input device, keyboard, and mouse device pointing to objects on a graphics display. CUBRICON produces output for three output devices: high-resolution color graphics display, monochrome display, and speech output device. The primary path that the input data follow is indicated by the numbered modules

FIGURE 2.1
SYSTEM OVERVIEW

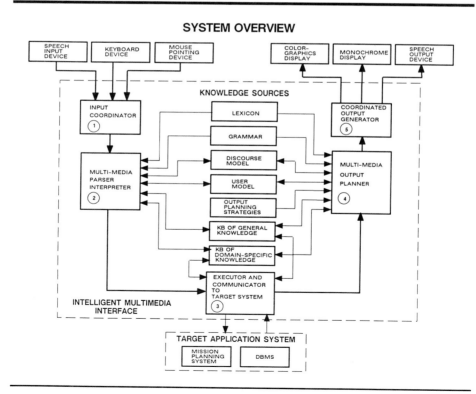

in the figure: (1) Input Coordinator, (2) Multi-media Parser Interpreter, (3) Executor/Communicator to Target System, (4) Multi-media Output Planner, and (5) Coordinated Output Generator. The Input Coordinator module accepts input from the three input devices and fuses the input streams into a single compound stream, maintaining the temporal order of tokens in the original streams. The Multi-media Parser/Interpreter is an augmented transition network (ATN) that has been extended to accept the compound stream produced by the Input Coordinator and to produce an interpretation of this compound stream. Appropriate action is then taken by the Executor module. This may be a command to the mission planning system, a database query, or an action that entails participation of the interface system only. An expression of the results of the action is then planned by the Multi-media Output Planner for communication to the user. The Output Planner is a generalized ATN that produces a multi-media output stream representation with components targeted for different devices (e.g., color graphics display, speech device, monochrome display). This output representation is translated into visual/auditory output by the Coordinated Output Generator module. This module is responsible for producing the multi-media output in a coordinated manner in real time (e.g., the Output Planner module can specify that a certain icon on the color graphics display must be highlighted when the entity represented by the icon is mentioned in the simultaneous NL output).

The CUBRICON system includes several knowledge sources to be used during processing, including:

1. A lexicon
2. A grammar defining the language used by the system for multi-media input and output
3. A discourse model
4. A user model
5. A knowledge base of output planning strategies to govern the composition of multi-media responses to the user
6. A knowledge base of information about generally shared world knowledge
7. A knowledge base of information about the specific task domain of tactical air control

These knowledge sources are used for both understanding input to the system and planning/generating output from the system. They are discussed in more detail in the next section.

The CUBRICON system is implemented on a Symbolics Lisp Machine with a mouse pointing device, a color graphics monitor, and a monochrome monitor. Speech recognition is handled by a Dragon Systems VoiceScribe 1000. Speech output is produced by a DECtalk speech production system. CUBRICON software is implemented using the SNePS semantic network processing system [Shapiro79a; Shapiro81; Shapiro87], an ATN parser/generator [Shapiro82a], and Common Lisp. SNePS is a fully intensional propositional semantic network and has been used for a variety of purposes and applications [Maida85; Shapiro82c; Shapiro87; Neal86; Neal87]. SNePS provides:

1. A flexible knowledge representation facility in the semantic network formalism
2. Representation of rules in the network in a declarative form so they can be reasoned about like any other data
3. A bidirectional inference subsystem [Shapiro82b] that focuses attention toward the active processes and cuts down the fanout of pure forward or backward chaining
4. A simulated multiprocessing control structure [McKay80]
5. Special nonstandard connectives [Shapiro79b] to model human reasoning processes
6. Existential, universal, and numerical quantifiers [Shapiro79c]

2.5 KNOWLEDGE SOURCES FOR MULTI-MEDIA LANGUAGE PROCESSING

2.5.1. The Lexicon and Grammar

A lexicon is the collection of all morphemes, tokens, and signals that carry meaning in a given language. The CUBRICON system's lexicon consists of words, graphic figures, and pointing signals. The grammar defines how the morphemes, tokens, and signals of the lexicon can combine to form legal composite language structures. An example of a multimodal language structure that is legal according to the CUBRICON grammar is a noun phrase. A noun phrase consists of the typical linguistic syntax (e.g., determiner, followed by zero or more modifiers, followed by a noun) accompanied by zero or more pointing signals (pointing to objects on the graphics display). The lexicon and grammar together define the multimodal language used by the system.

2.5.2. The Discourse Model

Continuity and relevance are key factors in discourse. Without these factors, people find discourse disconcerting and unnatural. The attentional discourse focus space representation [Grosz78; Grosz85; Grosz86; Sidner86] is a key knowledge structure that supports continuity and relevance in dialogue. CUBRICON tracks the attentional discourse focus space of the dialogue carried out in multi-media language and maintains a representation of the focus space in two structures: a main focus list and a display model.

The main focus list includes those entities and propositions that have been explicitly expressed (by the user or by CUBRICON) via natural language, pointing, highlighting, or blinking. The display model represents all the objects that are "in focus" because they are visible on one of the monitors. CUBRICON is based on the premise that graphics are an integral part of its language, along with natural language and other forms of text and pointing. The CUBRICON system treats objects presented on the graphics displays as having been intentionally "expressed" or "mentioned." All objects on the graphics display are "in focus," and CUBRICON maintains a representation of all these objects in the form of a display model. The display model consists of two levels: (1) a list of windows per monitor and, (2) for each window, a list of all the objects visible in the window. This display model is used in a manner analogous to the use of the main dialogue focus list.

The dialogue attentional focus space representation is used for determining the interpretation of anaphoric references [Sidner86] and definite descriptive references [Grosz81] expressed by the user in natural-language. In the CUBRICON system, the main dialogue focus list is consulted in determining the referent of a pronoun. In the case of a definite reference, if an appropriate referent is not found in the main dialogue focus list, CUBRICON consults the display model. The motivation for this is the fact that when a person expresses a definite reference, such as "the airbase," with just one such object in view (as on a graphics display), and none have been discussed, then the person most likely refers to the one in view, even though he or she may know about several others.

We have not addressed the problem of understanding an input phrase (e.g., "the airbase") when more than one such object is in view and none have been discussed in the human-computer dialogue. The phrase is ambiguous, but a reasonable approach would be to interpret the phrase as referencing the one in view that is most relevant to the user's task.

The discourse model is used during output generation also. When CUBRICON composes a reference for an entity as part of a NL sentence, it consults the discourse model. If the entity is represented in the display model as being visible on one of CUBRICON's windows, then the system uses a deictic dual-media expression to refer to the entity in the output sentence. The deictic expression consists of a phrase, such as "this airbase," and the simultaneous blinking/highlighting of the airbase as the system's means of pointing to the object. If the entity is the most salient of its gender according to the main focus list, CUBRICON uses a pronoun to refer to the entity.

2.5.3. The User Model

Many aspects of a user are highly relevant to interface technology. These aspects include level of expertise in the current task, perspective based on the user's role, his or her value system, degree and nature of impairedness due to fatigue or illness, and preferences concerning mode of communication. Carberry [Carberry87] provides a brief summary of recent research on user modeling. A special issue of *Computational Linguistics* [Kobsa88] provides more in-depth discussion of issues in user modeling. To address all of these different aspects of user modeling is, of course, beyond the scope of this project. The aspects of the user that are most relevant in the CUBRICON system are (1) the importance rating that the user attaches to the different entity types relevant to each given task, which we call the user's *entity rating system;* and (2) the task in which the user is currently engaged.

CUBRICON includes a representation of the user's entity rating system as a function of the task being addressed by the user. For a given task being carried out by the user, the entity rating system representation includes a numerical importance rating (on a scale from 0 to 1) assigned to each of the entity types used in the application task domain. The numerical rating assigned to a given entity type represents the degree of importance of the entity to the user. Associated with the entity rating system is a *critical threshold value;* those entities with ratings above this threshold value are critical to the current task, and those with ratings below the threshold are not. The CUBRICON design provides for the entity rating system representation to change automatically under program control in the following manner: (1) When the user's task changes, the system replaces the current entity rating list with the standard initial rating list for the new task. (2) When the user mentions an entity whose rating is below the critical threshold, its rating is reset to equal the critical threshold to reflect the user's interest in the entity and its seeming relevance to the current task. In the current implementation, CUBRICON performs the second function, but the implementation of the first is not complete.

The user's entity rating system plays an important role in composing responses to the user. The entity rating system representation is used in determining what information is relevant in answering questions or responding to commands from the user. The system is used in selecting ancillary information to enhance or embellish the main concept being expressed and to prevent the user from making false inferences that he or she might otherwise make. The entity rating system is also used in organizing the form in which information is presented.

As an example of the first function, if the user instructs the system to "Display the Fulda Gap region," CUBRICON uses the entity rating system representation to determine what objects within the region should be displayed. If the user is a military mission planner, then displaying all the country cottages in the region, for example, is irrelevant. Thus, the objects that the system selects from its database for display are airbases, missile sites, and targets, for example. Section 2.8 presents examples of the use of this entity rating system representation in interactive dialogue between a user and the CUBRICON system.

CUBRICON includes a simple representation of the current task in which the user is engaged. CUBRICON's mode of response to the user is affected by whether or not the user's task has just changed. The CUBRICON team is developing a task hierarchy: a decomposition of the user's main tasks into sub-tasks. This a priori task knowledge can be used by CUBRICON to help track the discourse focus, manage the displays, and anticipate the needs of the user.

2.5.4. Knowledge Bases: General and Domain-Specific

The CUBRICON system includes knowledge bases containing general and domain-specific information. General information includes world knowledge applicable across different task domains; domain-specific information is applicable to the particular task domain of the target information system being used as a "back end" for the interface system. Crucial information included in the knowledge bases is that concerning the presentation or expression of the entities/concepts known to the system. The knowledge base includes information on how to express an entity in its unified verbal/graphic language. This includes the words and symbols used to express an entity, specification of which symbols are appropriate under which conditions, and determination of when particular colors are to be used.

2.6 MULTI-MEDIA LANGUAGE UNDERSTANDING

CUBRICON accepts language consisting of coordinated simultaneous natural language and pointing (via a mouse device) to objects on a graphics display. The use of pointing in combination with natural-language forms a very efficient means of expressing a definite reference. This enables a person to use a demonstrative pronoun as a determiner in a noun phrase and simultaneously point to an entity on the graphics display to form a succinct reference. Thus, a person is able to say "this SAM system" and point to an entity on the display to disambiguate which of several SAM systems is meant. The alternative, using natural language only, would be to say something like "the SAM system at 10.35 degrees longitude and 49.75 degrees latitude" or "the SAM system just outside of Kleinburg." The use of pointing references combined with natural language is efficient since the cognitive process of generating the dual-media reference would be much shorter than the generation of the NL-only reference. The result is a reduction in the cognitive workload for the user.

The CUBRC team has developed a formal grammar defining the syntax of the multi-media language. The grammar is implemented in the form of a generalized ATN. The traditional ATN, which takes a linear textual input stream, has been modified so that it takes a multi-media input stream with components from the different input devices. Input from the devices is accepted and fused into a compound stream, and information is maintained as to which point gesture(s) occurred with (or between) which word(s) of the sentence. Each noun phrase or locative adverbial phrase can consist of zero or more words of text along with zero or more pointing references to objects on the displays (there must be at least one point reference or one word). The pointing input that is a component of a noun phrase or locative adverbial can occur anywhere within the phrase—as the first token(s), between the NL words of the phrase, or as the last token(s).

In the CUBRICON system, four types of objects can be referenced via pointing:

- A geometric point within any window (e.g., a map or graph)
- An entity represented by an icon
- A table entry
- A window on one of the monitors

The following sentences illustrate the type of input accepted by the CUBRICON system. These inputs presuppose that a map is displayed on the color graphics screen, with icons representing various entities. Each "<point>" represents a point to an object or location on one of the graphics displays. The system's responses to such input will be discussed in Section 2.7, where output planning and generation is discussed.

Interrogative

"Where is the 43d Soviet Tank Battalion?"

"What is the mobility of this <point> SAM?"

"Is this <point> the base for these troop battalions <point>$_1$ <point>$_2$ <point>$_3$?"

Imperative

"Display the East-West Germany region."

"Display the aimpoints within this <point> airbase."

"Present the OCA1001 mission plan."

Use of such dual-media references entails certain problems, however. A point by the user can be ambiguous if it is to an area where two or more graphical figures or icons overlap. Also, the user may inadvertently miss the object to which he or she intended to point. Figure 2.2 shows overlapping extents for an airbase and a SAM system. If the user points to the overlapping area, the point has two interpretations. However, a NL reference spoken simultaneously with the point can disambiguate the pointing reference. For example, if the phrase "this airbase" is spoken in conjunction with the point to the overlapping extents of Figure 2.2, the dual-media reference is no longer ambiguous. On the other hand, the user may intend to point to the Allstedt airbase but may either inadvertently point to the nearby SAM icon instead or totally miss all the icons with the point gesture. The CUBRICON methodology includes features for handling these problems.

Some systems use default techniques to handle ambiguous pointing. For example:

FIGURE 2.2
RECTANGULAR ICON EXTENTS THAT OVERLAP

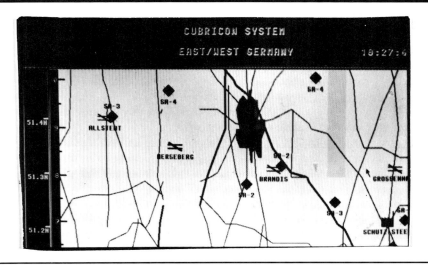

1. A point returns the entity represented by the "top" or "foremost" icon, where the system has a data structure it uses to remember the order in which icons are "painted" on the display (i.e., which are further in the background and which are foremost in the foreground).
2. The icons or entities are assigned weights representing importance, and the icon with the largest weight is selected as the interpretation of an ambiguous point.
3. The icon whose "center" is closest to the location pointed to is selected.

Combinations of these techniques can also be used. A serious disadvantage of these point interpretation techniques is that it is difficult, if not impossible, for certain icons to be selected via point references. Such default techniques were deliberately not used in the CUBRICON system. CUBRICON's acceptance of natural language accompanying a point gesture overcomes the limitations of such weak default techniques and provides a more flexible referencing capability.

CUBRICON uses several of the knowledge sources discussed in Section 2.5 in determining the referent of a combined NL and pointing reference. The following examples illustrate the CUBRICON methodology.

In the first example, determination of the referent depends primarily on the use of the task domain knowledge represented in the knowledge base combined with the ancillary visual discourse focus representation called the display model (see Section 2.5.2).

User: "What is the status of this <point> airbase?"

When the phrase "this <point> airbase" is parsed, the system uses the point coordinates to determine which icons are touched by the point. Then the display model is searched to retrieve the semantic network nodes representing the objects graphically displayed by the "touched" icons. Within the knowledge base, the system has a representation of the category to which each object belongs, as well as a representation of the airbase concept. From the hierarchy of the knowledge base, the system determines which of the objects selected by the point gesture are airbases, and it discards the others. If the user has pointed to at least one airbase, the system uses this (these) airbase instance(s) as the referent of the dual-media noun phrase. If the user has pointed at no airbases, the system performs a bounded incremental spatial (geographical) search for an airbase to use as the referent.

The second example entails the use of the syntax and semantics of the sentence processed thus far, along with the knowledge base, to determine the referent of the phrase "this <point>." Here the concept of "mobility" is the critical item of information.

User: "What is the mobility of this <point> ?"

From the display model, the system retrieves the objects represented by the icons that were touched by the point gesture. From the syntax of the noun phrase "the mobility of this <point>" and the semantics of the word "mobility" as represented in the knowledge base, the system deduces that mobility is a property (as opposed to a subpart or some other possible relation that could exist between the concepts mentioned) of the object mentioned in the prepositional phrase. The system then determines which of the objects selected by the point gesture have a property called mobility by consulting the knowledge base. The other objects selected by the point gesture are discarded. The resulting set is used as the referent of the phrase "this <point>." If the set is empty, the system performs a bounded incremental search in the geographical area of the user's point gesture to find an object with the property "mobility."

The case frame indicated by the main verb of a sentence is another source of information that CUBRICON can use to determine the referent of a dual-media phrase. The case frame of the main verb can provide constraints on the fillers of the frame slots. A simple example of the use of such constraints is provided in the following example:

User: "Zoom in on this <point>."

For CUBRICON, the semantics of the "zoom in" command require either an object with components that can be presented in enlarged form or a location (that can be represented by a pair of coordinates). If the point gesture touches an icon representing an entity that can be displayed in enlarged form, then the referent of the point is that entity. The system would consult the knowledge base to determine if this is the case. Otherwise, the system assumes that the referent is the location designated by the point, and it displays an enlargement of the area around the point.

Section 2.8 discusses additional examples from a user-computer dialogue to illustrate the CUBRICON methodology for parsing and interpreting dual-media input. This topic is discussed more fully in [Neal88b; Neal89].

2.7 PLANNING THE MULTI-MEDIA RESPONSE

The CUBRICON system design provides for output in the form of coordinated speech, text displayed on a CRT, and pictorial information on a color graphics display. The system uses the ATN methodology for generation as well as understanding. ATNs have been used to generate text by Simmons & Slocum [Simmons72], in the XCALIBUR system [Carbonell85], and by Shapiro [Shapiro75, Shapiro82a]. In this project, this ATN methodology is being expanded to generate language in the form of text, graphics, or a text/graphics combination from the semantic network knowledge bases.

A multi-media language provides a wider range of choices for the formulation of an expression for a given concept than a single-media language, such as natural language used in isolation. There are alternative ways of expressing a given concept in a strictly textual language. For example, George Bush can be referred to as "George Bush," as "the President of the United States," or as "the Commander in Chief of the Armed Forces of the United States." If language is extended to include graphics as well, then Mr. Bush could be referred to by pointing to his picture, by creating/displaying his image as a reference, or by a combination of text and graphics. Thus, a reference can be composed of a proper noun, a noun phrase with modifiers, a graphic form with features of color, size, and location on a display, and so on. Furthermore, the graphic features "modifying" a form or shape can communicate meaning just as do the adjectives and relative clauses that modify a head noun of a noun phrase.

The Multi-Media Output Planner composes the response that is to be produced to the user by the Output Generator in coordinated multiple modalities. The Output Planner determines the media and modalities for expressing the response information to the user, but it then must determine whether the resources are available to do so. If they are not, the Planner must take appropriate action to modify the state of the resources, modify the information to be expressed, and/or select different modalities for expressing the information before composition of the output can be accomplished.

The CUBRICON design includes the following output modalities, in isolation or in combination: color graphics/pictorial displays, tables, histograms, written NL prose, spoken natural language, and fill-in-the-blank forms. This list does not exhaust the possibilities, of course, but it provides a good, varied selection with which to "prove our concept" and upon which to build.

Selection of the most appropriate modalities for expressing information in the CUBRICON system is based on the nature and characteristics of the information. Our system design is based on the premise that graphic/pictorial presentation is always desirable. The following is a brief summary of the selection criteria.

1. Color graphics are selected whenever the CUBRICON system knows how to represent the information pictorially.
2. A table is selected when the values of common attribute(s) of several entities must be expressed.
3. A histogram is selected when a quantitative attribute of several entities must be displayed in a comparative form.
4. A predefined form is selected when the task engaged in by the user requires it.
5. Natural-language prose is selected for the expression of a proposition, relation, event, or combination thereof when the knowledge structures being expressed are heterogeneous. Natural language can be presented in either spoken or written form. *Spoken natural language* is selected for

   ■ Dialogue descriptions to assist the user in comprehending the presented information. These include explanations of graphic displays or display changes and verbal highlighting of objects on the displays (e.g., "The enemy airbases are highlighted in red").

   ■ Warnings to alert the user of important events that have taken or are about to take place (e.g., new critical information comes into the application system database, and the system notifies user: "The XXX airbase has been damaged by enemy shellfire").

   ■ Informing the user about the system's activity (e.g., "I'm still working" when the user must wait for output from the system).

   ■ Short expressions of relatively nontechnical information that can be remembered when presented serially (e.g., a "yes"/"no" answer to a user's question).

   Written natural language is selected for longer technical responses that would strain the user's short-term memory if speech were used (see [Miller56]).

Most frequently, multiple modalities are desirable for expressing a body of information to the user. For example, to inform the user about the movements of a certain tank battalion, a desirable presentation might be a spoken explanation and coordinated drawing on a graphic map display showing movements of the battalion, as well as a printed textual summary with ancillary information on the monochrome display. The multiple modalities should be selected to complement and enhance one another. Andriole [Andriole86] has used "graphic equivalence" effectively, employing dual displays or split screens to present the same material in different forms to aid user comprehension and problem solving performance. We are not restricting the system to presenting the *same* material in different forms; instead, our system presents related material or different aspects of a given event or concept in different forms/modalities (as appropriate, based on the nature and characteristics of the information). We are also not restricted to graphic display presentations.

Our top-level output planning process is summarized as follows. This planning process presupposes that the primary relevant information has been obtained for response to the user.

1. For each information item or cluster, determine the ideal modality for its expression. Graphic/pictorial presentation is always desirable. Natural language can always be used as a last resort if no other modality is available.

2. Determine whether the resources are available to express the information as desired. For a color graphics display, find out if the items to be expressed graphically are already present on the display (e.g., if objects of interest in a geographical domain are already displayed on a map). If so, no additions are necessary. If not, is there room to add them in their "natural" position? That is, can the desired objects be inserted in the area already available on the graphics display without changing the area shown, or does the displayed area need to be extended or changed totally? Similar issues arise for a monochrome display. For a speech output device, resources are always available.

3. If the desired resources are not available, modify the state of the resources. The desired resources would be "not available" in at least two cases: (a) The physical device is not functional (e.g., needs repair), or (b) the device (e.g., a display) already contains critical information that cannot be disrupted or covered by a window. For the graphics displays, if all the items to be expressed graphically are not on the display, then the system must compose a new display. Using terminology for a geographical display, the possible cases are:

    ■ *Zoom out* with intelligent addition of relevant ancillary objects to fill in the new area to maintain consistency throughout the display.

    ■ *Zoom in* with intelligent addition of relevant objects to create an intelligible display.

    ■ *Pan* to a different area, maintaining consistency in the types of objects displayed.

    ■ Employ a combination of these procedures.

    ■ Display a different disjoint area: (a) Completely replace the display with the new "area," or (b) open a window on the monitor to show new information.

4. If resources are still not available to accommodate the information to be expressed, try modifying the information. Trim the amount of infor-

mation by filtering on the basis of relevance with regard to user model and/or discourse model.

5. If the information still cannot be expressed in the given modality due to insufficient resources, select another modality and go back to step 2.

6. Compose the output, having resolved resource constraints.

The methodology discussed in this section is fully implemented, with the exception of the histogram modality. The processes for the modality selection and for resolution of resource problems are undergoing refinement to maximize generality and extend their functionality. The next section discusses working examples from a dialogue with the system. The examples illustrate some of the functionality of the system.

2.8 SAMPLE DIALOGUES

This section presents short sample dialogues to illustrate the functionality and processing discussed in the previous sections. The dialogues are concerned with mission planning and situation assessment in a tactical air control domain. Consider the following initial user input to the CUBRICON system:

> *User*: "Display the Fulda Gap region."
> *CUBRICON*: (Refer to Figure 2.3)
> Speech output:
> - Statements to direct the user's attention to the appropriate monitor as information is displayed. Just before the region is displayed on the color graphics monitor:
> "Look at the color graphics screen. The Fulda Gap region is being presented."
> Just before the table is presented on the monochrome monitor:
> "The corresponding table is being presented on the monochrome screen."
> Color graphics display:
> - Map of the Fulda Gap region with main roads, major cities, waterways, and national boundaries
> - Icons representing entities within the Fulda Gap region, that are above the critical threshold according to the entity rating system for the user's task, superimposed on the map
> Monochrome graphics display:
> - Table of relevant entity attributes for those entities on the map display

The planning and composition of output for the user depends on the nature of the information, the discourse context, and the user model. Since

FIGURE 2.3
THE DISPLAYS COMPOSED BY THE SYSTEM

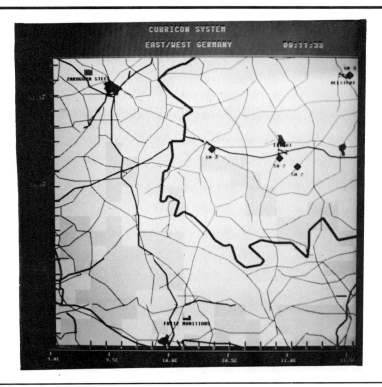

this sample command is the initial input, the process is simpler than for
other cases. The CUBRICON system knows that a region can be represented
graphically and therefore chooses graphics as the primary modality for display. Regions are represented in the CUBRICON knowledge base with an
associated boundary. The boundary is retrieved by the system, and the main
roads, major cities, waterways, and national borders are displayed on the color
graphics display. These items are displayed by use of the RADC MAP Display System [Hilton87]. The CUBRICON system then searches its knowledge
base for task-specific objects within the region to be displayed. The selection
of these objects is based on the user model discussed in Section 2.5, which
consists of the user's entity rating system: a task-dependent assignment of
importance ratings to the objects in the task domain. The system does not
display all entities it knows about in the region, but only those that lie above
the criticality threshold for the particular task in which the user is engaged (a
subtask of planning an air strike mission). Thus, the system decides to display
all airbases, surface-to-air missile (SAM) sites, and critical factories and plants,
but not objects such as food production plants or minor industries that are

FIGURE 2.3 (Cont.)

Entities in the Region

Item	Disposition	Latitude	Longitude	Name	Mobility
fighter base	enemy	50.970N	10.960E	erfurt	--
fighter base	enemy	51.400N	11.460E	allstedt	low
SA-2	enemy	50.933N	10.933E	--	low
SA-3	enemy	50.883N	11.083E	--	high
SA-3	enemy	50.983N	10.366E	--	high
steel plant	friendly	51.403N	11.516E	zaragoza steel	--
munition factory	friendly	49.991N	10.152E	fritz munitions	--

=> display the FG region.
=> ▮

[Mon 11 Jul 8:56:22] pawlicki   CL SHEPs: User Input   SEN4 not germane to mission planning. The resulting color map display is shown in Figure 2.3*a*.

Based on the information provided by the user model, the system knows the important attributes of each object. These attributes are not displayed or communicated via the map display but have been selected as relevant, so the system must determine a modality for presenting this information. Since this information consists of lists of objects with different values of common attributes, the system determines that a table presentation is appropriate. The system composes a table showing the important attributes of the displayed objects. The number of attributes (columns of the table) is constrained by available space. The resultant table is displayed on the monochrome display and is shown in Figure 2.3*b*.

To further illustrate the CUBRICON system's modality selection and output composition process, we will consider the next user input. The user queries the system about the location of the Dresden airbase in a manner that provides no instruction to the system as to how to present the information (e.g., map, natural language only).

User: "Where is the Dresden airbase?"
CUBRICON: (Refer to Figure 2.4.)
  Speech output:
  ■ Statements to direct the user's attention to the appropriate monitor when a major window is presented. As the map is expanded on the color monitor:
    "The map on the color graphics screen is being expanded to include the Dresden airbase."
        As the table is presented on the monochrome monitor:
        "The corresponding table is being presented on the mono-chrome screen."
  ■ After the map is expanded, a statement to direct the user's attention to the Dresden airbase on the map:
    "The Dresden airbase is located here <point>."
    The word "here" is accompanied by a visual point gesture in the form of a blinking airbase icon and the addition of a pointing text box.
  Color graphics display:
  ■ Map of the Fulda Gap region with added area that includes the Dresden airbase
  ■ Main roads, major cities, waterways, and national boundaries (as before, but across the whole map, showing old and new areas)
  ■ Icons representing entities within the new map area displayed that lie above the critical threshold on the entity rating system for the user's task

FIGURE 2.4
MAP AND TABLE MAINTAINING CONTEXT AND CONSISTENCY

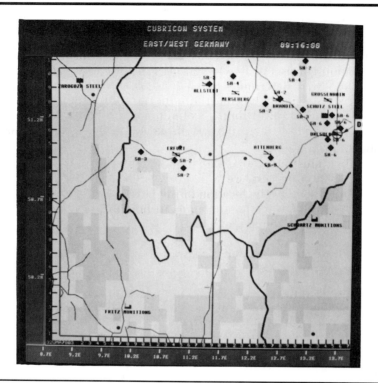

- The Dresden airbase icon presented in a blinking and highlighted manner (the blinking is temporary and is coordinated with the speech)

Monochrome graphics display:

- Table of relevant entity attributes (same table as before, but expanded to include the new entities added to the map covering the extended area)

As discussed in Section 2.7, whenever possible the CUBRICON system prefers to present information graphically, with ancillary information presented simultaneously in another modality. Since CUBRICON knows how to display an airbase graphically (it has an icon associated with the class in the knowledge base), and since each particular airbase in the knowledge base has an associated geographical location, the system will display the airbase on the color graphics map, with additional information displayed in another modality. If the Dresden airbase were already displayed on the color map display, the system would choose to blink the particular airbase

FIGURE 2.4 (Cont.)

Entities in the Region

Item	Disposition	Latitude	Longitude	Name	Mobility
fighter base	enemy	51.100N	13.700E	dresden	- -
fighter base	enemy	51.330N	11.960E	merseberg	- -
fighter base	enemy	51.310N	13.530E	grossenhain	- -
fighter base	enemy	50.980N	12.510E	atzenberg	- -
fighter base	enemy	51.400N	11.460E	allstedt	- -
fighter base	enemy	50.970N	10.960E	erfurt	- -
fighter base	enemy	51.310N	12.660E	brandis	- -
SA-2	enemy	51.283N	12.466E	- -	low
SA-2	enemy	51.550N	13.133E	- -	low
SA-2	enemy	51.316N	12.716E	- -	low
SA-2	enemy	50.883N	11.083E	- -	low
SA-3	enemy	50.933N	10.933E	- -	high
SA-3	enemy	51.250N	12.566E	- -	high
SA-3	enemy	50.950N	11.516E	- -	high
SA-3	enemy	50.983N	10.366E	- -	high
SA-4	enemy	51.473N	12.953E	- -	low
SA-4	enemy	51.450N	11.916E	- -	low
SA-6	enemy	51.016N	13.586E	- -	high
SA-6	enemy	51.066N	13.536E	- -	high
SA-6	enemy	51.133N	13.733E	- -	high
SA-6	enemy	51.166N	13.520E	- -	high
SA-6	enemy	51.216N	13.603E	- -	high
steel plant	enemy	51.211N	13.480E	schutz steel	- -
steel plant	friendly	51.421N	9.344E	zaragoza steel	- -
munition factory	enemy	50.561N	13.320E	schwartz munitions	- -
munition factory	friendly	49.991N	10.152E	fritz munitions	- -

=> Display the FG region.
=> Where is the Dresden airbase?
=> ▮

[Mon 11 Jul 6:43:02J pavllcki   CL SHEPS: User Input   SCHCK icon as its way of pointing to the object and would accompany this pointing action with a spoken response. If the Dresden airbase could be added to the current map, CUBRICON would do so and direct the user's attention to the airbase icon. However, the Dresden airbase is outside of the region shown in the map display currently on the color CRT. Therefore, the system must decide how to show the airbase. What map should be displayed?

In composing a new map on which to display the Dresden airbase, the system has some choices: open a window on the color graphics display showing the area around the Dresden airbase, replace the old map on the CRT with a new map of the area around the Dresden airbase, or compose a new map including both the old map and the region around the Dresden airbase.

An important guideline to which the CUBRICON system tries to adhere is to maintain the context of the user-computer dialogue. With regard to the graphic displays, this means that the system tries to retain the most recently discussed or mentioned objects on the displays in order to maintain continuity in the dialogue. The discourse focus space representations, (see Section 2.5) are the key knowledge sources in this process. The system composes a new map containing the objects on the old map as well as the Dresden airbase. The algorithm that the system uses to determine the boundary for a new map of this type is to find the smallest rectangle that encloses the objects on the current map plus the new objects to be displayed and then add a small border area around all sides. This essentially extends the area shown to include both the old and the new objects.

A key feature of the CUBRICON system is that it can display any rectangular region within a "master map" boundary containing the East-West Germany region. That is, the system can select any degree of longitude for the eastern or western boundary of the map to be displayed and any degree of latitude for the northern or southern boundary (within the confines of the master map). For any such map, as indicated previously, the non-domain-specific items such as roads, major cities, waterways, and national boundaries are displayed by the RADC MAP Display System.

Another important guideline to which the CUBRICON system adheres is to maintain consistency throughout a display to prevent the user from making false inferences about what is or is not located within the region. In the case of our map display, this means that there should be consistency in the types of objects shown across the entire map. If SAMs are displayed in the old region, then they should be displayed in the newly added map area; the same holds for other types of objects. If this is not done, the user would probably infer that there are no SAMs in the new area since none appear on the display. Figure 2.4a shows the new map display composed by the CUBRICON system in response to the user's input "Where is the Dresden airbase?" The rectangular outline within the map is used to indicate the previously displayed area. This provides graphic context: the new entities are shown in the context of the previously displayed area. Guided by the consistency principle, the system also modifies the tabular presentation that is on the monochrome display. Both displays are also shown in Figure 2.4.

As discussed in Section 2.6, the CUBRICON system accepts NL input with coordinated pointing to objects on the graphics display. As an example of this multi-media input, the user can enter:

User: "Is this <point> a steel plant?"
where the point touches on or near an icon on the map display.
CUBRICON:
Speech: "No, it is a munitions factory."

CUBRICON decides to respond in natural-language since the information to be expressed is short and relatively nontechnical (refer to the modality selection process discussed in Section 2.7). The system uses a pronoun to refer to the object referenced by the user since it is the most salient object according to the system's discourse focus space list (refer to Section 2.5.2).

The following example illustrates CUBRICON's ability to infer the referent of a pointing gesture that misses the intended icon. It also illustrates CUBRICON's ability to respond in highly integrated speech and graphics.

User: "What is the mobility of this <point>$_1$<point>$_2$<point>$_3$?"
where each point is a mouse point by the user on the map display. The first point touches the wrong icon, and the third touches no icon at all.
CUBRICON:
Speech output with coordinated color graphics:
"The mobility of this <blinking icon>$_1$ sam is low, the mobility of this <blinking icon>$_2$ sam is high, and the mobility of this <blinking icon>$_3$ sam is high."
For each SAM reference, the particular SAM icon blinks as the system's method of pointing to it. Next to each SAM icon, a small text box is added to provide a terse written summary of the requested information.
Monochrome display—small NL window:
"Point 1: The icon you pointed at does not have the property 'mobility,' but a nearby referent has been found."
"Point 3: Your point gesture did not touch any objects on the display; however, a nearby object with the property 'mobility' has been found."

The mouse handler returns representations of the objects touched by the point, if any exist. CUBRICON examines each of the returned objects to determine if it has a mobility property. The first point gesture touched an airbase icon but no SAM icons. CUBRICON deduces that the referent cannot be the airbase, since airbases are not mobile according to its knowledge base. Therefore, the system performs an incremental geographic bounded search around the location of the user's point gesture to find an object with the property "mobility." It is successful in finding a nearby SAM. The second point gesture touched a SAM icon, so the system simply retrieves the value of its mobility property from the knowledge base. The third point gesture touched no icons at all. Therefore, CUBRICON performs another incremental geographic bounded search to find a nearby object with the mobility property. It finds a SAM and determines the value of its mobility from the knowledge base. For each of the two point gestures that touched no object with the mentioned property, the system prints a message in the NL window on the monochrome display to inform the user of its activity.

When composing a response to the user, the system first selects the modalities in which to respond. As per the criteria discussed in Section 2.7, the system decides to answer in natural language since the information is not very voluminous. Since the entities (i.e., the SAMs) are visible on the display map, the system points to each one (by blinking the appropriate icon) as it is referenced in the NL response. Also, since the information is technical and the user may subsequently want to refer back to it, CUBRICON decides to present a terse printed version also. This is done by placing a small text box near each SAM icon with a simple statement of its mobility. Figure 2.5, included primarily to illustrate the next user-computer interaction, also shows the printed NL response from this example.

In our demo script, the user then requests:

User: "Zoom in on this <point> point."

where the point is a mouse point somewhere on the map.

CUBRICON: (Refer to Figure 2.5)

Speech output:

Statements to direct the user's attention to the appropriate monitor as information is displayed. As the new map window is added to the color monitor:

"Look at the color graphics screen. The window being generated contains the zoomed in area."

As the new table is added to the monochrome monitor:

"The corresponding table is being presented on the monochrome screen."

Color graphics display:

A new map window is created containing a magnification of the area around the location of the user's mouse point. Due to the size requirement, this window is placed so that it overlaps the original map window.

Monochrome graphics display:

Table of relevant entity attributes for those entities on the map display. This table is placed on the monochrome monitor in a position that matches the position of its related map window on the color graphics monitor.

FIGURE 2.5
NEWLY COMPOSED MAP AND TABLE DISPLAYS

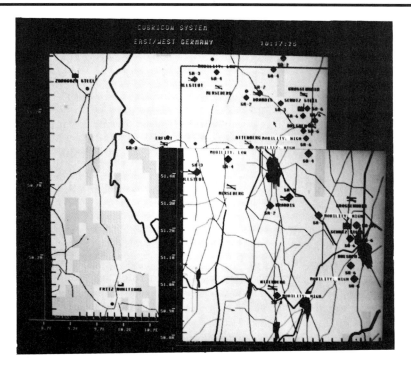

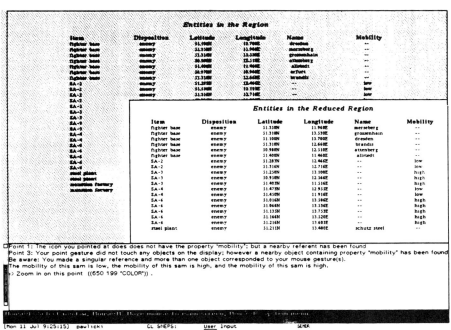

Entities in the Region

Item	Disposition	Latitude	Longitude	Name	Mobility
fighter base	enemy	51.000N	13.700E	dresden	--
fighter base	enemy	51.310N	13.530E	merseberg	--
fighter base	enemy	51.310N	11.530E	grossenhain	--
fighter base	enemy	50.900N	12.510E	attenberg	--
fighter base	enemy	51.400N	11.460E	allstedt	--
fighter base	enemy	50.970N	10.946E	erfurt	--
fighter base	enemy	51.310N	12.660E	brandis	--
SA-2	enemy	51.283N	13.446E	--	low
SA-2	enemy	51.316N	12.199E	--	low
SA-2	enemy	51.316N	13.710E	--	low

Entities in the Reduced Region

Item	Disposition	Latitude	Longitude	Name	Mobility
fighter base	enemy	51.330N	11.960E	merseberg	--
fighter base	enemy	51.310N	13.530E	grossenhain	--
fighter base	enemy	51.100N	13.700E	dresden	--
fighter base	enemy	51.310N	12.660E	brandis	--
fighter base	enemy	50.900N	12.510E	attenberg	--
fighter base	enemy	51.400N	11.460E	allstedt	--
SA-2	enemy	51.283N	12.465E	--	low
SA-2	enemy	51.316N	12.716E	--	low
SA-3	enemy	51.250N	13.100E	--	high
SA-3	enemy	50.950N	12.366E	--	high
SA-3	enemy	51.403N	11.516E	--	high
SA-4	enemy	51.473N	12.953E	--	low
SA-4	enemy	51.450N	11.916E	--	low
SA-6	enemy	51.016N	13.506E	--	high
SA-6	enemy	51.046N	13.536E	--	high
SA-6	enemy	51.133N	13.753E	--	high
SA-6	enemy	51.166N	13.520E	--	high
SA-6	enemy	51.216N	13.603E	--	high
steel plant	enemy	51.211N	13.400E	schutz steel	--

☐ Point 1: The icon you pointed at does does not have the property "mobility"; but a nearby referent has been found
Point 3: Your point gesture did not touch any objects on the display; however a nearby object containing property "mobility" has been found
Be aware: You made a singular reference and more than one object corresponded to your mouse gesture(s).
The mobility of this sam is low, the mobility of this sam is high, and the mobility of this sam is high.
▸) Zoom in on this point ((650 199 "COLOR")) .

CUBRICON correctly interprets the point as referring to a geometric point location, even though the user's point gesture touches some icon on the display. This is due to the NL phrase "this point" accompanying the mouse point gesture. The system interprets the statement as an instruction to magnify an area around the location of the point. The system uses a predefined "radius" to determine the area to magnify. CUBRICON then draws a box around the area to be magnified so that the user can follow its activities. At this point the system has a couple of choices: It can repaint the existing map window with the new area, or it can open a window to show the new area. Since CUBRICON's task model does not indicate that the user's task has changed, it assumes that the original map is still relevant. It therefore opens an additional window to show the new area, as illustrated in Figure 2.5a. To present attributes of the entities on the new map that are not communicated via the color graphics map and to maintain consistency, CUBRICON displays a table of the important attributes of the entities visible on the new map. To maintain positioning consistency on the two monitors, CUBRICON places the table window on the monochrome monitor in a position that closely matches the position of the new map window on the color monitor.

In this section we have discussed examples to (1) illustrate some of the key functionality of the CUBRICON system, (2) show how some of the important CUBRICON knowledge sources are used, and (3) show how the important human factor guidelines are applied by the system. The functionality illustrated includes the ability of the system to accept and understand a multi-media noun phrase that consists of a textual noun phrase accompanied by a pointing reference; use natural language to infer the intended referent of an "ill-formed" dual-media expression; select the modalities for presentation of information to the user; select relevant information to present to the user; compose the multi-media presentations, particularly map graphics and tables; and use coordinated speech and pointing gestures for output. The CUBRICON knowledge sources used in the examples of this section include the nature and characteristics of the information to be expressed, the knowledge bases, the discourse model, and the user model. The guidelines discussed in the examples were the maintain-context guideline and the consistency guideline.

2.9 CURRENT STATUS AND FUTURE DIRECTION

As stated in Section 2.2, CUBRICON is implemented on a Symbolics Lisp Machine with a mouse pointing device and both a monochrome graphics monitor and a color graphics monitor. The Dragon Systems VoiceScribe 1000 speech recognition system and the DECtalk speech production system are both fully functional in the CUBRICON hardware suite of equipment.

The CUBRICON software modules discussed are implemented and functioning. These modules include: the lexicon and grammar for parsing and interpreting input consisting of NL speech or keyboard text with simultaneous coordinated pointing to objects on the graphics displays; the executor that retrieves information from the target information system for presentation to the user; the process of selecting media/modalities for the presentation of information to the user; the processes of intelligently composing map displays and tables; the process of generating simultaneous coordinated speech and pointing gestures during output; and the knowledge sources, including the knowledge bases, discourse model, and user model.

The CUBRICON team is continuing its development of the processes discussed in this paper as well as developing new functionality. Areas in which the team is continuing current work and/or planning future development include:

1. Extending and refining the system's automated process of selecting the appropriate media/modalities for expressing responses to the user
2. Enhancing the user model and developing the task hierarchy
3. Adding additional modalities (e.g., predefined forms for mission planning) to the CUBRICON repertoire
4. Extending and refining the process of determining whether the desired resources are available and, if not, either modifying the state of the resources or the information to be expressed, or selecting different modalities for expressing the information
5. Extending the functionality of the multimodal output generator to produce more sophisticated, highly integrated natural language and graphics at the discourse and sentence level, including the coordinated presentation of time- and space-dependent activities and events (e.g., planned movements of military forces)

2.10 SUMMARY

This paper discussed the architecture of the CUBRICON system, the key functionality of the system, the important knowledge sources used by the system, multi-media language understanding, the system's process for composing multimodal output, examples illustrating some of the system's key functionality and processing methodology, and the current status and future direction of the CUBRICON project.

Key functionality of the system includes the ability to handle simultaneous input in natural language and graphics pointing, automated selection of media/modalities for output presentation, and automated composition of multi-media responses to be conveyed to the user.

The knowledge sources used by the CUBRICON system are the lexicon and grammar, the discourse model, the user model, the knowledge bases of general world and application-specific knowledge, the nature and characteristics of the information to be presented, guidelines for enhancing human comprehension, and the constraints or limitations of the hardware input and output devices.

The system's parsing/interpretation of input consisting of simultaneous coordinated natural-language and graphics pointing gestures was discussed with emphasis on the system's ability (1) to use natural-language to disambiguate pointing to objects on a graphics display and (2) to infer the intended referent of a dual-media expression in which the user misses the object to which he or she intended to point.

The system's output composition process includes selection of appropriate modalities and media, determination of whether resources are available, subsequent modification of resources or information to be expressed (if necessary), modification of selected output modalities/media (if necessary), and composition of the output.

Examples were presented to illustrate some of the key functionality of the CUBRICON system, to show how the CUBRICON knowledge sources are used, and to show how two important guidelines for enhancing human comprehension are applied by the system.

CUBRICON is being developed as part of the Intelligent Multi-Media Interfaces Project. This project is devoted to the development of interface technology that integrates speech, natural-language text, graphics, tables, and pointing gestures for human-computer dialogues. The objective of the project is to develop interface technology that uses the media/modalities intelligently in a flexible, context-sensitive, and highly integrated manner.

ACKNOWLEDGMENTS

The other members of the CUBRC team are J. Byoun, Z. Dobes, D. Funke, J. Lammens, M. Summers, and C. Thielman.

The RADC MAP Display System was initially developed by Lt. Mike Hilton (RADC), who graciously arranged for us to use it.

REFERENCES

[Aceves84] Aceves, J. J. G., Poggio, A., and Eliott, D. 1984. *Research into Multimedia Message System Architecture, Final Report.* Proj. No. 5363. Menlo Park, CA: SRI International.

[ACM88] ACM. 1988. *Communications of the ACM: Special Issue on HyperText,* 31(7).

[Allgayer89] Allgayer, J., Jansern-Winkeln, R., Reddig, C., and Reithinger, N. 1989. Bidirectional Use of Knowledge in the Multi-modal NL Access System XTRA. *Proceedings of IJCAI-89,* Detroit, pp. 1492–1497.

[Andriole86] Andriole, S. J. 1986. Graphic Equivalence, Graphic Explanations, and Embedded Process Modeling for Enhanced Process Modeling for Enhanced

User-system Interaction. *IEEE Trans. on Systems, Man, and Cybernetics*, 16 (6), 919–926.

[Arens88] Arens, Y., Miller, L., Shapiro, S., and Sondheimer, N. 1988. Automatic Construction of User-Interface Displays. *Proceedings of AAAI-88*, pp. 808–813.

[Arens91] Arens, Y., Miller, L., and Sondheimer, N. 1991. Presentation Design Using an Integrated Knowledge Base. In present volume.

[Carberry87] Carberry, S. 1987. First International Workshop on User Modeling. *AI Magazine*, 8(3), 71–74.

[Carbonell85] Carbonell, J. G., Boggs, W. M., Mauldin, M. L., and Anick, P. G. 1985. An Integrated Natural Language Interface. In Andriole, S. (ed.), *Applications in Artificial Intelligence.* Petrocelli Books, pp. 227–245.

[Cheikes88] Cheikes, B. A., and Webber, B. L. 1988. The Design of a Cooperative Respondent, *Proceedings of The Workshop on Architectures for Intelligent Interfaces: Elements and Prototypes*, J.W. Sullivan and Tyler, S.W. (eds.), Monterey, CA, March, pp. 3–17.

[Conklin87] Conklin, J. 1987. Hypertext: An Introduction and Survey. *Computer*, 20(9), 17–41.

[Egan89] Egan, D. E., Remde, J. R., Gomez, L. M., Landauer, T. K., Eberhardt, J., and Lochbaum, C. C. 1989. Formative Design-Evaluation of SuperBook. *ACM Transactions on Information Systems*, 7(1), 30–58.

[Feiner82] Feiner, S., Nagy, S., and van Dam, A. 1982. An Experimental System for Creating and Presenting Interactive Graphical Documents. *Trans. Graphics*, 1(1), 59–72.

[Feiner89] Feiner, S., and McKeown, K. R. 1989. Coordinating Text and Graphics in Explanation Generation. *Proceedings of the DARPA Speech and Natural Language Workshop*, Cape Cod, MA, pp. 424–433.

[Grosz78] Grosz, B. J. 1978. Discourse Analysis, in Walker, D., (ed.), *Understanding Spoken Language.* New York: Elsevier North-Holland, pp. 229–345.

[Grosz81] Grosz, B. J. 1981. Focusing and Description in Natural Language Dialogues. In Joshi, A., Webber, B. and Sag, I. (eds.), *Elements of Discourse Understanding.* New York: Cambridge University Press, pp. 84–105.

[Grosz85] Grosz, B. J., and Sidner, C. L. 1985. Discourse Structure and the Proper Treatment of Interruptions. *Proceedings of IJCAI*, pp. 832–839.

[Grosz86] Grosz, B. J. 1986. The Representation and Use of Focus in a System for Understanding Dialogs. In Grosz, B. J., Jones, K. S., and Webber, B. L. (eds.), *Readings in Natural Language Processing.* San Mateo, CA: Morgan Kaufmann, pp. 353–362.

[Hilton87] Hilton, M. L. 1987. Design and Implementation of the MAP Display System. RADC Report.

[Hollan91] Hollan, J., Rich, E., Hill, W., Wroblewski, D., Wilner, W., Wittenburg, K., and Gruden, J. 1991. An Introduction to Hits: Human Interface Tool Suite. In present volume.

[Kaplan82] Kaplan, S. J. 1982. Cooperative Responses from a Portable Natural-Language Database Query System, In Brady, M. (ed.), *Computational Models of Discourse.* Cambridge, MA: MIT Press, pp. 167–208.

[Kass91] Kass, R., and Finin, T. 1991. General User Modeling: A Facility to Support Intelligent Interaction. In present volume.

[Katz84] Katz, A. 1984. An Experimental Internetwork Multimedia Mail System. *Proceedings IFIP 6.5 Working Conf. Computer Message Services.* Nottingham, England.

[Kobsa86] Kobsa, A., Allgayer, J., Reddig, C., Reithinger, N., Schmauks, D., Harbusch, K., and Wahlster, W. 1986. Combining Deictic Gestures and Natural Language for Referent Identification. *Proceedings of the 11th International Conference on Computational Linguistics.* Bonn, FR Germany.

[Kobsa88] Kobsa, A., and Wahlster, W. (eds.), 1988. *Computational Linguistics: Special Issue on User Modeling.* Cambridge, MA: MIT Press.

[Maida85] Maida, A. S., and Shapiro, S. C. 1985. Intensional Concepts in Propositional Semantic Networks. In Brachman, R. J., and Levesque, H. J. (eds.), *Readings in Knowledge Representation.* San Mateo, CA: Morgan Kaufmann, pp. 169–190.

[Mason88] Mason, J. A., and Edwards, J. L. 1988. Explicit Models in Intelligent Interface Design. *Proceedings of the Workshop on Architectures for Intelligent Interfaces: Elements and Prototypes.* Sullivan, J. W. & Tyler, S. W. (eds.) Monterey, CA, March, pp. 151–167.

[McKay80] McKay, D. P., and Shapiro, S. C. 1980. MULTI—A LISP-Based Multiprocessing System. *Conference Record of the 1980 LISP Conference.* Stanford Univ., pp. 29–37.

[Miller56] Miller, G. A. 1956. The Magical Number Seven Plus or Minus Two. *Psychological Review,* 63, 81–97.

[Neal86] Neal, J. G., and Shapiro, S. C. 1986. Knowledge Representation for Reasoning about Language. In Boudreaux, J. C., Hamill, B. W., and Jernigan, R. (eds.), *The Role of Language in Problem Solving.* New York: Springer-Verlag, pp. 27–47.

[Neal87] Neal, J. G., and Shapiro, S. C. 1987. Knowledge Based Parsing. In Bolc, L., (ed.), *Natural Language Parsing Systems.* New York: Springer-Verlag, pp. 49–92.

[Neal88a] Neal, J. G., Bettinger, K. E., Byoun, J. S., Dobes, Z., and Thielman, C. Y. 1988. An Intelligent Multi-media Human-Computer Dialogue System. *Proceedings of the Workshop on Space Operations, Automation, and Robotics (SOAR-88).* Dayton: Wright State University, pp. 245–251.

[Neal88b] Neal, J. G., Dobes, Z., Bettinger, K. E., and Byoun, J. S. 1988. Multi-modal References in Human-Computer Dialogue. *Proceedings of AAAI-88,* pp. 819–823.

[Neal89] Neal, J. G., Thielman, C. Y., Dobes, Z., Haller, S. M., and Shapiro, S. C. 1989. Natural Language with Integrated Deictic and Graphic Gestures. *Proceedings of the DARPA Speech and Natural Language Workshop,* Cape Cod, MA, pp. 410–423.

[Neches86] Neches, R., and Kaczmarek, T. 1986. *AAAI-86 Workshop on Intelligence in Interfaces.* USC/Information Sciences Institute, August 1986.

[Press86] Press, B. 1986. The U.S. Air Force TEMPLAR Project Status and Outlook. *Western Conf. on Knowledge-Based Engineering and Expert Systems,* Anaheim, CA, pp. 42–48.

[Reithinger87] Reithinger, N. 1987. Generating Referring Expressions and Pointing Gestures. In Kempen, G. (ed.), *Natural Language Generation.* Dordrecht: Nijhoff, pp. 71–81.

[Roth91] Roth, S., Mattis, J., and Mesnard, X. 1991. Graphics and Natural Language as Components of Automatic Explanation. In present volume.

[Shapiro75] Shapiro, S. C. 1975. Generation as Parsing from a Network into a Linear String. *AJCL,* microfiche 33, pp. 45–62.

[Shapiro79a] Shapiro, S. C. 1979. The SNePS Semantic Network Processing System. In Findler, (ed.), *Associative Networks: The Representation and Use of Knowledge by Computers,* New York: Academic Press, pp. 179–203.

[Shapiro79b] Shapiro, S. C. 1979. Using Non-standard Connectives and Quantifiers for Representing Deduction Rules in a Semantic Network. Invited paper presented at *Current Aspects of AI Research,* seminar held at the Electrotechnical Laboratory, Tokyo.

[Shapiro79c] Shapiro, S. C. 1979. Numerical Quantifiers and Their Use in Reasoning with Negative Information. *Proceedings of IJCAI,* pp. 791–796.

[Shapiro81] Shapiro, S. C., and SNePS Implementation Group. 1981. *SNePS User's Manual.* Buffalo, NY, SUNY CS Dept.

[Shapiro82a] Shapiro, S. C. 1982. Generalized Augmented Transition Network Grammars for Generation from Semantic Networks. *AJCL,* 8(1), 12–25.

[Shapiro82b] Shapiro, S. C., Martens, J., and McKay, D. 1982. Bi-directional Inference. *Proceedings of the Cognitive Science Society,* pp. 90–93.

[Shapiro82c] Shapiro, S. C., and Neal, J. G. 1982. A Knowledge Engineering Approach to Natural Language Understanding. *Proceedings of ACL,* pp. 136–144.

[Shapiro87] Shapiro, S. C., and Rapaport, W. 1987. SNePS Considered as a Fully Intensional Propositional Semantic Network, *Proc. AAAI-86,* pp. 278–283; in McCalla, G., and Cercone, N. (eds.), *Knowledge Representation,* New York: Springer-Verlag.

[Shepard89] Shepard, S. J. 1989. A New Approach to Hypertext: MINDS. *AI Expert,* 4(9), 69–72.

[Sidner86] Sidner, C. L. 1986. Focusing in the Comprehension of Definite Anaphora. In Grosz, B. J., Jones, K. S., and Webber, B. L. (eds.), *Readings in Natural Language Processing,* San Mateo, CA: Morgan Kaufmann, pp. 353–362.

[Simmons72] Simmons, R., and Slocum, J. 1972. Generating English Discourse from Semantic Networks. *CACM,* 15(10), 891–905.

[Sullivan91] Sullivan, J. W., and Tyler, S. W., (eds.) 1991. *Intelligent User Interfaces,* present volume.

[Thomas85] Thomas, R. H., Forsdick, H. C., Crowley, T. R., Schaaf, R. W., Tomlinson, R. S., Travers, V. M., and Robertson, G. G. 1985. Diamond: a multimedia message system built on a distributed architecture. *IEEE Computer,* December, 65–78.

[Wahlster91] Wahlster, W. 1991. User and Discourse Models for Multimodal Communication. In present volume.

[Young91] Young, R. L. 1991. A Dialogue User Interfaces Architecture. In present volume.

CHAPTER **3**

USER AND DISCOURSE MODELS FOR MULTIMODAL COMMUNICATION

WOLFGANG WAHLSTER

Computer Science Department,
German Research Center for Artificial Intelligence,
University des Saarlandes

ABSTRACT

In face-to-face conversation humans frequently use deictic gestures parallel to verbal descriptions for referent identification. Such a multimodal form of communication is of great importance for intelligent interfaces, because it simplifies and speeds up reference to objects in a visual context. Natural pointing behavior is very flexible, but possibly ambiguous or vague, so that without a careful analysis of the discourse context of a gesture there would be a high risk of reference failure. The subject of this paper is how the user and discourse models of an intelligent interface influence the comprehension and production of natural language with coordinated pointing, and conversely how multimodal communication influences the user model and the discourse model.

This research was partially supported by the German Science Foundation (DFG) in its Special Collaborative Programme on AI and Knowledge-Based Systems (SFB 314).

After a brief description the deixis analyzer of our XTRA system, which handles a variety of tactile gestures, including different granularities, inexact pointing gestures, and pars-pro-toto deixis, we present some empirical results of an experiment that investigates the similarities and differences between natural pointing in face-to-face communication and simulated pointing using our system. This paper focuses on consequences of this investigation for our present work on an extended version of the deixis analyzer and a gesture generator currently under development. We show how gestures can be used to shift focus and how focus can be used to disambiguate gestures. Finally, we discuss how the user model affects the decision of the presentation planning component to use a pointing gesture, a verbal description, or both, for referent identification.

3.1 INTRODUCTION

In face-to-face conversation humans frequently use *deictic gestures* (e.g., the index finger points at something) parallel to verbal descriptions for referent identification. Such a *multimodal* form of communication can improve human interaction with machines, because it simplifies and speeds up reference to objects in a visual world.

The basic technical prerequisites for the integration of pointing and natural language are fulfilled by high-resolution bit-mapped displays and window systems for the presentation of visual information; various pointing devices such as mouse, light-pen, joystick, and touch-sensitive screens for deictic input; and the DataGlove™[Zimmerman87] or even image sequence analysis systems for gesture recognition. But the remaining problem for artificial intelligence is that explicit meanings must be given to natural pointing behavior in terms of a formal semantics of the visual world.

Unlike the usual semantics of mouse clicks in direct manipulation environments, in human conversation the region at which the user points is not necessarily identical with the region to which he or she intends to refer. Following the terminology of Clark, we call the region at which the user points, the *demonstratum*; the descriptive part of the accompanying noun phrase, the *descriptor* (which is optional); and the region to which he or she intends to refer, the *referent* [Clark83]. In conventional systems there exists a simple one-to-one mapping of a demonstratum onto a referent, and the reference resolution process does not depend on the situational context. Moreover, the user is not able to control the granularity of a pointing gesture, since the size of the predefined mouse-sensitive region specifies the granularity.

Compared to that, natural pointing behavior is much more flexible, but also possibly ambiguous or vague. Without a careful analysis of the *discourse context* of a gesture there would be a high risk of reference failure, as a deictic operation does not cause visual feedback from the referent (e.g., inverse video or blinking as in direct manipulation systems).

The subject of this paper is how the user and discourse models of an intelligent interface influence the comprehension and production of natural language with coordinated pointing to objects on a graphics display and conversely how multimodal communication influences the user and discourse models.

Figure 3.1 outlines the basic architecture of an intelligent interface with multimodal input and output. For the sake of clarity, we have omitted all aspects of processing components and knowledge base that are not relevant to the topic of this paper.

Before we review previous research on the combination of natural language and pointing and describe some current approaches related to our work, let us briefly introduce the basic concepts of user and discourse models.

FIGURE 3.1
THE BASIC ARCHITECTURE OF AN INTELLIGENT MULTIMODAL INTERFACE

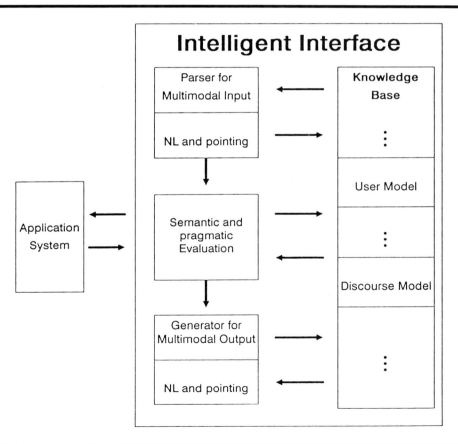

3.2 USER MODELS AND DISCOURSE MODELS

A reason for the current emphasis on user and discourse models [Wahlster86, Kobsa89] is the fact that such models are necessary prerequisites in order for a system to be capable of exhibiting a wide range of intelligent and cooperative dialogue behavior. Such models are required for identifying the objects to which the dialogue partner is referring, for analyzing a nonliteral meaning and/or indirect speech acts, and for determining what effects a planned utterance will have on the dialogue partner. A cooperative system [Wahlster84] must certainly take into account the user's goals, plans, and prior knowledge about the domain of discourse, as well as misconceptions the user may possibly have concerning the domain.

We use the following definitions [Wahlster88]:

- A *user model* is a knowledge source containing explicit assumptions about all aspects of the user that may be relevant to the dialogue behavior of the system.

- A *user modeling component* is that part of a dialogue system that performs the following functions:

1. To incrementally build up a user model
2. To store, update, and delete entries in it
3. To maintain the consistency of the model
4. To supply other components of the system with assumptions about the user

- A *discourse model* is a knowledge source that contains the system's description of the syntax, semantics, and pragmatics of a dialogue as it proceeds.

- A *discourse modeling component* is that part of a dialogue system that performs the following functions:

1. To incrementally build up a discourse model
2. To store and update entries in it
3. To supply other components of the system with information about the structure and content of previous segments of the dialogue

It seems commonly agreed upon that a discourse model should contain a syntactic and semantic description of discourse segments, a record of the discourse entities mentioned, the attentional structure of the dialogue including a focus space stack, anaphoric links, and descriptions of individual utterances on the speech act level. However, there seem to be many other ingredients needed for a good discourse representation that have not yet been determined in current discourse theory.

An important difference between a discourse model and a user model is that entries in the user model must often be explicitly deleted or updated, whereas in the discourse model entries are never deleted (except for phenomena related to forgetting). Thus according to our definition above, a belief revision component is an important part of a user modeling component.

This does not imply that the discourse model is static and only the user model is dynamic. The discourse model is also highly dynamic (consider, e.g., focus shifting), but it lacks the notion of logical consistency that is important for belief revision and default reasoning in a user modeling component. The discourse model is like an annotated trace of the various levels of the system's processing involved in understanding the user's utterances and generating its own dialogue contributions.

3.3 RELATED WORK ON DEICTIC INPUT

Although in an intelligent multimodal interface the "common visual world" of the user and the system could be any graphics or image, most of the projects that combine pointing and natural language focus on business forms or geographic maps.

To the best of our knowledge, Carbonell's work on SCHOLAR represents the first attempt to combine natural language and pointing in an intelligent interface [Carbonell70]. SCHOLAR, a tutoring system for geography, allowed simple pointing gestures on maps displayed on the terminal screen. NLG [Brown79] also combined natural language and pointing using a touch screen to specify graphics with inputs like (1).

(1) Put a point called A1 here <touch>.

Woods and his co-workers developed an ATN editor and browser that can be controlled by natural-language commands and accompanying pointing gestures at the networks displayed on the screen [Woods79].

In SDMS [Bolt80] the user can create and manipulate geometric objects by natural language and coordinated pointing gestures. The first commercially available multimodal interface combining verbal and nonverbal input was NLMenu [Thompson86], where the mouse could be used to rubber band an area on a map in sentences like (2).

(2) Find restaurants, which are located here <pointing> and serve Mexican food.

All approaches to gestural input mentioned so far in our brief review were based on a simple one-to-one mapping of the demonstratum onto a referent and thus have not attacked the central problems of analyzing pointing gestures.

Recently, several research groups have more thoroughly addressed the problems of combining nonverbal and verbal behavior. Several theoretical studies and empirical investigations about the combination of natural language and pointing have been published [Hayes86, Hinrichs87, Reilly85]. Working prototype systems have been described, which explore the use of complex pointing behavior in intelligent interfaces.

For example, the TACTILUS subcomponent[1] of our XTRA system [Kobsa86], which we will describe below in more detail, handles a variety of *tactile gestures*, including different granularities, inexact pointing gestures, and *pars-pro-toto deixis*. In the final case, the user points at an embedded region when actually intending to refer to a superordinated region.

In the DIS-QUE system [Wetzel87] the user can mix pointing and natural language to refer to student enrollment forms or maps. The deictic interpreter of the T^3 system [Scragg87] interacts with a natural language interpreter for the analysis of pointing gestures indicating ship positions on maps. In addition it can utilize continuing or repeated deictic input. CUBRICON [Neal91] is yet another system that simultaneously handles input in natural language and pointing to icons on maps, using language to disambiguate pointing and using pointing to disambiguate language.

While the simultaneous utilization of both verbal and nonverbal channels provides maximum efficiency, most of the current prototypes do not use truly parallel input techniques, since they combine *typed* natural language and pointing. In these systems the user's hands move frequently back and forth from the keyboard to the pointing device. Note, however, that multimodal input makes even natural-language interfaces without speech input more acceptable (fewer keystrokes) and that the research on typed language forms the basis for the ultimate speech-understanding system.

3.4 A CLASSIFICATION OF TACTILE POINTING GESTURES

For a study of the semantics and pragmatics of pointing, it is important to distinguish between two types of gestures:

- Pointing at *graphic models of objects* in the domain of discourse (e.g., geographic maps, icons for an office environment). In this case, the *detailed structure* of an icon is not relevant for the interpretation of a pointing gesture. For example, pointing at the lid of the trash icon causes the same effect as pointing at the can.

- Pointing at *objects* of a visual domain (e.g., forms, texts, graphics, formulas, images). In principle, *every pixel* on the screen can be a *separate reference object* in this case. For example, in our XTRA system (see Section 3.5 following) gestures can refer to all parts of the tax forms.

---

[1] In 1984 in the proposal for the XTRA project, I described the basic architecture of a flexible multimodal interface with a gesture analysis component. Since 1985, we have been working on the integration of pointing and natural language. The current version of TACTILUS was designed and implemented by J. Allgayer.

Today, most multimodal interfaces combining natural language and pointing belong to the first category (see Section 3.3 preceding). In this case, the interpretation and generation of pointing gestures are much easier than in the second category.

On the other hand, many of the subtleties of natural pointing come into their own only in the second case (see also [Schmauks87]). Moreover, that category covers a much wider range of possible applications.

Another fundamental distinction, which is independent from the classification introduced above, is whether the system deals with a static or a dynamic visual domain:

- Pointing at *fixed* and *static* visual objects on the screen (e.g., an icon for an airport on a map, a region of a tax form). In this case pointing gestures refer to *directions, locations*, or *objects*.
- Pointing at *dynamic* and *animated* visual objects on the screen (e.g., an animated ship icon on a map, a moving car in an image sequence). The pointing gestures can refer to *events* (e.g., "This U-turn was not allowed").

One limitation of the current prototypes is that the presented visual material is fixed and finite, so that the system builder can encode its semantics into the knowledge base. While some of the recent NL interfaces respond to queries by generating graphics, they are not able to analyze and answer follow-up questions about the form and content of these graphics, since they do not have an appropriate representation of its syntax and semantics. Here one of the challenging problems is the *automatic formalization of synthetic visual information* as a basis for the interpretation of gestural input.

3.5 XTRA: AN INTELLIGENT MULTIMODAL INTERFACE TO EXPERT SYSTEMS

XTRA (eXpert TRAnslator) is an intelligent multimodal interface to expert systems that combines natural language, graphics, and pointing for input and output. As its name suggests, XTRA is viewed as an intelligent agent, namely a translator that acts as an intermediary between the user and the expert system. XTRA's task is to translate from the high-bandwidth communication with the user into the narrow input/output channel of the interfaces provided by most of the current expert systems.

The present implementation of XTRA provides natural language access to an expert system, which assists the user in filling out a tax form. During the dialog, the relevant page of the tax form is displayed on one window of the screen, so that the user can refer to regions of the form by tactile gestures. As shown in Figure 3.2, there are two other windows on the right part of the display, which contain the natural language input of the user (upper part) and the system's response (lower part). An important aspect of

FIGURE 3.2

THE COMBINATION OF NATURAL LANGUAGE, GRAPHICS, AND POINTING
IN XTRA

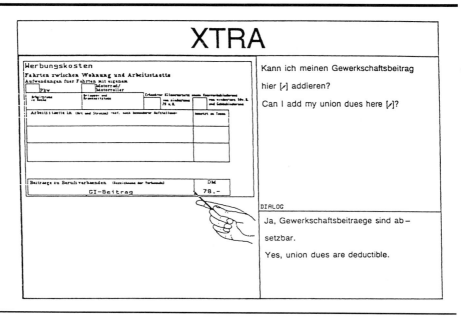

the communicative situation realized in XTRA is that the user and the system share a common visual field—the tax form. As in face-to-face communication, there is no visual feedback after a successful referent identification process. Moreover, there are no predefined 'mouse-sensitive' areas, and the forms are not specially designed to simplify gesture analysis. For example, the regions on the form may overlap, and there may be several subregions embedded in a region of the form.

XTRA uses a unification-based parser for German, which is distinguished from similar parsers in that it is able to parse multimodal input. As Figure 3.3 shows, XTRA's parser treats pointing gestures as terminal symbols in the input stream. These symbols are then mapped onto the preterminal category "deictic."

In its full generality, the parsing of multimodal input is a complicated subject in its own right, and even a modest exposition of this topic would be beyond the scope of the present paper.

The syntax and semantics of the tax form are represented as a directed acyclic graph, called *organization graph*. It contains links to concepts in a terminological knowledge base encoded in SB-ONE, a representation language in the KL-ONE paradigm. The nodes of the organization graph represent

FIGURE 3.3

A CHART PRODUCED BY XTRA'S PARSER FOR MULTIMODAL INPUT

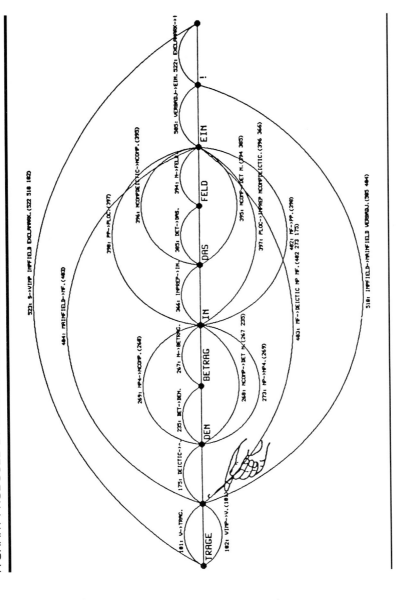

various types of regions of the form, and the edges describe relations such as "geometrically embedded" or "conceptual part of." Four types of nodes are used in this graph:

- *Value regions*, where data can be entered by the user (e.g., the region where the number 78 has been typed in; see Figure 3.2)
- *Label regions*, which provide captions for value regions and framed regions (e.g., the string DM above the number 78 in Figure 3.2)
- *Framed regions*, which highlight rectangular parts of the form (e.g., the box containing the string DM in Figure 3.2)
- *Abstract regions* as aggregations of conceptually related, but not necessarily adjacent parts of the form (e.g., the column of three boxes above the DM box in Figure 3.2)

In addition to the direct interpretation of a gesture, where the demonstratum is simply identical to the referent, TACTILUS provides two other types of interpretation. In a pars-pro-toto interpretation of a gesture the demonstratum is geometrically embedded within the referent. In this case, the referent is either a framed region that contains smaller regions, or an abstract region. An extreme case of a pars-pro-toto interpretation in the current domain of XTRA is a situation where the user points at an arbitrary part (pars in Latin) of the tax form intending to refer to the form as a whole (pro toto in Latin). Another frequent interpretation of gestures is that the demonstratum is geometrically adjacent to the referent: the user points, for instance, below or to the right of the referent. Reasons for this may be inattentiveness or the attempt to gesture without covering up the data in a field.

The user first chooses the granularity of the intended gesture by selecting the appropriate icon from the pointing mode menu or by pressing a combination of mouse buttons and then performs a tactile gesture with the pointing device symbolized by the selected mouse cursor. The current implementation supports four pointing modes (see Figure 3.4):

- Exact pointing with a pencil
- Standard pointing with the index finger
- Vague pointing with the entire hand
- Encircling regions with the '@'-sign

The deixis analyzer of XTRA is realized as a *constraint propagation* process on the organization graph described above. A pointing area of a size corresponding to the intended granularity of the gesture is associated with each available pointing mode. A plausibility value is computed for each referential candidate of a particular pointing gesture according to the ratio of the size of the part covered by the pointing area to the size of the entire region. The

FIGURE 3.4
THE POINTING MODE MENU

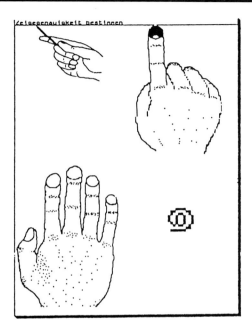

result of the propagation process is a list of referential candidates consisting of pairs of region names and plausibility values.

Since pointing is fundamentally ambiguous without the benefit of contextual information, this list often contains many elements. Therefore, TAC-TILUS uses various other knowledge sources of XTRA (e.g., the semantics of the accompanying verbal description, case frame information, the dialog memory) for the disambiguation of the pointing gesture (see [Allgayer86] and [Kobsa86] for further details).

3.6 NATURAL VERSUS SIMULATED POINTING: SOME EMPIRICAL RESULTS

In order to evaluate the strengths and limitations of the deixis analyzer described above, an experiment[2] was carried out. The main objective of the

---

[2] It should be noted that in what follows we present only some preliminary results and that the final evaluation of all the data obtained from the experiment is not yet available. The experiment was designed by M. Wille with the help of D. Schmauks and Th. Pechmann.

experiment was to investigate the *similarities* and *differences* between the following:

- *Natural pointing* in face-to-face communication with an advisor
- *Simulated pointing* using the TACTILUS component of the XTRA interface

In this experiment, 32 subjects were asked to fill in two pages of the German income tax forms using data about a fictitious person. The information about this person was provided by the experimenter in textual form.

While the first page of the tax form was presented as a hard copy and was filled out using a pencil, the second page was displayed on the screen of a Lisp machine and was filled out using TACTILUS. The complete experiment consisting of 16 hours of dialog sessions was video- and audio-taped.

The tape transcriptions consist of an analysis of both the spoken and typed or written expressions and the accompanying gestures along with their temporal interdependency.

1200 gestures were identified and classified along the following dimensions (selection only):

> device :: = pencil | finger | hand | mouse arrow (screen only)
> movement :: = point | underline | encircle
> exactness :: = precise | borderline | vague
> directness :: = tactile | visual (hardcopy only)
> location :: = exact | above | below | left | right

Considering first the data for which there was no marked difference between natural and simulated pointing, two main results of the experiment should be noted:

- The low frequency (< 1%) of the following types of pointing gestures:
  using the hand/hand icon as a pointing device
  encircling
- The high frequency of pointing *below* the demonstratum.

Let us now turn to the results of the first part of the experiment, where the subjects used a pencil to fill in a hard copy of the tax form. The most important findings for natural pointing were the following:

- The high frequency of underlining (about 30%). The data showed the following order of frequency for the dimension "type of movement": point > underline > encircle.
- The preference of the subjects for using the pencil as a pointing device.

- The high frequency of pointing at the borderline of the demonstratum (about 36%).
- The frequency of using pointing device for focusing (see Section 3.7).
- The large percentage of visual pointing gestures (about 60%) as compared to tactile pointing gestures.

An encouraging result of the experiments with TACTILUS was that after a short training period (1–2 mins) even subjects without any computer experience were able to use the system to perform the specified task. There were two important observations in this part of the experiment:

- The low frequency of underlining (1.6%)
- A greater number of gestures (830) than in the natural setting (370)

It is quite clear that the higher frequency of pointing in the dialog sessions with TACTILUS can be explained by the fact that in this setting the subjects had the additional task of positioning the input cursor, which required extra pointing.

Most of the design decisions for TACTILUS were supported by the findings from the experiment. It became evident that the important prerequisites for truly natural interaction in a multimodel mode are the following:

- *Context-sensitive interpretation* of pointing gestures (i.e., no one-to-one mapping of the demonstratum onto the referent)
- A *user model* and *discourse model* together with *assertional* and *terminological knowledge* for the interpretation of *ambiguous* pointing gestures

In addition, it was concluded that the ability to deal with a variety of tactile gestures, including different granularities and inexact pointing, to evaluate pointing gestures *below* the demonstratum and to cope with pars-pro-toto deixis is a positive feature of the current implementation that should be extended in future versions of the system.

On the other hand, the data suggest that in our current work on an improved version of TACTILUS the hand icon should be removed and that we need not make an effort to extend the mechanisms for the interpretation of encircling gestures (e.g., by allowing circles around arbitrary polygons), since these options were used extremely seldom. It also became clear that the interpretation of focusing gestures must be included in an improved version of the system, since this use of pointing was often observed in the natural setting but could not be handled by TACTILUS.

The high frequency of visual pointing gestures on the 2D tax forms showed that the 3D analysis of the position and orientation of the pointing device (e.g., by using a DataGlove™) is a promising direction for further improvements of the current system. With two DataGloves and the option to type with the gloves or to use speech input, truly parallel input becomes possible.

Finally, some comments are in order concerning the extent to which these findings may be generalized. The situation investigated in this study was highly restricted. The study was limited to 2D demonstrata with a permanent location. 3D and moving objects were excluded as targets for pointing actions. Another limitation of the present study concerned the nature of the experimental task, which was basically data entry. There is a large variety of situations in which people use deictic gestures that could not be studied in the present experiment.

3.7 THE INFLUENCE OF POINTING GESTURES ON THE DISCOURSE MODEL

In the experiment reported above, pointing was used not only for referent identification but also to mark or change the *dialogue focus*, for example, to control or shift *attention* during comprehension. As we noted in section 3.2, focus is an important notion in a discourse model, since it influences many aspects of language analysis and production. For example, focus can be used to disambiguate definite descriptions and anaphora [Grosz81].

Figure 3.5 gives an example of the disambiguation of a definite description using a focusing gesture. Without focus the definite description 'the A' is ambiguous in the given visual context, since three objects are visible which could be referred to as 'A' (one in each row of the table displayed in Figure 3.5). Together with the gesture of pointing at row Y, which marks this row as a part of the immediate focus, the definite description can be disambiguated, since there is only one 'A' in the focused row.

As in the case of gestures for referent identification, the effect of a focusing gesture can also be produced by a *verbal paraphrase*. For the example presented in Figure 3.5, a meta-utterance like 'Now let's discuss the entries in row Y' would have the same effect on the discourse model and help to disambiguate the subsequent definite description.

As we noted earlier, without a discourse context most pointing gestures are ambiguous. In the example above, we have seen that a discourse context can be established not only by verbal information but also by gestures. Thus there is a twofold relation between gestures and focus. Gestures can be used to shift focus, and focus can be used to disambiguate gestures.

From this it follows that in *simultaneous pointing actions* two communicative functions of pointing can be combined: focus shifting and reference. The following two types of simultaneous pointing can be identified:

- One-handed input:

    Focusing act: For example, the pencil is put down on the form, so that it points to a particular region on the form.

FIGURE 3.5
FOCUSING GESTURE DISAMBIGUATING THE QUESTION "WHY SHOULD I DELETE THE 'A'" '

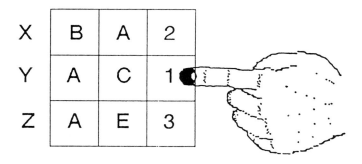

> Referential act: A subsequent pointing gesture refers to an object in the marked region.

- Two-handed input (see also [Buxton86]):

> Focusing act: For example, the index finger of one hand points to a region of the form.

> Referential act: The index finger of the other hand points to an object in the marked region.

Figures 3.6 and 3.7 illustrate the use of focusing gestures for the disambiguation of referential gestures. Note that in both situations displayed in Figures 3.6 and 3.7 the index finger points at the same location on the form and that the utterances combined with these referential gestures are identical. The cases shown in both figures differ only in the location of the pencil used for focusing.

Let us explore the processing of these examples in detail. Since the referential gesture with the index finger is relatively inexact, TACTILUS computes a large set of possible referents. The head noun, "numbers," of the verbal description that accompanies the pointing gesture imposes two restrictions on this set of possible referents. Since there are only four numbers displayed on the part of the form shown in Figures 3.6 and 3.7, the semantics of the noun restricts the solution space to the power set of $\{3, 4, 7, 5\}$, and the plural implies that only sets with at least two elements are considered in this power set. Finally, the position of the index finger on the form makes the interpretations $\{3, 7, 5\}, \{3, 4, 5\}, \{3, 4, 7\}$ and $\{4, 5, 7\}$ implausible, so that the resulting set of plausible referential readings becomes $\{\{3, 4\}, \{4, 5\}, \{3, 4, 7, 5\}\}$, where $\{3, 4, 7, 5\}$ is a typical example of a pars-proto-toto reading.

FIGURE 3.6

SIMULTANEOUS POINTING GESTURES

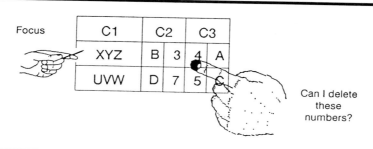

This means that there remain three possible interpretations before we consider the focusing gesture. It is worth noting that this is one of the cases where the combination of verbal and nonverbal information in one reference act does not lead to an unambiguous reading. Here information from the discourse model helps to clarify what is meant. In Figure 3.6 the pencil points at the row beginning with XYZ, so that this row and all its parts become focused. Now the intersection of the set of plausible referents and the currently focused objects results in the unique interpretation {3, 4}. Similarly, in Figure 3.7 the pencil is pointing at the block of columns called 'C3', so that the intersection of the focused elements with the results of the referential analysis is again a unique interpretation, namely {4, 5}, but it differs from the set of referents found for the gestural input shown in Figure 3.5. These examples once again emphasize the basic premise of our work, that pointing gestures must be interpreted in a highly context-sensitive way and that all approaches supposing a one-to-one mapping of the demonstratum onto the referent will fail in complex multimodal interactions.

FIGURE 3.7

SIMULTANEOUS POINTING GESTURES WITH DIFFERENT FOCUS

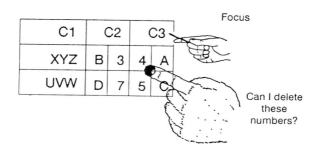

FIGURE 3.8
INTRINSIC INTERPRETATION OF 'REPLACE THE BOX BY THE RIGHT CIRCLE'

As we have seen, each focusing gesture modifies the discourse model. Another example of the impact of such focus information on the comprehension process is the effect of gestures on the selection of the *intrinsic* or *extrinsic use of spatial relations*. It is well known that the interpretation of spatial expressions depends on the selected frame of reference (for a more complete discussion of the intrinsic versus extrinsic use of spatial prepositions see [Retz-Schmidt88]).

One way to establish a reference frame is to use an intrinsic orientation. For example, consider the interpretation of the definite description 'the right circle' in Figure 3.8. Since there are three circles in the shared visual world of the user and the system, the interpretation of 'right' is crucial for finding the correct referent. In this case, the normal reading direction selecting from left to right forms the basis for an intrinsic interpretation as a default, selecting Circle 5 as the referent of the noun phrase.

Another way to establish a frame of reference is the use of a certain point of view for the extrinsic interpretation of spatial relations. The pointing gesture at Box 2 shown in Figure 3.9 overrides the default interpretation used for Figure 3.8. The focus information in the discourse model resulting from the gesture should cause the system to favor an interpretation

FIGURE 3.9
EXTRINSIC INTERPRETATION OF 'REPLACE THE BOX BY THE RIGHT CIRCLE'

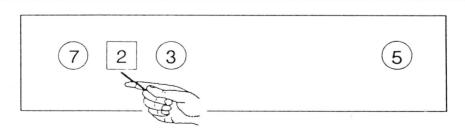

where 'the right circle' refers to Circle 3. In this example, the position of the pointer induces a reference frame for the interpretation of the spatial description.

Note that in this situation the pointing gesture at Box 2 is redundant with respect to the referent identification process for the noun phrase 'the box'. Because only one box is visible, a unique referent can be determined without considering discourse information.

3.8 USER MODELING FOR PRESENTATION PLANNING

As we noted at the outset, an intelligent interface should be able not only to analyze multimodal input, but also to generate multimodal output. The design of XTRA's generator allows the simultaneous production of deictic descriptions and pointing actions [Reithinger87]. Because an intelligent interface should try to generate cooperative responses, it has to exploit its user model to generate descriptions tailored to users with various levels of expertise.

One important decision that a multimodal presentation planner has to make is whether to use a pointing gesture or a verbal description for referent identification. Let us use an example from our tax domain to explore the impact of the user model on this decision.

Suppose the system knows the concept 'Employee Savings Benefit' and an entry in the user model says that the current dialog partner seems to be unfamiliar with this concept. When the system plans to refer to a field in the tax form, which could be referred to using 'Employee Savings Benefit' as a descriptor, it should not use this technical term but a pointing gesture to the corresponding field. This means that in the conversational context described (3) would be a cooperative response, whereas (4) would be uncooperative.

(3) You can enter that amount here [↗] | in this [↗] field.
(4) You can enter that amount as employee savings benefit.

To summarize that point, if the system knows that a technical term which could be used to refer to a particular part of the tax form visible on the screen is not understandable to the user, it can generate a pointing gesture, possibly accompanied by a mutually known descriptor.

In the following, we discuss a particular method of user modeling, called *anticipation feedback*, that can help the system to select the right granularity of pointing when generating multimodal output. Anticipation feedback loops involve the use of the system's comprehension capability to simulate the user's interpretation of a communicative act that the system plans to realize [Wahlster86]. The application of anticipation feedback loops is based on the implicit assumption that the system's comprehension procedures are similar to those of the user. In essence, anticipation on the part of the system means answering a question like (5).

(5) If I had to analyze this communicative act relative to the assumed knowledge of the user, then what would be the effect on me?

If the answer to this question does not match the system's intention in planning the tested utterance, it has to replan its utterance, as in a generate-and-test loop. Figure 3.10 shows an extremely simplified version of a multimodal description planning process with an anticipation feedback loop for user modeling. Let us assume that the generator decided to plan a deictic description of an object X, to which the systems intends to refer. The result of the de-

FIGURE 3.10
AN ANTICIPATION FEEDBACK LOOP FOR PRESENTATION PLANNING

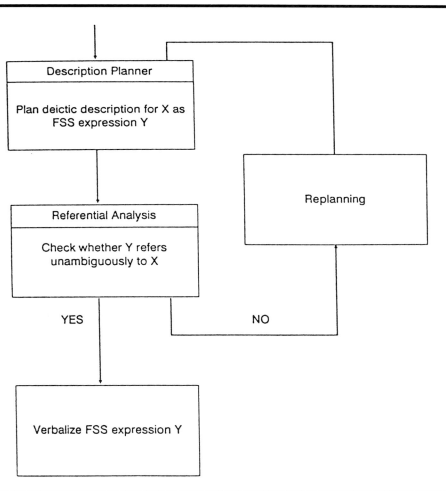

scription planning process is a an expression Y of the functional-semantic structure (FSS) together with planned gesture. The FSS is a surface-oriented semantic representation language used on one of the processing levels of the how-to-say component of XTRA's generator.

This preliminary deictic description is fed back into the system's analysis component, where the referent identification component together with the gesture analyzer TACTILUS try to find the intended discourse object. If the system finds that the planned deictic description refers unambiguously to X, the description is fed into the final transformation process before it is outputted. Otherwise, an alternative FSS and/or pointing gesture has to be found in the next iteration of the feedback process (Figure 3.10).

Now let us use a concrete example to follow the feedback method as it goes through the loop. Suppose that the system plans to refer to the string 'Membership Fees' in the box shown in Figure 3.11. Also assume that the presentation planner has already decided to generate an utterance like 'Delete this [↗]' together with the pointing gesture shown in Figure 3.12.

For a punctual pointing gesture the system chooses the pencil as a pointing device. In this case, the exact position of the pencil was selected according to XTRA's default strategy described in [Schmaucks88]: the pencil is below the entry, so that the symbol does not cover it.

When this pointing gesture is fed back into the gesture analyzer of the referent identification component, the set of anticipated reference candidates might be {'Fees', 'e', 'Membership Fees'} containing only elements that can be 'deleted' (the current version of TACTILUS does not deal with characters or substrings of a string). Since the system has detected that the planned gesture is ambiguous, it starts replanning and then selects the index finger icon as a pointing gesture with less granularity (Figure 3.12). This time, the result of the feedback process is unambiguous, so that the system can finally perform the pointing action.

FIGURE 3.11
PLANNED POINTING GESTURE

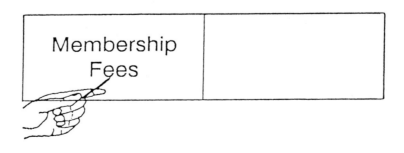

FIGURE 3.12
POINTING GESTURE AFTER REPLANNING

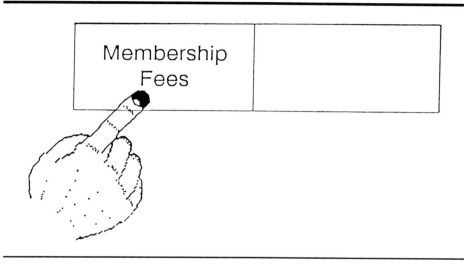

3.9 CONCLUSIONS

We have shown how the user and discourse models of an intelligent interface influence the comprehension and production of natural language with coordinated pointing to objects on a graphics display, and conversely how multimodal communication influences the user model and the discourse model.

First, we described XTRA as an intelligent interface to expert systems that handles a variety of tactile gestures, including different granularities, inexact pointing, and pars-pro-toto deixis, in a domain- and language-independent way. Then we discussed several extensions to the XTRA's deixis analyzer and presented our approach to generating multimodal output.

We showed how gestures can be used to shift focus and focus can be used to disambiguate gestures, so that simultaneous pointing actions combine two communicative functions: focus shifting and reference. We explored the role of user modeling for presentation planning and described how the user model can be exploited to generate multimodal descriptions tailored to the user's level of expertise.

Finally, we discussed anticipation feedback as a particular method of user modeling that can help the system to select the right granularity of pointing when generating multimodal output.

Some of the questions that have to be answered through future research on intelligent multimodal interfaces are the following:

■ How can we deal with pointing gestures which refer to events? When there are dynamic and animated objects on the screen, the restriction of current prototypes, that is, that the presented visual material is fixed and static, is no longer viable.

■ How can we handle pointing in 3D space? In the current systems the deictic space is two-dimensional and all objects are completely visible, so that tactile pointing is always possible.

■ How can we cope with complex pointing actions, for example, a continuous movement of the index finger (underlining something, specifying a direction or a path) or a quick repetition of discrete pointing acts (emphatic pointing, multiple reference)?

References

[Allgayer86] Allgayer, J., and Reddig, C. 1986. Processing Descriptions Containing Words and Gestures—A System Architecture. In Rollinger, C.-R. (ed.), *Proceedings GWAI/ÖGAI 1986.* Berlin: Springer, pp. 119–130.

[Bolt80] Bolt, R. A. 1980. Put-That-There: Voice and Gesture at the Graphics Interface. *Computer Graphics*, 14, 262–270.

[Brown79] Brown, D. C., Kwasny, S. C., Chandrasekaran, B., and Sondheimer, N. K. 1979. An Experimental Graphics System with Natural-Language Input. *Computer and Graphics*, 4, 13–22.

[Buxton86] Buxton, W., and Myers, B. A. 1986. A Study in Two-Handed Input. In *Proc. CHI'86 Human Factors in Computing Systems*, New York: ACM, pp. 321–326.

[Carbonell70] Carbonell, J. R. 1970. *Mixed-Initiative Man-Computer Dialogues.* BBN Report No. 1971. Cambridge, MA: Bolt, Beranek and Newman.

[Clark83] Clark, H. H., Schreuder, R., and Buttrick, S. 1983. Common Ground and the Understanding of Demonstrative Reference. *Journal of Verbal Learning and Verbal Behavior*, 22, 245–258.

[Grosz81] Grosz, B. 1981. Focusing and Description in Natural Language Dialogues. In Joshi, A., Webber, B., and Sag, I. (eds.) *Elements of Discourse Understanding.* New York: Cambridge Univ. Press, pp. 84–105.

[Hayes86] Hayes, P. J. 1986. Steps towards Integrating Natural Language and Graphical Interaction for Knowledge-based Systems. *Proceedings 7th European Conference on Artificial Intelligence*, Brighton, Great Britain, pp. 436–465.

[Hinrichs87] Hinrichs, E., and Polanyi, L. 1987. Pointing The Way: A Unified Treatment of Referential Gesture in Interactive Discourse. *Papers from the Parasession on Pragmatics and Grammatical Theory at the 22nd Regional Meeting*, Chicago Linguistic Society, Chicago, pp. 298–314.

[Kobsa86] Kobsa, A., Allgayer, J., Reddig, C., Reithinger, N., Schmauks, D., Harbusch, K., and Wahlster, W. 1986. Combining Deictic Gestures and Natural Language for Referent Identification. In *Proceedings 11th International Conf. on Computational Linguistics*, Bonn, Germany, pp. 356–361.

[Kobsa89] Kobsa, A., and Wahlster, W. (eds.), 1989. *User Models in Dialog Systems*. New York: Springer.

[Neal91] Neal, J. G., and Shapiro, S. C. 1991. Intelligent Multi-Media Interface Technology. In present volume.

[Reilly85] Reilly, R., (ed.) 1985. *Communication Failure in Dialogue: Techniques for Detection and Repair*. Dublin, Ireland: Deliverable 2, Esprit Project 527, Educational Research Center, St. Patrick's College.

[Reithinger87] Reithinger, N. 1987. Generating Referring Expressions and Pointing Gestures. In Kempen, G. (ed.) *Natural-Language Generation*, Dordrecht: Kluwer, pp. 71–81.

[Retz-Schmidt88] Retz-Schmidt, G. 1988. Various Views on Spatial Prepositions. In *AI Magazine*, 9 (2) 95–105. Also appeared as: Report No. 33, SFB 314, University of Saarbrücken, Computer Science Department.

[Schmauks87] Schmauks, D. 1987. Natural and Simulated Pointing. In *Proceedings 3rd European ACL Conference*, Copenhagen, Denmark, pp. 179–185.

[Schmauks88] Schmauks, D., and Reithinger, N. 1988. Generating Multimodal Output—Conditions, Advantages, and Problems. In *Proceedings 12th International Conference on Computational Linguistics*, Budapest, Hungary, pp. 584–588.

[Scragg87] Scragg, G. W. 1987. *Deictic Resolution of Anaphora*. Unpublished paper, Franklin and Marshall College, P.O. Box 3003, Lancaster, PA 17604.

[Thompson86] Thompson, C. 1986. Building Menu-Based Natural Language Interfaces. *Texas Engineering Journal*, 3, 140–150.

[Wahlster84] Wahlster, W. 1984. Cooperative Access Systems. *Future Generation Computer Systems*, 1, 103–111.

[Wahlster86] Wahlster, W., and Kobsa, A. 1986. Dialog-Based User Models. In Ferrari, G. (ed.), *Proceedings of the IEEE*, 74 (7), 948–960.

[Wahlster88] Wahlster, W. 1988. Distinguishing User Models from Discourse Models. In Kobsa, A., and Wahlster, W. (eds.) *Computational Linguistics*. Special Issue on User Modeling, 14 (3), 101–103.

[Wetzel87] Wetzel, R. P., Hanne, K. H., and Hoepelmann, J. P. 1987. *DIS-QUE: Deictic Interaction System-Query Environment*. LOKI Report KR-GR 5.3/KR-NL 5, Stuttgart, Germany: Fraunhofer Gesellschaft, IAO.

[Woods79] Woods, W. A., et al. 1979. *Research in Natural Language Understanding*. Cambridge, MA: Annual Report, TR 4274, Bolt, Cambridge, MA: Beranek and Newman.

[Zimmermann87] Zimmermann, T. G., Lanier, J., Blouchard, C., Bryson, S., and Harvill, Y. 1987. A Hand Gesture Interface Device. *Proceedings CHI'87 Human Factors in Computing Systems*, New York: ACM, pp. 189–192.

CHAPTER 4

THE CONTRIBUTING INFLUENCE OF SPEECH AND INTERACTION ON HUMAN DISCOURSE PATTERNS

SHARON L. OVIATT *and* **PHILIP R. COHEN**
Artificial Intelligence Center, SRI International

ABSTRACT

The present chapter provides an empirical comparison of the discourse organization, referential characteristics, and performance efficiency of task-oriented language occurring in three different communication modalities: interactive speech, noninteractive speech, and interactive keyboard. The commonalities are evaluated between (1) the two spoken modalities, in contrast with keyboard, and (2) the two interactive modalities, in contrast with the noninteractive one. Implications are discussed for the development of future interfaces and technology that are either based on speech or involve limited interactivity.

This research was supported primarily by the National Institute of Education under contract US-NIE-C-400-76-0116 to the Center for the Study of Reading at the University of Illinois and Bolt Beranek and Newman, Inc., and in part by a contract from ATR International to SRI International. Authors' current address: Artificial Intelligence Center, SRI International, 333 Ravenswood Avenue, Menlo Park, CA 94025

4.1 INTRODUCTION

Communication channels physically constrain the flow and shape of human language just as irresistibly as a river bed directs the river's current. Escarpments speed the current, sculpting jetties and whirlpools. Meadows encourage evenness, a certain recumbency. The flow becomes a deafening cascade as it passes over granite bolders, and is abruptly arrested behind man-made dams. In short, the river is molded, rendered navigable or not, through the physical medium of its own bed. Although communication modalities may be less visually compelling than the terrain surrounding a river, it is a mistake to assume that they are any less influential in shaping the language transmitted within them.

Understanding the influence of communication modalities begins with an identification of their landmark features, and of the observable impact of these features on language. The present chapter focuses on two fundamental and potentially orthogonal landmarks that shape the nature of a communication modality: transmission through speech, and interaction between conversants. One goal of this chapter is to provide a comparison of the discourse and performance characteristics of instructions presented in three different modalities, each of which was classified according to the presence or absence of the following: (1) Speech and (2) Interaction. A second goal is to begin constructing an analytical framework from which predictions can be made about the separate impact of speech and interaction on specific aspects of discourse and performance. If we can predict what the desirable qualities will be of proposed technologies that are based on different communication modalities, then we will be more able to optimize the design of future applications.

In the present research, telephone, audiotape, and keyboard instructions were compared for teams in which an expert instructed a novice on how to assemble a hydraulic water pump. The spoken modalities were telephone and audiotape, which contrasted with typed input via keyboard. The two modalities with interactive capability included telephone and linked keyboard, whereas the audiotape instructions were transmitted noninteractively. A final partitioning of the modalities was based on the presence of *interactive speech*. For this contrast, the telephone modality, which was unique in its natural combination of both the speech and interaction components, was distinguished from audiotape and keyboard. A comprehensive set of discourse and performance characteristics was examined, including referential, organizational, and efficiency measures. For each measure, the differences in magnitude were compared among all three modalities, and these data were analyzed to determine whether the characteristic predominated when speech was present, when interaction was present, or only when these factors occurred together in interactive speech. Table 4.1 illustrates the logical partitioning and predicted data pattern among modalities for those characteristics considered to be influenced by speech, interaction, or interactive speech.

TABLE 4.1
PREDICTED PATTERNS FOR MODALITY
CHARACTERISTICS INFLUENCED BY SPEECH,
INTERACTION, AND INTERACTIVE SPEECH

	Audiotape	Telephone	Keyboard
Speech	$+$[a]	$+$	$-$
Interaction	$-$	$+$	$+$
Interactive Speech	$-$	$+$	$-$

[a] The *directionality* (i.e., as indicated by $+$ or $-$) of predicted magnitude differences among modalities for speech, interaction, and interactive speech characteristics is inconsequential. For example, either a $-$ $+$ $+$ or a $+$ $-$ $-$ pattern among modes for a given feature indicates the association of that feature with interaction.

Previous research on communication modalities has focused primarily on establishing descriptive characterizations of individual modalities. Although this research has occasionally viewed modalities in terms of their underlying factors, it has not followed through any given theoretical perspective with the empirical comparisons needed to link particular discourse and performance patterns with the proposed underlying factors. As a result of this limitation, as well as a lack of research on how the interaction factor influences communication, research to date has not considered the relative influence of speech and interaction on the characteristics of a modality. Nonetheless, general descriptions of spoken and written communication provide some basis for predicting which characteristics may be associated with the presence of speech. Among other things, speech has been described as less concise, more repetitious, more replete with pronouns, more rapidly delivered, and associated with faster task performance [Blass75; Chafe82; Chapanis77; Stoll76]. The present research predicts, on this basis, that the two spoken modalities, by comparison with the keyboard one, are more likely to display a greater number of words, more personal pronouns, and faster novice assembly time. Since interactive speech has been reported to be more efficient than noninteractive speech [Oviatt91], this further distinction is incorporated in the present prediction that interactive speech should display the fastest novice assembly time, followed by audiotape, and then keyboard. In addition, recent research has indicated that frequent repetitions are primarily a feature of noninteractive speech, rather than interactive speech or speech in general [Oviatt91]. On the basis of this qualification, the prediction is made that repetitions are more likely to vary with the presence or absence of interaction, not speech. Finally, since temporally oriented organizational markers such as "Okay, next..." have been found to introduce almost all assembly segments in both interactive and noninteractive spoken modalities [Oviatt91], the prediction is made that such temporal markers are more likely to be characteristic of speech than interaction. If this is true, then the present comparison should find that they occur at a lower rate in the keyboard modality.

Although noninteractive human speech is the required input for a variety of innovations in progress, such as voice mail and automatic dictation devices [Gould82; Gould83a; Gould83b; Jelinek85; Nicholson85] the organization of human discourse and performance under conditions of restricted interactivity is still poorly understood. In our study contrasting the transmission of instructions in interactive and noninteractive spoken modalities [Oviatt90], we identified differences in discourse organization, referential characteristics, and performance efficiency. For example, descriptive elaborations and repetitions were much more prevalent in the noninteractive audiotape mode, as were introductions of upcoming actions and summary descriptions. Furthermore, the absence of interaction in spoken discourse corresponded with reduced performance efficiency. Referential differences between interactive and noninteractive speech also have been highlighted by earlier studies demonstrating the role of "concurrent feedback" in progressively reducing the length of referring expressions that are repeated during dialogue [Krauss64, Krauss66]. The present research predicts that the rate of elaborations, repetitions, action introductions, and summaries all will be influenced primarily by the presence or absence of interactive feedback within a modality. In particular, the interactive telephone and keyboard exchanges that include confirmation feedback are predicted to contain fewer of these features than noninteractive audiotape.

With respect to the introduction of new objects, telephone dialogue has been characterized as more indirect and fine-grained descriptions than either interactive keyboard [Cohen84] or noninteractive audiotape [Oviatt91]. Telephone dialogue also has been described as more indefinite than audiotape in its use of determiners to introduce new objects [Oviatt91], although this comparison has yet to be made with keyboard. For purposes of the present research, then, it was clear in advance that the habitual use of separate indirect requests for identification of new objects depends on the presence of interactive speech. Based on this background information, as well as on the observed concordance between indirection and indefiniteness of description [Oviatt91], it is predicted that experts will habitually use more indefinite determiners to introduce new objects in telephone than in keyboard interactions. That is, it is predicted that indefinite reference to new objects likewise will predominate during interactive speech.

4.2 OVERVIEW OF EMPIRICAL STUDY

4.2.1. Method

For the present research purposes, data from thirty subjects, fifteen experts and fifteen novices, were examined and compared. These subjects represented a subset of the total of fifty who participated in a larger study, partial results of which have been reported elsewhere [Cohen84; Oviatt91]. The fifteen novices had been randomly assigned to experts to form a total of fifteen expert-novice pairs. All subjects were paid student volunteers. For five of the pairs the expert related instructions by telephone, and an interactive telephone dialogue ensued as the pump was assembled. For another five pairs the expert's spoken instructions were recorded by audiotape, and later the novice assembled the pump as he or she listened to the expert's taped monologue. For the last five pairs the expert typed instructions on a keyboard, and a typed interactive exchange then took place between the participants on linked CRTs. The fifteen pairs of participants were randomly assigned to the telephone, audiotape, and keyboard conditions.

Each expert participated in the experiment on two consecutive days, the first for training and the second for instructing the novice. During training, experts were informed that the purpose of the experiment was to investigate modality differences in the communication of instructions. They were given a set of assembly directions for the hydraulic pump kit, which were written as a list of imperatives, along with a diagram of the pump's labeled parts. Approximately twenty minutes was permitted to practice putting the pump together using these materials, after which the subject practiced administering the instructions to a research assistant. If a subject was doubtful or experienced difficulty during practice, training continued for an additional ten to fifteen minutes.

During the second session the expert was informed of a modality assignment. Then the expert was asked to explain the task to the novice partner and to make sure that the partner built the pump so that it would function correctly when completed. The expert was allowed to view the water pump parts for reference while giving instructions, although touching the pieces was prohibited. The novice received instructions similar to the expert's regarding the purpose of the experiment, and was supplied with all the water pump parts and a tray of water for testing.

In the telephone condition the expert spoke through a standard telephone receiver, and the novice listened through a speakerphone so that his or her hands would be free for assembly. The expert and novice were located in adjacent rooms. In the audiotape condition a cassette recorder was used for recording and playback of the expert's instructions. The novice was tested after recording and was at liberty to rewind and review sections of the tape. Keyboard teams typed their instructions on Elite Datamedia 1500 CRT terminals connected by the Telnet computer network to a computer at Bolt Beranek and Newman, Inc. The terminals were linked so that whatever was typed on one would appear on the other. Simultaneous typing was possible and did occur. Participants were informed that their typing would not appear instantaneously on their partner's terminal and, in fact, response times averaged 1 or 2 seconds with occasional longer delays due to system load. For all three modalities assembly of the pump was videotaped. Written transcriptions were available as a hard copy of the keyboard exchanges, and were composed from audio-cassette recordings of the monologues and co-ordinated dialogues, the latter of which had been synchronized onto one audio channel beforehand. Signal distortion was not measured in either spoken modality, although no subjects reported difficulty with inaudible or unintelligible instructions and < 0.2%, or 1 in 500 recorded words, were undecipherable to the transcriber and experimenter. In all cases, the participants were aware that their behavior would be recorded for later study by the researchers.

4.2.2. Sample Transcripts

Discourse fragments are provided below to illustrate all three modalities. Each sample includes instructions on how to assemble two parts.

Telephone Dialogue Segment

Expert:	"Now, do you see a little pink plastic piece?"
Novice:	"Yeah, yeah."
Expert:	"With two holes?"
Novice:	"Yeah."
Expert:	'Okay. You have your blue cap in front of you?"
Novice:	"Yeah."
Expert:	"Setting down with the two little prongs sticking up?"
Novice:	"Yeah."
Expert:	"Okay, take that little pink plastic piece, and the two holes in the plastic piece—"
Novice:	"Mm–hm."
Expert:	"—go over the two little notches."
Novice:	"Does it matter whether the shiny side or the dull side of the pink thing's up?"
Expert:	"No, it doesn't matter."
Novice:	"Okay."
Expert:	"And put it so that it's covering the hole in the bottom of that little cap. Kinda fits hard, doesn't it?"
Novice:	"Little bit tight, yeah. Okay."

Audiotape Monologue Segment

Expert:	"So the first thing to do is to take the metal with the red thing on one end and the green cap on the other end. Take that and then look in other parts— there are three small red pieces. Take the smallest one.

> It looks like a nail—
> a little red nail—
> and put that into the hole in the end of the green cap.
> There's a green cap on the end of the silver thing.
> Take the little red nail and put it in the hole in the end
> of the green cap."

Keyboard Interaction Segment

Expert: "Now take the blue cap with the two prongs sticking out and fit the little piece of pink plastic on it. Okay?"

Novice: "Okay."

4.2.3. Results

Within the research framework described, the data from all three conditions were collected, and then scored and analyzed for their discourse and performance characteristics. Detailed methods for coding, second scoring, and analyzing the dependent measures are summarized elsewhere [Oviatt91]. All dependent measures reported in this chapter had reliabilities ranging above .86. The basic statistical comparisons were based on *apriori* t or Fisher's exact probability tests [Siegel56].

Aspects of Discourse and Performance Influenced by Speech

Among the discourse characteristics that were influenced solely by the presence of speech were overall wordiness, use of personal pronouns, and the habitual introduction of individual discourse segments with temporal markers such as "Okay, next..." That is, evaluation of these dependent measures revealed that the interactive and noninteractive speech modes did not differ significantly and that, after collapsing data from the speech modes, the contrast between the speech and nonspeech modes was a significant one. With respect to discourse length, the audiotape and telephone experts spoke an average of 875 and 845 words, respectively, compared with only 303 words in keyboard ($t = 5.87$, $df = 12.19$, $p < .0001$, one-tailed, with separate variance estimates). Likewise, personal pronouns were uttered at the average rate of 4.14 and 4.41 per 100 words in the audiotape and telephone transcripts, by comparison with only 1.64 in keyboard ($t = 4.03$, $df = 13$, $p < .001$, one-tailed). Finally, whereas almost all discourse segments were introduced with temporal markers in the audiotape and telephone modes, or an average of 96.3% and 98.6%, respectively, only 43.0% received such initial marking in the keyboard mode. All five experts in the two speech modalities met the criterion of producing nine or more introductory markers, while only one of five keyboard experts did so—a significant departure from chance based on Fisher's exact probability test ($p = .02$).

With respect to performance, efficiency was enhanced quite substantially by the presence of speech, although interaction contributed further to the efficiency of the spoken modalities. Whereas the average assembly time for the audiotape and telephone novices was 530 and 417 seconds, respectively, novices using interactive keyboard required an average of 1,485 seconds to construct the same water pump (t = 3.71, df = 4.13, p < .01, one-tailed, with separate variance estimates).

Aspects of Discourse and Performance Influenced by Interaction

Discourse characteristics that were influenced solely by the presence of inter-action included descriptive elaboration and repetition, as well as the preva-lence of action introductions and summaries. For this collection of dependent measures, analyses revealed that the two interactive modes did not differ sig-nificantly, although the combined data from the interactive modes was sig-nificantly different from that of the noninteractive mode. With respect to referential characteristics, experts operating in the noninteractive audiotape modality elaborated their descriptions at the rate of 3.94 per 100 words, which was a significantly higher rate than the 2.09 and 1.36 elaboration rates pro-duced by telephone and keyboard experts, respectively (t = 4.74, df = 13, p < .0005, one-tailed). Perseverative elaborations[1] occurred at the average rate of .86 per 100 words in noninteractive audiotape, whereas they were nonex-istent in keyboard and nearly nonexistent in telephone (.075 per 100 words), this latter contrast a significant one (t = 3.27, df = 4.18, p < .02, one-tailed, with separate variance estimates). Furthermore, descriptive reversions[2] were found exclusively in the noninteractive audiotape modality. Expert repeti-tions also occurred at a significantly higher rate in noninteractive audiotape, which had .65 repetitions per 100 words, compared with .15 and .13 in the interactive telephone and keyboard modes (t = 3.19, df = 13, p < .005, one-tailed).

With respect to organizational features, both action introductions (e.g., "Now we are going to assemble the base of the pump") and descriptive sum-maries (e.g., "Okay, so at the moment you are going to have this body of the pump with the plunger in it, and the red cap at the top with the base

---

[1] The definition and coding of elaborative phenomena such as perseverations is outlined in detail in [Oviatt91]. Descriptive perseveration refers to continued elaboration of a piece de-scription *after* the expert has explained how to assemble the piece, but within the same discourse assembly segment (see Sample Transcripts section for context of the following audiotape perse-veration: "There's a green cap on the end of the silver thing."). A discourse assembly segment refers to a segment of discourse in which the expert provides instructions for attaching two parts or subassemblies as part of an individual assembly step.

[2] Descriptive reversion refers to an elaborative pattern in which the expert describes a new piece in a direct and definite manner, but then downshifts to an indirect and indefinite elabora-tion about the same piece (e.g., Audiotape expert: "...you take *the* L-shaped clear plastic tube, *another* tube, there's *an* L-shaped one with a big base...").

on it, and standing on this pedestal, this plastic pedestal") were significantly more prevalent in the noninteractive than the interactive modalities. In noninteractive audiotape, experts introduced upcoming actions an average of 3 times per transcript, compared with once in interactive telephone and none in interactive keyboard. The contrast between action introductions in audiotape and telephone was significant (t = 1.91, df = 8, p < .05, one-tailed). Likewise, descriptive summaries were issued at the rate of .47 per 100 words in the noninteractive audiotapes, compared with .17 in interactive telephone and none in the interactive keyboard. The difference between audiotape and telephone summaries again was significant (t = 2.03, df = 8, p < .04, one-tailed.)[3]

The opportunity for speaker interaction further strengthened performance efficiency beyond the level afforded by speech alone. This is reflected in the fact that, while novices in the two spoken modalities performed much faster than keyboard novices, those in the interactive telephone modality also worked significantly faster than audiotape novices, with average assembly times of 417 and 530 seconds, respectively, (t = 1.87, df = 8, p < .05, one-tailed).

Unique Discourse Characteristics of Interactive Speech

Some aspects of referential and illocutionary style appeared only when the combined resources of speech and speaker interaction were both present, as represented in the relatively natural telephone modality. In the introduction of new piece descriptions, four of the five telephone experts met the criterion of introducing nine or more new pieces with an indefinite determiner, whereas none of the five audiotape or keyboard experts did so, a significant difference based on Fisher's exact test (p = .02). Four of the five telephone experts also used a separate indirect request for piece identification when introducing nine or more of the pieces, although none of the five audiotape or keyboard experts made a separate request of this type. Again, this was a significant difference based on Fisher's (p = .02). Instead, audiotape and keyboard experts adopted a more definite and direct style, one in which they immediately requested that the novice assemble the newly introduced piece.

Table 4.2 summarizes the discourse and performance characteristics that were influenced primarily by speech, by interaction, or by the confluence of both of these factors.

---

[3] Although interactive keyboard clearly provided an even more pronounced contrast with respect to both introductions and summaries, parametric analyses were precluded due to nonoccurrence. However, if experts in audiotape and keyboard were classified according to whether or not they used introductions, and again according to whether they used summaries, both classifications would reveal 5 of 5 audiotape experts and 0 of 5 keyboard experts as having qualified as producers of at least one introduction or summary, which constitutes a significant departure from chance based on Fisher's, p < .01.

TABLE 4.2
DISCOURSE AND PERFORMANCE CHARACTERISTICS INFLUENCED
BY SPEECH, INTERACTION, AND INTERACTIVE SPEECH

	Spoken Modalities	Interactive Modalities	
	Audiotape	Telephone	Keyboard
Speech			
Speed of Assembly Time	+	+ +	−
Number of Words	+	+	−
Personal Pronouns	+	+	−
Initial Temporal Markers	+	+	−
Interaction			
Number of Elaborations	+	−	−
Perseverations	+	−	0
Reversions	*	0	0
Repetitions	+	−	−
Introduction of Actions	+	−	0
Summary Descriptions	+	−	0
Interactive Speech			
Separate Requests for ID of New Pieces	−	+	−
Indefinite Reference to New Pieces	−	+	−

++ and + and − specify greatest, greater, or lesser amounts of a feature, respectively, with each of these distinctions statistically significant (p less than .05).

0 and * designate a nonexistent or sometimes present feature.

4.3 DISCUSSION

One of the more remarkable features of spoken language modalities was confirmed to be the sheer copiousness of their output. By comparison, typed interaction was very abbreviated, almost telegraphese. In spite of their verbosity, the speech modalities were characterized by substantially faster novice assembly times. This efficiency advantage for speech ranged approximately three-fold, with task completion in the spoken modalities averaging seven to nine minutes, whereas keyboard novices required over twenty-four minutes for the same task. Previous research has reported an efficiency advantage for spoken modalities of approximately two-fold over written and typed exchanges [Chapanis77], based on two-person cooperative assembly and geographical location tasks. These data substantiate what has been the general conjecture that speech may be a particularly apt selection for use with hands-on tasks in which typing or writing otherwise would detract from overall performance time. Furthermore, they establish the margin of advantage for hands-on tasks as falling within the two- to three-fold range. Future research on tasks of practical interest other than assembly tasks could contribute further specifics on the natural advantages that make speech a powerful modality. A clearer perspective on these issues will be vital as we strive to harness speech fully for technological purposes.

Apart from their verbosity and efficiency, spoken language modalities also elicit frequent use of personal pronouns, irrespective of whether direct speaker interaction and feedback is present or not. In the past, the very high rate of pronouns in interactive speech has been construed as an index of personal involvement between the participants [Chafe82]. If this were true, then modalities permitting more direct speaker interaction, including clarification subdialogues and confirmation exchanges, should generally be characterized by a profusion of personal pronouns. However, in the present research, the rate of personal pronouns produced by experts was substantially lower during keyboard interactions, by a factor of 2.6. Perhaps equally disconcerting to the "direct involvement" viewpoint, personal pronouns were as frequently used by experts in the noninteractive audiotape modality as they were by those engaged in interactive telephone dialogues. In short, the present data provide evidence implicating speech, not interaction, as the common modality factor underlying frequent use of personal pronouns.

One possible explanation for this finding is that there is a strong tendency in spoken language modalities for speakers to create a subjective sense of direct interaction and involvement with a partner, even when the modality itself actually precludes any such opportunity. For example, it has been argued that audiotape experts fabricate a mute listener [Oviatt91], perhaps as an aid in composing instructions.[4] As they interact with this fictitious partner, evidently suspending the realities of the known time delay in audiotape communication, they have been found to engage in residual requests for confirmation, followed by comments typical of interactive responses (e.g., Audiotape expert: "Okay, you got that? Good.") These data on the characteristics of audiotape experts' speech highlight the possibility that there exists subjective gravitation toward fully interactive speech, or an attempt on the speaker's part to recreate a more natural and familiar form of collaborative interaction. Evidently, this is one strategy that audiotape experts use to cope with the strain induced by noninteractive performance requirements. The extent to which people create interactional placeholders when using limited interaction modalities needs to be investigated if we desire accurate user models that are capable of predicting the discourse and performance patterns of future language technology. To date, the user modelling literature has not addressed the relation between modality constraints and the performance models of users.

---

[4] [Goffman81] has aptly described people's subjective sense that engaging in solitary monologues feels distinctly like a failure of decorum, especially if observed publicly. In this sense, audiotape talk can be viewed as a sort of technologically induced social impropriety, which results from the delamination of speech from its usual interactional framework.

By contrast with speech, the presence or absence of interaction was associated mainly with referential features of the discourse. By comparison with telephone dialogues and keyboard interactions, noninteractive monologues were distinguished principally by the extensiveness of their elaborative and repetitive description. These profusely elaborative descriptions focused on the pieces and actions that formed the essence of the present assembly instructions. They also contained more unique elaborative patterns, such as perseverated and reverted elaborations of pieces. These latter elaborative phenomena gave the impression of being out-of-sequence parenthetical additions that disrupted the smooth continuity of the audiotape discourse. For a variety of reasons outlined by [Oviatt91] this collection of referential characteristics rendered the noninteractive audiotape modality far less integrated and predictably sequenced than either of the interactive modalities, and, as such, it created more inferential strain for listeners in this modality. Finally, performance efficiency clearly was eroded by lack of speaker interaction and feedback, although the magnitude of the interaction effect on efficiency was relatively small in comparison with the influence of speech.

These basic differences in discourse organization and performance efficiency have implications for the successful design of various applications using interactive and noninteractive input. For example, technology based on noninteractive dictation will be prone to excessive elaboration and repetitiveness that slow down and undermine the coherence of messages, contributing to inefficient processing by the recipient or system. Such communications also will tend toward poorer integration and less predictable structuring, requiring more effort by the recipient to resolve their meaning. When written output is desired, noninteractive speech will lead to poor copy that requires labor-intensive editing, a disadvantage that must be weighed with respect to the initial advantages of spoken input. In fact, the major current impediment to the acceptability of such systems is the unavailability of technically adequate editing facilities [Ades86]. To reduce the impact of these outlined difficulties on professional communications such as voice mail and other automatic dictation devices, it may be strategic to limit such technology to brief and informal tasks, and to ones that do not emphasize planning or reviewing during transmission. In fact, the recommendation for brevity accords with the usage patterns and preferences reported in recent voice mail and filing studies [Nicholson85; Gould83a], which indicated a tendency for users to limit noninteractive messages to under one minute in length.

Above a certain threshold, language systems slower than real-time will elicit user input that has similar characteristics to noninteractive language. When system responding is slow and, in addition, prompt confirmations to support the user-system "dialogue" are not forthcoming, then users will elaborate and repeat themselves [van Katwijk79]. For practical purposes, that is, users are unable to distinguish between a slow response and no response at all, so their strategy for coping with both situations is similar. Ultimately, to improve both dictation technology and delayed-response language systems, the most direct solution may be to design methods of confirmation feedback that effectively inhibit speaker elaborations, along with the discourse convolutions and inefficiency that they precipitate [Oviatt91].

Speech and interaction each were associated with different patterns of discourse organization. Audiotape experts provided more organizational enhancements in the form of introductions of upcoming actions and summary descriptions than did experts in either interactive modality. These organizational reinforcements may have assisted in offsetting the relative lack of integration and predictability in audiotape discourse by focusing the more rambling audiotape descriptions. By contrast, experts in the spoken language modalities habitually provided local temporal markers, such as "Okay, then . . . ," before describing each individual assembly action, whereas keyboard experts did not. In short, organizational enhancements that occurred due to the absence of speaker interaction operated at the propositional level, through explicit advance introduction or reviewing of main points. Instead, the organizational fortification in spoken modalities was temporal in nature, perhaps simply because visual sequencing of the assembly instructions is not possible in speech as it is in written or typed modes.

The discourse characteristics that surfaced exclusively during interactive telephone speech, but not in modalities in which either speech or interaction were absent, centered on the referential and illocutionary style used to introduce new pieces. Basically, experts engaging in a telephone dialogue habitually introduced new water pump pieces in an indefinite and indirect manner, using a more fine-grained series of illocutionary steps. Telephone experts typically decomposed new piece descriptions into two parts: identify and act. As step one, they indirectly requested identification of a piece, which the novice then confirmed, before they progressed to step two—more detailed instructions for picking up, orienting or acting on the piece. In contrast, both audiotape and keyboard experts maintained a more emphatic and direct illocutionary style. These experts were more presumptuous of the novice's initial recognition of new pieces, as reflected in their definite descriptions of them, and they were more assertive about immediately instructing the novice to act on new pieces in a particular way. These data suggest that the use of an indirect and indefinite illocutionary style, one that imparts instructions through a more fine-grained series of illocutionary steps that are each confirmable, is a relatively fragile discourse pattern that relies on the confluence of both speech and interaction.

One implication of the habitually directive style of both noninteractive and nonspeech modalities, which is at odds with the indirection of dialogue, is that users risk creating misleading impressions of their attitude toward the task and the message recipient. This may be especially problematic for communication in professional settings, in which the need to observe status distinctions is generally emphasized. For example, potential users may be reluctant to send messages to higher status individuals such as managers using voice mail or other noninteractive modalities that encourage a directive, brusk, or impatient tone. Future research in this area could begin with careful observation of natural usage patterns for technology prone to such problems, and could determine whether the outlined stylistic phenomena are amenable to training.

This chapter has described several basic ways in which speech and interaction each mold the current of language flowing within a communication modality. The long-term goal of the present approach is to construct a model capable of predicting the advantages and disadvantages of different communication modalities for future language interfaces and technology. Such a model can provide one source of guidance in the selection and design of proposed systems. However, unique discourse features always can be expected to emerge that are not derivable in any simple way from underlying modality factors, which was evident from the patterns of interactive speech. As a result, research with prototype systems will be required in order to refine or correct anticipated outcomes. Information generated by empirical models, and supplemented with performance results collected during iterative design, will speed the process of crafting future language systems that are habitable, high quality, and relatively enduring.

REFERENCES

[Ades86] Ades, S., and Swinehart, D. C. 1986. Voice Annotation and Editing in a Workstation Environment. In *Proc. AVIOS '86: Voice I/O Systems Applications Conference*, Alexandria, VA: American Voice I/O Society, September, pp. 13–28.

[Blass75] Blass, T., and Siegman, A. W. 1975. A Psycholinguistic Comparison of Speech, Dictation and Writing. *Language and Speech*, 18, 20–34.

[Chafe82] Chafe, W. L. 1982. Integration and Involvement in Speaking, Writing, and Oral Literature. In D. Tannen (ed.), *Spoken and Written Language: Exploring Orality and Literacy*, 3, pp. 35–53. Norwood, NJ: Ablex Publishing Corp.

[Chapanis77] Chapanis, A., Parrish, R. N., Ochsman, R. B., and Weeks, G. D. 1977. Studies in Interactive Communication: II. The Effects of Four Communication Modes on the Linguistic Performance of Teams During Cooperative Problem Solving. *Human Factors*, 19(2), 101–125.

[Cohen84] Cohen, P. R. 1984. The Pragmatics of Referring and the Modality of Communication. *Computational Linguistics,* 10(2), 97–146.

[Goffman81] Goffman, E. 1981. *Forms of Talk*. Philadelphia, PA: University of Pennsylvania Press.

[Gould82] Gould, J. D. 1982. Writing and Speaking Letters and Messages. *International Journal of Man-Machine Studies*, 16(1), 147–171.

[Gould83a] Gould, J. D., and Boeis, S. J. 1983. Human Factors Challenges in Creating a Principal Support Office System—The Speech Filing System Approach. *ACM Transactions on Office Information Systems*, 1(4), 273–298.

[Gould83b] Gould, J. D., Conti, J., and Hovanyecz, T. 1983. Composing Letters with a Simulated Listening Typewriter. *Communications of the ACM*, 26(4), 295–308.

[Jelinek85] Jelinek, F. 1985. The Development of an Experimental Discrete Dictation Recognizer. *Proc. IEEE*, 73(11), 1616–1624.

[Krauss64] Krauss, R. M., and Weinheimer, S. 1964. Changes in Reference Phrases as a Function of Frequency of Usage in Social Interaction: A Preliminary Study. *Psychonomic Science*, 1(1), 113–114.

[Krauss66] Krauss, R. M., and Weinheimer, S. 1966. Concurrent Feedback, Confirmation, and the Encoding of Referents in Verbal Communication. *Journal of Personality and Social Psychology*, 4(3), 343–346.

[Nicholson85] Nicholson, R. T. 1985. Usage Patterns in an Integrated Voice and Data Communications System. *ACM Transactions on Office Information Systems*, 3(3), 307–314.

[Oviatt91] Oviatt, S. L., and Cohen, P. R. 1990. Discourse Structure and Performance Efficiency in Interactive and Noninteractive Spoken Modalities. *Computer Speech and Language*.

[Siegel56] Siegel, S. 1956. *Nonparametric Methods for the Behavioral Sciences*. New York, NY: McGraw-Hill.

[Stoll76] Stoll, F. C., Hoecker, D. G., Kruger, G. P., and Chapanis, A. 1976. The Effects of Four Communication Modes on the Structure of Language Used During Cooperative Problem-Solving. *Journal of Psychology*, 94(1), 13–26.

[VanKatwijk79] VanKatwijk, A. F., VanNes, F. L., Bunt, H. C., Muller, H. F., and Leopold, F. F. 1979. Naive Subjects Interacting with a Conversing Information System. *IPO Annual Progress Report*, 14, 105–112.

PART II

MODELS, PLANS, AND GOALS

CHAPTER 5

AN INTELLIGENT INTERFACE ARCHITECTURE FOR ADAPTIVE INTERACTION

SHERMAN W. TYLER, JON L. SCHLOSSBERG,
ROBERT A. GARGAN JR., LINDA K. COOK,
and **JOSEPH W. SULLIVAN**
Lockheed AI Center, Research and Development Division

ABSTRACT

This chapter describes CHORIS, the Computer-Human Object-oriented Reasoning Interface System, a generic architecture for intelligent interfaces developed by the Intelligent Interfaces research group of the Lockheed Artificial Intelligence Center. This system is designed to enable a wide range of users to interact effectively with varying types of complex applications. The overall approach for CHORIS has been to design a set of domain-independent reasoning modules driven by domain-specific knowledge bases. The necessary knowledge bases include explicit models of the user (including canonical and role-based stereotypes), the domain (objects, relations, commands, and high-level tasks), and the interface itself. The reasoning modules include the following: the Input/Output Manager, supporting a wide range of forms of user input and output, including natural language, graphics, and voice; the Plan Manager, interpreting user actions within a plan-based context in an attempt to infer user intentions and directly assist users in achieving high-level goals; the Adaptor, modifying interface features to best suit the current user and that user's ongoing tasks; and the Presentation Manager, reasoning how best to present system information to the user and basing its decision on the nature and intended use of the information. In addition, efforts have been undertaken to develop a tool kit, which would support the acquisition of the needed knowledge bases from an application expert, in order to facilitate the process of building intelligent interfaces for new domains. This chapter discusses the operation and utility of these components in the context of the current prototype domain of emergency management.

5.1 INTRODUCTION

A human-computer interface can potentially fulfill three key roles in support of the user: (1) it can help the user accomplish intended goals on the target system; (2) it can enable the user to understand how both the target system and the interface operate; and (3) it can magnify the capabilities of the user. For both pragmatic and theoretical reasons there is increasing interest among researchers and developers in creating intelligent interfaces to achieve these roles. The pragmatic reasons for this growing interest are clear. For one thing, there is an ever widening range of computer system users, with both highly computer-knowledgeable and quite naive users often served by the same interface. Furthermore, the systems with which users must interact are becoming ever more complicated. In complex space systems, for example, users must control and understand enormously involved operations, while receiving a flood of information, and must frequently do so in a very short period of time to avoid catastrophe. In this situation the computer must act intelligently, taking into account knowledge of the user and of the current circumstances to provide the user with information at the right level of detail to make quick decisions and to execute those decisions as easily as possible.

The theoretical reasons for pursuing the study of intelligent interfaces are also apparent. An intelligent interface at its developmental extreme is an intelligent agent that embodies some of the key capabilities of a human assistant: observing and forming models of the world and the user; inferring user intentions based upon those observations; and formulating plans and taking actions to help the user achieve those intentions. Thus, to build an intelligent interface or agent requires a confrontation of some of the key problems in artificial intelligence.

Aside from facilitating the accomplishment of useful tasks, the interface can also have the goal of promoting understanding of the target system. In this role it serves, in the most general case, as an intelligent tutoring system. To teach users about complex systems requires a tutor who is both an expert in regard to the system and an accomplished instructor. In most cases there are far too few human individuals with these qualifications who are available to devote the time and attention necessary for each trainee. This suggests the use of computers as training devices. However, traditional computer-assisted instruction is not sufficient for this purpose, since such systems lack any true tutoring capability. All users are treated in the same manner; a separate program is required for each type of training; and that program cannot be easily altered when problems arise or the target system of the training changes. The alternative is to build intelligent tutoring systems. Such systems are characterized by explicit knowledge of the domain, of the user, and of how to accomplish various generic tasks (diagnosis, operation) within that domain, as well as an explicit indication of the curriculum to be taught to the user and the teaching procedures available for so doing. These systems are capable of adapting their training regimen to the characteristics of the individual and of maximizing the progress of that individual towards the training goal; they can also be fairly easily modified as changes are required.

One major problem with intelligent interface systems is that their development currently necessitates large expenditures of time and money by accomplished programmers and domain experts. To alleviate this problem, tools can be designed to help the domain expert describe the application-specific knowledge, which is then translated by the tool into the form required by the interface. In this way the knowledge can be acquired more easily and without the tool user having to know any implementation details about either the interface or the driving knowledge bases. Therefore, one extension of interface work focuses on how to design such tools to facilitate the construction of powerful interface systems.

This chapter attempts to provide one perspective on the research presented at the workshop by describing CHORIS, the Computer-Human Object-oriented Reasoning Interface System developed by the Intelligent Interfaces Project of the Lockheed Artificial Intelligence Center. That system provides one way of viewing the main components of an intelligent interface and learning how they interact. Some rudimentary tools have also been developed to acquire the knowledge needed to implement a working version of CHORIS for a new application. The sections that follow summarize the CHORIS architecture and the various types of knowledge upon which it relies. They also present an example interaction, a more detailed treatment of each major functionality of CHORIS, and a brief depiction of the evolving set of interface design tools.

5.2 MAIN COMPONENTS OF AN INTELLIGENT INTERFACE

Research reported in the chapters of this book grew out of an effort to determine the vital elements of an architecture for intelligent interfaces. While the authors naturally offer differing points of view on this question, certain common themes emerge. First, it is generally agreed that an intelligent interface should be both knowledge-based [Hollan91] and modular [Norman91]. Second, it should be able to infer and evaluate user plans and intentions [Young91] and adapt its behavior to the individual user and the user's current task [Kass91; Tyler88]. Knowing user goals and plans for achieving those goals provides a powerful context for interacting with the user, allowing the system to carry out many actions on behalf of the user without requiring the usual detailed and error-prone commands. The system can also do sophisticated error detection and correction, finding flaws in the user's plans based on knowledge of the application. In addition, an intelligent interface should support multimodal input [Neal91; Wahlster91], permitting users to communicate with the system through several parallel channels, mixing, for example, pointing operations and natural language text in making a single request. This facilitates interaction by assuring that users can map their tasks to actions that are more natural and require less effort than would be the case if only a single input mode was supported. The planning of information presentation in multiple output modalities [Arens91; Feiner91; MacKinlay91] is

FIGURE 5.1
INTELLIGENT INTERFACE ARCHITECTURE

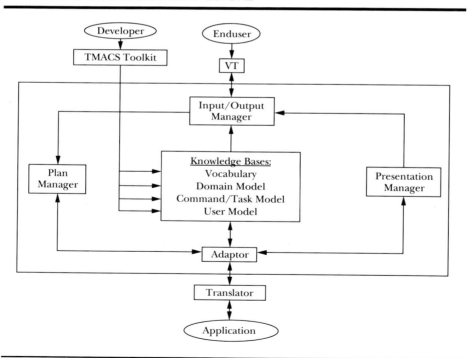

also a powerful interface function. Instead of displaying the results of system queries in some fixed manner, the interface reasons, based on its knowledge of the user and the user's current goals, as well as the nature of the information itself, how best to show the information so that the user detects the relevant relations.

An architecture which incorporates these key functions of an intelligent interface is shown in Figure 5.1. The interface is viewed as a module distinct and separate from the target application, and operates as a set of general functions that rely on a number of different knowledge bases to facilitate the operation and learning of the target system by the user. The following sections provide details about each of the main elements composing this architecture. An example will first be offered of how a user interacts through an existing implementation of the interface. Subsequent sections will describe how each of the various components of the interface contribute to the efficacy of this interaction. Because the construction of the driving knowledge bases can be onerous, tools that facilitate defining the different kinds of knowledge used by the interface are also important. Three such tools developed for CHORIS are sketched following the component descriptions. The final section of this book contains a more complete examination of several powerful knowledge-based interface design tools.

5.3 EXAMPLE

This section illustrates some of the capabilities of our system by tracing a sample interactive session. The current CHORIS domain is an emergency crisis management system. In this application, the user views a map of a geographic area and must respond appropriately when some emergency situation arises (e.g., earthquake, hazardous material spill, medical disaster).

Figure 5.2 shows a full screen view of CHORIS. The largest portion of screen real estate is devoted to a map of the area surrounding the incident, for example, the San Francisco Bay area. Also given large areas of real estate are the Agenda, which provides a flattened view into the underlying command and task structure; the Event Logger, which facilitates necessary bookkeeping of the hundreds of individual incidents that occur during major crises; and the Network Communication Facility, which provides a straightforward capability for interaction among geographically disparate sites.

Also initially present on the screen is a set of map commands that were determined to be appropriate and useful actions for this user. A text input window is presented that allows the user to enter natural language questions. Finally, an icon dock provides access to CHORIS' other facilities. The following sample session depicts an Emergency Operations Center (EOC) officer using many of these facilities to retrieve information in preparation for an evacuation.

FIGURE 5.2
A FULL-SCREEN SNAPSHOT OF THE INTELLIGENT INTERFACE

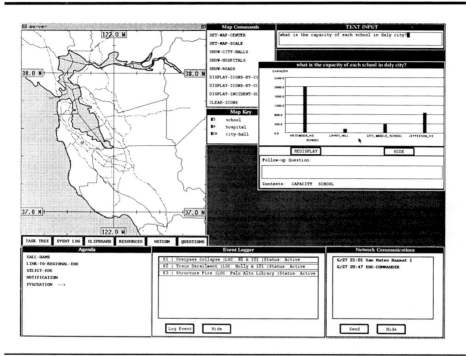

To begin the interactive session, the user navigates through the subcommands of the evacuation task as presented in the Agenda. With the help of population models contained in the emergency management application, the user determines the number of people affected, the number of people needing evacuation, and finally the number of people needing transportation.

Next, the user must determine appropriate reception centers (evacuation destinations). Since the incident occurred in the south part of San Mateo County, the EOC officer begins searching for a reception center in Daly City (in the north part of the county, just below San Francisco). The officer asks the system, via the natural language capability, "What is the capacity of each school in Daly City?" CHORIS informs the user that there are four schools in Daly City: Westmoor, Lippitt Hill, City Middle School, and Jefferson. To present the capacities of these schools most effectively to the user, CHORIS reasons a barchart is appropriate. This response window is depicted in Figure 5.2.

The officer then wishes to follow up on this information and retrieve the address of each school. The user accomplishes this command in CHORIS by asking a follow-up question (at the bottom of the response window of Figure

FIGURE 5.3
A FOLLOW-UP RESPONSE WINDOW

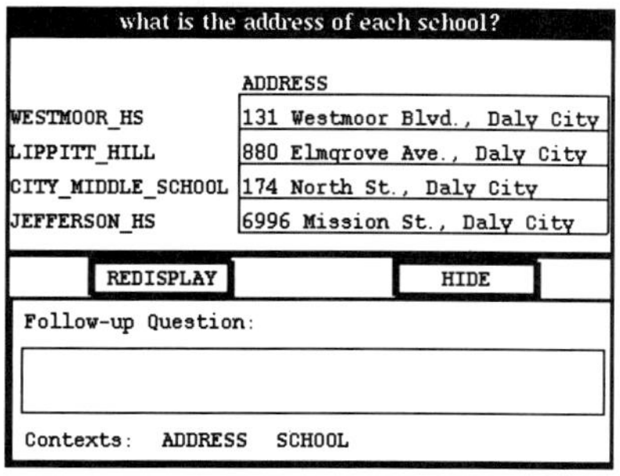

5.2), "What is the address of each school?" In response to this query the system produces a table of the four schools and their addresses (Figure 5.3).

The user might then ask to see the four Daly City schools on the map. This can be accomplished by the officer selecting the *Display Icons by City*. Next, the user might ask the system to plan a route from the affected area to a proposed reception center. CHORIS presents the planned route both visually on the map and textually as a list of instructions.

Finally, the user would finish up the evacuation task by determining the number of transportation units, allocating these units through the resource allocator, calling the Red Cross, and notifying on-site personnel as well as the media of the evacuation route and destination.

The next sections provide some details on how each major component of the CHORIS intelligent interface contributed to this example interaction.

5.4 MODELING: THE MAJOR KNOWLEDGE BASES

For a computer system to be intelligent in the broadest sense, it must be able to call upon a variety of techniques and knowledge in order to make its decisions about how to modify the user interface as the situation changes. In considering what types of knowledge might be of use for this purpose, a wide view of the elements of a human-computer system is needed. Table 5.1 presents one such view. Four main aspects of the interface are shown in the far left column of that table. For each aspect, there are both abstract components, which embody general knowledge about that aspect, and the more specific context, which captures what [Clancey86] has called the *situation-specific model*, that is, the current state of that aspect in the running system.

To demonstrate how each of these types of knowledge might be realized and utilized within an operational intelligent interface, attention is now di-

TABLE 5.1
MAJOR ASPECTS AND COMPONENTS OF INTERFACE

Aspect	Abstract Components	Context
World/Application	Possible objects in world; Possible operations on objects; High-level tasks mapping goals to operations and objects in world	Current state of world = existing objects and available operations
Communication	Possible interface objects; Possible operations on interface objects (ordering; physical actions); Mapping between interface and world	Current screen contents = existing interface objects and available interface operations
User	Semantic knowledge structure; Episodic knowledge structure; Preferences; Abilities	Knowledge of abstract components and context of world and communication aspects
Instruction	Curriculum; Teaching procedures	Current state of curriculum and of executing teaching procedure

rected to the prototype interface developed for the emergency crisis domain. In that prototype, each of the first three types of knowledge bases is represented as a set of objects in the CLOS language (work is currently under way on adding an instructional knowledge base, but this is at an early stage). The *world*, in this case, is the set of objects and operations on those objects that are appropriate for emergency planning and response. These items are each represented as separate objects in the interface. There are sufficient methods and data structures to show and manipulate these objects in iconic form on a map of the immediate area. This knowledge serves three significant functions: it allows users to view directly the behavior of the *world*; it supports interactions through direct manipulation of the icons; and it allows mixed-mode input through combined natural language (see following) and pointing operations involving these icons.

There are also objects representing the commands for acting on the world in ways such as establishing collection areas or moving resources. These objects contain enough information to support users in a variety of interactive modes. They describe, for example, how to construct a form for users to provide the parameters for a command in natural-language phrases.

CHORIS also has knowledge of high-level tasks users might typically perform on the target system, in this case, the crisis-management system. High-level tasks are sequences of commands that are carried out in some ordered way to accomplish a single general goal on the system. As the example in the previous section illustrated, an Emergency Operations Center (EOC) officer may need to plan an evacuation. This involves determining information about the people to be evacuated, determining a destination, determining a route, and notifying all of the affected individuals. The system is able to represent all these steps as one object and so support even the naive user in executing the high-level task directly. This is done by presenting the user with a menu of the task steps and their current states; when selected, these entries either execute as commands or expand into their substeps depending on the point of the user in the task. Thus, the task object must hold information on the substeps of the task, how these are related, and how to describe the task step to the user. The task knowledge base provides the mapping from the high-level tasks of the system to the necessary underlying commands.

The second main type of knowledge base holds information on the state of communication with the user, that is, the contents of the interface and the state of the dialogue. Each possible screen object (such as windows, forms, and menus) is represented as a separate object, and there is a display object that contains pointers to each of the objects currently on the screen.

The third source of knowledge concerns the users of the system. There are three levels of models describing the user. At the most general level, the canonical user model summarizes the preferences and abilities of human users (see section on Response Planner). Then there are stereotypes for the different types of emergency response personnel, such as an EOC officer or Incident (on-site) officer. By placing users within one of these stereotypes, the interface can infer default values for many of the user model variables without having to rely on lengthy observations of that user's behavior on the system (see [Rich79] for details). Finally, there are individual user models describing each particular user of the system. A wide range of variables in these models captures details of the user's abilities and preferences, as well as the user's past interaction history (commands and tasks executed, errors made, help requested, etc.). Through sets of inference rules (see following), the interface can use this information to determine the user's knowledge of both the domain and the interface itself, and can modify its behavior accordingly. Thus, in the previous example, the model of the current user initially inherits many of its values based on the fact that the user is an EOC officer. Additionally, the queries executed by the user are recorded in the user model. Had the user chosen to override the interface's decision to present the initial information as a bar chart, this, too, would be added to the model. The interface can use this information to determine the user's knowledge of the domain and the interface, as well as the user's response preferences, and modifies its behavior accordingly.

All the interface modules use one or more of these knowledge bases, generally through interactions with the Adaptor module, to achieve their ends. Two of the modules perform basic functions. The Virtual Terminal (VT) provides device independence, transforming device-specific input into a generic form for interface processing and similarly altering the generic output of the interface to suit the specific device. The Translator formats commands issued by the system and sends them on to the target application for execution. The remaining four interface modules constitute the core of the interface. Each of these modules embodies a vital intelligent interface functionality. In the remaining sections, these four modules are more fully described.

5.5 INPUT/OUTPUT MANAGER

The primary purpose of the Input/Output Manager is to integrate multi-modal input (e.g., mouse picks and natural language) into a single logical representation that can be used by the interface to reason about the user's actions. On the output side, it takes the high level commands from the Presentation Manager and translates them into the lower level generic operations required by the Virtual Terminal. A major focus has been on integrating the natural-language (NL) processor into the overall architecture, having it serve as a usable tool for obtaining information and for taking actions. This component aims at making it easier for users to communicate intent. Supporting NL and mixed modes of input allows for naturalness of interaction; the user is free to use the direct manipulation or NL descriptions, whichever is easier.

This work built on the natural language processor *Chat-80* [Pereira83] developed by Fernando Pereira. Chat-80 is a natural-language query-answering system implemented in Quintus Prolog. The research done in modifying Chat-80 was done in collaboration with Fernando Pereira and Phil Cohen of the AI Lab at SRI International. The modifications to Chat-80 consisted of adding the capability to (1) interpret deictics (pointing acts as with the mouse to elements on the screen) that are inserted directly into the lexical string being entered by the user; (2) process imperative sentence structures to support NL annotation of commands using forms; and (3) maintain a graphical representation of the discourse context for anaphor resolution. This section presents a brief examination of this component (for detailed information, see [Cohen89]).

Deixis — In everyday language, deictic utterances, consisting of words such as *this, that,* and *those,* typically accompanied by a pointing gesture, are often employed to point out something directly. Deictics can reduce referential ambiguity and enable succinct NL input by increasing the communication bandwidth. In the CHORIS interface, a preprocessor handles the insertion of deictics into the natural language input window.

An example of the use of deictic reference in the emergency-management domain would be the user typing "What is the capacity of these schools *pick pick pick?*". The three "picks" would be mouse selections from the graphical depiction of the schools on the map and would produce a query with the system's names for each *pick* entered in the NL string. Equivalently, the user could have typed the full name of each of the schools.

As can be seen from the example, the use of deictics provides an elegant way to combine the generality of NL with the specificity inherent in the graphic items depicted on the computer screen to provide the user a more natural method of interaction.

NL Annotated Commands—A common feature of user interfaces developed in the last few years is to have mouse sensitive "menu" commands (e.g., **DELETE, MOVE, OPEN**) that, when selected, activate a prescribed action. Often these commands require the entry of an argument, either by selecting a mouse sensitive item on the screen, or by typing in the argument (e.g., the **OPEN** command would require the entry of a file name as the argument). Modifying Chat to handle imperative sentences enhanced the user's flexibility in specifying commands and increased the degree of structure provided by the system to support user command entry.

At present three levels of commands have been implemented: (1) the standard method as described above, which is the most structured and least flexible; (2) a forms-based version that allows the user to enter NL phrases in the argument slots—this method provides the structure of the standard method, but adds considerable flexibility in specifying the arguments; (3) complete NL entry of command as an imperative sentence—this method has minimal structure but maximal flexibility. The forms mode of command entry provides the user with a fairly high degree of structure. The command options are selectable from a permanent menu or submenus thereby making clear the legal command options and reducing the burden on the user's memory. By adding the option of using NL phrases as the arguments, the user now has flexibility in specifying the command arguments and can easily initiate actions which would be most cumbersome within a direct manipulation style of interface.

Graphical Anaphor Resolution—Anaphora occurs when a speaker uses certain words (anaphors) to *refer back* to people, objects, events, etc. that were previously mentioned in the discourse context. Although anaphora is used effectively in conversations, the heavy reliance on memory can contribute to misunderstanding and confusion when the memories ('discourse models' in linguistic terms) of the listener and speaker do not correspond. When an NL processor is the 'listener' this problem is exacerbated (the maintenance of a good discourse model is computationally very expensive).

As the NL requirements for various domains were analyzed, many situations were found to benefit from the capability to use anaphoric references. For example, the EOC officer might be searching for a hospital to be designated as the primary care facility. To do this, he might begin asking questions that become increasingly more specific. In these situations the individual is branching down a decision tree in pursuit of a solution to the problem. That is, he is establishing a dynamic discourse model in which each question builds on the previous questions and their answers.

To accomplish this task using a standard database query language would require the user to build longer and longer queries as the questions become more and more specific. A more parsimonious approach is one that permits the user to ask simple NL queries that refer to elements of the discourse context established by previous questions.

To avoid the computational problems associated with currently offered processing solutions to discourse models, a graphics-based method for explicitly maintaining and presenting a discourse model was developed. Figure 5.3 shows an example of a window that is generated in response to an NL query. These windows are the basic elements of the graphical discourse model. Each window has attached to it *Contexts* that allow the user to ask follow-up questions referring to items that are in a particular context. This restricts Chat's query planner to query the database only about those items that are in the current context. In the example window the context is SCHOOL. To ask a question just about the schools shown in the example window, the user would select SCHOOL and then type the question after the prompt "FOLLOW UP:" in the figure. The system's response would be just for those schools.

A question history window displays the interrelationship among all the questions that have been asked. It can be called up as a system facility by opening the "Questions" icon. If the user needs to ask another question in relation to a previous one, for example, that response can be chosen from the Question History Window and the system will redisplay that window. The user can then enter a new follow-up question in the contexts available at that point. The system will display the response, and the question will be added to the Question History Window.

CHORIS provides the user with the capability to make anaphoric references to previously answered questions by combining a graphic context environment with NL. Because the system handles the context, the user no longer has to build more and more specific queries. The graphics interface makes clear what the current context is and the series of questions that led up to the current response.

5.6 PLAN MANAGER

The primary function of the Plan Manager is to assist the user on the target application through knowledge about typical plans for achieving high-level goals. Operating from knowledge of the user's current goals and plans, the interface can accomplish the following: detecting and trying to correct global errors, errors in user plans that would not otherwise be regarded as mistakes; completing high-level tasks, as by filling in default parameters and directly executing the system commands composing the plan steps; interpreting ambiguous requests; indicating the current state of an executing plan; and in general helping the user in mapping high-level goals into the low-level commands of the application.

Such a plan-based approach requires three critical elements: (1) a declarative representation of plans; (2) routines for utilizing such representations to assist users in their interactions, as described above; and (3) within the interface, the reasoning ability to determine what particular goals users are trying to achieve. Substantial progress has been attained on the first two elements. A useful way of representing plans as a separate knowledge base within the interface was developed. Plans are represented as object hierarchies, with each object standing for a substep of the plan. Figure 5.4, for example, shows a simplified view of the substep hierarchy for the *Manage Earthquake* task. Thus, when a user logs on to the system and defines the incident as an earthquake, this task is invoked. The top of the tree represents the high-level goal itself, nonleaves constitute substeps of the plan for achieving that goal, and, at the lowest level of the hierarchy, the leaves stand for actual commands that can be given to the system.

Each step of the task, as an object, is described by a number of variables or slots. The most critical variable is a list of the immediate substeps of the given step and of the interrelationships among those substeps. The interrelationship information includes the required preceding and following substeps of a given substep, as well as the minimum and maximum number of executions of that step permitted in executing the task.

The second main element of the Plan Manager, namely, the routines to support users based on their current goals, has also been realized to a significant degree. Thus, the interface can consider the commands and arguments to commands provided by the user, compare those with the constraints on the task substep's parameter values, and thereby detect global

FIGURE 5.4
AN EXAMPLE COMMAND AND TASK HIERARCHY

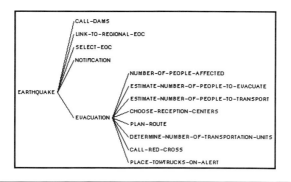

errors. This same mechanism allows the interface to make reasonable guesses about what default parameters are appropriate for the current task step, and to provide these automatically for the user. In this way ambiguous commands and incomplete commands can be specified without the need for precision and completeness on the user's part. The interface can also provide an indication of the current state of the plan. This is done either textually by changing the font of executed commands in the Agenda or graphically by displaying the task hierarchy in a separate window on the screen with the currently executing step highlighted and those steps already executed shown boxed. The current interface prototype supports executing several tasks at once, or suspending the execution of one plan and resuming it at another time.

The missing element of the Plan Manager is the ability to infer user goals from the sequence of low-level commands entered by the user. At present, the interface simply activates its task support when the user directly indicates the task he wishes to execute by choosing it directly from a menu on the screen. One of our short-term goals is to incorporate some aspects of this missing element. However, even in its current state, the Plan Manager adds considerably to the overall utility of the interface.

5.7 ADAPTOR

When the range of user abilities and roles is large, or there are varying constraints on task execution (as rapid versus self-paced response times), having a single interface for all situations is inadequate. Different users will need more or less descriptive information on interface features, will require varying commands in interacting with the system, and will operate best when their view of the domain is tailored to their role and when the format of the information returned from the system supports the kind of decisions they must make. Therefore, another powerful capability for an intelligent interface is the ability to adapt its own features to the needs and preferences of the current user and the user's present task.

There are three key issues that must be addressed in designing and implementing the Adaptor: when to adapt, what to adapt, and how to adapt. Our approach to these three issues, as well as a discussion of the major components of the Adaptor, will now be considered.

When to adapt—Dialogue Phases. To answer the first question of when to adapt, the system must have some way of looking at the dialogue that permits detecting changes in the current dialogue state that warrant adaptation of the dialogue as the next state is entered. In the Adaptor, this issue can be resolved by viewing the interaction of the user and the computer system as consisting of a series of interaction events, with each event in turn composed of a set of distinct dialogue phases (see [Benbasat84]). An interaction event is an atomic unit that brackets the actions from when a user enters a request or command until the system returns a response. In the basic sequence of phases, the user enters some input, such as a natural language request (InputNLPhase), the response is sent on to the system for execution (ExecutionPhase), and the response of the system is displayed to the user (SystemResponsePhase). Looking at the dialogue as a series of interaction events, each composed of such phases, provides a way of organizing the Adaptor so that: (1) it is triggered at the appropriate times, for example, when an event causes the dialogue to enter a new phase; and (2) the adaptive mechanism can be applied in a discrete fashion, considering only what can be adapted in the interface for the impending dialogue phase. This leads to the second issue for the Adaptor.

What to Adapt—Dimensions of Interface Variability. To determine what to adapt, the interface needs to know what the possible range of options is for each major attribute of the interface at any given point in the dialogue, and must be able to select any appropriate combination of those features for dynamic realization. Much of the power of the Adaptor arises from its interaction with the other interface modules: calling upon the user model to interpret ambiguous input, reduce the search space of possible user intentions, and indicate how best to organize the interface to meet user preferences. In isolation, the Adaptor in the emergency management prototype of the interface currently considers four primary dimensions of variability. The first is the screen view of the geographic area, that is, the map. The system can present various geographic areas and can scale these to varying levels of detail, depending on the needs of the user. The interface is also able to vary the commands provided to the user for direct or forms-based execution, and can similarly vary the high-level tasks made available in the agenda or task hierarchy windows. An EOC officer, for example, could be directly supported in taking the necessary steps to handle an earthquake incident. The interface can also select certain facilities, such as the Event Logger or the Network Communications Facility (see following), to be open by default for a given user. Finally, the interface can vary the way in which data is presented to the user, showing users information in their preferred mode of viewing.

How to adapt—Main components. Figure 5.5 shows the major components of the Adaptor and how they interrelate. Each of these components is instantiated in the interface as a separate object or group of objects (in software terms). Aside from the knowledge bases, the main components of the Adaptor are these: the Monitor, which updates each of the different knowledge bases as conditions change; the Accessor, which provides generic functions for obtaining information from each of the knowledge bases, allowing other interface components to use the knowledge bases without having to know the internal details of their structure; the dialogue phases, each of which has parameters describing how the interface should look when that phase is entered as well as rule sets for adapting the interface for that phase; and an ExecutiveRouter, which decides, when an interface event occurs, what the

FIGURE 5.5
THE MAIN ADAPTOR COMPONENTS

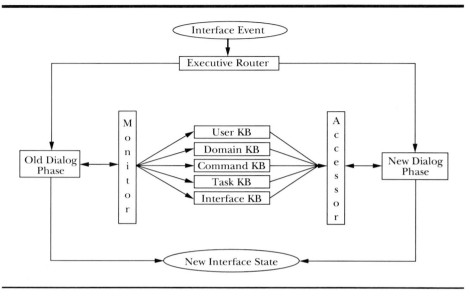

new dialogue phase should be, and coordinates the overall operation of the other Adaptor components.

How to adapt—Operational details. In general terms, adaptation occurs as follows (see Figure 5.5). When a significant interface event occurs, the Executive Router is called. Based upon the current dialogue phase and the nature of the event, this component determines what the next dialogue phase should be. The original dialogue phase is then called upon. It typically updates some of the knowledge bases, recording in the user model, for example, that a given command was successfully executed from a form by the user. The old phase also adjusts the interface if necessary, by removing interface features associated with that phase (e.g., a particular menu or form). The Executive Router then calls upon the new dialogue phase. The new phase exercises the most fundamental mechanism of adaptation by firing its particular set of rules. These rules consult the state of the appropriate knowledge bases through the Accessor, and based on the contents of these knowledge bases, the main parameters of that dialogue phase are set (details on the form of the rule sets for each dialogue phase transition can be found in [Tyler86, Tyler88]). The new dialogue phase then determines what features should be present in the interface based on the values of its parameters, and the interface is accordingly modified. The resulting action can range from something very simple, such as constructing a form for filling in the arguments to a command, to something much more complex, such as defining the context for a high-level task. Providing task context involves displaying graphically the task substeps and their states (e.g., executed or still to be accomplished), inferring default parameters and actions, dynamically designing menus of substeps, and interpreting user actions in terms of the selected task.

The impact of this module can be seen in a number of the features of the example screen of Figure 5.3. First, because the user is concerned with emergencies throughout a given region, the view provided by the map (left window) shows the entire Bay Area at a relatively low level of detail. Furthermore, the set of map commands offered in the menu attached to the map have been filtered to include only those actions this user would likely want to perform (e.g., looking at the locations of city halls as possible EOC locations). The system also determines how to show information to the user based upon that user's needs. Therefore, Figure 5.2 shows a barchart, facilitating detection of trends. Another type of user or task might suggest instead that actual values were more important than trends, in which case, the interface would display the data as a table instead.

None of the decisions made by the interface are final, however. The user is given the option of making other choices. Hence, under the *Map Commands* menu, there is an entry called *Additional Commands* which allows the user to select a command not on the immediate menu. If the user selects a particular command from that additional list, then that fact is recorded in the user model. If the command is selected often enough, the interface will automatically add it to the main menu. Similarly, when the system generates a response, as in Figure 5.3, the user can use the mouse to bring up a menu of possible alternative ways of showing the same data. If one of these is selected, the data is redisplayed in that format, and the user model is updated; enough such selections can lead to a decision by the interface to modify the way it shows such data by default (this is also discussed in the next section). The overriding objective of the adaptor module, then, is to assure that the interface is modified to best suit a given individual's needs, thereby easing the user's burden in accomplishing tasks on the system.

5.8 RESPONSE PLANNER

The final module of the intelligent interface is the response planner. A response planner is needed for several reasons. First, different users prefer to see the same kinds of information in different fashions. Additionally, there are many different types of modalities, and techniques within those modalities, which are accessible. A response planner can examine the data returning from the application and determine the most appropriate modality and modality technique(s) for presenting the information. Finally, the response planner removes the requirement that designers continually redesign and implement the output side of an application each time the system requirements change.

There are three steps to planning a response—(1) expressiveness, (2) effectiveness, and (3) adaptation. These steps are incorporated into the selection of modality as well as one or more techniques within the chosen modality for presenting the information to the user.

Rather than describing modality selection and technique selection (which is discussed more fully in [Gargan88]), this paper presents the basic process in terms of the three steps introduced above.

Expressiveness.   Expressiveness is a measurement of a presentation technique's ability to present the given information [Mackinlay86]. During this test, the Response Planner examines and compares the information to the constraints of the various presentation techniques. For instance, during technique selection, if there are two fields, one containing numerical information and the second holding symbolic information, and some relationship exists between those two fields, then a bar chart can be used to fully express the information.

Effectiveness.   The effectiveness step compares the expressive techniques and modalities within the context of human perception and understanding. Values used for comparison come from a user model that has inherited the values from the canonical user model. The canonical model contains general perceptual information [Cleveland84; Hochberg86; Tukey86] (size of bars in bar charts, line widths, spacing, frequency, etc.) and information comparing relative values of one technique versus another [Clark86; DeSanctis84]. For example, the bar chart's effectiveness step checks for the number of bars. The greater the number of bars the more difficult it is to distinguish the relationships between any two bars.

Adaptation.   The last step in the response planning process is to adapt the response to the individual user. Here the techniques that have passed the effectiveness test are ordered based on how well each technique can support the user's intention. Finally, the response planner presents the information using the technique within that list that the user prefers. So, for example, one user may prefer to see specific numerical information in a table, while another might prefer a bar chart for that same data.

The response planner considers a variety of techniques and modalities each time the user issues a query or a command to the interface in a similar process. As a result, it is unnecessary for an interface designer to specify all possible layouts at the outset. This means that as the users or the underlying application change, it is not necessary to "redesign and construct" the output of the interface.

5.9 INTELLIGENT INTERFACE DESIGN TOOLS

A long-term goal of the intelligent interfaces project is to develop a set of tools so that persons unfamiliar with the implementation details of the interface can still easily specify the nature of their application and have an intelligent interface produced automatically for that application. To support this process requires interacting with users through menus, graphs, and simple editing windows to obtain the information needed to define the domain-specific knowledge bases that drive the intelligent interface. The complete tool kit would require tools for defining the vocabulary appropriate for the domain, for listing the commands and tasks available, and for enumerating the important attributes of the user and domain models. At the current time, work has been completed on the vocabulary acquisition tool, domain model tool, and command and task knowledge base tool. This work also includes an effort to integrate these tools along with a user model tool into a tightly coupled tool kit. In the sections that follow, each of the three tools along with the design of an integrated tool kit are discussed.

5.9.1. Vocabulary Acquisition Tool

The Vocabulary Acquisition Tool assumes that the domain modeler lacks expertise with the particular representation language underlying the system and lacks familiarity with linguistic terminology. The vocabulary tool must acquire domain-specific knowledge without relying on linguistic terminology such as "transitive verb," "inflectional forms," "argument structure," etc. This tool utilizes ideas developed by others concerned with the general issue of vocabulary acquisition, including work in the HITS project at MCC [Hollan91] and the TEAM system developed at SRI International [Grosz86].

The Vocabulary Acquisition Tool supports the defining and modifying of nouns, verbs, adjectives, and prepositions. The tool is also invoked when an end user enters a word unknown to the system. Currently, the tool functions in conjunction with the Chat-80 natural-language understanding system [Pereira83], but the routines that write definitions to PROLOG are the only ones customized to Chat-80. An extensive, context-sensitive help system is provided to support novice users of this tool.

A detailed example of a definition for the verb *move*, as in the sentence "A bus moves evacuees to a location," is now presented. The user first enters the new verb, and the system scans its lexicon for existing definitions. If one or more previous definitions are found, the user can edit one of them or enter a new definition. For this example, *move* has not been previously defined.

Using morphological rules of English, the system attempts to guess the correct inflectional forms of the verb: third person singular, past form, present participle, and past participle. Each verb form is presented in upper-case letters in a general sentence using the new verb being defined. If the system guesses the verb form incorrectly, the user corrects the spelling.

Next, the user types in a sentence, using either known objects or existential phrases, specifying a use of the word. Using the sentence mentioned above, "A bus moves evacuees to a location," and assuming all other words beside *moves* have been defined, the system can deduce that *moves* is being defined transitively (takes a direct object) and that it takes a prepositional phrase argument. The system also guesses at the type of the arguments from this sentence. From the existing domain model, the tool would already know that a *bus* is a **transportation object**, *evacuees* are **people**, and *location* is a **place**. Often the arguments to a verb can be more general than the system infers automatically, so the user has the ability to edit the definition explicitly.

A second method of specifying the arguments in the sentence is to use existential phrases, as in "An ambulance moves a patient to a hospital." In this case, the types of arguments are directly specified by the user, but again, they can be edited as necessary.

Alternatively, the user can directly examine the domain model and graphically select the types of the verb's argument from there. This method has been found to be confusing to an initial user but, since it is much faster, may be used by more experienced vocabulary tool users. Help is available to assist the novice in using these three methods.

The majority of the development for the Vocabulary Acquisition Tool has gone into verb acquisition, since verbs require the most complex information for natural-language processing systems. This tool has undergone several stages of development and has been subjected to some informal user testing.

5.9.2. Domain Model Tool

The Domain Model Tool supports users by insulating them from knowledge representation terminology and from the particular representation language underlying the given system. This tool allows developers either to define a new domain model or to refine an existing one.

The design of the Domain Model Tool is similar to that of other CHORIS tools in that graphical techniques are used to solicit information from the user. For instance, rather than putting the user into a text editor to describe each concept in the domain, the user is given the freedom to create one or more concepts, link them together graphically, and provide any attributes needed to describe those concepts at any point in the interaction.

The existing Domain Model Tool provides a mechanism whereby a user knowledgeable about the domain, but not about interface design, can easily build the CHORIS domain model. One of the design goals of this tool was to give the user flexibility in defining the elements of the domain model in any order.

The user specifies the concepts in the domain. Currently, after a concept is created, an English word of the same name is also created. Other actions can occur in any order in the Domain Model Tool after at least one concept has been defined: describing concepts with attributes, describing concepts graphically, and linking concepts together.

An example highlighting these features of the Domain Model Tool is as follows. First, a user graphically creates the concept, **resource**. The tool then guesses the English word *resource* is an appropriate word to map to this concept. Similarly, the user creates an **ambulance** concept. At any time, the user could open a form on one of the concepts and add attributes describing the concept. The user further states that an ambulance is a kind of resource graphically by drawing a line from the **ambulance** concept to the **resource** concept. Finally, the user might create **MPA-1** as an instance of an **ambulance**.

The current state of the Domain Model Tool allows users to create and modify concepts graphically and instantiate those concepts appropriately. This tool has been used by the CHORIS developers to maintain the domain model underlying the CHORIS system.

5.9.3. Command and Task Knowledge Base Tool

Another important tool for developing an intelligent interface, the Command and Task Knowledge Base Tool, supports the description of the commands and tasks that can be performed. Defining the actions available in an application is done through a two-stage process. The user first specifies what attributes are important for understanding actions within the application (a generic definition of a command or task). For example, one attribute might be "Menu Description," which could be a string used to describe the command in a menu. The user then gives values to the attributes in the generic definition to describe each individual action. For instance, the "Menu Description" attribute might be given the value "Clear Map" for a command to remove all icons from a map displayed on the screen. In what follows, the first stage will be referred to as "property definition" and the second as "structure definition."

The set of properties that may be specified during this stage fall under two categories, depending on their types. A property may be a simple type (e.g., string) or complex type (e.g., list). In addition to the type, there is other information that is needed for each property. The complete specification for each property includes the following: (1) the property name; (2) the property type, which is depicted as a tree, and limits the range of values acceptable for the property; (3) the prompt string, which is used to prompt for the value; and (4) a help message, which is to be used to provide explanations of the value type.

Structure definition is used to incrementally build the hierarchical structure of a knowledge base and to fill in the values for the properties that are implicitly attached at the leaves based on the properties' types. When prompting the user for the values, the structure definition phase makes use of the information provided from the property definition phase. Thus, the developer, during this stage, defines each application action and its particular attributes, with the earlier property definition serving to insure that attribute values are of the appropriate type. The top-level interaction window for this stage displays the set of all entered commands. The editor, when invoked for a leaf, lays out the properties that exist for that leaf using the information that was provided through property definition. Each property's value is labeled with the corresponding prompt string, and the user selects the property's slot to edit its value. The user is given the help message describing what kinds of values are expected when the corresponding sensitive region on the window is selected. Also, general help on the overall use of the editor can be invoked at any time by the user.

5.9.4. An Integrated Tool Kit

This section presents the design of and some of our experience with an integrated tool kit for CHORIS [Tyler90]. This tool kit consists of the three tools detailed in the previous section: the Domain Model Tool, the Vocabulary Acquisition Tool, the Command and Task Model Tool, along with a User Model Tool. First, general features and benefits of an integrated tool kit are presented followed by an illustrative example of the advantages of a tightly integrated tool kit.

General Features

The most obvious general benefit of an integrated tool kit is a consistent "look and feel" to the individual tools. This allows developers primarily familiar with one tool to be, by extension, familiar with all the tools. Examples of this consistency include similar mouse clicking, consistent help accessing and help text style, similar screen layout, and so on.

A second general advantage is the coordination of similar tasks. This feature can be extremely helpful, since frequently it is the case that, while one tool is in use, some piece of knowledge will be needed from another tool. Rather than forcing the developer to define each type of knowledge separately, the tool kit can greatly facilitate the developer's job by recognizing and supporting this coordination. This coordination also leads to a completeness verifier for certain types of knowledge; if every time one type of knowledge is added, any related type of knowledge is also defined, completeness can be assured.

Finally, an integrated tool kit can automate many of the steps of knowledge acquisition. Frequently, the system can guess from one piece of knowledge what another piece of related knowledge will be. Presenting the tool user with this guess and allowing editing can be a powerful development aid.

An Example

This section describes the design of TMACS (Tool for Model Acquisition in CHORIS), a system that integrates the individual CHORIS tools into a tool kit. This example describes the process of defining an application action for use in the CHORIS interface. The definition begins in the Command and Task Model Tool and other tools are invoked to enter related knowledge, as TMACS reasons appropriate.

In isolation, the Command and Task Model Tool requires the user to provide, from memory or with the aid of some hardcopy document, a detailed description of the arguments or parameters of a given command or task. However, with an integrated tool kit, the developer is given access to the knowledge representation expertise of the Domain Model Tool, the linguistic knowledge of the Vocabulary Acquisition Tool, and the modeling knowledge of the User Model Tool.

For the example of TMACS in operation, a situation is considered in which the developer wants to define the domain action *move* within the emergency planning and response system. Within TMACS, the developer first indicates that an application action called **move** is being described. Immediately, the Domain Model Tool is invoked to aid the user in specifying the parameters for this new command. For the example, the developer states that **resources** *are moved* from one **location** to another **location**. This is accomplished, via the Domain Model Tool, by selecting the appropriate nodes from a graphical presentation of the domain model.

After the parameters have been defined, the Vocabulary Acquisition Tool is invoked. TMACS has enough information to make plausible guesses as to the English verb that maps to this command, the argument structure, and types of the verb.

Initially, the system assumes that the name of the command is the same as the English verb that invokes this command. If this assumption is not correct, the developer can easily correct it. Next, using linguistic rules, TMACS guesses the various inflectional forms of the verb. TMACS also examines the number of arguments to infer the verb's argument structure. Further, the system copies information about the nodes that were selected as parameters to the command to use as the semantic types to the word *move*.

Once the action is fully defined, TMACS requests knowledge about this command for user modeling purposes. With the **move** command, it might be the case that only certain types of users (e.g., EOC officers) have the authorization to execute such a command. This information is collected in the stereotype categories within the User Model Tool.

During this process, the user has the full power of any of the tools at his disposal. For instance, if the type of one of the parameters was not predefined, the user can proceed to define the information through the Domain Model Tool and to describe the necessary lexical information. A more detailed discussion of the integration between the Domain Model Tool and the Vocabulary Acquisition Tool is presented elsewhere [Tyler90].

The above example highlights only some of the possible points of tool interaction within the TMACS integrated tool kit. Many other logical points of interaction among the various tools could be offered to further demonstrate the clear advantages of integrating the tools for CHORIS knowledge acquisition into a single coherent system.

5.10 CONCLUSION

This overview of the CHORIS work has been intended to convey an idea of the characteristics of the main components of an intelligent interface and an idea of how they might work together in an integrated system. This work has attempted to isolate and implement the main functionalities of an intelligent interface. In the process, the capabilities of multimodal input, interpretation of user input in terms of plans and goals and adaptation of interface features to the individual user, and dynamic reasoning about how to present system information, have all been found to play an important role in enhancing the utility of the interface. The chapters to follow will provide greater detail and differing perspectives on these interface functions, including a substantial final section on interface design tools. Taken together, the research detailed in this book encompasses many of the key issues in intelligent interface design.

REFERENCES

[Arens91] Arens, Y., and Miller, L. 1991. Presentation Design Using An Integrated Knowledge Base. In present volume.

[Benbasat84] Benbasat, L., and Wand, Y. 1984. A Structured Approach to Designing Human-Computer Dialogues. *International Journal of Man-Machine Studies*, 21, 105–126.

[Clancy86] Clancy, W. J. 1986. From Guidon to Neomycin and Heracles in Twenty Short Lessons. *AI Magazine*, 7(3), 40–60.

[Clark86] Clark, N. 1986. The Language of Data: Tables and Graphs as Exposition. In *Proceedings ICRISAT*, pp. 113–120.

[Cleveland84] Cleveland, S., and McGill, R. 1984. Graphical Perception: Theory, Experimentation, and Application to the Development of Graphical Methods. *Journal of the American Statistical Association*, 79(387), 531–554.

[Cohen89] Cohen, P. R., Sullivan, J. W., Dalrymple, M., Gargan, R. A., Jr., Moran, D. B., Schlossberg, J. O., Pereira, F. C. N., and Tyler, S. W. 1989. Synergistic Use of Direct Manipulation and Natural Language. In *Proceedings of CHI '89*, Austin, TX, May, pp. 227–233.

[DeSanctis84] DeSanctis, G. 1984. Computer Graphics as Decision Aids: Directions For Research. *Decision Sciences*, 15, 463–487.

[Feiner91] Feiner, S. 1991. An Architecture for Knowledge-Based Graphical Interfaces. In present volume.

[Gargan88] Gargan, R. A., Jr., Sullivan, J. W., and Tyler, S. W. 1988. Multimodal Response Planning: An Adaptive Rule Based Approach. In *CHI 1988 Proceedings*, May, pp. 229–234.

[Grosz86] Grosz, B. J., Appelt, D. E., Martin, P., and Pereira, F. 1986. *TEAM: An Experiment in the Design of Transportable Natural Language Interfaces*. Technical Report 356R, SRI International. October.

[Hochberg86] Hochberg, J., and Krantz, D. H. 1986. Perceptual Properties of Statistical Graphs. In *Proceedings of the Section on Statistical Graphics of the American Statistical Association*. pp. 211–214. This paper is a subpaper in the paper: "Three Perspectives on Statistical Graphs: A Basis for Defining Evaluation Criteria" by Nancy Clark. pp. 29–35.

[Hollan91] Hollan, J., Rich, E., Hill, W., Wroblewski, D., Wilner, W., Wittenberg, K., and Grudin, J. 1991. An Introduction to HITS: Human Interface Tool Suite. In present volume.

[Kass91] Kass, R. and Finin, T. 1991. General User Modelling: A Facility to Support Intelligent Interaction. In present volume.

[MacKinlay91] MacKinlay, J. 1991. Search Architectures for the Automatic Design of Graphical Presentations. In present volume.

[MacKinlay86] MacKinlay, J. D. 1986. *Automatic Design of Graphical Presentations*. PhD thesis. Stanford University, December. Report number: STAN-CS-86-1138.

[Neal91] Neal, J. G., and Shapiro, S. C. 1991. Intelligent Multi-Media Interface Technology. In present volume.

[Norman86] Norman, D. A. 1986. Cognitive Engineering. In Norman, D. A., and Draper, S. W. (eds.), *User Centered System Design—New Perspectives on Human-Computer Interaction*, pp. 31–61. Hillsdale, NJ: Lawrence Erlbaum Associates.

[Pereira83] Pereira, F. C. N. 1983. *Logic for Natural-Language Analysis*. Technical Report Technical Note 275, SRI International, January.

[Rich79] Rich, E. 1979. *Building and Exploiting User Models*. PhD thesis. Carnegie-Mellon University, April.

[Tukey86] Tukey, P. A. 1986. A Data Analyst's View of Statistical Plots. In *Proceedings of the Section on Statistical Graphics of the American Statistical Association*. This paper is a subpaper in the paper: "Three Perspectives on Statistical Graphs: A Basis for Defining Evaluation Criteria" by Nancy Clark. pp. 21–29.

[Tyler86] Tyler, S. W. 1986. *SAUCI: A Self-Adaptive User-Computer Interface*. PhD thesis. University of Pittsburgh, October.

[Tyler88] Tyler, S. W. 1988. *Sauci: A Knowledge-based Interface Architecture*. In *CHI 1988 Proceedings*, May. pp. 235–240.

[Tyler90] Tyler, S. W., and Schlossberg, J. L. 1990. *TMACS: A Knowledge Acquisition Toolkit for Intelligent Interfaces*. CHI '90 Invited Poster, Seattle, WA, April.

[Walhster91] Wahlster, W. 1991. User and Discourse Models for Multimodal Communication. In present volume.

[Young91] Young, R. L. 1991. A Dialogue User Interface Architecture. In present volume.

CHAPTER 6

GENERAL USER MODELING: A FACILITY TO SUPPORT INTELLIGENT INTERACTION

ROBERT KASS
Center for Machine Intelligence

TIM FININ
Paoli Research Center, Unisys Corporation

ABSTRACT

An important component of adaptable interactive systems is the ability to model the system's users. Previous systems have relied on user models tailored to the particular needs of that system alone. This paper presents the notion of a *general user model*, and describes some of our research on building a general user modeling facility that could be used by a variety of applications. This

This chapter describes work that was performed (in part) while the authors were at the Department of Computer and Information Science at the University of Pennsylvania, where it was supported by DARPA grant N00014-85-K-0018 and grants from the Army Research Office and the Digital Equipment Corporation.

work focuses on the representation, maintenance, and acquisition issues of modeling long-term beliefs of the user, and describes a general facility for accomplishing these tasks.

6.1 INTRODUCTION

User modeling is an important component of many systems that seek to adapt their behavior to users in order to interact more intelligently. This modeling may involve design criteria for an interface, such as human factors analysis [Norman86] (where the user is modeled by system designers when making decisions about the form of user-system interface), or it may involve using a model dynamically (where knowledge about the user is utilized to direct system behavior in an interaction). This paper discusses only the second aspect of user modeling. To provide a clear foundation for that discussion, the following definition, taken from [Wahlster86], will be used as a starting point.

A *user model* is a knowledge source in a system that contains explicit assumptions on all aspects of the user that may be relevant to the behavior of the system.[1]

Unfortunately, because user models are just one component that contributes to intelligent interaction, the user modeling aspects of interactive systems have frequently been left unexplored, or systems have employed simple, domain-specific models. This paper describes our ongoing research on the feasibility and effectiveness of *general user models*: models that have a well-defined set of capabilities that can be used in diverse situations and systems. To this end, Section 6.2 discusses when user models are needed for intelligent interfaces, and how they may be used. Section 6.3 describes the characteristics of an "ideal" general user modeling facility, whereas Section 6.4 and Section 6.5 present work we have done on the issues of user model maintenance and acquisition—focusing on models of the user's beliefs. Section 6.6 discusses how stereotypes, the classification techniques of Section 6.4, and with the implicit model acquisition techniques of Section 6.5, can be integrated, and describes a particular problem of arbitrating between conflicting beliefs about the user in such a system.

6.2 THE IMPORTANCE OF USER MODELING

User models are not needed for all man-machine interactions, or even all intelligent interfaces. User models are only beneficial to a system if it has one or more of the following characteristics [Kass86]:

---

[1] Wahlster and Kobsa's original definition was presented in the context of natural language systems only. The definition here has been expanded to include user models in any context.

- The system seeks to *adapt* its behavior to individual users;
- The system assumes *responsibility* (or shares responsibility with the user) for ensuring the success of user-system communication;
- The class of potential system users, or the potential uses of the system, is *diverse*.

Several contributors to this book describe systems that have these requirements. For example, the systems described by [Hollan88] and [Young88] modify their behavior based on their perception of user needs. Similarly, the Bridge tutor for novice programmers [Bonar88] requires a model of students' plans to help it decide what to do, and UC, the Unix Consultant [Chin88] must reason about user's goals and knowledge when generating advice in response to user questions. Further, user models may be employed by expert systems to tailor their explanations to individual users [Sleeman85; Kass88b; Paris88a]. In general, an interactive system may need to reason about a user's beliefs, goals and plans, preferences and attitudes, or capabilities to understand his or her actions and control the system's own behavior.

Systems that can benefit from a user modeling facility are not necessarily classified by a particular form of interaction. In fact, any system that strives to be *cooperative* (as described in [Cheikes88]) can benefit from a user model. For example, user models have been of help in identifying potential obstacles in a user's plan [Allen80], recognizing when a user's query does not reflect the user's underlying goals [Pollack86], tailoring responses according to the user's perspective [McKeown85b] or knowledge [Paris88b], or correcting user misconceptions [McCoy88]. Figure 6.1 illustrates a taxonomy of uses for a user model.

6.3 THE IDEAL GENERAL USER MODEL

Although user models have been employed in many types of interactive systems, the models have been specifically crafted for each application, usually by the explicit coding of domain-related goals, plans, or knowledge that system users are expected to have. This hand-crafting is unfortunate, because building a user modeling facility requires a substantial amount of effort. This section examines the characteristics of an *ideal* general user modeling facility, focusing on dimensions for measuring the generality of a user modeling system, and the facilities that any general user modeling system should have.

Is it possible to produce a general user modeling facility so multiple systems can benefit from a single design effort? Our ultimate answer is yes, general user modeling is practical. Although the ideal system described here may not be realized, significant features of the ideal model can be achieved and used effectively.

FIGURE 6.1
USES FOR KNOWLEDGE OF THE USER

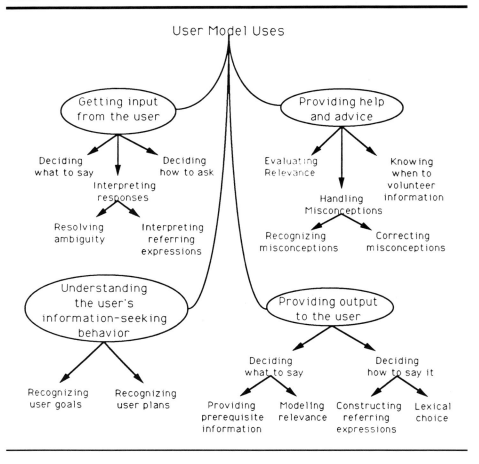

6.3.1. Dimensions of Generality

User models may be general with respect to three dimensions: the range of users, the forms of interaction, and the underlying system domain. *User generality* is usually a requirement of any user-modeling facility because user models are generally employed (and most beneficial) when a range of users deal with the system, or when the system strives to adapt its behavior to individual users. Thus, interaction and domain generality are the unique features of an ideal general user-modeling facility. A user model has *interaction generality* if it can be used with a variety of interaction modes, such as structured interactions or mixed initiative dialog, and can be used with various modes of communication, such as natural language, menus, speech, and graphics. A *domain general* user modeling facility can be used with applications having a range of knowledge bases, such as diagnostic systems for medicine, mechanical devices, and electronic components.

6.3.2.   User Modeling Facilities

A general user modeling system must provide three types of user modeling facilities: representation and maintenance facilities for the contents of the model, access facilities for other components of the system or interface, and acquisition facilities for building the model [Kass86].

Representation and Maintenance

Any user modeling facility requires a knowledge base to represent its beliefs about user goals and plans, preferences and attitudes, capabilities, and beliefs about the world and other agents. A user model's representation requirements differ from most knowledge-based systems, however, in that user models are inherently volatile. Not only is new information added as an interaction proceeds, but old knowledge about the user must be revised as well. Thus, the maintenance facilities for a general user model must be able to retract beliefs about the user and resolve conflicts in those beliefs.

Access

A user model is present in a system as a service; it provides information about the system's users. How other components in the system access this information can vary widely. The user model might provide information about users *descriptively*, serving as a knowledge base of information about the user and retrieving this information in response to queries from other components in the system. A user model might also be used *prescriptively*, to simulate the behavior of the user so that the system can "run the model" to see how a user might be expected to behave. In this case, other system components may propose hypothetical additions to the user model, seeking to learn the effects of these changes on the state of the user. An example of the prescriptive use of a user model is *anticipation feedback* in generating elliptical responses [Wahlster86]. In this case a potential system response is generated and given to the user model to test whether the response can be understood by the user.

   Both descriptive and prescriptive methods for accessing the user model are *passive*; other system components initiate the interaction with the user model. The user modeling facility might also be an *active* participant in the system, volunteering information to other components when it decides the information is important. For example, an active user modeling facility might monitor the user model, notifying other system components when it achieves a certain state. Such a state might occur when the modeling facility notifies a system component that a belief revision that changes the belief status of information previously provided to the component has occurred in the user model.

Acquisition

Representation, maintenance, and access facilities are of little use if the user model contains no information about the user. Methods for acquiring knowledge about the user may vary: knowledge may be explicitly encoded in the user model before it is ever used, other system components may update the user model directly (by making assertions to the user model's knowledge base), or the general user modeling facility may actively acquire its own information. Active model acquisition, in turn, can be implicit or explicit. The user modeling facility may have access to some representation of the interaction between user and system and may use this to update its model of the user (implicit acquisition), or the user-modeling facility may have its own goals about what it would like to know about the user (such as information that would resolve a belief conflict) and may generate its own request for information from the user (explicit acquisition).

For a user modeling facility to be truly general, it must be able to support all of the capabilities described above. Thus, the ideal general user model is a "toolbox" of capabilities for user modeling. It has the versatility to support a variety of demands from the overall system and the flexibility to acquire the information it needs in the best manner possible.

Our work has focused on the representation and maintenance, and acquisition facilities for general user modeling. Representation and maintenance of information about the user is central to any user modeling activity, whereas the acquisition of such information has been a major bottleneck to effective user modeling. We have also focused on modeling *long term* user information, such as the beliefs a user holds about the world or about the system domain. Such beliefs tend to persist over time, so the user model formed for an individual can be useful in many separate user-system interactions. The next two sections describe some of our efforts towards building a general user modeling facility.

6.4 GUMS—A GENERAL USER-MODELING SHELL

GUMS, a General User Modeling Shell, is intended to provide a basis for experimentation with the representation and maintenance issues of general user modeling [Finin86; Finin88]. GUMS is designed to serve as a utility for a set of application programs (see Figure 6.2). For each application GUMS keeps a knowledge base of user models relevant to that application. Applications are responsible for acquiring information about the user and supplying it to GUMS to update the user model. Likewise, the application queries GUMS to obtain information about the user, although demons can be used to accomplish the task of informing an application when specific changes occur in the user model.

FIGURE 6.2
A GENERAL ARCHITECTURE FOR A USER MODELING UTILITY

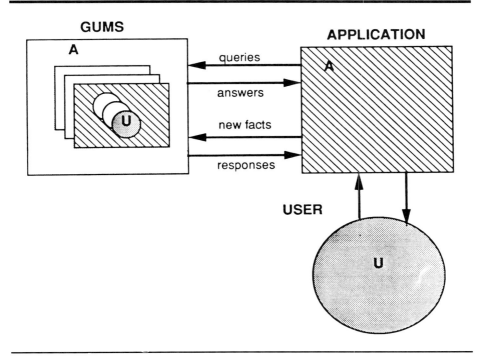

6.4.1. Representation

User modeling is most useful in situations in which a system must draw many plausible conclusions about the user on the basis of a small amount of definite knowledge. Thus, *default reasoning* [Reiter80] is an appropriate method for representing user model information. GUMS uses three default reasoning techniques to represent its beliefs about user knowledge: stereotypes, explicit default rules, and failure as negation. These three techniques capture generalizations of different grain size: they form a hierarchy with respect to the strength of their conclusions. Stereotypes capture generalizations about large classes of users. Within a stereotype, explicit default rules may express stereotypic norms that might vary for individuals of that class. Failure as negation is the weakest form of default reasoning, needed to gather weak evidence for beliefs about the user when stronger methods do not exist.

Stereotypes consist of a set of facts and rules believed to apply to a class of users. These facts and rules might be *definite*, meaning they necessarily apply to all users of that class, or *default*, specifying initial beliefs about users of that class that can be overridden. The definite information in a stereotype forms a sort of definition for the stereotype, by specifying information that must be believed about users for them to be a member of that class.

Stereotypes can be organized in hierarchies, where one stereotype, S1, subsumes another, S2, if everything true in S1 is necessarily true in S2. Thus, a stereotype can inherit information from more general stereotypes in the hierarchy. A model of an individual user is represented as a leaf-node in the hierarchy. Individual user models can have specific information associated with them, in addition to inheriting the facts and rules from subsuming stereotypes in the hierarchy. This information, however, is constrained to be *definite* and *unitary*, that is, it must consist of definite, fully instantiated facts. A hierarchy of stereotypes and individual user models is illustrated in Figure 6.3. Ideally, users and stereotypes should be able to inherit information from

FIGURE 6.3

A HIERARCHY OF STEREOTYPES AND INDIVIDUALS

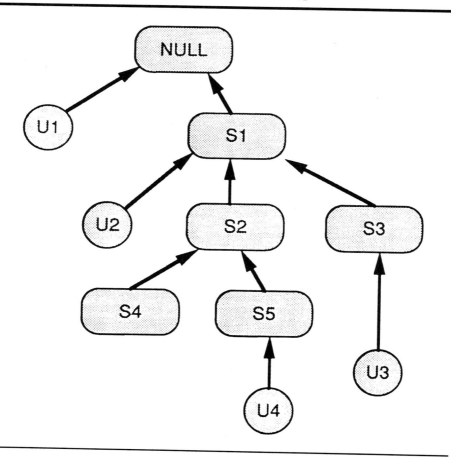

several immediate subsumers, as in a lattice, but this initial implementation limits the hierarchy to be a tree.

6.4.2. Maintenance

As new information about a user is supplied to GUMS, the individual user model must be updated, potentially creating inconsistencies in the model. The task of the maintenance facility is to update the individual user model and restore the consistency if necessary. Some inconsistencies are easy to resolve. If a new, definite fact about the user is asserted, contradicting a default assumption, the definite information is believed. Thus, default facts inherited from stereotypes, conclusions of default rules, and conclusions from failure as negation are overridden by definite facts about the user.

A more difficult conflict to resolve is one between a new, definite, fact and a definite fact inherited from a stereotype. In this case again the definite fact asserted about the user is believed, but steps must be taken to resolve the conflict with the stereotype. Because a definite fact is a defining characteristic of a stereotype, a conflict of this form means the user has been classified incorrectly in the stereotype hierarchy. Thus, this form of conflict requires a *reclassification* of the individual user model.

Reclassification can be either domain dependent or domain independent. Domain dependent methods are useful when reasons for a misclassification are understood. For example, as a user learns about the domain, the appropriate stereotype for representing his knowledge will change. Domain dependent reclassification can use knowledge of the user's expected "growth path" to select a new stereotype. A powerful domain independent reclassification method could implement a technique similar to concept classification in the KL-ONE family of representation languages [Brachman85]. The definite facts in a stereotype provide a set of features for classification. A KL-ONE style classifier would consider all possible stereotypes and find the set of most specific subsuming stereotypes with definite beliefs present in the individual user model. Although feasible, this approach may be computationally expensive. GUMS implements a simpler scheme; when a conflict is encountered, the ancestors of the current stereotype are searched in order of specificity (moving up the tree) until one is found that does not conflict with the individual user model.

GUMS enables general user modeling by providing applications with an environment containing a set of user modeling facilities. Applications using this environment take advantage of these facilities, instead of re-creating them. Thus, GUMS centralizes control of the access and maintenance of information about the user, similar to the way knowledge base systems and data base systems centralize the control of these functions for knowledge and data.

6.5 IMPLICIT USER MODEL ACQUISITION

In addition to the representation and maintenance of long term user beliefs addressed in GUMS, our work has also focused on the problem of *acquiring* a model of the user's beliefs, and included an implementation of GUMAC, a General User Model Acquisition Component [Kass87; Kass88a]. In GUMS, beliefs about the user were acquired in two ways: by explicitly encoding beliefs in the stereotypes and individual user models, and by assertions made by the application. Although GUMS can support the user-modeling requirements for many applications, a great deal of effort is required to make use of it. Not only must the application designers discover and implement a system of domain related stereotypes, but (because the application is responsible for populating the individual models of users with facts representing their beliefs) they must also design and implement some kind of knowledge acquisition strategy. Thus, the problem of acquiring user knowledge can be a significant bottleneck for general user modeling.

6.5.1. Explicit Versus Implicit Acquisition

The acquisition problem in GUMS, as in most user modeling systems, is the need to encode a large amount of information about the potential system users. Currently, several user model acquisition techniques that emphasize the *explicit* acquisition of information about the user are used. One approach, used in the BLAH system [Weiner80)] which generates tailored explanations of a system's reasoning, requires the users themselves to build the user model. A second approach is used by UMFE [Sleeman 85], a User-Modeling Front End for an explanation component of NEOMYCIN, that asks a series of questions to determine the user's knowledge of concepts that might appear in an explanation in order to present the explanation in terms the user understands. The most common approach, though, is to pre-encode a set of stereotypic user models and to try to identify which stereotypes are appropriate for particular users. Unfortunately, the first two techniques require explicit action by the user to build the user model and require self-representations that may not accurately describe the user. Although the use of stereotypes can avoid explicit model-building activity by users, it requires the system builders to encode a potentially large number of stereotypes—a task that may take more time than building the domain knowledge base itself.

An alternative to explicit user model acquisition is to build the model implicitly as the user interacts with the system. Implicit acquisition avoids the explicit encoding bottleneck and can reduce the burden on the application as well. If the user modeling facility takes full responsibility for acquiring the user model, applications do not need to reason about what information should be asserted about the user. Furthermore, if the user modeling facility's acquisition capability is application independent, then general user modeling is a practical method for providing user modeling capabilities to a variety of applications.

Implicit user model acquisition has not been pursued extensively because it has generally been considered to be too slow to build a useful, robust model and too uncertain in the conclusions it makes. Our research suggests that this need not be the case. In particular, for specific forms of user-system interaction many basic assumptions about the user's behavior can be made that provide a foundation for drawing many conclusions about the user's beliefs.

6.5.2. User Model Acquisition Rules

This implicit acquisition approach has been implemented in GUMAC, which focuses on providing a set of user-modeling facilities for *cooperative advisory systems* (systems that advise the user and seek to be as helpful as possible) that allow the user to volunteer information and that communicate in natural language. Rather than providing a shell in which applications can be built, GUMAC implements the user-modeling facilities of a system as a separate module as illustrated in Figure 6.4. Given this model, GUMAC has four sources of information for acquiring a model of user beliefs: (1) the user's behavior that is observable by the system, (2) the system's behavior that the

FIGURE 6.4
THE GUMAC INTERACTIVE SYSTEM MODEL

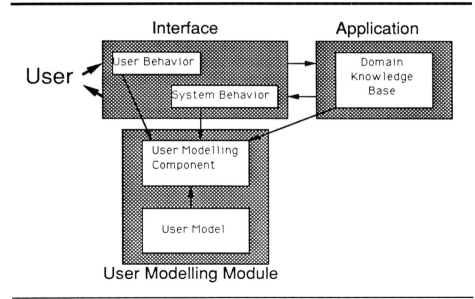

User Modelling Module

user can observe,[2] (3) the system's domain model, and (4) the current model of the user.

The implicit acquisition technique used by GUMAC has been implemented as a set of *user model acquisition rules*. These rules are domain independent, supporting the feasibility of general user modeling.[3] The rules were inspired by transcripts of over 100 conversations between a human expert and people seeking advice concerning their personal financial investments.[4] The rules capture reasonable methods that an expert might use to draw conclusions about the beliefs of the user. In fact, from a short dialogue between the system and a user, they are capable of building a model sufficiently robust to enable it to tailor its explanations to that user [Kass88a; Kass88b].

The implicit acquisition rules rely on basic assumptions about the user and the user's behavior. For example, one set of rules,[5] the *cooperativity* rules, assumes the user is cooperating with the system and thus is observing Grice's Maxims for cooperative communication [Grice75]. The *relevancy rule*, based on Grice's maxim of relation "Be relevant," allows the system to draw conclusions about the user's knowledge of the system's reasoning. If the maxim of relation is being obeyed then the system expects users to believe that the statements they make are relevant to their current conversational goals. In the type of expert system advisory interactions assumed in this work the system (which controls the interaction) establishes these goals, usually by asking the user a question. Thus, cooperative users will respond with information they believe is relevant to accomplishing the system's goals. In general form, the rule is stated as follows:

$$\mathrm{coop} - \mathrm{agent(User)} \wedge \mathrm{do(User, Act)} \wedge \mathrm{current} - \mathrm{goal(System, G)} \rightarrow$$

$$\mathrm{Bel(User, subgoal(Act, G))}.$$

Thus, in the following dialogue taken from the transcripts, the caller believes that all the information she provides is relevant to determining how to take her supplemental annuity.

(1) C.   I just retired December first, and in addition to my pension and social security I have a supplemental annuity, which I contributed to while I was employed, from the state of New Jersey mutual fund. I'm entitled to a lump sum settlement, which would be between $16,800 and $17,800, or a lesser life annuity and the choices of the annuity would be $125.45 per month. That would be the maximum with no beneficiaries.

(2) E.   You can stop right there, take your money.

---

[2] Both (1) and (2) are obtained by gaining access to the interface component's internal representations of the statements made by users and the system.

[3] Thus, interaction generality has been abandoned in the effort to obtain domain-general user model acquisition.

[4] The transcripts were made by Martha Pollack and Julia Hirschberg from the radio talk show "Harry Gross: Speaking about Your Money" broadcast on station WCAU in Philadelphia, February 1–5, 1982.

[5] See [Kass88a] for a complete presentation of the rules.

If this dialogue took place between a user and an investment advisory system, the user-modeling module would assert that the user believes that each of these items is relevant to the goal of deciding how to take the annuity, even though the system knows that some of the information is, in fact, not relevant.

Other acquisition rules make assumptions about reasoning that the user is likely to do. In general, one cannot assume that the user will believe all of the logical consequences of his current beliefs (i. e., assume *consequential closure*). Instead, an approximate model of the inferences any user would be likely to draw is needed. Our model includes, for example, rules to cover the transitivity of subsumption relations (if the users know A is a kind of B, and B is a kind of C, then they will infer that A is a kind of C) and inheritance of properties of concepts.

Another group of rules focuses on assumptions about the user's human behavior. For example, the *agent rule* considers the situation where the system knows the user has performed a particular action. The fact that the user was the agent of this action is significant, because it means the user himself must know of the action, know of any necessary substeps of the action, and know all the information related to performing that action. For example, if the user says, "I just rolled over two CD's," he or she must not only know about the rolling over action, but also that CD's have a due date, that they are obtained from banks, and so on. Thus, the Agent Rule can be a quite powerful way of determining a large amount of information about the user's beliefs. The rule states:

$$\text{achieved(User, Act)} \rightarrow$$

$$\text{Bel(User, goal(Act))} \land \forall p(\text{property(Act, p)} \supset \text{Bel(User, property(Act, p)))} \land$$

$$\forall g(\text{necessary} - \text{subgoal(g, Act)} \supset (\text{Bel(User, subgoal(g, Act))}) \land$$

$$\text{Bel(User, goal(g))} \land \forall p(\text{property(g, p)} \supset \text{Bel(User, property(g, p)))))}.$$

Here, "necessary-subgoal(A, B)" is needed because there may be more than one way to achieve a goal. A necessary subgoal is one that must be performed, no matter what plan is used to accomplish the goal. Thus, the necessary subgoals constitute the intersection of the steps of all possible plans to achieve the goal.

In summary, a significant problem in acquiring user models can be overcome through the use of implicit acquisition techniques. The acquisition rules developed in our work are domain independent, thus they enable more practical general user models to be built.

6.6 INTEGRATING STEREOTYPES AND IMPLICIT ACQUISITION

Although the contrasts between explicit and implicit user model acquisition techniques are emphasized in Section 6.5, these methods can complement each other. Despite the problems with explicit acquisition and the advantages of implicit acquisition methods, in many situations it is still desirable to encode domain-specific knowledge about users. This section describes how GUMAC integrates the implicit acquisition rules with the GUMS framework, resulting in a powerful, extensible general user modeling facility that benefits from both acquisition approaches.

The key to integrating the implicit acquisition rules with GUMS is recognizing that the rules are *default* rules, sanctioned by specific assumptions about the user. Thus, the acquisition rules can be viewed as elements of very general stereotypes. For example, a stereotype for the class of "cooperative agents" contains the cooperativity rules, including the Relevancy Rule, as default rules. Other general stereotypes include "rational agent," containing rules modeling the user's reasoning capabilities, and "communicative agent," containing rules specific to communication. These stereotypes distinct from the domain specific stereotypes, form an independent hierarchy in a stereotype lattice. Thus, for an investment advisor system, a hierarchy of stereotypes such as in Figure 6.5 might be used.

With this notion of general stereotypes it is useful to distinguish between two types of rules a stereotype may contain: rules believed to be used *by* the users in their own reasoning (user inference rules) and rules *about* users needed by the system to make conclusions about them (model acquisition rules). For example, the Relevancy Rule reasons *about* users' beliefs, but a transitivity rule, although it can be used to draw conclusions about the user's beliefs, is assumed to be used *by* the users in their own reasoning. Any of these rules may be held as definite or default beliefs.

FIGURE 6.5
A HIERARCHY CONTAINING GENERAL AND DOMAIN INDEPENDENT STEREOTYPES

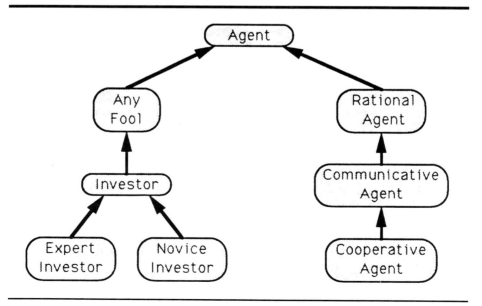

No representational distinction is made between domain independent and domain dependent stereotypes, enabling two additional, potentially powerful user modeling capabilities. First, model acquisition and user inference rules that are domain-specific can be included in stereotypes. One of the problems with building stereotypes is the number of facts that must be included in the stereotype. Domain specific model acquisition rules enable the user-modeling facility to infer these facts implicitly, so they do not need to be encoded explicitly.

The second capability involves the encoding of explicit facts in general stereotypes. A problem with many interactive systems is their limited knowledge of the world. If a body of common sense knowledge that all users are assumed to know is available in a very general stereotype, it could relieve the brittleness problem of such systems. Such a stereotype of common sense knowledge might be called the *any fool stereotype*, after McCarthy's notion that this is the knowledge "any fool" would know [McCarthy80].

6.6.1. Integration Problems

Some problems arise, however, when implicit acquisition methods are integrated with the stereotype hierarchy of GUMS. Two that we have encountered are discussed here, with our thoughts on potential solutions for the problems.

One problem with very general stereotypes, such as "cooperative agent," is the lack of defining facts about members of that class. In GUMS, the hierarchy of stereotypes is determined by the definite facts contained in the stereotypes, but for a stereotype such as "cooperative agent," useful defining facts are rare. Users might belong to the class of cooperative agents if the property "cooperative" can be applied to them, but such a user property is as difficult to define and as hard to acquire. Thus, it is not feasible to wait to discover the fact "cooperative(U)" before classifying U as a cooperative agent.

This difficulty can be avoided by initially classifying the user beneath all of the domain independent stereotypes. Consequently, GUMAC initially assumes the user is a rational, communicative, and cooperative agent, so the defining facts of these stereotypes are not needed in order to use them. Thus, for an investment advisory system, a user might originally be assumed to be an "initial agent" and a "novice investor," as in Figure 6.6. It might be necessary, however, to retract the assumption that a general stereotype applies to a user. For example, this might be necessary when the cooperativity rules consistently make conclusions that are contradicted by other, more certain, beliefs about the user. We do not know of a general method for distinguishing when one or more default rules in a stereotype should be retracted, and when belief in the stereotype as a whole should be retracted.

A second problem involves conflicting beliefs about the user. In GUMS new information about the user was supplied by the application and GUMS assumed it was definite knowledge. Thus, most of the belief conflicts encoun-

FIGURE 6.6
INITIAL CLASSIFICATION FOR AN INVESTMENT ADVISORY SYSTEM USER

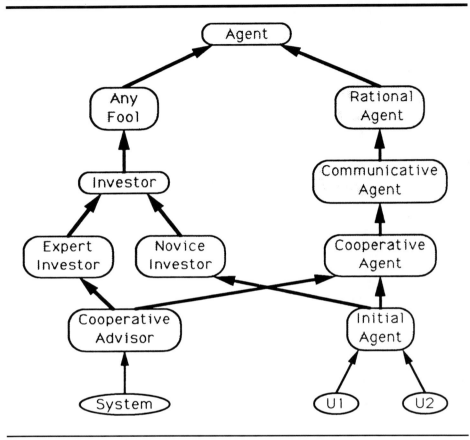

tered by GUMS are between definite knowledge from the application, and definite or default knowledge assumed by stereotype subsumption. Conflicts between definite and default knowledge are easy to resolve: believe the definite knowledge. In GUMS a conflict with definite knowledge from a stereotype is also straightforward; belief in the stereotype is dropped, and the hierarchy is traversed upward until a stereotype consistent with the definite knowledge about the user is found.

The simple resolution techniques in GUMS do not extend well to the integrated version of the system. First, the assumption that assertions from the application are definite is a simplification. Most of the assertions made by the implicit acquisition rules are default conclusions. Second, the stereotype hierarchy in GUMS is a tree, whereas GUMAC requires a lattice to reflect the inheritance of several independent sets of assumptions about the user. Thus, GUMAC may have conflicts between stereotypes that are incomparable.

Some of these problems can be handled by applying a heuristic that attempts to maximize the number of assumptions about the user after a conflict is resolved—this heuristic is used implicitly in GUMS. The stereotype hierarchy in GUMS represents an ordering based on the amount of information assumed about the user: stereotypes at the top of the tree contain few assumptions, whereas those at the bottom inherit the assumptions from higher stereotypes in addition to their local assumptions, so they contain more assumptions. When a conflict is encountered that requires a stereotype to be dropped, GUMS traverses up the tree, trying to find the stereotype with the most information that is consistent with the definite beliefs about the user.

A similar method can be used in GUMAC: when a conflict between stereotypes arises, the system should retract the stereotype that leaves the maximum number of assumptions about the user intact. Because several stereotypes may concurrently draw conclusions about some facts, this means the stereotype that makes the least number of unique conclusions about the user should be retracted.

6.7 CONCLUSION

General user modeling is an attractive approach to providing interactive systems with information about their users. Our work in this area indicates that general user modeling is not only feasible, but practical. The GUMS system demonstrates how a set of facilities for user modeling can be provided in the scope of an environment for building interactive applications. Further, work on implicit acquisition indicates that the acquisition bottleneck can be overcome in a domain independent manner. Thus, a general user modeling facility for supporting cooperative advisory systems is a practical possibility.

REFERENCES

[Allen80] Allen, J. F., and Perrault, C. R. 1980. Analyzing Intention in Utterances. *Artificial Intelligence*, 15, 143–178.

[Bonar91] Bonar, J., and Liffick, B. W. 1991. Communicating with High-Level Plans. In present volume.

[Brachman85] Brachman, R. J., and Schmolze, J. G. 1985. An Overview of the KL-ONE Knowledge Representation System. *Cognitive Science*, 9, 171–216.

[Cheikes88] Cheikes, B. A. and Webber, B. L. 1988. The design of a cooperative respondent. In *Proceedings of the Workshop on Architectures for Intelligent Interfaces: Elements and Prototypes*, pp. 3–18.

[Chin89] Chin, David N. 1989. KNOME: Modeling What The User Knows in UC. In Kobsa, A. and Wahlster, W. (eds.), *User Models in Dialog Systems*. Berlin and New York: Springer Verlag, pp. 74–107.

[Finin86] Finin, T., and Drager, D. 1986. GUMS$_1$: A General User Modeling System. In *Proceedings of the 1986 Conference of the Canadian Society for Computational Studies of Intelligence*, pp. 24–30.

[Finin89] Finin, T. 1989. GUMS—A General User Modeling Shell. In Kobsa, A., and Wahlster, W. (eds.), *User Models in Dialog Systems*. Berlin and New York: Springer Verlag, pp. 411–430.

[Grice75] Grice, H. P. 1975. Logic and Conversation. In Cole, P., and Morgan, J. L. (eds.), *Syntax and Semantics, 3*, pp. 64–75. New York: Academic Press.

[Hollan91] Hollan, J., Rich, E., Hill, W., Wroblewski, D., Wilner, W., Wittenburg, K., and Grudin, J. 1991. An Introduction to HITS: Human-Interface Tool Suite. In present volume.

[Kass86] Kass, R., and Finin, T. 1986. User Models in Intelligent Interfaces: Why They Are Needed, Problems with Their Implementation. In B. Neches and T. Kaczmarek, (eds.), *AAAI-86 Workshop on Intelligent Interfaces*, pp. 48–50.

[Kass87] Kass, R., and Finin, T. 1987. Rules for the Implicit Acquisition of Knowledge about the User. In *Proceedings of the Sixth National Conference on Artificial Intelligence*, pp. 295–300.

[Kass88a] Kass, R. J. 1988. *Acquiring a Model of the User's Beliefs From a Cooperative Advisory Dialog*. PhD thesis, Department of Computer and Information Science, University of Pennsylvania.

[Kass88b] Kass, R., and Finin, T. 1988. The Need for User Models in Generating Expert System Explanations. *International Journal of Expert Systems,* 1(4), 345–375.

[McCarthy80] McCarthy, J. 1980. Circumscription—A Form of Nonmonotonic Reasoning. *Artificial Intelligence,* 13(1), 27–40.

[McCoy88] McCoy, K. F. 1988. Reasoning on a Highlighted User Model to Respond to Misconceptions. *Computational Linguistics,* 14(3), 53–63.

[McKeown85] McKeown, K. R. 1985. Tailoring Explanations for the User. In *Ninth International Conference on Artificial Intelligence*, pp. 794–798.

[Norman86] Norman, D. A., and Draper, S. W., (eds.) 1986. *User Centered System Design: New Perspectives in Human-Computer Interaction*. Hillsdale, NJ: Lawrence Erlbaum Associates.

[Paris88a] Paris, C. L. 1988. Generation and Explanation: Building and Explanation Facility for the Explainable Expert System Framework, July. Presented at the Fourth International Workshop on Natural-Language Generation.

[Paris88b] Paris, C. L. 1988. Tailoring Object Descriptions to a User's Level of Expertise. *Computational Linguistics*, 14(3), 64–78.

[Pollack86] Pollack, M. E. 1986. *Inferring Domain Plans in Question-Answering*. PhD thesis, Department of Computer and Information Science, University of Pennsylvania.

[Reiter80] Reiter, R. 1980. A Logic for Default Reasoning. *Artificial Intelligence,* 13(1), 81–132.

[Sleeman85] Sleeman, D. H. 1985. UMFE: A User Modeling Front End Subsystem. *International Journal of Man-Machine Studies,* 23, 71–88.

[Weiner80] Weiner, J. L. 1980. BLAH, a System Which Explains its Reasoning. *Artificial Intelligence*, 15, 19–48.

[Wahlster86] Wahlster, W., and Kobsa, A. 1986. Dialog-based User Models. In *Proceedings of the IEEE*, 74(7).

[Young91] Young, R. L., 1991. A Dialogue Model for User Interfaces. In present volume.

CHAPTER 7

COMMUNICATING WITH HIGH-LEVEL PLANS

JEFFREY BONAR
GUIdance Technologies, Inc.

BLAISE LIFFICK
Millersville University

ABSTRACT

Everyone knows that really powerful computer systems are too hard for novices to use while easy-to-use systems are too clumsy and have too few features to be useful to experts. What if this were not so? That question motivates this work. In our approach we give users a very high-level programming language for expressing their intentions to a computer system. By *high-level* we mean a language that is informal, vague, contains much implicit information, and is designed to represent goals of interest to a particular class of users. Our high-level language makes assumptions about the user's background knowledge and overall intentions. We propose an approach that

This work was supported by the Office of Naval Research under contract numbers N00014-83-6-0148 and N00014-83-K0655 and by the the Air Force Human Resources Laboratory under contract number F41689-84-D-0002, Order 0004. Any opinions, findings, conclusions, or recommendations expressed in this report are those of the authors, and do not necessarily reflect the views of the U.S. Government. Copyright © 1990 Jeffrey G. Bonar explicitly structures knowledge to capture the experience and intentions of a domain expert without programming skill. We call the knowledge structures *plans*. Bridge, an intelligent tutor that teaches programming, is presented as an example of how the framework is implemented in a working system. We conclude by discussing a new system that provides a high-level plan language interface to a spreadsheet.

7.1 INTRODUCTION

Everyone knows that really powerful computer systems are too hard for novices to use while easy to use systems are too clumsy and have too few features to be useful to experts. What if this were not so? That question motivates this work. Our particular interest is experts in a particular domain who have no experience with computers, for example, stock brokers, medical doctors, and managers of large projects. How can we build a powerful and productive interface that will satisfy both experienced and novice computer users?

In our approach we give users a very high-level programming language for expressing their intentions to a computer system. By *high-level* we mean a language that is informal, vague, contains much implicit information, and is designed to represent goals of interest to a particular class of users. The language is high-level because the users need not be concerned with the details of how a computation proceeds, only with the purpose for which the computation is initiated. Our notion of a high-level programming language is quite different from what is used in automatic programming research (see, for example, [Balzer85]). In automatic programming, *high-level programming* means highly formal logic specifications that omit all but the most essential aspects of a description of a task. We, on the other hand, are interested in the sort of heuristic, vague, and partially implicit specifications used by humans with other humans. Instead of stripping out the contextual from the computational, we put in as much context as possible, relating the computations to a particular user's everyday experience.

Our high-level language makes assumptions about the user's background knowledge and overall intentions. This is consistent with our interest in providing interfaces to professionals and domain experts who have no computer experience. Our system must take such a user's specification—most likely a specification that requires assumptions about intentions and background knowledge to remove vagueness and inconsistencies—and derive an implementation using the primitives provided by a standard computer system.

We propose an approach that explicitly structures knowledge to capture the experience and intentions of a domain expert without programming skill. We call the knowledge structures *plans*.[1] Plans represent a vocabulary of ac-

---

[1] The word *plans* is used here in the sense of "a method for achieving an end; an often customary method of doing something," not in the more common artificial intelligence sense of "a scheme or program for making, doing, or arranging something." Definitions are from [Websters [75].

tions organized around the interests, intentions, and experience of many different classes of users. The plans and the language that combines these plans are the backbone of the intelligent interface.

Contrast our approach to a more typical intelligent interface approach that monitors low-level user actions, attempting to infer higher-level intentions. These inferences are typically implemented with partial matching schemes, based on a catalog of user goals and subgoals (see, for example, [Johnson86a]). The inferences allow the system to complete user actions, correct errors, or provide tutorial assistance. This approach to inference of user intentions has proved to be quite difficult; goal/subgoal catalogs need to be extensive and even then performance is not robust.

Our approach, with a high-level plan language, turns the typical approach on its head. Users work by specifying and arranging high-level plan structures. The system performs low-level actions to accomplish what is specified by the high-level plans.

What does the scheme outlined above have to offer an experienced user? An experienced computer user, by definition, has a deeper understanding of the computer system and takes more responsibility in directing it in its actions. The expert does this in exchange for improved performance and extra functionality. For an expert, consider a hierarchy of plans instead of a single set of high-level plans. At the top of the hierarchy are the vague, high-level plans of domain experts with little computer experience. At the bottom is something close to a modern programming language. Users are free to use any components they like. Moving one link down in the hierarchy corresponds to the user taking one step down in the ease-of-use versus performance/functionality continuum. Computer novices always work at the top; computer experts work at the bottom; everyone else uses the plans from the middle that provide the best trade-off from their perspective.

The rest of this chapter begins with a discussion of the dilemma between the novice and expert users of computer systems. Next, a framework for a system built from a hierarchy of plans is described. Bridge, an intelligent tutor for teaching programming, is presented as an example of how the framework is implemented in a working system. We conclude by discussing a new system that provides a high-level plan-language interface to a spreadsheet.

7.2 THE DILEMMA OF INTELLIGENT INTERFACES

Upon first consideration, one might want to design an intelligent interface that would present a task to users as intuitively as possible. The interface should present the computer system so as to allow human users to think in exactly the way they are used to thinking. Each feature of the system should be presented using terms and conventions familiar from previous experience working without the computer-based support. The advantages of this approach are obvious: the human user begins to use the computer system with little or no training. The features of the computer system are exactly as the user would expect—straightforwardly understandable by appealing to earlier experience.

While having appeal, the intuitive approach presented above has an obvious drawback. An interface that merely matches the user's expectations is stuck with those expectations. In particular, the user can never go beyond those expectations to use more powerful facilities than that expectation allows. Consider, for example, implementing a word processor as a computerized typewriter. Slavish attention to this metaphor would give a word processing tool with little of the power we expect from word processors. We would, for example, need to type <RETURN> at the end of every line, use a special brushlike mouse cursor to "white out" mistakes, and insert a new diskette at the end of every page. Similarly, if computer based spreadsheets merely provided a convenient grid for laying out numbers—the role of manual spreadsheets—they would not be best-selling personal computer applications.

The dilemma, then, is between usability and functionality. Intelligent interfaces should make an application easier to use and understand. Merely applying the intelligence to anticipating and matching every expectation of the user leaves the system doing no more than the user already expects it to do. The question is this: How can we build interfaces that allow graceful progression from the novice's use of a system to more sophisticated use of a system?

7.3 OUR APPROACH

We approach the intelligent interface dilemma by allowing large sets of automated operations called plans. Each set of plans is customized to a particular class of users—managers, secretaries, and statisticians, for example. A beginner uses these plans as black boxes, with no understanding of their internal construction. This is possible because the plans have been designed to be simple, intuitive, and directly applicable to particular tasks of interest to that user.

For example, managers might be given a set of plans that would help them to organize projects. For each project, the plans would provide tools for representing subtasks, personnel, applicable resources, deadlines, and so on. The plan set provides fixed capabilities for organizing the project elements, modeling changed deadlines, and creating reports. The details of these capabilities are based on the standard kinds of organizations, models, and reports used by that manager or organization.

Inevitably, the appeal of standard operations wears off. Our user may now be more sophisticated through experience with the plan set. Many users are likely to be frustrated with the lack of flexibility inherent in the fixed set of plans. This is the position of normal experienced users of most computer software—stuck with the system that was delivered. Even if the system was very well designed, it cannot be tailored to the particular evolving needs of each user.

We propose a new mode of use. Consider that each of the plans provided to the manager is constructed of a few slightly lower level, slightly less powerful, slightly more general plans. The icons that represent the initial set of operations can be *opened up*, presenting a small network of the lower-level icons, connected together to describe the behavior of the icon that was opened (see Figure 7.1). If a user is dissatisfied with a particular form of the high-level icon, he or she can easily open up the icon and redesign its behavior with the lower-level icons. Essentially, this creates a new operation that is now available for use. In the project management tool example, the manager might modify the way project tasks are described, or how resources are allocated to a project.

The user need not do this sort of modification. It is done only when the user is sufficiently dissatisfied with the current plan set to be willing to do the work required to understand the next level of complexity. If the plan sets are carefully designed, opening up a plan should correspond to exactly one more level of flexibility and complexity. That is, there is exactly one new thing that must be learned in order to master the lower-level operations. In practice, there will be many levels of plans defined by lower-level plans. By providing many levels, we can give users a smooth continuum from easy-to-use and intuitive to sophisticated and flexible. In essence, the user can become as sophisticated a computer user as he or she desires.

Note that we are not suggesting the classic knowledge representation approach that builds a large collection of frames at various levels of generality, and interlinks them in various useful ways. The approach used here focuses on how to build a series of usable system elements that, while complete at a certain level of functionality, also provide a scaffolding for higher levels of functionality (lower-level plans in Figure 7.1). This approach is very much like that used in a college-level science textbook. In fact, the most compelling precedents for a plan-based approach are well designed technical curricula.

In such technical curricula, ideas are carefully layered into a series of chapters and sections, one or two new ideas per section. An oversimplification presented in one chapter is sufficiently accurate to support the ideas and tasks discussed in that chapter. A later chapter corrects the oversimplification, leaving those ideas from the earlier chapter in place, though now more accurately grounded. Furthermore, in correcting the oversimplification, the later chapter fills in capabilities and extends applicability in ways not anticipated in the earlier chapter. This approach is typical of most introductory college science, math, and engineering textbooks. We are proposing the plan-based interface approach as a way to extend the idea to sophisticated computer systems. We see the design of a plan network comparable in complexity to the design of a standard piece of curricula, and therefore requiring certain skills.

FIGURE 7.1
A SCHEMATIC OF THE INTERFACE DESIGN APPROACH ADVOCATED IN THIS ARTICLE

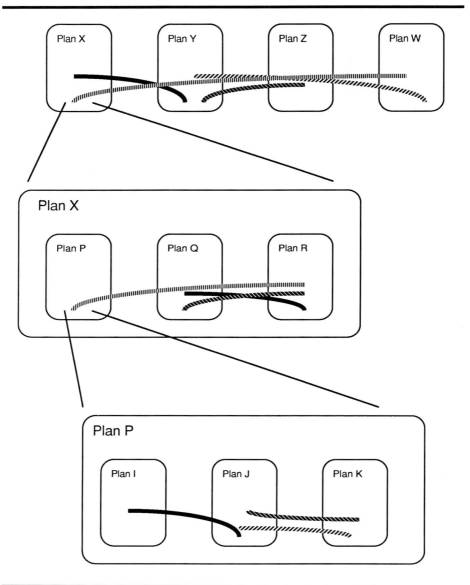

An approach like this nicely meets the needs of novice and casual users. Few users are willing to sit still to learn a sophisticated system. Fewer still are willing to start with the most basic programming elements and build up solutions to real tasks from scratch. Our approach begins with intuitive solutions to real world tasks and allows a user to learn only as much as is required to customize those solutions to the user's needs.

The approach outlined above is sufficiently high-level and vague to evoke little disagreement. However, a number of important questions are not addressed:

- How are plan contents determined?
- How are the various plan links, including the *open-up* link, implemented?
- How does a user handle the complexity of searching through and organizing the many plan objects that would be available in any realistic system?

Although we have no general answer to those questions, the rest of the article presents two specific examples to illustrate how an overall system might work. One example is drawn from an intelligent tutor that teaches programming in Pascal. The second example is drawn from an intelligent spreadsheet system. Based on our experience with these two domains, a general system is currently under development. The general system is discussed briefly in the concluding section.

7.4 THE BRIDGE TUTOR

Research into how novices learn programming reveals that understanding the semantics of standard programming languages is not the main difficulty of novice programmers. Instead, success with programming seems to be tied to a novice's ability to recognize general goals in the description of a task, and to translate those goals into actual program code (see, for example, [Eisenstadt81, Mayer79, Soloway84].) In Bridge we built a programming environment that supports a novice in working with plans that describe the goals and subgoals typical of programming tasks. By using plans that describe programming goals, Bridge allows for initial novice conceptions of a problem solution that are informal and sketchy. The Bridge environment features an iconic plan-programming language with editor facilities to control execution and support debugging. A complete discussion of Bridge can be found in [Bonar88]. The name comes from an intended bridge between novice and expert conceptions of programming.

Bridge supports a novice in the initial informal statement of a problem solution, subsequent refinement of that solution, and final implementation of the solution as programming language code. This is accomplished in three phases, discussed in detail in the rest of this section. These phases correspond to three levels of the hierarchy presented in Section 7.3. Phase I is the highest level—simple, intuitive, and made up of simple English phrases. Phase II takes each English phrase in phase I and elaborates it with an iconic plan. These plans have more detail and more finely-articulated interconnections between the program elements. The phase II plans are high-level, but they require some of the details needed in a normal programming language. Finally, phase III takes the phase II plans and elaborates them with normal Pascal code.

To illustrate Bridge use, we discuss a student working on the *Ending Value Averaging problem:*

> Write a program which repeatedly reads in integers until it reads in the integer 99999. After seeing 99999, it should print out the correct average without counting the final 99999.

In this section, a summary of each of the phases is presented, followed by a discussion of how that phase fits into the framework presented in Section 7.3.

7.4.1.   Bridge Phase I: Informal Natural-Language Plans

The first phase of Bridge involves an informal statement and refinement of the goals for the code. Empirical evidence [Bonar85, Kahney82, Soloway89] suggests that novice programmers bring a vocabulary of programming-like plans from everyday experience with procedural specifications of activities expressed in natural language. These plans come from experience with step-by-step instructions such as "Check all the student scores and give me an average," or "See that hallway? If any doors are open, close them." These informal plans, however, are often extremely difficult for novices to reconcile with the much more formal plans used in standard programming languages. Note, for example, that both example phrases involve an iteration without any specific mention of a repeated action.

In phase I we provide a plan language based on simple natural-language phrases typically used when people write step-by-step instructions for other people. For example, a student can construct the phrase "...and so on... until 99999 is seen." Figure 7.2 shows an example with several such phrases. Such phrases represent the highest level at which a student can express intentions to the system. Because of the ambiguity in such phrasings, Bridge must understand the student's intentions based on several possible naive models of programming. For example, a common naive model of looping allows a student to construct a loop with a description of the first iteration followed by the phrase "and so on." Based on the particular phrasings constructed by the student, Bridge infers a particular naive model.

FIGURE 7.2
PHRASES FROM A PHASE I BRIDGE SOLUTION

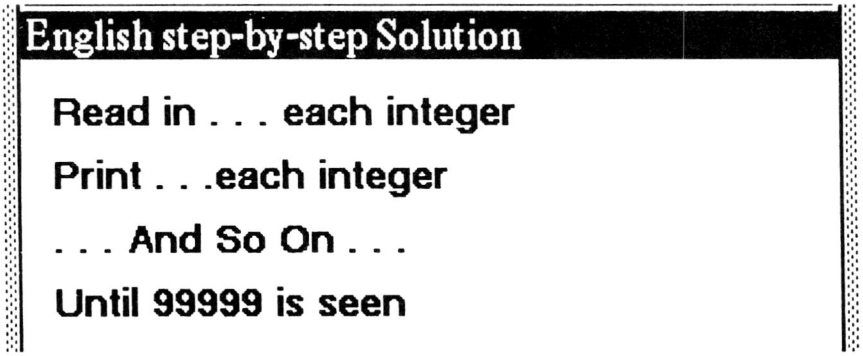

English step-by-step Solution

Read in . . . each integer

Print . . .each integer

. . . And So On . . .

Until 99999 is seen

Bridge supports three different naive models of programming loops:

- Declarative restatement—The loop is not explicitly mentioned at all. All reference to values assumes that they are available as needed: for example, "Compute the sum divided by the count," or just "Compute the average."
- Aggregate operator—The looping operations are subsumed by operators that act over entire data structures: for example, "Add all the integers and divide by how many there were."
- And-so-on loop—Mention is made of getting individual data values, as opposed to the aggregate values at the aggregate operator level. A looping construct is also mentioned, such as "Continue until 99999 is seen." At the *and-so-on* level, however, the solution does not specify detailed coordination among the individual steps within the loop. Very characteristic is a specification of the first iteration of the loop followed by the phrase "and so on," or something similar to this.

Based on our empirical work [Bonar85], these models subsume most of the misconceptions novices have about simple programming loops. Although there are many different English phrases used by novices, a simple pattern-matching approach to parsing the phrases is sufficient for distinguishing among the three models for each of the different plans.

Since Bridge's task is to teach programming, detection of such a naive model results in a tutorial suggestion from Bridge. The architecture underlying Bridge could as easily respond to the user's naive model directly without attempting to teach the user the correct specification. In this more advisory mode, the system would insist on a more fully developed model only when the user's specification was incomplete or lacking key details.

In terms of the multilevel plan approach discussed in Section 7.3 and illustrated in Figure 7.1, the first phase of Bridge is an implementation of the highest level of plans. Each plan stands for the kinds of operations and mental models normally expressed in English language step-by-step specifications written by nonprogrammers. The naive looping models represent the implicit knowledge required to understand the objects being manipulated by the user. The language is quite simple; only ordering and nesting links are possible between the plans. Data communication links between the plans are implicit, reflecting the structure of natural-language specifications.

7.4.2. Bridge Phase II: Iconic Programming Plans

In the second phase of Bridge a programming student refines the informal description of phase 1 into a series of semi-formal iconic programming plans. Figure 7.3 shows the Bridge screen as the student is working in phase II. In this phase the plans are schemalike structures which describe how goals are transformed into actual programming code (see [Soloway84] for a detailed discussion of these plans).

Plans have various elements that interrelate with the elements of other plans. So, for example, a counter plan has *initialize, increment,* and *use* elements, each with a particular relationship to the loop containing the counter. This interaction of elements often results in the plan implementation being dispersed across the program in standard programming constructs. A running total, for example, is implemented in Pascal with four statements that are dispersed throughout a program: a variable declaration, an initialization above a loop, an update inside that loop, and a use below the loop. [Spohrer85] has shown that plan-to-code translation errors account for many mistakes made by students.

In the second phase of Bridge, students focus on relating various plan elements. However, they have no need to compromise the fundamental plan structure or to introduce the syntactic complexity required by standard programming code. Figure 7.4 shows a typical phase II solution to the Ending Value Averaging problem. Each plan is represented by a single icon. There are two kinds of links between the plan elements. Control flow links are expressed by attaching puzzle tabs to puzzle slots. Data flow links are expressed by moving the small tiles with "ears" from the data source to the data destination. This is the way, for example, that the value of the COUNTER plan is associated with the average computation in the COMPUTE plan.[2]

---

[2] A problematic design issue arises with the data value tiles. We would like to have shown the data flow graphically, but found the screen too cluttered when a line was drawn from each data source to each data destination. Although we experimented with approaches that showed these links only when requested by the student, we ultimately abandoned graphical data links in favor of overall simplicity.

FIGURE 7.3

THE BRIDGE SYSTEM WHILE A STUDENT IS CONSTRUCTING A PHASE II
SOLUTION, BASED ON A COMPLETE PHASE I SOLUTION

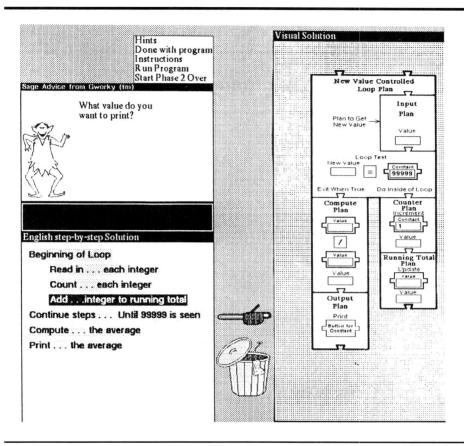

The plan icons shown in Figure 7.4 illustrate what we mean by "understandable based on previous experience." Although the plans in Figure 7.4 assume the reader is a programming student, they are designed to skirt various tricky technical issues that should be the problem of the compiler designers, not the problem of novice programmers.

For example, the NEW VALUE CONTROLLED LOOP plan does not explicitly specify the order of the steps inside the loop body: (1) new value fetch, (2) the test of that new value, and (3) the body following "Do Inside of Loop." While this is an immediate concern to most experienced programmers, it is not an issue for beginning programmers. Nonprogrammers have a very well developed model of a loop that gets a data item, checks its

FIGURE 7.4
A TYPICAL PHASE II SOLUTION IN BRIDGE

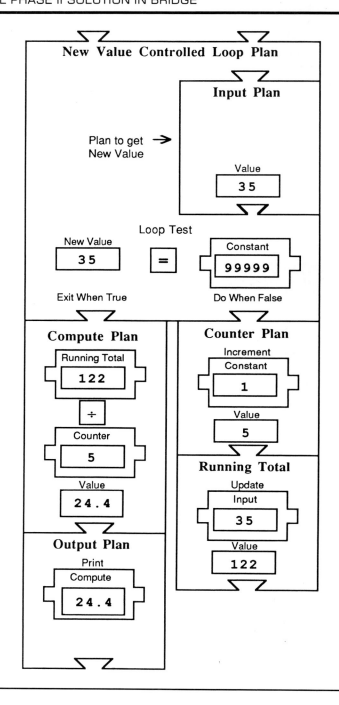

applicability, and then proceeds only if the data item is usable (see [Soloway83, Bonar85]). There are good reasons most programming languages don't provide such a construct, but those reasons do not make sense when we can present the novice with a library of plans adapted to his or her needs.

Just as phase I of Bridge represents the highest level plans, closest to the understanding of a nonprogrammer, phase II represents a lower-level plan. The transition from phase I to phase II, then, represents an implementation of *opening up* top-level (phase I) plans. In the current Bridge system the student must complete a phase I plan specification and then must *open up* that specification to implement a phase II elaboration of the original specification. As the student works in phase II, links back to phase I are always available. In a nontutorial version of the interface, the phase II plan language would allow for refinement of the informal plans specified in phase I. However, it would not require the complexity of a specification of the actions actually performed by the machine. The links in phase II express potential connections between elements of the plans, as described in the preceding paragraphs. Also, note that the phase II plans can be executed by the Bridge tutor. Students using Bridge are encouraged to fully understand and test their phase II programs.

7.4.3. Bridge Phase III: Pascal Code

The third phase requires the Bridge student to translate the plan-based description of phase II into actual Pascal code. Students are provided with a Pascal structure editor (much like that of [Garlan84]), and an interpreter with a stepping mode. In this phase the user no longer works with plans, but with a standard programming language. In a nontutorial version of the interface, this phase would be omitted.

7.4.4. Diagnosis with Plans

Any intelligent interface needs to infer user intentions from user behavior. In particular, the system must infer all mental activity from the actual actions performed by the user. In teaching computer programming, for example, a standard intelligent tutor must reconstruct the student's entire mental activity from the time he or she sees a program specification to the time he or she actually enters code into the machine. Such a reconstruction must account for both the correct and incorrect knowledge used by the student during design and implementation.

A tutor's reconstruction of a student's program is based on at least two capabilities. First, the tutor must have the capability to assist students in breaking the high-level goals of the problem statement into lower-level goals. Second, the tutor must have the capability to translate low-level goals into program code. Within an intelligent tutor, these two capabilities would typically be represented as search space operators that transform one kind of knowledge structure into another. In addition to correct versions of these operators, the tutor must contain buggy versions representing common student misconceptions.

Using a knowledge base of correct and buggy operators a tutor can, in principle, use search techniques to reconstruct plausible accounts for incorrect and ambiguous student specifications. This approach has been powerfully demonstrated in the programming tutor PROUST [Johnson86a]. While the approach works, it is very costly in terms of both search time and knowledge engineering. The accomplishments of PROUST must be weighed against the large cost in knowledge engineering time—several hundred hours per problem tutored [Johnson86b]. This knowledge engineering is particularly cost ineffective because the student sees so little of the results. Specifically, operators describe how to apply programming knowledge, but some students never see the knowledge engineering that has been captured in these operators. Inside of PROUST, these operators are optimized for the the search task. They are not available in a form that could be presented to students or used to assist students as they work toward a solution.

Bridge uses a different approach to reconstructing the student's intentions. Instead of attempting to use only one step to reconstruct a student's entire reasoning from problem statement to final code, Bridge has the student prepare intermediate solutions in plan languages. These solutions correspond to particular levels in the process of moving from problem specification to goals to code. This alleviates many of the difficulties of the PROUST approach. The search is more manageable because it has been broken up into a series of much smaller searches. In each of the smaller searches there are fewer relevant operators to try and the difference between the user's reasoning and the solution the tutor is trying to reconstruct is not as great.

In addition, the Bridge approach simplifies the knowledge engineering. The fewer operators in each search, the smaller the overall catalog of operators to be specified. In addition, the smaller search spaces make it easier to tell when the space of possible correct and incorrect versions has been covered.

7.5 DESIGN OF A PLAN LANGUAGE

In this section we detail a formal specification for Bridge phase II plans. This specification is not implemented in the current version of Bridge. Instead, it is derived from the experience with Bridge. It is our first attempt to create a plan language that formally captures vague, heuristic, and informal plans. The plan language supplies a systematic semantics that describe how plans execute, how new plans are designed, and how plans are translated into standard programming constructs. See [Bonar90] for a more detailed treatment of this material.

7.5.1. Goals for the Plan Language

As detailed in the previous section, Bridge allows a student programmer to work by describing successively more complex plan combinations. There are four main objectives for the plan languages that express these combinations:

1. The plan language should allow users to make use of their preconceptions about the domain. Unless users can recognize how their own understanding of a task fits into the planning language, they will find it impossible to formulate usable specifications.
2. The plan language should support users in becoming familiar with a collection of plans. Eventually, the user would begin to think in terms of the more formal phase II plans, not the informal phase I plans. Not only is there a catalog of plans, but students are able to create their own plans. This learning will be transparent and effortless, primarily because the plans present a more effective set of distinctions for dealing with a problem.
3. The plan language should, when appropriate, support novice users in learning how to implement plans with lower-level plans or actions that more closely resemble the programming language of the system being interfaced. Note that we take as given that an intelligent interface will never be as flexible as a user directly specifying actions at a lower level of detail. That is, some flexibility and generality is always lost when dealing with high-level plans.
4. For those who are learning the basics of the system being interfaced, the plan language should support the use of plan-like composition. Plans, which are easily read and understood, can be seen as the essence of good design. We want the users of the system to gain an appreciation for using these plans.

7.5.2. Plan Representation

We begin with the iconic plan language shown in Figure 7.4, which shows a series of plan icons connected together to produce the average of a series of numbers. This series is read from the user, and it stops with the value 99999. Each icon represents a single plan. Icons are constructed to suggest puzzle pieces that can be connected together in a finished program. Control flow is suggested by the top-to-bottom order in which pieces are connected. Data flow is suggested by the user moving a *value* icon from the plan supplying a value to the plan using that value. For example, in Figure 7.4 the user moves a value icon from the Input plan to the *update slot* of the RUNNING TOTAL plan. More details on the visual plan language appear in [Bonar90].

Certain relationships are expressed visually in Figure 7.4. Our formalism, based on object-oriented programming, is designed to capture such relationships expressed visually in Figure 7.4, but in a way that lends itself to formal manipulation. For each type of plan there is a class that specifies the local data and operations of that plan. Instances of a plan class can then be created, each with their own copy of the local data. The user organizes these instances into a particular execution order. Figure 7.5 shows a piece of the formalism describing the iconic plans in Figure 7.4.

FIGURE 7.5
A FORMAL DESCRIPTION OF RUNNING TOTAL AND COUNTER PLANS

Running Total Plan

ParentClass
Loop Action Plan

Slots
Total:	*value*	
Addend:		
Initial:	*initially*	0

Initialization

```
Total := Initial
```

Execution

```
Total := Total + Addend
```

Constant Running Total Plan

ParentClass
Running Total Plan

Slots
Increment:	*class*	Integer,
	rename	Addend

Counter Plan

ParentClass
Constant Running Total Plan

Slots
Count:	*rename*	Total
Increment:	*constant*	1

Each plan is represented with up to four parts:

1. PARENTCLASS—For purposes of taxonomy and inheritance, this section provides a link indicating a hierarchical relationship among plans. If this section is missing, there is only the default parent class to the plan.
2. SLOTS—Each plan can have zero or more slots, which specify data or plan links. One data slot can be distinguished as the *value slot* for this plan.[3] A plan's value can be used by other plans. So, for example, the value slot of the RUNNING TOTAL plan is used in the computation of an average. The slots provide a method for referring to other plans. Slots are used, for example, to refer to the plans executed in the body of a loop.
3. INITIALIZATION—This section contains executable code that is performed once when control first flows through the plan. As a special condition, when control flows through a loop plan, it fires its initialization section and the initialization sections of all plans contained in its body.
4. EXECUTION—This section contains executable code that is performed whenever control flows through the plan.

The code given in the INITIALIZATION and EXECUTION sections is expressed in a simple procedural code. The most critical kind of statement in these sections is the **EXECUTE** message which initiates the execution of a plan specified within a slot. At higher levels of the plan hierarchy, EXECUTION sections consist almost entirely of **EXECUTE** messages. At the lower levels (like the plans in Figure 7.5) the EXECUTION sections look more like normal procedural code. Plans whose EXECUTION sections that have only **EXECUTE** messages are considered *pure plans* because they can be manipulated formally by the system. That is, the system can manage the users, traversal up and down the hierarchy and keep track of exactly what they do and do not know at any given time.

Plans with procedural code other than **EXECUTE** messages in their EXECUTION sections are at the bottom of the plan hierarchy. This code can easily be translated into a standard programming language. Although the system cannot reason about this low-level code, the users can have access to it, allowing them to examine the way a plan is implemented in a standard programming language.

7.5.3. Inheritance

Each plan must specify a parent class explicitly. This provides a linkage for the inheritance mechanism. Slots are inherited from all predecessors, but may be renamed or redefined. Note in the example given in Figure

---

[3] Only one slot from each plan can be designated as the value. This is designed to be a simplified way of referring to the plan. That is, the value slot answers the question, "What is the one value that sums up the role the plan is playing in the program?"

7.5 that the COUNTER plan has inherited (and renamed) the TOTAL slot from the RUNNING TOTAL plan, although the intervening plan (CONSTANT RUNNING TOTAL) does not explicitly reference it. In addition, the COUNTER plan inherits TOTAL's designation as the distinguished value of the RUNNING TOTAL plan. Note that the CONSTANT RUNNING TOTAL plan has also redefined the inherited ADDEND slot (ADDEND.INCREMENT) to specify a constant. The COUNTER plan further constrains this plan to default to the value 1.

The INITIALIZATION and EXECUTION sections can also be inherited. In this case, both are inherited by successors of the RUNNING TOTAL plan. The renaming and redefining mechanisms specify that the COUNTER plan will inherit

```
Count := Count + 1
```

without explicitly defining it this way. In addition, it allows us in conversation with the user to describe the "1" as an increment rather than as an addend.

7.6 A MORE COMPLEX EXAMPLE

Figure 7.6 shows the representation of the ending value averaging loop (EVAL) plan and its components. This plan is used to calculate the average of a series of values entered by the user. In this example, the LOOP, BODY, AVERAGE, and OUTPUT slots contain links to other plans, and they use a procedure header-style mechanism for referring to other plans. Note that it is possible to pass values to linked plans. For instance, in the AVERAGE slot, the AVERAGE plan receives the values of TOTAL and COUNT; the AVERAGE plan uses these values to compute a value for the slot. The OUTPUT slot sends this average to the OUTPUT plan.

Slots can be executed by sending them an **EXECUTE** message. This is illustrated in the EXECUTION section on the EVAL plan. The meaning of this code is that the slots identified are to be executed sequentially.

Note that the LOOP slot contains code that references the SENTINEL LOOP plan. This SENTINEL LOOP plan is a child class of the NEW VALUE CONTROLLED LOOP plan. The SENTINEL LOOP plan does not have any executable sections, but does define three new slots that are used during execution.

Finally, note that the code for performing the actual looping action appears only in the NEW VALUE CONTROLLED LOOP plan. The EVAL plan and the SENTINEL LOOP plan push this detail down a level so that it can be hidden from the user. In this case, this executable code is inherited by the SENTINEL LOOP plan, where the values given in its slots (which are references to other plans) are used to fill in the blanks of the code. In this way, a child class plan can redefine slots that have been originally defined in its parent plan.

FIGURE 7.6
A FORMAL DESCRIPTION OF THE LOOP IN THE ENDING VALUE AVERAGING
PROBLEM

Ending Value Averaging Loop Plan

Slots

Loop	*use* Sentinel Loop Plan
Body	*use* Running Total Plan(*import* Total),
	use Counter Plan(*import* Count)
Average	*use* Average(*export* Total, Count, *import* Average)
Output	*use* Output Plan(*export* Average)

Execution

```
Execute ==> Loop
Execute ==> Average
Execute ==> Output
```

Sentinel Loop Plan

ParentClass
    New Value Controlled Loop Plan

Slots

New Value	*use* Input Plan(*import*)
Sentinel	*class* Integer
Test	*use* Test Plan(*export* NewValue, Sentinel, NotEquals, *import*)

New Value Controlled Loop Plan

Slots
    New Value
    Test
    Body

Execution
    loop
```
        Execute ==> NewValue
        Execute ==> Test
```
    if not Test *then exit*
```
        Execute ==> Body
```
    endloop

The BODY of the loop in the executable code given in the NEW VALUE CONTROLLED LOOP plan actually comes from the EVAL plan. In this way, the actual contents of the loop body can be customized to fit the requirements of particular plans. In this case, it is the EVAL plan that should define that the body of the loop contains a RUNNING TOTAL and a COUNTER. The SENTINEL LOOP plan is not responsible for this detail, since its only concern should be how to construct a loop that repeats until some sentinel value is reached.

7.6.1. Using the Plans

We intend that a novice initially uses plans at the highest possible level, constructing programs by selecting from a menu of plan icons, and connecting the icons together to produce a problem solution. However, it is intended that students examine the plans themselves, either through curiosity or need. Eventually, the students will wish to modify existing plans and to create customized versions for their own needs.

This is all consistent with the goals expressed above. In addition, such manipulation of the environment is supported by the representation of plans already outlined. The user can navigate the hierarchy of plans in two distinctly different ways. Figure 7.7 shows a graphical representation of the EVAL plan and its components, as derived from the formal plan descriptions. The students are able to navigate such a structure and, as their ability grows, they are able to modify the contents of the plans identified.

A second way that the plans might be navigated, changing to a different point of view, is through the class hierarchy. Figure 7.8 shows how this might be represented graphically. By navigating this representation, users move from more specific levels (such as the COUNTER plan) to more general ones (up to, for instance, the RUNNING TOTAL plan). They can also examine how slots have been renamed or redefined (as in the case of the ADDEND.INCREMENT slot).

The hierarchy of Figure 7.7 can be considered as orthogonal to the one shown in Figure 7.8. It represents additional detail that the user can explore for a deeper understanding of programming plans. Traversing these levels also lets users explore the plan taxonomy. In this way the user gains a more sophisticated view of the programming environment and available programming tools.

7.7 A SPREADSHEET PLAN LANGUAGE

We are generalizing the Bridge Plan system to address issues in the development of a spreadsheet tutor. With the spreadsheet system we are attempting to build a plan-based intelligent interface that focuses not on teaching, but on intelligent support an expert who is not experienced with spreadsheets.

FIGURE 7.7
A GRAPHICAL REPRESENTATION OF THE EVAL PLAN AND ITS COMPONENTS

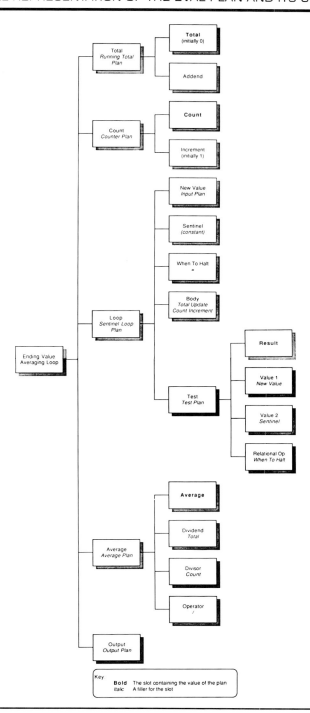

FIGURE 7.8
A GRAPHICAL REPRESENTATION OF CLASS HIERARCHY

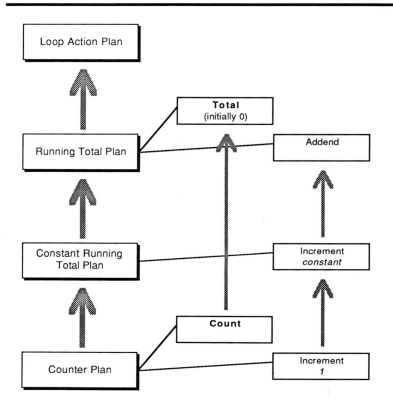

Loop Action Plan

Total
(initially 0)

Addend

Running Total Plan

Constant Running
Total Plan

Increment
constant

Count

Counter Plan

Increment
1

Key

Plan

Slot for a plan (tied to the plan by a solid line)
    bold - the slot used for a plan's value
    italics - the value or value constraints for the slot

Slot inheritance

Plan inheritance

Traditionally, a spreadsheet is an oversized piece of paper made up of rows and columns intersecting to form boxes which contain words or numbers. Functionally, the spreadsheet serves as a structure for performing financial calculations, testing assumptions, and analyzing results. Electronic spreadsheets also consist of intersecting rows and columns; but they are stored and displayed on a computer. Certain cells are defined with a formula that references other cells. The cell displays the value computed by the formula. Any change in a cell referenced in the formula causes the formula to be recomputed and the new value displayed. Computer-based spreadsheets allow for effortless changes. When one number on the spreadsheet is changed, either to make a correction or perform some analytic forecasting function, many other values might depend upon it and therefore also need to be changed. What would be a very tedious job by hand can be done with speed, accuracy, and ease on a computer.

The typical user of a spreadsheet is an expert in some domain, typically a business or engineering specialty, and a novice computer user. This seems to be a very common class of users, making spreadsheets a crucial application for intelligent interfaces. The dilemma of whether or not to use an intelligent interface is particularly relevant in this situation:

- On the one hand, an intelligent spreadsheet would not look like a spreadsheet at all, because the expert has only particular situations and tasks to be accomplished with the spreadsheet. Instead, the system would present a set of forms representing basic calculations and capabilities corresponding to these situations and tasks. These could be selected and pieced together.

- On the other hand, we do not want to limit our experts and would like to give them ways to understand and use the full functionality inherent in a spreadsheet.

Spreadsheets are an interesting domain, not only because of the people who typically use them, but also for another reason. A study reported in [Brown87] gave six experienced spreadsheet designers four spreadsheet tasks of moderate complexity (2–6 hours). Forty-three percent of the resulting spreadsheets had serious errors in the results predicted by the spreadsheet. This is a troubling result, suggesting that standard spreadsheet languages are too low-level and error-prone for reliable use with tasks of even moderate complexity. The plan-based approach to intelligent interfaces discussed in this article can address this problem. For most spreadsheet tasks being done by typical spreadsheet users, it would not be necessary to build low-level formulas and links. Instead, a series of spreadsheet plans would be assembled. As the plans are assembled, they would compile themselves into standard spreadsheet formulas and load themselves into an actual spreadsheet. If a user wanted to explore or modify details, or was forced by an

Spreadsheet Plans

    Input Table

        Labels

            Time Sequence

            Participant List

            Subproject List

            Main – Fixed Cells

            Horizontal – Fixed Cells

            Vertical – Fixed Cells

        Records

            Horizontal – Fixed Cells

            Vertical – Fixed Cells

        Parameters

            Labels

            Values – Variable Cells

    Output Table

        Input Table augmented with horizontal and vertical extensions –
        Variable Cells

    Output Report

        Computed Values – Variable Cells

        Records

            Horizontal – Fixed Cells

            Vertical – Fixed Cells

        Labels

            Time Sequence

            Participant List

            Subproject List

            Main – Fixed Cells

            Horizontal – Fixed Cells

            Vertical – Fixed Cells

unusual problem to specify a particular detail, he or she could interact with the spreadsheet directly, but only in a very local and particular context.

For such a scheme to work, it is necessary that we actually find spreadsheet plans of sufficient generality to apply to the task. To do this, we examined several how-to books on using spreadsheets in business (for example, [Anderson87; Clark86]). We studied many spreadsheets used for business tasks like income statements, checkbook accounting, sales summary, purchase summary, operating expenses summary, and cash flow summary. The study yielded surprisingly few plans in use. The most common plans are summarized in Figure 7.9. That figure shows a set of plans, grouped at the highest level as INPUT TABLE plans, OUTPUT TABLE plans, or OUTPUT REPORT plans.

Figure 7.9 shows the plans and plan components found in common business world spreadsheet plans. For example, almost all spreadsheets had an INPUT TABLE plan, with axis based on a time sequence, sequence of names, or sequence of subprojects.

A plan-based spreadsheet interface has been implemented and is fully documented in [Namasivayam88]. For the most part, a user works by selecting standard spreadsheet plans (like those listed in Figure 7.9) and linking those plans together. The user supplies problem-dependent data and some problem-dependent formulas. The current system cannot examine problem-dependent information, but does allow the user to package that new information as a new, specialized plan. When a user actually modifies data on the spreadsheet, as opposed to on the plan forms, the system tracks those changes. Although the system has no real understanding of what the user did, it does understand that the user modified a particular cell of an instantation of a standard plan. That modification is tracked for the user.

Note that spreadsheet macros as provided with most commercial spreadsheets do not provide the capabilities of plans. The macros are much like procedure calls in a conventional language—while they allow many standard commands to be combined into one new command, they do not allow a higher-level view of the actual task being accomplished with the spreadsheet.

7.8 RELATED WORK

The most notable work in the development of a plan formalism is the plan calculus used in the Programmer's Apprentice [Rich90; Rich81; Shrobe79; Waters78]. The main emphasis of this formalism is the "analysis, synthesis, and verification of programs" [Rich81]. Although these are important issues, they are not the concern of our own system. There is little to suggest that the plan calculus can be used effectively by novice programmers to construct their own plans, to modify available plans, or to understand programming plans themselves. Although we have a great deal of respect for the plan calculus, it does little to address how users who are not computer experts can be given more powerful computer systems.

The BOXER system [diSessa85] should also be contrasted with the work discussed here. BOXER is a programming system for novices with a single goal. It seeks to identify a minimal set of constructs that are computationally complete, provide a powerful set of capabilities, and yet, through a visual metaphor, are intuitively appealing to novices. DiSessa's work presents an extremely carefully crafted compromise between the two horns of the dilemma of intelligent interfaces presented at the beginning of the paper. We have chosen, instead, to look for a way to live with and even exploit that dilemma.

7.9 CONCLUSION

We have sketched a formalism that allows novice programmers to program with plans. The formalism neatly specifies the behavior of a high-level visual plan language. In addition, the formalism allows students to connect plans to their informal experience, implement plans in a conventional programming language, and define new plans based on previously defined plans. The formalism provides a scheme for realizing a high-level planning language for use as an intelligent interface.

Although we are pleased with Bridge and the Spreadsheet interface, we know that this work is only a beginning. In particular, we have only given the first steps toward a full-scale plan interface, as discussed in the early sections of the paper. Anoosh Shahidi [Shahidi90], one of Bonar's students, has begun Ph.D. work toward such a full-scale version.

ACKNOWLEDGMENTS

Many thanks to Robert Cunningham for his stunning implementation of Bridge. Our thanks to A. Namasivayam who has implemented the spreadsheet interface and to Mary Lewis who developed the spreadsheet plan set.

An anonymous reviewer from the 1988 Intelligent Interfaces Workshop provided extremely thoughtful comments, helping a great deal to shape the final form of this paper. Comments from the organizers of the workshop were also very helpful.

REFERENCES

[Anderson87] Anderson, L., and Cobb, D. 1987 *1-2-3 For Business*. Que Corporation, Indianapolis, Indiana.

[Balzer85] Balzer, R. 1985. "A 15 Year Perspective on Automatic Programming." *IEEE Transactions of Software Engineering*, SE-11 November, pp. 1257–1267.

[Bonar85] Bonar, J., and Soloway, E. 1985. "Pre-programming Knowledge: A Major Source of Misconceptions in Novice Programmers." *Human-Computer Interaction*, 1, 133–161.

[Bonar88] Bonar, J., Cunningham, R., Beatty, P., and Weil, W. 1988. *Bridge: Intelligent Tutoring With Intermediate Representations*. Technical Report, Learning Research and Development Center, University of Pittsburgh. Copies also available by writing to J. Bonar.

[Bonar90] Bonar, J., and Liffick, B. 1990. A Novice Visual Programming Language. In Chang, S. K. (ed.) *Principles of Visual Programming Systems*, Englewood Cliffs, NJ: Prentice Hall, pp. 326–366.

[Brown87] Brown, P. S., and Gould, J. D. 1987. An Experimental Study for People Creating Spreadsheets. *Transactions on Office Information Systems*. 5(3), 258–272.

[Clark86] Clark, R., and Swarsey, P. 1986. *The Compleat IBM Spreadsheeter*. Englewood Cliffs, NJ: Prentice Hall

[DiSessa85] DiSessa, A. 1985. A Principled Design for an Integrated Computational Environment. *Human-Computer Interaction*, 1, 1–47.

[Eisenstadt81] Eisenstadt, M., Laubsch, J., and Kahney, H. 1981. "Creating Pleasant Programming Environments for Cognitive Science Students". In *Proceedings of the Third Annual Cognitive Science Conference*. Berkeley, CA.

[Garlan84] Garlan, D. B., and Miller, P. L. 1984. "GNOME: An Introductory Programming Environment Based on a Family of Structure Editors." In *Proceedings of the Software Engineering Symposium on Practical Software Development Environments*, Association for Computing Machinery.

[Johnson86a] Johnson, L. 1986. *Intention-Based Diagnosis of Novice Programming Errors*. Palo Alto, CA: Morgan Kaufman.

[Johnson86b] Personal communication.

[Kahney82] Kahney, H., and Eisenstadt, M. 1982. "Programmers' Mental Models of Their Programming Tasks: The Interaction of Real World Knowledge and Programming Knowledge." In *Proceedings of the Fourth Annual Conference of the Cognitive Science Society*, pp. 143–145.

[Mayer79] Mayer, R. E. 1979. "A Psychology of Learning BASIC." *Communications of the Association for Computing Machinery* 22(11), pp. 589–593.

[Namasivayam88] Namasivayam, S. 1988. *A Plan-Based Spreadsheet System*. Masters Thesis, Department of Computer Science, University of Pittsburgh.

[Rich81] Rich, C. 1981, 1986. A Formal Representation for Plans in the Programmer's Apprentice. In *Proceedings of the 7th International Joint Conference on Artificial Intelligence*, Vancouver, Canada, 1981. Also in *Artificial Intelligence and Software Engineering*, Rich, C., and Waters, R. C. (ed.). Morgan Kaufmann Publishing, 1986, pp. 1044–1052.

[Rich90] Rich, C., and Waters, R. C. 1990. *The Programmer's Apprentice*. New York, NY: ACM Press.

[Shahidi90] Shahidi, A. 1990. The Visual Plan Language System. Ph.D. Dissertation Proposal. For copies, write to the author at Sverdrup Technology, Inc., 2001 Aerospace Parkway, Brook Park, OH, 44142, phone 216/891-2213.

[Shrobe79] Shrobe, H. 1979. Dependency Directed Reasoning for Complex Program Understanding. Ph.D. Thesis, MIT/AI/TR-503, April.

[Soloway83] Soloway, E., Bonar, J., and Ehrlich, K. 1983. "Cognitive Strategies and Looping Constructs: An Empirical Study." *Communications of the ACM*, November.

[Soloway84] Soloway, E., and Ehrlich, K. 1984. Empirical Studies of Programming Knowledge. *IEEE Transactions of Software Engineering*, SE-10, pp. 569–609.

[Soloway89] Soloway, E., and Spohrer, J. 1989. *Studying the Novice Programmer*. Hillsdale, NJ: Lawrence Erlbaum Associates.

[Spohrer85] Spohrer, J., Soloway, E., and Pope, E. 1985. A Goal/Plan Analysis of Buggy Pascal Programs. *Human-Computer Interaction*, 1, pp. 163–207.

[Waters78] Waters, R. C. 1978. Automatic Analysis of the Logical Structure of Programs. Ph.D. Thesis, MIT/AI/TR-492, December 1978.

[Waters85] Waters, R. C. 1985. "The Programmer's Apprentice: A Session with KBEmacs." *IEEE Transactions of Software Engineering*, SE-11.

[Websters75] 1975. *Webster's New Collegiate Dictionary*. Springfield, MA: G&C Merriam Company.

CHAPTER 8

A DIALOGUE USER INTERFACE ARCHITECTURE

ROBERT L. YOUNG
Schlumberger Laboratory for Computer Science

ABSTRACT

Current user interfaces cast users into one of two roles: telling a system everything it must do, or answering questions and obeying commands that it presents to them. In neither case is it possible for a dialogue to emerge between user and system. We describe a set of strategies to bring dialogue-like structure to user-system interaction. These strategies are based on explicitly representing the "plans" of programs *and* explicitly introducing those plans into the interface. Both programs and users can conveniently communicate how their actions relate to these plans. A data graphics presentation editor provides an example.

8.1 INTRODUCTION

Computer users have available to them ever-increasing numbers of "flops," "lips," and pixels. In spite of this increase in sheer power, the computer is rarely more than a passive servant, at best doing *exactly* what a user requests, and no more. Although the goal of constructing systems that display a significant amount of autonomy in carrying out complex tasks is extremely desirable, it is also quite long-range. It should be noted that human associates displaying this highly desirable behavior are also rare. Nonetheless, assistants can and do prove valuable to one engaged in problem solving activities.

User interfaces create a user's view of the underlying systems they serve. The best of today's interfaces are typically only thin veneers over the systems themselves. Although they may be concerned with making specific interactions easy, they rarely address the much more important problem of bringing coherence to a user's extended interactions with a system.

To better understand what is missing from current interfaces, contrast their style of interaction with the interactions among someone engaged in problem solving and human associates. A fundamental difference is the nature of the communication: humans engage in *dialogues in context* among themselves, whereas they communicate with their computers using impoverished "context-free" languages (including languages containing interactive user signals, such as mouse clicks). Some essential elements of human dialogue in context are:

- There is a shared context (or several contexts) that persists through time; a discussion does not start from scratch.

- Communication is usually accomplished through dialogue, not stand-alone utterances. This creates a transient context specializing the persistent shared context.

- Working dialogue is only loosely structured, admitting apparent *non sequiturs* and allowing either party to direct the discussion.

- Questions, as well as their answers, are frequently expressed in ways that are ambiguous if examined in isolation but are unambiguous in the context of their occurrence. The communicators select the most likely choice (after clarifying, if necessary, rather than doing something unacceptable).

- Dialogues include modes of expression that enable brevity and facilitate communication; comparative references are very important, and pictures and drawings frequently supplement natural language.

In summary, dialogues are structures knitting together preexisting and transient elements that significantly facilitate communication.

An implication of these observations is that a user of a computer system must be able to communicate with the system via dialogues of this kind, if the system is to rise above the level of a very sophisticated toolkit and become a problem solving environment for the user. Does this mean that intelligent user interfaces must await the solution of the "natural language dialogue" problem? No, it is possible to draw on dialogue as a metaphor for user interfaces without tackling all of its complexity. (See Chapters 2 and 9 for descriptions of user interfaces supporting "real" natural-language dialogues.) In fact, the language of interaction may remain quite unnatural and contain useful interactive gestures (e.g., using a mouse) and elements (e.g., menus). [Terveen90] also observes that the model of human conversation may influence the structure of interfaces, without being literally realized.

In the next section, we will briefly examine the predominant styles of user interfaces, establishing some points of comparison for possible user roles. Following this, we present the proposed dialogue-based architecture. Experimentation with user interfaces based on this proposed architecture was made feasible by an enabling computational environment, which we will then describe. Finally, the organization of a sample interface displaying many of the desired characteristics will be discussed.

8.2 CURRENT INTERFACES

User interfaces have experienced radical changes in recent years. Wide use of bit-mapped displays and mice have resulted in significant increases in the graphic presentation of information, and interfaces that require users to do practically no typing are well known. However, none of these techniques addresses the basic problem of how to raise the level of interaction to a dialogue. We will briefly characterize the current state of interactive interfaces with respect to the user's role. A thought-provoking, and much more detailed, examination is found in the collection [Norman86b]. [Norman86a], [Laurel86], [Hutchins86], [Reichman86], and [Brown86] are especially relevant.

Current systems tend to provide users one of two distinct roles in the interaction: in one role the system is in charge, and in the other the user is in control. When a user invokes a typical application, the program almost always initiates interactions, and the sequence in which the interactions occur is under the program's control. An advanced interface for an application may provide users with very easy modes of interaction (e.g., menus and active graphics), answer validation, and convenient ways to request canned, explanatory help messages about the meaning of the pending interaction. However, a user rarely has a means of questioning the interface about the implications of available choices or of gaining other information about future interactions that the program has "planned"— much less exerting any influence over this scenario. A program's predetermined sequence of actions is usually rigidly established as a matter of programming and design convenience. The ways in which a program depends on the assumed sequence of interactions are frequently difficult for a user to understand. Such global knowledge about a program's operation comes only from documentation and (more frequently) prior experiences.

A user is typically in control for interactions with executives and editors. Interfaces supporting this mode of interaction can usefully be thought of as varying along a dimension of *predominant communication style*. At one end is single-line user input in specialized command languages, and at the other are highly symbolic/iconic communication schemes. The former is the norm for interacting with executives (whether operating systems or subsystems) and is so prevalent [1] that it needs no elaboration. The second group of programs, which we call editors, encompass a wide range of interface styles, all characterized by a user interacting with a model through one or more continuously displayed views. Examples of this class include the text editor EMACS [Stallman84], the MetaClass[2] knowledge-base editing environment [Smith87] (see further discussion in Section 8.4), and "direct manipulation interfaces," where communication is solely through interactive manipulation of iconic model elements (e.g., the Pinball Construction Set program [Budge83]).

These three examples lie at significant points on the spectrum of design possibilities with respect to reliance on iconic/symbolic communication. EMACS relies on text and commands from a user to examine and alter text files, utilizing the continuously displayed image of the text to provide feedback to the user. It does not provide the user with any iconic access to operations.

MetaClass provides alteration and examination facilities for knowledge bases (KBs) including their constituent elements (e.g., objects, slots, facets). It makes extensive use of its workstation environment, providing many kinds of graphs and other visual presentations of the current state of the KB and using the mouse for a majority of the possible types of interactions. Menus are the primary mechanism for invoking operations, although there is extensive use of active screen areas (which depict parts of the KB model) to select targets and obtain menus.

When direct manipulation is the predominant communication style, a user must always perform some action that symbolically designates the model operation desired. In the domain of pinball game construction, this means that construction operations are done by moving iconic components into place.

In neither the controlling nor the controlled role does a user have any real opportunity to communicate with a system about goals, plans, or intentions. When a system is asking the questions, its user must translate these motivating concerns into a pattern of responses that will further them. A user in charge interactively performs sequences of tasks that collectively accomplish goals. Yet the system has no knowledge of these goals and can offer the user no guidance or support in achieving them. At most, the system may maintain histories recording *what* a user did, but not *why*.

Notice that this problem is independent of the predominant communication style that the interface uses. A direct-manipulation interface suffers from the same weakness as one using single-line commands. In their discussion of direct-manipulation interfaces, Hutchins et. al. [Hutchins86] draw a distinc-

---

[1] There are a few notable exceptions, such as the interfaces for SmallTalk and Apple's Macintosh.

[2] MetaClass is a trademark of Schlumberger, Inc.

tion between "conversational" and "model world" interfaces. This choice of terminology seems particularly misleading. The so-called conversational approach is more suggestive of a foreign traveler communicating exclusively through phrases extracted from a guidebook than it is of true conversation. On the other hand, introduction of models that can be used as a basis for communication between a user and a system is a major advance. Insofar as these models are best thought of and manipulated via graphic means, the direct-manipulation style is exactly right. What remains undone is to enable true conversation—dialogue—between user and system *about* relevant model worlds, including the domains of user motivations and plans. By treating user interaction as a dialogue, one can move the level of system assistance higher, to span more extended interactions. However, this additional structure must be introduced without reducing a user's flexibility and freedom if it is to result in a net enrichment of the environment.

8.3 A DIALOGUE ARCHITECTURE FOR USER INTERACTION

8.3.1. Persistent Context

A user interface that allows a user to carry on a dialogue with a system will have access to knowledge bases describing the entities, activities, goals, and evaluation criteria of the system's subject domain. This body of knowledge provides the kernel persistent shared context. These KBs capture only domain knowledge (whatever the domain) and are independent of user interaction. This independence enables their reusability wherever this domain knowledge context is needed. Although domain knowledge is sharable among users, each user has unique characteristics. Therefore, the persistent context should include KBs describing a user, including information such as personal preferences and idiosyncrasies, as well as long-term plans. Collectively, this knowledge is available to the interface from the very start of an interaction.

8.3.2. Transient Context

For user interaction to be carried out in a dialogue-like fashion, the persistent context must be supplemented with a transient context that captures the history and state of the present (extended) interaction. This need cannot be met with simple history lists of occurrences. Such lists do not provide coherence to actions that have already occurred, nor do they readily suggest actions likely to occur. Coherence can be found only in plans that relate actions to each other, and to a user's goals. The problems of planning, as well as plan and goal recognition, in user interfaces are open research issues; Chapter 9 illustrates our current understanding of these issues. Nonetheless, there are practical ways to introduce the utility of plans and goals into user interface architecture now. We propose explicitly representing the task structure of interaction sequences in advance. The set of tasks to be accomplished involving user interaction, and their interrelationships, are all represented as are ultimate goals. Such plans provide a structure for the sequence of interactions. As steps are begun and then completed, the history and state of interaction are maintained as progressive instantiation of the plan. This representation provides the much-needed structure for history and enables predictions about other actions yet to be done.

The user interface need not be able to *infer* what the user is trying to do; rather, the style of interaction should make it totally natural and very easy for the user to state explicitly which task is being undertaken at appropriate times. Graphic depiction of the current plan, including both completed and undone steps, offers the potential of keeping the user clearly aware at all times of the current state. Thus, the user has a readily available structured history (and proposed future) and need not manage the purpose of actions mentally or have them managed opaquely by underlying applications.

Interaction plans must be able to represent (1) hierarchical decomposition of tasks into their subtasks, (2) tasks requiring arbitrary iteration, and (3) parallelism of unordered tasks. Hierarchical structure brings clarity to plans by identifying intermediate tasks. Iteration arises out of the need to allow arbitrary repetition on a user's part. Without parallelism, a plan in progress would force artificial sequentiality onto the tasks a user must accomplish. Maintaining task parallelism brings the user much more freedom in selecting what to do and when to do it; the user is constrained only by the true requirements of the plan. (For example, a piece of information cannot be used before it is provided. This is an intrinsic, not an artificial, ordering.)

8.3.3. Contextually Sensitive Communication

Two general strategies are employed to improve the quality of interactions, with the structures just discussed providing context and coherence. The first strategy is to interpret questions and their answers with respect to their composite contexts. A question such as "How does *x* work?" should sometimes elicit a one-line description, and sometimes a complex functional presentation. Which is best depends on who is asking, what is asked about, and why the question is being asked. Since the interface could have a significant amount of knowledge about each of these factors, all communications should be filtered by heuristics that transform the information accordingly.

The use of comparisons can be very effective but can occur only in an environment with context. Regardless of which kind of answer the system would propose for the preceding question, a better response might be "It works just like *y*," if the user has recently either used *y* (indicating an understanding of it) or asked about *its* functionality. Current help facilities never respond to queries in this way because they have no structured memory.

The second strategy is to support multiple forms of information expression. To maximize the advantage offered by this expressive variety, the process of deciding what to say should be kept separate from that of determining exactly how to say it. A piece of information that the system wishes to present to the user might be presented textually or graphically. The choice can be influenced by the complexity of the information, the user's personal preferences, and even the current state of the interaction. In the preceding example, the very simple description of x's function might be realized textually, whereas the complex functional description could well appear as a diagram. Although failure to maintain a separation of form and content does not preclude sensitivity to informational complexity and user preferences, it does make it nearly impossible to adapt to the context of the presentation.

8.3.4. Help: Explanation and Browsing

"Help" is an especially important user request. It should be available at all times, and it could be a significantly more effective service if the response generated were more tailored to the user and the current situation. We propose having interaction plans provide assistance by including an explicit "help" task that may be repeated as often as, and whenever, the user desires. Although an ideal environment can always respond directly and usefully to a user's need for information, realistically there will always be information that a system is unable to present and questions that the user is unable to ask. Context-sensitive explanations are provided whenever possible, but the system must provide the user powerful browsing capabilities for the remaining situations. The system responds by providing some (intelligently selected) active display or complex of displays for the user. In browsing, the user takes most of the responsibility for extracting information from these displays. Basic browsing facilities include text substring- and keyword-oriented searches for facts, models, and so on. A query language or sets of specialized menus might help the user navigate through available knowledge bases.

8.3.5. Summary

To summarize, the proposed architecture uses two sources of information to establish and maintain the context of interactions with a user:

- Persistent context—provided by preexisting KBs capturing domain- and user-specific information
- Transient context—provided by ongoing instantiation of interaction plans (visible to the user)

This context provides the environment in which two interaction strategies are applied:

- Input interpretation and output generation should be context-sensitive.
- Multiple modes of expression, distinct from the content expressed, should be available.

Finally "help" is an especially interesting facility to consider because it is almost universally valuable and is a likely candidate for improvement.

A number of other chapters present proposals for interfaces able to carry on dialogues with users. In particular, Chapters 2 and 9, by Chin, and by Neal and Shapiro, respectively, are quite relevant. Each of these proposals introduces some dialogue elements similar to those discussed here, with a particular research focus. Chin wants to construct *autonomous agents* and is centrally concerned with the very difficult problem of detecting user goals—a problem explicitly avoided in this chapter. Neal and Shapiro wish to support multi-media dialogues, with natural language and gesturing as input and graphics and text as output. This goal is clearly very similar to that motivating the second strategy discussed in Section 8.3.3.

Chapter 7, by Bonar and Liffick, presents research on interfaces, for nonexpert programmers, that support communication by means of high-level plans. This is a very similar use of plans to that in our proposal. They argue that plans are an easily understood concept, suitable for communication with both novice and expert users. Whereas novices are content simply to use the plans that are available, experts are able to open and customize them. These plans are depicted in the interface in highly visual, easily understood ways. The authors' recognition of the communication value of plans, independently of the plans' origins and justifications, and of the possibilities arising from portraying plans centrally in user interfaces concurs with the proposal set forth here.

8.4 THE ENABLING ENVIRONMENT

The dialogue interface architecture just described may leave the impression that a significant expenditure of effort is required even to begin investigating its feasibility. Fortunately, this is not true, thanks to an existing computing and research environment that contains some essential ingredients. There is a large community building knowledge-based systems using a common object-oriented representation system, Class.[3] (Class was previously called Strobe.) These systems typically use KBs to structure the domain knowledge required and are organized around these KBs. Furthermore, in attempting to achieve knowledge reusability, knowledge drawn from different domains is represented in correspondingly different KBs. There is also a serious commitment to separating user interfaces from applications. An interaction substrate, MetaClass [Smith87], is a standard part of the environment. (MetaClass was previously called Impulse.) It supports the construction of object-oriented interfaces, which communicate with their applications via messages between KBs. Finally, there is an extension to MetaClass, Ida [Young87;Smith87], which provides support for interactive user interfaces requiring graphic

---

[3] Class is a trademark of Schlumberger, Inc.

depiction of data. The entire Class-based environment is known as HyperClass.[4]

Work supporting both automatic programming and interactive problem solving has provided a Class-based representation of algorithms, CONFIG, with an interactive interpreter and examination facility. The class of supported control patterns is well suited to the needs of user interaction plans discussed previously. In particular, parallelism is supported, and a distinction is maintained between the flow of data and the flow of control. This algorithm representation work (as well as the spirit of the current proposal) has been strongly influenced by earlier experiments with declarative task representation and its impact on user interface [Smith84].

A final focus of active work is browsing. This work [Carando88;Carando89] is concerned both with identifying knowledge that must be included in KBs to make them more "browsable" and with the interface issues of how users can request and perform browsing easily and effectively.

The degree to which this computing environment supports exploration of the proposed user interface architecture is clear. Domain KBs needed to provide persistent context are already developed. The desire to separate interaction and application already exists, as do facilities for nonprogrammatic representation of interfaces, including graphics. The representation of interaction plans can be done without expending the significant effort required to develop even a simple algorithm representation language. And, finally, exploration of browsing is already underway.

8.5 A SIMPLE EXAMPLE: THE IDA EDITOR

To illustrate the central ideas we are exploring, we will use a small, self-contained example: The Ida Editor, a system for interactively building custom Ida interfaces. Although the system described is not fully implemented, the necessary elements all exist and could perform as described. Ida is a Meta-Class extension providing an object-oriented framework for interactive data graphics interfaces. Conceptually, the process of building a custom display involves laying out the 2-D arrangement of components and identifying the special relationships, if any, that exist among these components. The components include plotting areas, axis labels, titles, help areas, and a variety of scrolling controls. Relationships include those between plotting areas and their labels, and those between a scroll control and its controlled scrolling areas. Even at the implementation level, the quantity of information needed for a custom display is relatively small; however, it is very detailed information, and errors are easily made. Although a presentation building program could be built conventionally, the problem is an interesting one for exploring the dialogue user interface architecture.

---

[4] HyperClass is a trademark of Schlumberger, Inc.

FIGURE 8.1
IDA LOG DISPLAY

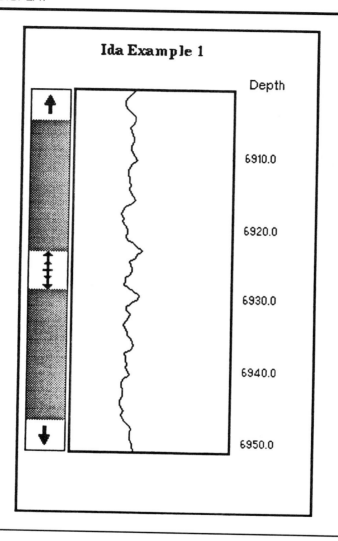

Figure 8.1 shows a very simple Ida display. The central rectangular *plot area* contains a plot of some data; it presents only one segment of the available data. Immediately to its right is the *y label area*, containing labels corresponding to the *y* scale used to plot the data (numeric "depth" values). The *scroll bar* on the left is used to alter the display by making other segments of the data visible in the plot area. Ida supports several types of scrolling, and this is reflected in the structure of the scroll bar. A user can drag the display at the

rate of cursor movement, make it move at variable scrolling rates, or simply "page" to an immediately adjacent segment of the data. The *title area*, at the top, is a simple, separate component of the display. We will use this display as an example for the discussions of the Ida Editor interface.

We stated earlier that a core persistent context is needed and should be provided by domain KBs. In fact, Ida is built around a KB that declaratively describes its domain of supported graphic interfaces. It contains representations of the basic components of displays and of the various relationships that may hold among them. A particular display is designed by deciding which elements are needed and how they should be laid out. For a wide range of displays, it is not necessary to *specialize* the basic elements Ida provides (e.g., plotting areas, scrolling mechanisms, types of labelings) by defining new classes, but they must be *parameterized* by supplying values for some of their attributes. Such parameters include the size and location of each component and other relationships, such as the areas to be scrolled by a specific scroll bar. Once a display is parameterized, it can be instantiated whenever needed, with the sets of data it is to display. Thus, Ida's KB provides the needed persistent context.

8.5.1. Architecture of the Editor

In moving into the domain of dialogue-like communication, the central problem is obtaining the structure of the transient context. Our proposal to solve this problem is to move "plans" into the realm of the explicitly declared. In the case of an application program, one way of doing this is to organize the program around an explicit declaration of its control and data flows. This is the architecture of the Ida Editor. CONFIG and its supporting environment [Kant88] provide tools for representing, viewing, and creating algorithms and their execution histories. The algorithms are composed of *modules, control flow links*, and *data flow links*. Modules may be simple, implemented directly in code, or they may be hierarchically structured, with submodules. Logical elements of an algorithm are captured using various specialized types of modules providing conditionals and loops.

Figure 8.2 shows a view of the algorithm developed for the Ida Editor. In this figure, boxes are used to represent modules, and small filled squares depict control ports, normally interconnected by solid lines depicting control flow links. Modules shown inside other modules are submodules of the outer modules. Other conventions of the figure will be described as they arise in the discussion.

The Ida Editor allows a user to construct the needed description for a customized presentation. The user may start from scratch or may use an existing presentation as the starting point. In Figure 8.2, the outermost box, *IdaEditor*, represents the entire program. Invocation of the program results in control reaching its entry control port. The small square inside *IdaEditor* and just to the left of the entry control port represents the flow of control

FIGURE 8.2

CONFIGURATION OF THE IDA EDITOR

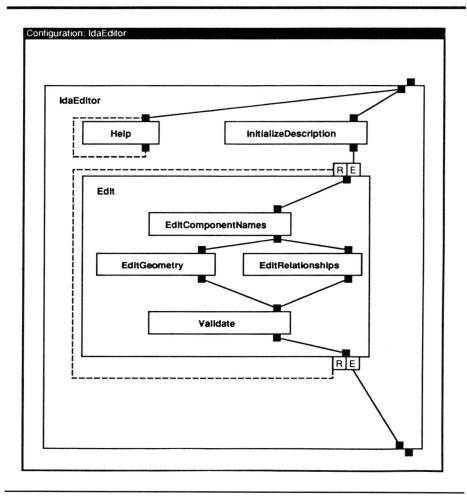

down into a module's submodules. In this case, control flows in parallel to the sub-modules *Help* and *InitializeDescription*. *Help* represents the program's "help" facilities and is a full-fledged program module. Advantages deriving from this design will be discussed in a later section. Help is available as soon the program begins.

The main task of the Ida Editor begins with *InitializeDescription*. The construction process consists of progressively refining a presentation description. The description may or may not be initially empty. The user then edits the description by iterating as many times as necessary through the following steps:

1.   Specify the components of the display by name.
2.   Specify geometric information for components.
3.   Specify nongeometric relationships that exist among components.
4.   Validate the entire description for consistency and completeness.

We will omit most details of the actual interface realization of these steps for now, examining them in the next section, on the user interface.

As already mentioned, *InitializeDescription* is one of the two submodules of *IdaEditor* to receive control immediately. It queries the user to learn if the initial description should be derived from an existing presentation. If so, that presentation exists in the KB and is directly accessible. If an existing presentation is to be modified by the current edit session, that fact is noted. Otherwise, the existing presentation is serving as a prototype and will not be changed. The presentation description is global to *IdaEditor* and does not appear explicitly in Figure 8.2.

From *InitializeDescription,* control flows to the *Edit* submodule, which is an *until* iteration module. The presence of an *R-E* box rather than the usual small square as *Edit*'s input control port depicts the distinction between initial entry (*E*) and repetition reentry (*R*). *Edit*'s output control port uses the same symbol to distinguish repetition (*R*) and exit (*E*). Repetition flow of control is depicted using a dashed line. *Edit* is composed of four sub-modules: *EditComponentNames, EditGeometry, EditRelationships,* and *Validate.*

EditComponentNames receives control immediately. It also is an *until* iteration module, but Figure 8.2 shows *EditComponentNames* only in an unexpanded form. It iterates, allowing the user to add, delete, or change any of the component names from the presentation description. These names have no predetermined meaning in Ida. They are used as a matter of convenience for users and assume meaning only when assigned roles that do have meaning. However, the names are the basis for building a new presentation from an existing one, so user consistency has practical advantages. Iteration continues until the user indicates satisfaction.

From *EditComponentNames* control flows to both *EditGeometry* and *EditRelationships.* These tasks follow establishment of the set of component names because those names are needed to perform either of them. However, the two tasks are unordered with respect to each other, and both become available to the user. Both *EditGeometry* and *EditRelationships* are also *until* iterations, allowing the user to repeatedly specify new information for the description until he or she elects to exit.

When control flows into *Validate* from both *EditGeometry* and *EditRelationships,* it becomes eligible for execution. *Validate* applies a set of consistency and completeness tests, and then either exits *Edit* if the tests are passed or iterates for the user to respond to the errors.

8.5.2. The User Interface

Let us now consider what is actually displayed to the user during the execution of *IdaEditor*. The interface uses three displays to communicate with the user. Figure 8.2 is one of the three. It shows the user the program's "plan of attack." Although *IdaEditor* is fairly simple in structure and interconnections, it should be apparent that much useful information is available to the user through this kind of display. The display also shows the user exactly where control is through the convention of inverting the lowest-level module currently executing.

The second display augments the first; it is a dynamic menu of modules currently available for execution: a module agenda. We previously stated that a module begins executing when control flow reaches it. However, to avoid overwhelming the user with competing interactions, the only action to occur when a module first becomes available for execution is the addition of the module's name to the agenda. Only when the user selects a module from the agenda is its name removed and its execution actually begun. If a user elects to start several modules in parallel and to deal with their simultaneous interactions, it is permissible.

The third display presents an execution history. Execution histories are constructed by CONFIG as the execution proceeds, and a module is entered into the history as it begins. Figure 8.3 shows a simple history display. Module instances have numeric suffixes to give them unique names. This history records a session in which the user built the Ida presentation of Figure 8.1 from scratch. (No existing description was given in *InitializeDescription-3*.) The user gave a valid description on the first try, so there is only a single instance of *Edit—Edit-4*. Since the presentation has four components, the user iterated in *EditComponentNames-5* four times, specifying their names. These iterations do not appear in the history, but their existence is signified by the "[*]" appended to the module instance name. The user can easily request expansion to show these suppressed iterations. *EditGeometry-6* and *EditRelationships-7* were performed to complete the presentation description. *Validate-8* was the final step, validating the complete description. History graphs are made more meaningful when it is possible to generate names like *LocatePlotArea-14* and *SpecifyScrollBar-19* for individual iterations. These names enable a user to more quickly identify a particular module instance of interest.

The history display is a user's interface to two facilities. First, CONFIG itself supports a number of module instance manipulations. These include examining a module's input data, as well as reexecuting the module with altered data values. Although the simplicity of the Ida Editor makes such selective reexecution less attractive, this sophisticated "redo" capability could lead to significant time savings for a user of an application containing complex modules with expensive submodules.

The second facility accessed through the history display is a framework for task-centered screen management. Multi-window systems enable users to make extremely large amounts of information available on their screens si-

FIGURE 8.3
IDA EDITOR HISTORY

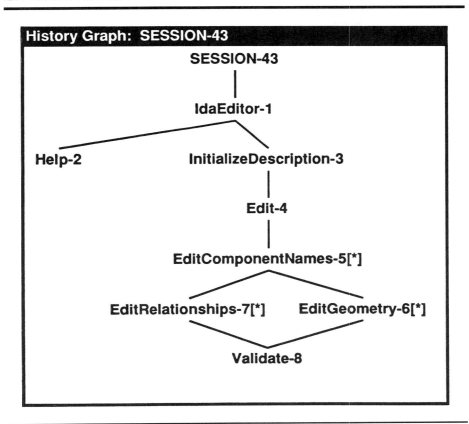

multaneously (or as close to simultaneously as bringing the appropriate window into view). But, as Laurel [Laurel86] observes, this new resource simply multiplies the burden faced by users of a single-window CRT. A user must be able to determine the implicit state of every window and must also manage the physical location of windows on the screen, remembering where needed windows are at all times. A user interacts through windows to make progress on current goals. The display of an explicit history, capturing the transient context of a user's dialogue with a system, is the ideal place to organize windows. As windows (including menus and other transient displays) are opened for various interactions, they are added to a *task windows* set associated with the current task.[5] From the history graph, the user can request collective

---

[5] Ideally, all windows appearing to the user are added to this set, but those windows opened by preexisting services that do not provide convenient access to the identity of the windows they use will fail to conform.

closing or reopening of all task windows. Centralizing the management of this important resource in the history graph significantly furthers its role of bringing structure to interaction sequences with the user.

8.5.3. The Help Facility

IdaEditor's *Help* submodule is responsible for providing users with help. *Help* is exactly like the other submodules, and is executed only when selected from the module agenda menu. Each invocation of *Help* leaves a module instance in the history display. A user has two types of help available: *Describe* and *Monitor*. *Describe* allows a user to request any of a number of descriptions that might be useful during the process of constructing an Ida presentation. *Monitor* requests the creation of a task monitoring the current state of either the geometry or component relationships in the evolving presentation, for the duration of the session.

Users look at existing presentations to build new ones. The degree and kind of presentation customizing they do can vary widely. Allowing a proto-type specification in the *InitializeDescription* submodule is one way to support this style of work. The *Describe* facility is a second way. Through this facility, a user may request a description of either the presentation being constructed or any existing presentation. The description may be of the presentation's geometry, its relationships, or its part-whole structure. *Describe* responds to the request and then terminates. However, the fact that its module execution leaves a representation of the request in the history graph, combined with the use of that graph to organize communication windows, allows a user to conveniently reexamine the response display at a later time. Thus, the fa-miliar scenario of reobtaining the same information several times during the course of a complex sequence of interactions, because there is no convenient way to keep it available, is avoided.

Describe generates a snapshot that is accurate at the time it is produced, but *Monitor* provides a way to create a continually updated view. A user can select either geometry or relationships as the monitored aspect of the de-scription. *Help* then creates a task and dynamically links it to the appropriate submodule: *EditGeometry* or *EditRelationships*. It displays the current version of the selected information and then waits for an input via this newly estab-lished link. Each iteration of the linked module (indicating a change of the appropriate type) produces a notification for the monitoring instance. For each such input, the system refetches the display, keeping the user's informa-tion current for the duration of the session. The declarative representation of the algorithmic structure of the program makes this possible. The link-ages between modules are available for manipulation, thus enabling dynamic modifications without impacting the modules themselves (like a high-level "advise" facility). This monitoring capability allows users who wish to see a current display of the presentation to do so without having responsibility for keeping it current. Furthermore, these displays will not be forced upon users who do not wish to see them.

An immediate benefit of integrating help into the same architecture as the rest of the program is that help too has an interaction context, and its interactions can be made sensitive to this context. A simple example of this arises out of a MetaClass convention that organizes menus with the default version of an operation directly available in the menu. If a user wants one of the nondefault versions, middle-buttoning the basic menu item brings up a submenu containing more alternatives. This is a very handy scheme, except that the default is chosen a priori based on overall statistical frequency. In the Ida Editor, *Help* can change the default dynamically based on the user's current task. If a user selects *Monitor* while the current task is *EditRelationships*, the default meaning will be to monitor relationships. The overall effect is again to bring the user's and the system's actions together, as they are structured around the transient context.

Three modes of information presentation are available in the Ida Editor: text, directed graphs, and diagrams. Ida already has a facility for producing brief textual descriptions of presentation components and composing them dynamically into larger descriptions. Interactive directed-graph displays are well supported in the MetaClass framework, and Ida (used as part of the environment, as well as the target) can produce interactive diagrams. As mentioned, Ida presentations contain three especially important classes of information, all available to users. First, part-whole composition is a central notion in describing a data display. Second, explicit geometric information (the exact sizes and locations of component boundaries) is necessary for the user to know exactly what a display looks like. Third, a variety of symbolic relationships (e.g., scrolls, labels) exist among display components. Notice that any of these classes of information can be represented using any of the three presentation modes mentioned. In the Ida Editor, this choice is left to the user. Clearly, much deeper utilization of the context would be possible. For example, suppose a user requests a picture of the geometry of a presentation. If the system notices that a previous request produced a picture of almost identical information, it could respond by reopening that earlier picture and textually describing the small difference. Such strategies would avoid unnecessary work in producing graphic displays, conserve screen space, and help users note possibly useful similarities. Separating the *what* from the *how* while contextually communicating with users results in a framework supporting significant flexibility.

8.6 CONCLUSIONS

A dialogue user interface architecture has been described. We propose explicitly representing and interacting via graphically presented plans to elevate the level of communication between system and user. This approach is a pragmatic alternative to building agency into an interface (so it can recognize what users are doing without being told). We share the belief expressed by [Williams90] and [Wroblewski90] that a great deal of progress can be made by following this course. (But we stop short of arguing that work on agency is "harmful"; in fact, [Schoen88] reports research on this more difficult course for the specific problem of building knowledge-based systems in the Hyper-Class environment.) Interfaces with which users can carry on loosely structured dialogues represent progress in turning users' computing environments into problem solving environments. Explicit, flexible plans for extended interactions provide the user with support at a level typically unavailable, and do this without introducing artificial constraints for users. Collectively, the context of user interactions enables the user interface to provide more appropriate and informative communication.

A critical factor to the success of this proposal is the user interface to plans and histories. Determining the best presentations of the configuration and history displays will require experimentation, and the solution will almost certainly vary with the kinds of users and the kinds of tasks those users are doing. We have simply started with the interfaces provided by CONFIG as a matter of convenience. Meaningful use of user model KBs and the integration of browsing facilities with other help mechanisms will require much work.

Although our illustrations all are drawn from interactions with a single program, the Ida Editor, a user should be able to use the same tools to build operations and behaviors to customize his or her environment. That is, instead of using a single application program structured in CONFIG modules, a user could define configurations using existing programs as modules, capturing personal work styles and extending the benefits of working within a dialogue to system-level interactions. We are currently studying the domain of mechanical design, where an engineer would profit tremendously from a computational environment that supports the declaration of relationships among the many individual programs and computations typically performed. In an environment this complex, customization to support personal preferences and models is essential.

Acknowledgments

Reid Smith and Eric Schoen provided helpful comments on this paper. Discussions with Elaine Kant have helped clarify issues in constructing problem solving environments.

References

[Brown86] Brown, J. S. 1986. From Cognitive to Social Ergonomics and Beyond. Norman, D.A., and Draper, S.W. (eds.), In *User Centered System Design: New Perspectives on Human-Computer Interaction*. Hillsdale, NJ: Lawrence Erlbaum Associates, pp. 457–486.

[Budge83] Budge, B. 1983. Pinball Construction Set. Computer Program. San Mateo, CA: Electronic Arts.

[Carando88] Carando, P. J. 1988. Shadow: A System for Capturing Software Design Information in a Browsable Form. In *Proceedings of the Twenty-First Hawaii International Conference on Systems Science*, pp. 73–82.

[Carando89] Carando, P. J. 1989. Fusing Hypertext with AI. *IEEE Expert*, 4(4), 65–78.

[Hutchins86] Hutchins, E. L., Hollan, J. D., and Norman, D. A. 1986. Direct Manipulation Interfaces. In Norman, D. A., and Draper, S. W.(eds.), *User Centered System Design: New Perspectives on Human-Computer Interaction*. Hillsdale, NJ: Lawrence Erlbaum Associates, pp. 87–124.

[Kant88] Kant, E. 1988. Interactive Problem Solving Using Task Configuration and Control. *IEEE Expert*, 3(4) pp. 36–49.

[Laurel86] Laurel, B. K. 1986. Interface as Mimesis. In Norman, D. A., and Draper, S. W. (eds.), *User Centered System Design: New Perspectives on Human-Computer Interaction*. Hillsdale, NJ: Lawrence Erlbaum Associates, pp. 285–313.

[Norman86a] Norman, D. A. 1986. Cognitive Engineering. In Norman, D. A., and Draper, S. W. (eds.), *User Centered System Design: New Perspectives on Human-Computer Interaction*, Hillsdale, NJ: Lawrence Erlbaum Associates, pp. 31–61.

[Norman86b] Norman, D. A., and Draper, S. W., (eds.) 1986. *User Centered System Design: New Perspectives on Human-Computer Interaction*, Hillsdale, NJ: Lawrence Erlbaum Associates.

[Reichman86] Reichman, R. 1986. Communication Paradigms for Window Systems. In Norman, D. A., and Draper, S. W., (eds.), *User Centered System Design: New Perspectives on Human-Computer Interaction*. Hillsdale, NJ: Lawrence Erlbaum Associates, pp. 285–313.

[Schoen88] Schoen, E., Smith, R. G., and Buchanan, B. G. 1988. Design of Knowledge-Based Systems with a Knowledged-Based Assistant. *IEEE Transactions on Software Engineering*, 14(12), 1771–1791.

[Smith84] Smith, R. G., Lafue, G. M. E., Schoen, E., and Vestal, S. C. 1984. Declarative Task Description as a User Interface Structuring Mechanism. *Computer*, 17(9), 29–38.

[Smith87] Smith, R. G., Barth, P. S., and Young, R. L. 1987. A Substrate for Object-Oriented Interface Design. In *Research Directions in Object-Oriented Programming*, Cambridge, MA: MIT Press.

[Stallman84] Stallman, R. M. 1984. EMACS: The Extensible, Customizable, Self-Documenting Display Editor. In Barstow, D. R., Shrobe, H. E., and Sandewall, E. (eds.), *Interactive Programming Environments*. New York: McGraw-Hill, pp. 300–325.

[Terveen90] Terveen, L. 1990. Resources for Person-Computer Collaboration. In *Working Notes from the AAAI Spring Symposium on Knowledge-Based Human-Computer Communication*, Palo Alto, CA, March, pp. 122–124.

[Williams90] Williams, M. D. 1990. The Pragmatics of Knowledge-Based Interface Design. In *Working Notes from the AAAI Spring Symposium on Knowledge-based Human-Computer Communication*, pp. 132–135.

[Wroblewski90] Wroblewski, D., Hill, W. C., and McCandless, T. P. 1990. Agency Considered Harmful. In *Working Notes from the AAAI Spring Symposium on Knowledge-Based Human-Computer Communication*, pp. 141–142.

[Young87] Young, R. L. 1987. An Object-Oriented Framework for Interactive Data Graphics. In *Proceedings of the Second ACM Conference on Object-Oriented Programming Systems, Languages, and Applications*, Orlando, FL, October, pp. 78–90. [ACM *SIGPLAN Notices*, 22(12)].

CHAPTER 9

INTELLIGENT INTERFACES
AS AGENTS

DAVID N. CHIN
Department of Information and Computer Sciences
University of Hawaii at Manoa

ABSTRACT

An intelligent interface cannot just respond passively to its user's commands and queries. It must be able to take the initiative in order to volunteer information, correct user misconceptions, or reject unethical user requests. To do these things, a system must be an intelligent agent. UCEgo is the intelligent agent component of UC (UNIX Consultant), a natural-language system that helps the user solve problems in using the UNIX operating system. UCEgo provides UC with its own goals and plans. By adopting different goals in

This research was supported in part by the Office of Naval Research, under grant N0014-48-C-0732; the Defense Advanced Research Projects Agency (DoD), under DARPA Order No. 4871, monitored by Space and Naval Warfare Systems Command under contract N00039-84-C-0089; the National Science Foundation under grant #85-14890; and Hughes Aircraft grant #442427-59868.

177

different situations, UCEgo creates and executes different plans, enabling it to interact intelligently with the user. UCEgo adopts goals from its *themes*, adopts subgoals during planning, and adopts *metagoals* for dealing with goal interactions. It also adopts goals when it notices that the user either lacks necessary knowledge or has incorrect beliefs. In these cases, UCEgo plans to volunteer information or correct the user's misconception, as appropriate.

9.1 INTRODUCTION

There has been some debate concerning whether intelligent interfaces should be structured as agents or whether it is better to think of them as tools with intelligently organized direct-manipulation options available for the user. In the interface-as-agent view, the interface is seen as a separate entity that mediates between the user and the machine. The user tells the interface what to do, and then the interface acts on these instructions. In the competing interface-as-tool view, the interface is seen as directly representing the machine. The interface merely facilitates the user's direct manipulation of the machine. In this view, all user actions should have immediate, directly perceptible results.

Proponents of the interface-as-tool view point out that the agent view requires that the interface have a well-defined model of the dialogue between the user and the interface. This is difficult because dialogue models are poorly understood and users tend to have difficulty trying to learn the nature of the dialogue. Misunderstandings by users concerning the nature of the dialogue can lead to problems. For example, users may expect one of their entries to constitute an order to the interface, whereas the interface models the entry as a mere statement of fact (or vice-versa). Such misunderstandings are less likely in the direct-manipulation model because users usually see the effects of their actions immediately. Also, the similarity between user-interface dialogues and human-human dialogues tends to set up faulty expectations concerning the capabilities of the interface in the user's mind. Finally, the interface-as-agent view is too unconstrained since it allows the interface to perform unexpected actions as an agent.

On the other hand, the interface-as-agent proponents argue that dialogue is a natural interaction mode, and they point out that most computer operating systems have been successfully based on implicit dialogue models. However the strongest argument for viewing the interface as an agent relates to the added flexibility needed by intelligent interfaces. This paper will show that intelligent interfaces often need to behave as agents at least part of the time. In particular, whenever the interface has greater knowledge than the user, the interface may need to take the initiative (i.e., perform unexpected actions) in order to correct the user, volunteer information, or suggest alternative courses of action. This paper will expand on the argument that intelligent interfaces need to be agents and will describe a natural-language interface that implements some of these ideas.

9.2 CONSULTATION PROGRAMS

An intelligent interface cannot just respond passively to its user's instructions and queries. Rather, it must be able to take the initiative in its dialogue with the user. For example, consider a hypothetical intelligent interface that provides help in using the UNIX[1] operating system. A user would be able to ask such a system in English (or some other natural language) for advice about how to do things, for definitions of terminology, or for advice in solving problems. The consultant program would then provide solutions in English like a real human consultant would. Also like a human consultant, such a program may need to take the initiative during the consultation. For instance, consider the following user interaction with the hypothetical consultation program:

> *User:* What is chin's phone number?
> *Program:* I'm sorry, I do not know that. To find out, type 'finger chin'.

In the above interaction, the program does not know the answer to the user's query. A system that was not capable of taking the initiative in the consultation dialogue would simply inform the user that it failed to find an answer and then await further instructions from the user. However a more intelligent interface might make the additional suggestion shown above. Here, the program has *volunteered* additional information to the user about how to find out chin's phone number using the UNIX **finger** command. The ability to take the initiative in order to volunteer information is especially critical for consultation systems, because, by definition, such systems know more about their domains of expertise than their users, who may not even know enough to ask the right questions. So, an intelligent consultation system needs to be able to take the initiative in order to volunteer critical information that its user may not even know was pertinent.

Another example showing why an intelligent system needs to take the initiative in the dialogue with the user is shown below:

> *User:* What does ls −v do?
> *Program:* It lists the contents of your current directory.

The hypothetical program gives an answer that is literally correct, since the **ls** command actually ignores inappropriate flags such as $-v$. However, a consultant that provides only the above answer has failed to correct the user's incorrect preconception that the **ls** command has a $-v$ flag. So, although the user did not specifically ask whether **ls** has a $-v$ flag, a good consultant would not fail to provide the information that in fact **ls** does not have such a flag. Such a response is shown in the next dialogue:

---

[1] UNIX is a trademark of Bell Laboratories.

User: What does ls −v do?

Program: There is no −v option for ls.

This is a better answer even though it does not literally answer the user's question. In deciding to ignore the user's direct question and shift its attention to the user's misconception, the program has taken the initiative in the dialogue. This shows that a good consultant cannot just passively respond to the user; rather, it must have its own agenda.

In the previous dialogue, the better answer requires that the program realize that the user has a misconception. To do this, the system must first infer that the user believes that **ls** has a −v option and then realize that the user's belief conflicts with the program's knowledge. So, in general, a good consultant system must also model the user's knowledge and beliefs.

Even after a consultant system realizes that the user has a misconception, it must decide how to deal with the misconception. In the example of the −v flag, the system decides that it should inform the user of the facts in order to correct the user's misconception. In other cases, the system may choose to ignore the misconception, as in the following scenario:

User: How can I delete someone else's file when I don't have write permission on the file?

Program: I will not help you delete someone else's file, because that is unethical.

In the user's statement above, the user has assumed that one needs write permission on the file to delete it. This is not true. Rather, one needs write permission on the parent directory to delete the file. Regardless of what is the correct precondition, the program decides not to help the user because of ethical considerations. This also means that the program decides not to correct the user's misconception, so as to avoid helping the user delete someone else's file. This is an example of a decision by a consultant program to be uncooperative.

Of course a good consultant program cannot arbitrarily decide to be uncooperative. In the previous case, the decision to be uncooperative should be based on the fact that the user's goal of deleting someone else's file conflicts with the program's goal of preserving all users' files. In such cases, the program's goal of preserving files should win out over the program's desire to help the user who asked the question. These sorts of goals and goal interactions are needed to guide a consultant system properly.

9.3 INTELLIGENT AGENTS

The examples in the previous section have shown that a good computer consultation system cannot be a passive system that just answers the user's queries and follows the user's instructions literally. Rather, the consultant system must often take the initiative. This is because consultant systems should have greater knowledge in their field of expertise than users. As in the example in the previous section, the consultant may sometimes need to take the initiative to correct a user's misconceptions. Also, the consultant may need to take the initiative to provide needed information that the user did not explicitly ask for. Often the user does not even realize that such information is pertinent and so would never ask for it. A computer consultant system needs to have the human-like capability of taking the initiative in a dialogue rather than always responding to the user passively.

Previous efforts in natural-language systems that take the initiative have resulted in programs capable of *mixed-initiative* dialogues. Among the first of these, the SCHOLAR system [Carbonell70b; Carbonell70a] for CAI (Computer-Aided Instruction), could take the initiative to test the user on facts in its knowledge base. It also allowed the user to query the system about facts in its knowledge base. This type of mixed-initiative works only for limited situations, such as mutual quizzing. A system based on answering or generating quiz questions cannot be adapted to help the user solve problems, volunteer information pertinent to the user's problems, or detect misconceptions evident from the user's questions (as opposed to wrong answers from the user).

Each of the above approaches works to provide programs the capability to take the initiative in limited situations. However, neither approach is general enough to cover other types of situations where a program should take the initiative. For example, neither approach would allow a program to take the initiative to correct a user misconception.

The approach that I take is to view the program as an *agent*. That is, a consultation system should be viewed as a system that can perform actions. For a natural-language consultation system, acting consists of mostly *speech acts* [Austin62;Searle69], that is, acting by communicating with the user. Within this paradigm, taking the initiative in a dialogue translates into acting without the guidance of the user. An agent that has this capability of taking the initiative is called an *autonomous agent*.

A *rational agent* is an agent that behaves rationally. In AI programs, much as in popular psychology, this usually means that a program's behavior is determined by reasonable plans and goals and that the program attributes reasonable plans and goals to other rational agents. For example, PAM [Wilensky78] understood stories involving rational agents by analyzing the goals and plans of the characters. Also, TALE-SPIN [Meehan76] used plans and goals to create simple stories with rational agents as characters. In the problem-solving domain, robot planning programs (e.g., [Fikes71; Sacerdoti74]) have shown that planning is a good paradigm for programming robots as rational agents. In the realm of conversation, [Hobbs80] has argued that human conversation fits such a paradigm. So, a program that contains reasonable plans and goals and whose behavior is determined by those plans and goals can be considered a rational agent.

Within the planning paradigm, a *rational autonomous agent* is one that contains plans and goals that allow the agent to take the initiative in appropriate situations. The central problem in building autonomous agents is determining which situations require the agent to take the initiative. For a rational autonomous agent that is based on the planning paradigm, this problem translates to the problem of determining appropriate goals for the planner. Such a process is called *goal detection* [Wilensky83].

After a rational autonomous agent, henceforth called an *intelligent agent*, has detected appropriate goals, it is up to the planner of the intelligent agent to formulate a plan to satisfy these goals and then carry out the plan. Much work has been done in AI in the area of planning where the goals of the planner are provided by the operator. For example, [Newell72] formulated means-ends analysis as a general strategy for achieving given ends or goals. However, the all robot-planning programs assumed that the goals are given by the users. Likewise, in TALE-SPIN the programmer provided the initial goals of the characters. For story understanding, PAM was able to recognize a character's goals when directly stated in the narrative, or when the goal could be inferred from the characters' stated actions based on the assumption that the actions were part of the character's plan. As [Carbonell82] points out, none of these systems have systematically addressed the problem of goal detection, which is essential for building intelligent agents.

This paper will address the problem of building a natural-language computer consultation system that behaves as an intelligent agent. The UC (UNIX Consultant) system embodies such an intelligent agent.

9.4 UC, THE UNIX CONSULTANT

UC (UNIX Consultant) is an interactive natural-language consultant system for the UNIX operating system. UC is able to provide information about how to do things in UNIX, definitions about UNIX or general operating system terminology, and help in debugging problems with using UNIX. A short overview of UC follows. For more details on UC, the reader is referred to [Chin87], [Wilensky86], and [Wilensky84].

In a typical UC session, the user types questions in English to UC, and UC responds to the user in English. A schematic diagram of the flow of information among UC's various components is shown in Figure 9.1.

The input to UC is analyzed by the ALANA language analysis component of UC, which produces a semantic representation of the input. This representation is in the form of a KODIAK network (a semantic network representation language developed at Berkeley [Wilensky87]). Next, UC's concretion mechanism performs concretion inferences [Wilensky83; Norvig83] based on the semantic network. Concretion is the process of inferring more specific interpretations of the user's input than might strictly be correct on a logical basis. Such inferences might be motivated by the context of the utterance or

FIGURE 9.1
FLOW OF INFORMATION AMONG UC COMPONENTS

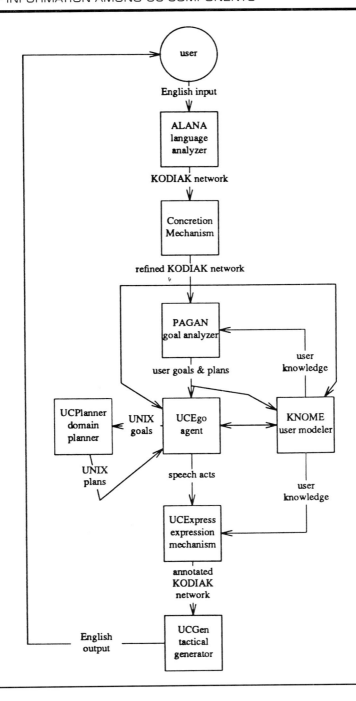

by culturally accepted usage biases. After concretion, the modified KODIAK network is passed to PAGAN, UC's goal analysis component. PAGAN deduces the user's actual goals. This includes inferring the user's high-level goals as well as the user's immediate goals. PAGAN also handles phenomena such as indirect speech acts.

After the initial analysis of the user's input, the UCEgo component of UC decides how UC should respond. UCEgo is the component of UC that implements an intelligent agent. It first determines what UC's own goals should be, then formulates a plan to achieve these goals, and finally carries out this plan. UCEgo detects its own goals based on the present situation, which may include varied factors such as the user's goals and the user's utterances, as well as UC's own goals, knowledge, and internal state.

Part of UCEgo's response may involve calling on the services of the UCPlanner component of UC. UCPlanner is a UNIX domain planner that creates plans for doing things in UNIX. Another component of UC that may be called by UCEgo is UCExpress. UCExpress uses the process of answer expression to refine the communicative plans produced by UCEgo. First, UCExpress prunes extraneous concepts from the answer, either when the user already knows the concepts or when the concepts are already part of the conversational context. Next UCExpress uses specialized formats such as similes and examples to express information to the user in a clear and concise manner. The result of UCExpress's processing is an annotated KODIAK network that is ready for generation into English by the UCGen tactical-level generator.

Another important part of UC is KNOME, the user-modeling component. KNOME encodes the knowledge and beliefs of the user. It also deduces what the user knows and believes, based on UC's conversation with the user. KNOME also models the extent of UC's own knowledge of UNIX. This is useful in differentiating between actual user misconceptions and cases in which UC's knowledge base is incomplete.

This paper will concentrate on the UCEgo component of UC and how it detects the right goals for UC in appropriate situations. By detecting the right goals, UC can respond intelligently to the user.

9.5 GOAL DETECTION

The central problem in building an intelligent agent is how to detect appropriate goals for the agent, goals that can then be used to guide the agent's actions. This process is called *goal detection* [Wilensky83].

Although considerable work has been done in the area of planning, very few planning systems have addressed the problem of how to detect appropriate goals for planning. In almost all planning systems, the high-level goals are provided by the human operators of the planners. An exception is described by [Allen79], whose system simulated a train station ticket agent. It detected goals based on an analysis of obstacles to a user's plans. By addressing these obstacles, the system could volunteer information that the user would need to achieve the user's plan. This approach addresses only a fraction of the general problem of goal detection. An analysis of obstacles to the user's plan does not address how these obstacle-related goals might interact with the system's other goals. Also, analyzing obstacles would not lead a system to detect user misconceptions and detect the goal of correcting the misconceptions. Even in terms of volunteering useful information to the user, an analysis of obstacles to a user's plans does not address the problem of when the system should volunteer an alternative plan.

The PANDORA planner [Faletti82] detected its own goals. It detected goals when actual or projected states conflicted with goals or plans and when certain frames describing situations were activated. For example, the goal of "find out about the world" was attached to the morning frame, which meant that PANDORA would try to read a newspaper in the morning. However, except for very simple frames, PANDORA did not address the problem of when is it proper to invoke frames and their associated goals. Also, because PANDORA existed in a self-contained simulated world, it did not address the problem of detecting goals when the system must interact with real users.

Schank and Abelson advocate *themes* as the origin of goals [Schank77]. However, themes give rise to only very high-level goals, such as being rich. Their theory does not explain how a program might proceed from these very high-level goals to lower-level goals, such as the goal of possessing a quarter that one sees on the sidewalk as opposed to a quarter that one sees in someone else's hand.

Once an agent has determined its goals, the relatively better-understood process of planning can be applied to satisfy them. The following sections describe how goals are detected by UCEgo.

9.6 TYPES OF SITUATIONS

In general, an agent may detect new goals whenever there is a change in an agent's environment or internal state. Any combination of factors in the agent's environment or internal state that leads to a new goal for the agent is called a *situation* after the terminology of [Wilensky83]. This section will classify the kinds of situations that lead UCEgo to detect new goals.

Since UC is a computer consultation system, UCEgo's environment is limited to a dialogue with the user on the subject of the UNIX operating system. So for UCEgo, situations are composed of combinations of UC's internal state, the user's statements, and information that might be derived from the user's statements, such as the user's plans and goals and the user's knowledge and beliefs. UC's internal state includes UC's domain knowledge, UC's own goals, and UC's *themes* [Schank77].

The situations that give rise to goals in the UC domain can be divided into five main classes:

1. themes → goals,
2. plans → subgoals,
3. goal interactions → metagoals,
4. gaps in the user's knowledge → goals,
5. user misconceptions → goals.

Themes can be considered as the internal motivations of an agent, so they are a prime source of new goals. Another source of goals is the planning process. As an agent plans for goals, the resulting plans may produce subgoals that the agent will need to adopt and plan to satisfy. When an agent has several goals, these goals may interact, giving rise to a *metagoal* [Wilensky83] which is a goal for dealing with the interaction among other goals.

Themes, plans, and goal interactions are universal sources of goals in that they are common to all intelligent agents. The other two sources of goals are somewhat more particular to a consulting environment. In a consulting environment, situations commonly arise wherein the state of the user's knowledge base (as deduced from conversing with the user) is not consistent with the consultant's knowledge base. One kind of inconsistency is detected when the consultant determines that the user lacks some necessary knowledge. Another kind of inconsistency is found when the consultant determines that the user's knowledge base conflicts with its own knowledge base, that is, that the user has a misconception. Both of these classes of situations are concerned with the user's knowledge, since the main task of a consultant is to impart information to the user. In other types of programs, a different focus may lead to other situation classes.

In UCEgo, each situation class is represented by a single KODIAK network pattern, which is used as the left-hand side of an *if-detected demon* [Chin87]. When a piece of KODIAK network matches such a pattern, the network is considered to represent a situation of the class, and the demon adds a new goal (also represented as a piece of KODIAK network) to UC's memory.

Unlike situation classes, goals in UC are explicitly represented in KODIAK using the has-goal relation, which has two aspectuals: *goal* and *planner*. A goal is modeled as a relation between an individual (planner) and some state (**goal**) that that individual wishes to achieve. There is no absolute category of goals, since a state cannot be said to be a goal unless some individual can be said to have that goal. This is not to say that there are not some states (e.g., having lots of money) that are habitually thought of as being goals. However, habitual goals encompass only a fraction of what is meant by the term *goal*. Almost any state can be a goal, provided only that some individual wishes to achieve that state. Thus treating goals as aspectuals of HAS-GOAL relations does capture the meaning of the term *goal*.

9.7 GOALS FROM THEMES AND PLANS

UCEgo has a number of themes that give rise to goals. These include life themes as well as role themes. An example of a life theme is UCEgo's stay-alive theme. This theme gives rise to the recurrent background goals of preserving the UC program and preserving the UNIX system. The stay-alive theme is also an instance of the *preservation theme* [Wilensky83], since it gives rise to preservation goals. An example of a role theme is UCEgo's consultant role theme. This gives rise to the recurrent goals of helping the user and being polite to the user. The goal of being polite is a background goal, since UCEgo does not attempt to plan for it immediately. On the other hand, the goal of helping the user is a foreground goal, because UC immediately tries to find ways to help the user.

Since all goals that arise from themes are detected when UC first starts up, it might seem that attributing these goals to themes is extraneous. However, themes are really quite useful. First of all, themes provide a relative-importance ordering for goals, which is useful in case of goal conflicts (see Section 9.8). This relative importance metric for goals can be used as the basis for a more complete theory that provides a calculus of goal values for an agent. Second, themes provide a means of organizing goals into related groups. For example, if UC were to provide other functions besides a UNIX Consultant, then the goals that arise from its consultant role theme could be added when UC starts working as a consultant and removed when UC stops working as a consultant.

The goals that arise from themes usually give rise to yet more goals, called subgoals, during the planning phase of UCEgo. In fact, all of UC's goals can ultimately be traced back to UC's themes, either directly or as subgoals of other goals that can be traced back to UC's themes.

9.7.1. Goals from Themes

When UC first starts up, it has a number of themes. These immediately give rise to goals for UC. The themes that have been found to be important for UC include the stay-alive and ethics life themes, and the consultant role theme. Other systems may find that different themes will be useful. Certainly, systems that are not consultation systems will have a different role theme than UC's consultant role theme.

The consultant role theme represents UC's job of being a UNIX consultant. It motivates UC to behave as a consultant to help the user. Therefore, the consultant role theme leads UCEgo to adopt the recurrent goal of helping the user. This goal is a recurrent goal, since once UC has helped the user, UC continues to have the goal of helping the user. Unlike other goals that arise from themes, the goal of helping the user is not a background goal. This means that UCEgo is constantly planning how to satisfy this goal.

Another aspect of being a consultant involves being polite to the client. So the consultant role theme leads UCEgo to adopt the recurrent background

TABLE 9.1
THEMES THAT GIVE RISE TO GOALS IN UC

Theme	goal
UC-consultant role theme	UC help user
	UC be polite to user
UC-stay-alive life-theme	preserve UC program
	preserve Unix system
UC-ethics life-theme	UC act-ethically

goal of being polite to the user. This goal is a recurrent goal, since UC never stops being polite to the user. It is also a background goal, since UCEgo does not try to plan how to be polite to the user. Instead, when a situation arises in which UC should be polite, this goal will become activated. Such social situations include greetings, farewells, and apologies.

The ethics life theme represents UC's desire to act ethically. It gives rise to UC's goal of ACT-ETHICALLY. Since UC cannot perform actions except for communicative acts, UC only has to worry about performing unethical communicative actions. For example UC worries about providing information to the user that will help the user perform an unethical act. In such situations, UCEgo detects a conflict between UC's goal of helping the user (from the consultant role theme) and UC's goal of ACT-ETHICALLY. Such goal interactions are described further in Section 9.8.

The stay-alive life theme is an instance of the preservation theme [Wilensky83], from whence arise preservation goals. This particular preservation theme represents UC's desire to preserve itself. As a result, it leads UC to adopt the goals of preserving the UC program and preserving the UNIX system on which UC runs. Other preservation goals that need to be taken into account in planning how the user should do things in UNIX (e.g., preserving the user's files and preserving the privacy of the user's files) are handled by UC's UNIX domain planner ([Luria85, Luria88]).

Themes in UC and the goals that they give rise to are summarized in Table 9.1.

9.7.2. Situations Leading to Subgoals

Except for goals that UC adopts from its themes, all of UC's other goals are subgoals or, less frequently, metagoals. This section will show how UCEgo adopts subgoals and will describe some of the subgoals found in UC. Other subgoals are introduced when appropriate in later sections.

Subgoals are created as part of the planning process. Many of UCEgo's plans contain steps that call for the achievement of a state. When UCEgo adopts such a plan, it adopts the subgoal of achieving that state.

An example of a particular subgoal is shown in Figure 9.2. The double circle represents an if-detected demon, and the arrows radiating inward toward the double circle represent the left-hand-side of the daemon, whereas the arrows radiating outward represent the right-hand-side of the daemon. This daemon allows UCEgo to adopt the user's goal of knowing something. It is triggered by a class of situations that consists of two parts:

1. UC has the goal of helping someone (UC-HAS-GOAL3).
2. That person wants (HAS-GOAL0) to know (KNOW2) something.

When UCEgo encounters a matching situation, it asserts that a plan for (PLANFOR3) helping (HELP1) the user (PERSON4) is to satisfy (SATISFY1) the subgoal of having the user know (KNOW2) what the user wants to know. This situation is a very common one for UC, because UC's users usually want to know something about UNIX.

UC's goal of acting ethically motivates another class of situations in which UCEgo detects a subgoal. When someone wants to know how to alter some-

FIGURE 9.2
IF-DETECTED DEMON FOR DETECTING THE SUBGOAL OF HAVING THE USER KNOW

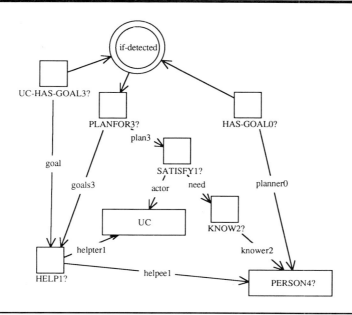

one else's file, an if-detected demon detects the subgoal of preventing that person from knowing how to alter someone else's file. More formally, the situation consists of five relations:

1. UC has the goal of acting ethically.
2. Someone (*?p1*) wants to know:
3. A plan for altering a file (altering includes the subclass of deleting).
4. The owner of the file is someone, *?p2*.
5. The owner (*?p2*) differs from the alterer (*?p1*).

When UCEgo detects such a situation, it asserts that a plan for acting ethically is to adopt the subgoal of preventing the first person from knowing how to alter the second person's file. Normally this type of situation occurs when the user asks UC how to alter someone else's file. UC should not help the user perform unethical actions, so in such cases, UC should not provide the user with such information. However this conflicts with UC's normal mode of operation in which UC adopts the user's goal of knowing in order to help the user. This results in an internal goal conflict for UC. Section 9.8 describes such goal interactions and how they are resolved.

In a sense, the meaning of high-level goals such as help-the-user, or act-ethically is defined by the set of situation classes in which UC adopts subgoals of these high-level goals. UC can only act to satisfy high-level goals when particular situations lead UC to adopt specific subgoals. It might seem that such high-level goals are superfluous, since one can always leave the high-level goals out of the situation and UC would continue to adopt the subgoals when appropriate. However, high-level goals serve several important functions. First, high-level goals help to organize related situations and subgoals. By removing a particular high-level goal from the system, one can disable an entire class of related situations or subgoals. Second, high-level goals allow the system to provide explanations about why it performed certain actions. When UC refuses to help the user delete someone else's file, it explains that it will not help because it is unethical. Finally, high-level goals help the system resolve conflicts between subgoals (see Section 9.8.2).

9.8 METAGOALS

Correcting user misconceptions or providing suggestions to the user do not necessarily require that the system have explicit goals of its own. Those types of responses can be provided by simpler systems that do not have goals and plans. However, a system based on planning for goals is more flexible, because it can much more easily handle interactions among goals. Goals can interact either negatively by conflicting or positively by overlapping. When UCEgo detects a situation where goals conflict or overlap, it creates a new goal for dealing with the goal interaction. Goals for dealing with other goals are called *metagoals* [Wilensky83].

Metagoals are not distinguished from other goals in the UC program either by representational differences or by differences in their processing. Of course, in discussing goals it is useful to make a distinction between metagoals and subgoals because these types of goals tend to originate from different kinds of situations and tend to have different subject areas.

Metagoals are also useful for controlling the planning and plan execution process. In UC, metagoals control when UCEgo tries to find out information for the user in situations in which UC does not know the information. Also, when UCEgo cannot find a prestored plan to satisfy one of UC's goals, UCEgo adopts the metagoal of knowing a plan for finding out a plan to satisfy this goal. This is an example of *metaplanning* [Wilensky83], since UC is planning to create a plan that is used to find another plan. For more details on metaplanning in UCEgo, see [Chin87].

9.8.1. Mutual Inclusion

Metagoals are used to deal with both positive and negative interactions between goals. One way in which goals can interact positively is through *mutual inclusion* [Wilensky83]. This describes situations in which a planner has the same or similar goals for different reasons. In such situations, the planner can merge the goals into a single goal. This saves resources, because the planner no longer has to plan several times nor execute many similar plans.

When UCEgo finds that it has two goals that are similar, it adopts the metagoal of merging the redundant goals. The redundant goals may actually be identical, or they may be just similar enough to be merged successfully into a single goal. For example, consider what happens when the user asks UC, "Is **cp** used to copy files?" and UC answers, "Yes."

In processing this query, UC's goal analysis component, PAGAN, deduces that the user's goal is to know whether **cp** is a plan for copying files. PAGAN also deduces that this goal has two possible parent goals (one or both of which might hold):

1. The user wants to know the effects of the **cp** command.
2. The user wants to know how to copy files.

To see why this added level of goal analysis is necessary, consider the slightly different query, "Is **cp** used to create files?" The answer to this query is *no*. However this is not a very good answer. In fact, any human consultant who only replied *no* in this case would be labeled uncooperative. The reason *no* is not a good answer for this query, whereas *yes* is a reasonable answer for the first query is because the *no* answer only superficially addresses the user's goals. It only addresses the user's immediate goal, to know whether or not **cp** is used to create files; it does not address either of the two possible goals that motivate that goal: The user wants to know the effects of the **cp** command, or the user wants to know how to create files, or both. To provide a more cooperative answer in such situations, UCEgo volunteers additional information by addressing the user's higher-level goals as well as the user's immediate goal. Volunteering information in such cases is described in Section 9.10.4.

The second query shows that UCEgo sometimes needs to address all of the user's goals rather than just the user's immediate goal. However, if UCEgo were to address all of the user's goals in the first query, it would end up providing three very similar, indeed redundant, answers to the user. UCEgo might approach this problem of redundant answers in one of two ways. It could always handle only the user's immediate goal and then volunteer more information only if it discovers that satisfying the user's immediate goal does not contribute to satisfying the higher-level goals that motivate the immediate goal. The problem with this approach is that it is fairly difficult to tell whether satisfying the immediate goal helps to satisfy the underlying goals. In fact, a planner will usually have to plan to satisfy the underlying goals before it can make such a judgment.

Since a planner must often plan for the underlying goals anyway, UCEgo uses the strategy of always planning to satisfy all of the user's goals and then noticing when these goals overlap to prevent redundant answers. Figure 9.3 shows the if-detected daemon that notices situations with potential goal overlap. Whenever UC has two different goals (UC-HAS-GOAL1 and UC-HAS-GOAL2) of wanting the user (PERSON1) to know something, and the answer (ANSWER-FOR1 and ANSWER-FOR2) for those queries are similar (implemented by the procedural test, UC-test-similar), then UCEgo adopts the metagoal (UC-HAS-GOAL3) of merging the redundant goals (MERGE-REDUNDANT-GOALS).

The procedural test, UC-test-similar, checks to see if the two goals are similar enough to be merged. It first matches the two answers to see if they are the same. If so, then the two goals can be merged. It also has knowledge that certain types of relations are similar enough that they convey essentially the same information. For example, HAS-EFFECT and PLANFOR are similar enough to be merged, provided of course that they relate similar concepts.

An example of merging goals occurs during the processing of the user query, "Is cp used to copy files?" By adopting all three potential user goals, UCEgo detects the three goals:

1. UC wants the user to know whether **cp** is used to copy files.
2. UC wants the user to know the effects of the **cp** command.
3. UC wants the user to know a plan for copying files.

UCEgo cannot tell that these goals are similar until after it has deduced the referent of the descriptions in UC's goals. For instance, the referent for the goal of knowing the effects of the **cp** command is an HAS-EFFECT rela-

FIGURE 9.3

IF-DETECTED DEMON FOR DETECTING OVERLAPPING GOALS

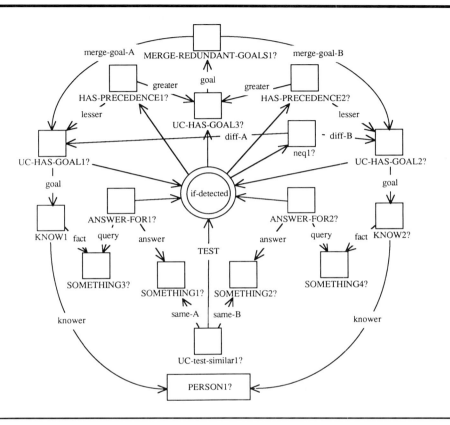

tion, whereas the referent of the goal of knowing a plan for copying files is a PLANFOR relation. These are similar albeit different relations, so they are candidates for merging. Since they both relate a UNIX-CP-COMMAND to a COPY-FILE-EFFECT, UC-test-similar decides that they can indeed be merged. Another type of similarity is found when one answer is contained in the other. In this example, the answer for the goal of knowing whether **cp** is a plan for copying files is the HAS-TRUTH-VALUE relation relating the truth value, *true*, and the proposition that the **cp** command is a plan for copying files. When comparing this answer, only the propositional content is compared. Eventually, all three goals are merged by discarding all but the immediate goal.

The final answer is shortened to just *yes*, rather than "Yes, **cp** is used to copy files." This is done since the proposition, "**cp** is a plan for copying files," is already part of the context (it is part of the user's query). Such processing is done by the UCExpress component [Chin87].

9.8.2. Goal Conflict

Goals can interact negatively by conflicting. When UCEgo detects a situation in which UC has two goals that conflict with one another, UCEgo adopts the metagoal of resolving the goal conflict. A frequent type of goal conflict situation is found when a planner wants both to achieve some state and to prevent that state from occurring. UCEgo detects such situations with the if-detected demon shown in Figure 9.4.

An example of a goal conflict situation is when the user asks UC, "How can I delete UC?" In this case, the usual flow of processing leads UCEgo to adopt the user's goal of having the user know a plan for deleting the UC program. This subgoal can be traced back to UC's goal of helping the user, which in turn arose from UC's consultant role theme (see Section 9.7.1).

In parallel to this, UCEgo also has a stay-alive life theme, which gives rise to UC's goal of preserving the UC program, that is, the UC executable file rather than the UC process—if UC wanted to preserve its process, it might refuse to tell the user how to exit UC. This goal is a *background goal* [Chin87], which means that UCEgo does not actively attempt to plan for the goal. Rather, the goal is considered only when UCEgo detects a relevant situation, such as in the present example. Whenever someone wants to know

FIGURE 9.4
IF-DETECTED DEMON FOR DETECTING GOAL CONFLICT

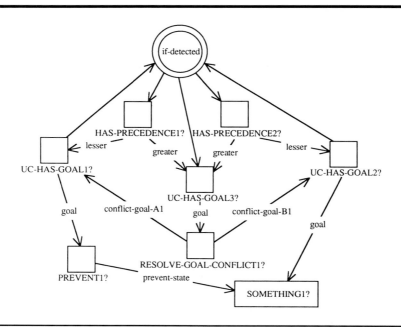

how to alter something that UC wishes to preserve, UCEgo adopts the subgoal of preventing the user from knowing how to do that. In this example, the user wants to delete (a specific kind of altering) the UC program, which UC wants to preserve. So, UCEgo adopts the subgoal of preventing the user from knowing how to delete the UC program.

At this point, these two lines of processing interact with a goal conflict. On the one hand, UC wants to help the user and hence wants the user to know how to delete it. On the other hand, UC wants to preserve the UC program and hence wants to prevent the user from knowing how to delete it. The goals of wanting the user to know and wanting to prevent the user from knowing serve to activate the conflict-detection demon shown in Figure 9.4. Activating the demon gives UC the goal of resolving the conflict. In this case, the metaplan of abandoning the lower-priority goal (helping the user) is used to resolve the conflict. To determine which goal is less important, UCEgo first searches for a direct precedence relationship (represented by a HAS-PRECEDENCE relation) between the two goals. If such a relation does not exist, then the search is expanded to include the causal parents of the goals. The search continues until the ultimate sources of the goals, which are usually UC themes, are included in the check for relative precedence relations. Since goal conflicts usually involve goals that originate from different UC themes and because all of UC's themes have an a priori relative precedence, UC-resolve-conflict is almost always able to decide which goal to abandon in order to resolve the conflict. In this case, UC's stay-alive life theme has greater apriori precedence than UC's consultant role theme, so UC abandons the lower-priority goal of helping the user by telling the user how to delete UC.

9.9 HANDLING USER MISCONCEPTIONS

User misconceptions are commonly encountered in systems like consultant programs where the system knows more than the user. A user is said to have a misconception when the user's beliefs conflict with what the consultation system knows. In order to respond properly in such cases, the consultant system must first determine that the user's beliefs conflict with what the system believes and then correct the user's misconception.

There has been considerable research on user misconceptions, both theoretical work on the types of misconceptions and concrete implementations of systems that can detect and correct some kinds of user misconceptions [Mays80, Webber83, Kaplan83, McCoy85, McCoy89, Marburger86, Quilici89]). However, none of these treat the interface as an intelligent agent. UC's agent approach allows greater flexibility in making principled decisions about when UC might wish to correct a user's misconception. For example, UC will decide that it should not correct a user's misconception when it would help the user do something that UC opposes.

9.9.1. Detecting Misconceptions in UC

User misconceptions are detected by UC during the processing of the user's query. Currently, UC handles only relational misconceptions, that is, misconceptions in which the user believes a relation holds between two objects when, in fact, such a relation cannot hold or does not happen to hold between those particular objects. UC does not handle object-oriented misconceptions, such as those for which [McCoy85] discusses correction strategies.

In processing the user's query, UC checks to see whether all relations mentioned by the user in the user's query have a counterpart in UC's knowledge base. For example, if the user asks, "What does ls −e do?" then UC's parser/understander understands part of this as a HAS-OPTION relation relating an instance of the **ls** command and an instance of the −e option. While looking for the effects of the command, UC finds that there is no corresponding HAS-OPTION relation between the **ls** command and the −e option in UC's knowledge base. At this point, UC suspects that the user may have a misconception.

In order to see whether the user actually has a misconception or whether UC just lacks information about this particular option of this command, UC checks with the KNOME subcomponent [Chin87, Chin89], which models the limitations of UC's knowledge base using *metaknowledge*. If KNOME has metaknowledge that UC knows all the options of this command, then UC knows that the user has a misconception. On the other hand, if the options of this command are not covered by KNOME's metaknowledge, then UC cannot assume that the user has a misconception. Instead, UC must assume that it lacks information about this command/option combination.

9.9.2. Correcting Misconceptions

After UC has determined either that the user has a misconception or that UC lacks knowledge, UCEgo decides how UC should reply to the user. When the user has a misconception, UCEgo tries to correct this misconception by denying that what the user mistakenly believes is the case. On the other hand, if UC determines that it lacks information, then UCEgo apologizes to the user for not knowing the answer to the user's query. These two types of responses are shown in the UC session of Figure 9.5.

In the first query, UC corrects the user's misconception that **who** has a −b option. It does this by first noticing that the user's usage of "who −b" translates into a *has-option* relation between a *UNIX-who-command* and a *-b option*. There is no equivalent *has-option* relation in UC's knowledge base, so UC suspects a possible user misconception. To see if this is the case or if UC just lacks knowledge about this particular option, UC consults the metaknowledge stored in KNOME. The appropriate metaknowledge in this case is the fact that UC knows all the options of all simple commands. Since **who** is a simple command, and since the *-b option* is not listed among the options

FIGURE 9.5

UC SESSION SHOWING DIFFERENT UC RESPONSES TO POSSIBLE
MISCONCEPTIONS

What does who -b do?

who does not have a -b option.

What does ruptime -t do?

I'm sorry, I do not know that.

---

of UNIX-*who-command* in UC's knowledge base, KNOME can infer that there
is no such option for **who**. Next, UCEgo decides that UC should correct the
user's misconception by denying the existence of a $-b$ option for **who**.

On the other hand, in the second query, UC professes ignorance about
the $-t$ option of the **ruptime** command. As in the previous query about **who**,
UC detects a possible misconception when it does not find a $-t$ option listed
for **ruptime** in its knowledge base. However, in this case, **ruptime** is a complex command, so the previous metaknowledge does not apply. There is no
metaknowledge about the options of complex commands (due to not enough
programming by UC's implementors rather than any inherent limitation of
UC), so UC cannot tell if **ruptime** has a $-t$ option. In order to be polite,
UCEgo apologizes to the user for not knowing.

9.10 FILLING GAPS IN USER KNOWLEDGE

A major difference between programs that purport to be consultants or tutors
and typical application programs is the fact that consultant/tutor programs
typically know more about their domain than their users. This leads to problems when users of a consultant system do not know enough to ask the right
questions. A tutoring system can usually avoid this problem by properly structuring tutoring sessions or by not providing the user with opportunities for
unconstrained inquiry. A consultant system, however, cannot utilize either
of these methods. It must be able to handle unconstrained inquiries from
the user in its domain and be prepared to deal with users that do not know
enough to ask the right questions.

One type of difficulty encountered by consultant systems in dealing
with users occurs when the user lacks some information that is useful for
the user's task. In such cases, the consultant should volunteer the information rather than waiting for the user to ask for it. Volunteering the
information solves the bottleneck problem that occurs when the user never
asks for needed information because the user does not realize than the
information is necessary.

9.10.1. Different kinds of Volunteered Information

In order to be able to volunteer information, a consultant system must do three things:

1. Determine that it would be helpful for the user to know some information.
2. Deduce whether the user already knows the information.
3. Inform the user when the system believes that the user does not know the information or when the system wants to remind the user of the information.

The kinds of information that might be volunteered by a consultant can be divided into three types: *warnings*, *suggestions*, and *elaborations*. Warnings are provided when the consultant believes there is a potential problem for the user. Suggestions are given to present alternatives and methodological hints to the user. Elaborations involve providing additional information that is relevant to the user's query. Each type of volunteered information is described in greater detail below.

9.10.2. Warnings

A consultant system should consider providing a warning to the user when the consultant believes that there may be a problem with the user's plans. Two factors come into play when deciding whether to give a warning. The first factor is the likelihood that the problem will actually occur. For example, if the user wants to print a file, the user's plan may fail if there is a power blackout or if the printer is out of ink. The chances of a problem caused by a power blackout are so unlikely that giving such a warning would be unreasonable. On the other hand, it may be reasonable to warn the user about the printer being out of ink if the consultant knows that the printer is currently low or out of ink or if this particular printer is so heavily used that it frequently runs out of ink.

Another factor in deciding whether to give a warning to the user is the consultant's belief about whether the user is already aware of the potential problem. Being aware of the problem implies that the user knows both that there is a potential problem with this type of plan and that this problem may arise in this case. If the consultant believes that the user is already aware of the potential problem, then the consultant does not need to warn the user. If the consultant believes that the user knows about this class of problem but might not apply this knowledge in this particular case, then the consultant should remind the user with a warning. In some cases, the potential problem may be important enough that the consultant may wish to remind the user even though the user is already aware of the problem.

Common warnings include telling the user about a plan's preconditions that are commonly violated and telling the user about a plan's deleterious sideeffects. An example of warning the user about a commonly violated precondition is:

User: How can I delete the directory named misc?

UC: Type 'rmdir misc.' However, rmdir works only if the directory is empty.

In the example, UC warns the user about a precondition of the **rmdir** plan, namely that the directory must be empty. This precondition is commonly violated, hence it is something that should be mentioned to the user. This can be contrasted to other preconditions of **rmdir,** such as the need for write permission on the directory containing the directory to be deleted. This precondition is much less frequently violated, so it need not be mentioned to the user. Such frequency information is stored as *concerns* [Luria87] by the UNIX domain planning component of UC. When the UNIX domain planner creates a plan, it passes along to UCEgo those preconditions that have a high degree of concern. UCEgo then decides whether to warn the user about the precondition, depending on whether or not KNOME believes that the user already knows that this type of problem may arise in this such plans. Since KNOME does not model the user's ability to apply general knowledge to individual cases, UCEgo can only assume that, if the user knows about this problem in general, then the user will know that it applies in this specific case. So UCEgo provides a warning only when KNOME believes that the user does not know about the precondition to the plan.

Warnings about a plan's deleterious side effects are handled in a similar fashion. The UNIX domain planner stores concerns about the side effects of plans and returns them along with the plan that it produced. In the following example, UC warns the user about one of **mv**'s deleterious side effects, namely that **mv** will overwrite files:

User: How can I move the file named new to the file named old?

UC: Type 'mv new old'. However, be careful, since if the file named old exists, it will be deleted.

9.10.3. Suggestions

Suggestions are provided by a system to present alternative plans to the user and to present methodological hints to the user. A trace of a UC dialogue in which UC volunteers a suggestion to the user is shown in Figure 9.6.

Since UC was not programmed with direct access to UNIX, UC does not know who is on the system. Hence UC apologizes to the user in order to be polite. However, UC does know how the user can find out who is on the

FIGURE 9.6

UC SESSION SHOWING UC VOLUNTEERING A SUGGESTION TO THE USER

 # Who is on the system?

I'm sorry, I do not know that.
To find out, type 'who'.

---

system, namely by using the **who** command. So, if UC believes that the user does not already know about the **who** command, UC will suggest this plan to the user. If UC were expanded to allow direct access to UNIX, then UC would not only tell the user who is on the system, but it would also volunteer information about the **who** command if UC did not believe that the user already knows about **who**.

Figure 9.7 shows the demon that detects the subgoal of having the user know how to find out something that the user wishes to know when the user

FIGURE 9.7

IF-DETECTED DEMON THAT SUGGESTS HOW TO FIND OUT INFORMATION

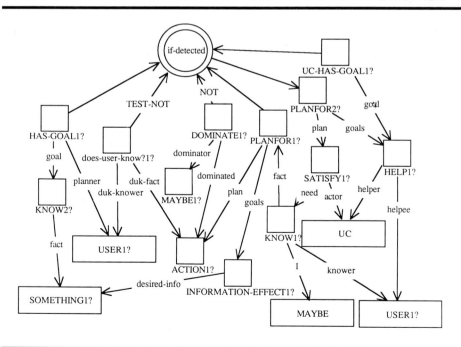

does not know this particular plan for finding out the required information (obviously, the user does know one plan for finding out, namely, ask UC).

This demon is activated in the following situations:

1. UC wants to help the user (UC-HAS-GOAL1).
2. The user wants to know something (HAS-GOAL1).
3. There is a specific (tested by the NOT DOMINATE1 test)[2] plan for finding out (INFORMATION-EFFECT1) the information.
4. The user does not know the plan (tested by the TEST-NOT, does-user-know?1, which represents a call to KNOME).

In such situations, the daemon asserts that a plan for helping the user is to adopt the subgoal of having the user know the plan for finding out the information.

The previous example shows how UCEgo proceeds when it fails to find a plan for a goal. It adopts the metagoal of finding a plan for that goal. In this case, UC does not know who is on the system, so it adopts the metagoal of knowing a plan for finding out who is on the system. UC's UNIX domain planner returns the plan of using the **who** command, which UC cannot use because it does not have direct access to UNIX. However, UC can suggest this plan to the user who does have access to UNIX and so can use the plan. The if-detected demon shown in Figure 9.7 suggests the plan (for helping the user) of adopting the subgoal of having the user know the **who** plan. Note that the daemon only suggests this plan if KNOME believes that the user does not already know about **who**. After all, it is possible that the user does know **who**, but instead decided to ask UC in order to find out the information (a plan that fails in this case). Some other examples of the same type are shown in Figure 9.8.

The last example shows a *reminder*-type suggestion. Reminders are given when the system believes that the user already knows some information but also that the user is likely to forget or ignore the information. In such cases, the system issues a reminder. In this example, KNOME believes that the user already knows about filing printer output in the boxes, so normally UCEgo would abandon the goal of suggesting that to the user. However, in this case it is likely that the user will shirk this duty, so UCEgo decides to provide the suggestion as a reminder.

In general, to issue a reminder-type suggestion requires that a system perform the following:

---

[2] The NOT designation allows encoding situations involving the absence of certain relations. The DOMINATE relation is a trick to allow the specification of additional category memberships for any node, or in this case, node ACTION1's lack of membership in the MAYBE category (which indicates that a concept is hypothetical).

FIGURE 9.8
UC SESSION SHOWING SUGGESTIONS BY UC

 # What is Chin's office?

I'm sorry, I do not know that.
To find out, type 'finger chin'.

 # What is the inode of the file named junk?

I'm sorry, I do not know that.
To find, type 'ls -i'.

 # How can I print a file on the laser printer?

Use lpr -Plz.
Don't forget to file the printer output in the boxes.

---

1. Detect some useful information for suggestion to the user.
2. Determine that the user is likely to forget or ignore the information.
3. Inform the user if the system believes that the user needs to be reminded of the information.

Whether a user is likely to forget or ignore information is represented in UC in a fashion similar to concerns [Luria87]. Facts that users are likely to forget or ignore are marked as needing reminders. Since UC will provide a reminder-type suggestion regardless of whether the user already knows the information, there is not the need to check for this as there is in other types of suggestions. On the other hand, UC does need to check whether it has direct evidence during the current session that the user is cognizant of the information. So, if the user has mentioned the information previously or if UC has previously reminded the user of the information, then UC does not provide a reminder-type suggestion to the user.

9.10.4. Elaborations

Elaborations are given when the user asks a simple yes/no question and the system volunteers more information than a simple yes/no answer. This type of volunteered information has been termed *overanswering* by [Wahlster83], who implemented overanswering in the HAM-ANS natural-language system. An example of elaboration produced by UC is shown in Figure 9.9.

Elaborations such as this require the system to recognize that the user not only has the goal of knowing whether **rn** is used to rename files but also that this goal is a subgoal of two possible parent goals, namely knowing the effects of the **rn** command and knowing how to rename files. In UC,

FIGURE 9.9

UC SESSION SHOWING AN ELABORATION IN UC'S RESPONSE
TO THE USER

 # Is rn used to rename files?

No, rn is used to read news.
To rename a file, use mv.

---

these deductions are made by UC's goal analysis component, PAGAN. After PAGAN has deduced the user's goals, UCEgo proceeds by adopting all of the user's possible goals. In cases where the answer is *yes*, both potential parent goals are satisfied by the simple answer of *yes*, so all three goals can be merged into a single goal (see Section 9.8.1), and no elaboration is needed. However, in Figure 9.9, a *no* answer satisfies only the user's immediate goal of knowing whether **rn** is used to rename files, and it does not satisfy either possible parent goal. In such cases, UCEgo proceeds to process both parent goals and produces answers to satisfy both. The parent goal of knowing the effects of the **rn** command is addressed by, "rn is used to read news." The other parent goal of knowing how to rename files is answered with, "To rename a file, use mv." When KNOME believes that the user already knows one of these elaborations, only the other elaboration is given to the user.

This goal-based approach to elaboration can be compared to the overanswering methodology of HAM-ANS. HAM-ANS used specific strategies such as filling optional deep case slots in the case frame associated with a verb used in the user's request. The problem with such non–goal-based approaches is that they are prone to volunteering information that the user may not actually be interested in. For example, when the user asks HAM-ANS, "Has a yellow car gone by?" HAM-ANS elaborates upon the *where* case-slot to produce the answer, "Yes, one yellow one on Hartungstreet." This is a good answer if the user were actually interested in where the yellow car passed by. However, if the user were interested in how long ago the car passed by, then an elaborative answer like, "Yes, fifteen minutes ago," would be much better. Likewise, if the user were interested in following the yellow car, then a better answer would be, "Yes, north on Hartungstreet."

In order to choose between such different elaborations, an analysis of the user's goals is needed. For example, if the user had prefaced the question by the statement, "My friend is supposed to pick me up here," then an analysis of the user's goals would show that the user is probably more interested in how long ago the yellow car passed by. On the other hand, if the user is a police officer chasing a vehicle, then the user is probably interested in following the yellow car. So, deciding how to elaborate a yes/no answer requires a goal-based elaboration strategy such as the one used in UC.

Besides being useful for deciding exactly how to elaborate a *yes/no* answer, a goal-based strategy also tells the system whether it is useful to elaborate at all. For example, when the user asks UC, "Is compact used to compact files?" then a simple answer of *yes* is quite sufficient. There is no need for UC to elaborate on this answer because it addresses all of the user's possible parent goals.

9.11 CONCLUSIONS

This paper demonstrates that an intelligent interface that knows more than its user needs to be an intelligent agent in order to respond properly to its user. An intelligent agent based on goals and plans is the most flexible, because such a system can more easily detect positive and negative goal interactions. Within this planning paradigm, the key problem for building an intelligent agent is how to *detect* the right goals for the agent in appropriate *situations*. Once an agent has adopted appropriate goals, planning to satisfy those goals is a better-understood problem.

ACKNOWLEDGMENTS

The work described in this paper was done at the University of California, Berkeley, as part of my Ph.D. thesis. I wish to thank Robert Wilensky, who supervised this work. I also wish to thank the past and present members of BAIR (Berkeley Artificial Intelligence Research) who have contributed in various ways to the UC project.

REFERENCES

[Allen79] Allen, J. F. 1979. *A Plan-Based Approach to Speech Act Recognition.* Ph.D. thesis, Department of Computer Science, University of Toronto. Also available as Technical Report 131, University of Toronto.

[Austin62] Austin, J. L. 1962. *How to Do Things with Words.* London: Oxford University Press.

[Carbonell70a] Carbonell, J. R. 1970. An Artificial-Intelligence Approach to Computer Assisted Instruction. *IEEE Transactions on Man-Machine-Systems,* MMS-11 (4), 190–202.

[Carbonell70b] Carbonell, J. R. 1970. *Mixed-Initiative Man-Computer Instructional Dialogues.* Ph.D. thesis, Massachusetts Institute of Technology. Also available as *Technical Report 1971,* Bolt Beranek and Newman.

[Carbonell82] Carbonell, J. G. 1982. Where Do Goals Come From? In *Proceedings of the Fourth Annual Conference of the Cognitive Science Society,* Ann Arbor, August, pp. 191–194.

[Chin87] Chin, D. N. 1987. *Intelligent Agents as a Basis for Natural Language Interfaces.* Ph.D. thesis, University of California, Berkeley. Also available as *Technical Report UCB/CSD 88/396,* Computer Science Division, University of California, Berkeley.

[Chin89] Chin, D. N. 1989. Knome: Modeling What the User Knows in UC. In Kobsa, A., and Wahlster, W. eds. *User Models in Dialog Systems.* Berlin: Springer-Verlag, pp. 74–107.

[Faletti82] Faletti, J. 1982. PANDORA-A Program for Doing Commonsense Planning in Complex Situations. In *Proceedings of the Second Annual National Conference on Artificial Intelligence,* Pittsburgh, August, pp. 185–188.

[Fikes71] Fikes, R. E., and Nilsson, N. J. 1971. STRIPS: A New Approach to the Application of Theorem Proving to Problem Solving. *Artificial Intelligence,* 2 (3–4), 189–208.

[Hobbs80] Hobbs, J. R., and Evans, D. A. 1980. Conversation as Planned Behavior. *Cognitive Science,* 4 (4), 349–377.

[Kaplan83] Kaplan, S. J. 1983. Cooperative responses from a Portable Natural Language Database Query System. In Brady, M., and Berwick, R. C. eds. *Computational Models of Discourse.* Cambridge, MA: MIT Press.

[Luria85] Luria, M. 1985. Commonsense Planning in a Consultant System. In *Proceedings, 1985 IEEE International Conference on Systems, Man, and Cybernetics,* Tucson, pp.602–606.

[Luria87] Luria, M. 1987. Expressing Concern. In *Proceedings of the 25th Annual Meeting of the Association for Computational Linguistics,* Stanford, CA, July, pp. 221–227.

[Luria88] Luria, M. 1988. *Knowledge Intensive Planning.* Ph.D. thesis, University of California, Berkeley.

[Marburger86] Marburger, H. 1986. A Strategy for Producing Cooperative Nl Reactions in a Database Interface. In *Proceedings of AIMSA-86,* Wana, Bulgaria.

[Mays80] Mays, E. 1980. Failures in Natural Language Systems: Applications to Data Base Query Systems. In *Proceedings of the National Conference on Artificial Intelligence,* Stanford, CA, August, pp. 327–330.

[McCoy85] McCoy, K. F. 1985. *Correcting Object-Related Misconceptions.* Ph.D. thesis, University of Pennsylvania, Department of Computer and Information Science, Moore School. Also available at *Technical Report MS-CIS-85-57.*

[McCoy89] McCoy, K. F. 1989. Highlighting a User Model to Respond to Misconceptions. In Kobsa, A., and Wahlster, W. eds. *User Model in Dialog Sytems.* Berlin: Springer-Verlag, pp. 233–254.

[Meehan76] Meehan, J. R. 1976. *The Metanovel: Writing Stories by Computer.* Ph.D. thesis, Yale University. Also available as *Yale University Computer Science Research Report #74* and through New York: Garland Publishing, 1980.

[Norvig83] Norvig, P. 1983. Frame Activated Inferences in a Story Understanding Program. In *Proceedings of the Eighth International Joint Conference on Artificial Intelligence,* Karlsruhe, West Germany, August, pp. 624–626.

[Newell72] Newell, A., and Simon, H. A. 1972. *Human Problem Solving.* Englewood Clifts, NJ, Prentice-Hall.

[Quilici89] Quilici, A. 1989. Recognizing and Responding to Plan-Oriented Misconceptions. In Kobsa, A., and Wahlster, W. eds. *User Models in Dialog Systems,* Berlin: Springer-Verlag, pp. 108–132.

[Schank77] Schank, R. C., and Abelson, R. P. 1977. *Scripts, Goals, and Understanding.* Hillsdale, NJ: Lawrence Erlbaum.

[Sacerdoti74] Sacerdoti, E. D. 1974. Planning in a Hierarchy of Abstraction Spaces. *Artificial Intelligence,* 5 (2), 115–135.

[Searle69] Searle, J. R. 1969. *Speech Acts; An Essay in the Philosophy of Language.* Cambridge, England: Cambridge University Press.

[Wahlster83] Wahlster, W., Marburger, H., Jameson, A., and Busemann, S. 1983. Over-answering Yes-No-Questions: Extended Responses in a Nl Interface to a Vision System. In *Proceedings of the Eighth International Joint conference on Artificial Intelligence,* Karlsruhe, West Germany, August, pp. 643–646.

[Webber83] Webber, B. L., and Mays, E. 1983. Varieties of User Misconceptions: Detection and Correction. In *Proceedings of the Eighth International Joint Conference of Artificial Intelligence,* vol. 2, pp. 650–652, Karlsruhe, West Germany, August.

[Wilensky84] Wilensky R., Arens, Y., and Chin, D. N. 1984. Talking to Unix in English: An Overview of UC. *Communications of the ACM,* 27 (6), 574–593.

[Wilensky78] Wilensky, R. 1978. *Understanding Goal-Based Stories.* Ph.D. thesis, Yale University. Also Available as *Yale University Computer Science Research Report #140,* New Haven.

[Wilensky83] Wilensky, R. 1983. *Planning and Understanding: A Computational Approach to Human Reasoning.* Reading, MA: Addison-Wesley.

[Wilensky86] Wilensky, R., Mayfield, J., Albert, A., Chin, D. N., Cox, C., Luria, M., Martin, J., and Wu, D. 1986. UC—A Progress Report. *Technical Report UCB/CSD 87/303.* Computer Science Division, University of California, Berkeley.

[Wilensky87] Wilensky, R. 1987. Some Problems and Proposals for Knowledge Representation. *Technical Report UCB/CSD 87/351.* Computer Science Division, University of California, Berkeley.

PART

DYNAMIC
PRESENTATION DESIGN

CHAPTER 10

GRAPHICS AND NATURAL LANGUAGE AS COMPONENTS OF AUTOMATIC EXPLANATION

STEVEN F. ROTH, JOE MATTIS, *and* **XAVIER MESNARD**
Robotics Institute
Carnegie-Mellon University

ABSTRACT

This paper presents an approach to the automatic explanation of changes in the results generated by quantitative modeling systems. These explanations combine both text and graphics, and therefore serve as a vehicle for exploring the interaction between these two modes of presentation. The approach integrates research from three different areas. Relevant content for explanations is determined using extensions of previous work on comparative analysis of financial models. Text discourse planning is performed by applying techniques of rhetorical modeling to the analysis of explanatory dialogues. Graphical presentation is accomplished by extending prior work on the automatic design of displays of quantitative data. An important issue is how the generality and application independence of these separate components can be preserved and still produce integrated responses. Therefore, this paper also presents an approach to coordinating textual and graphical presentations.

10.1 INTRODUCTION

Explanation of Quantitative Models. Understanding change is one of the most important and time-consuming tasks in the use of quantitative modeling systems. Users of these systems frequently ask questions like:

- "Why did the yearly budget projections increase from last month's estimate to this?"
- "Why did the end date of the project occur much later than expected?"
- "Why did the air-pollution index increase from scenario 1 to scenario 2, even though average wind speed increased?"

These questions reflect the fact that users of modeling systems typically create several sets of input data representing different assumptions, estimates, or events. The function of the system is to rapidly calculate results for each input set by propagating values through many variables via algebraic equations. Having generated the results, users must then examine the changes in values throughout their models and navigate through the equations to determine their causes. When algebraic models are integrated with other databases, users must also search for important attributes that help identify variables, as well as the processes and events with which they are associated.

Although analyzing change is an extremely commonplace activity for users of spreadsheet, database, scheduling, and other quantitative modeling packages, virtually no capabilities exist commercially for supporting it. Similarly, in contrast to the high priority given to research on explanatory capabilities for expert systems, relatively little research has occurred on explanation of change for quantitative modeling systems [Kosy84; Roth88; Roth90a].

As a result, the focus of our research has been the development of explanatory capabilities for quantitative models. Our goal has been a system that automatically produces explanations that (1) isolate portions of models relevant to understanding changes and their interaction; (2) determine the significance of changes; (3) determine supportive quantitative facts that are useful for understanding change in a domain; (4) describe important qualitative characteristics that identify, classify, and aggregate objects associated with variables that change; (5) compose texts that navigate through large models in a way appropriate to explanatory dialogues at computer terminals; and (6) design effective graphical displays that support explanation. The immediate goal of SAGE, a system for automatic and graphical explanation, was to provide these capabilities.

Automatic Presentation. Apart from being an important interface problem in its own right, explanation generation has also provided an excellent opportunity to study the problems of automatic graphics and text presentation. Effective explanations contain very different types of information and therefore require both modes of presentation. Natural language is useful for conveying causal relationships, summarizing and describing the interactions among changes, and focusing attention while navigating through large models. In contrast, graphical displays (including tables) are more effective when many quantities must be presented and compared and for portraying the hierarchical and relational dependencies underlying the equations (as in financial budgets and activity schedules). The need for both modes of presentation provided an excellent test bed for studying automatic, multimodal presentation.

Approaches to automatic presentation have varied along a continuum, which reflects the degree to which presentation knowledge is domain independent or specialized. For example, the work of [Neal91] and [Arens91] has required highly specialized graphical displays and corresponding presentation knowledge to deal with the unique requirements of interfaces for manipulating objects on geographic representations. At the other end of the continuum is work by [Mackinlay86; Mackinlay91], who demonstrated that combinations of conventional presentation graphics (e.g., bar and plot charts, graphs) could be designed automatically with domain-independent graphical knowledge. The advantage to the latter approach is the ability to use the same automatic presentation capabilities across many applications, although this work was limited to graphical displays.

Our approach to explanation involves developing general and independent components for selecting the content of explanations as well as for automatically designing graphical presentations and selecting and ordering sequences of assertions to be expressed textually. The generality of the text-discourse presentation component provides the ability to express explanations of different types of quantitative models. The independence of the graphics component enables it to be used to provide the presentation capabilities for other applications besides supporting explanations (e.g., a database query system).

The Need for Coordination. The price of maintaining the independence of these components is the difficulty of coordinating their operation in a system that must produce both text and graphics, especially over the course of an explanatory dialogue. Solving the coordination problem requires distributing content between the two modes and designing combinations of text and graphics that are structurally compatible and that refer to each other appropriately. These capabilities require an architecture that allows coordinated operation and feedback between graphical design and text discourse planning.

This paper presents our approach to explanation of quantitative models and an approach to automatic multimodal presentation. We also present an architecture for coordinating the design of textual and graphical presentations. Section 10.2 describes the domain in which this work occurred and the types of quantitative models that are to be explained. Section 10.3 provides an overview of our approaches and a review of related research. Sections 10.4, 10.5, and 10.6 describe components for selecting the content, composing text discourse sequences, and designing graphical displays, respectively. Finally, Section 10.6 describes an analysis of the coordination problem and an architectural solution.

10.2 PROBLEM OVERVIEW: EXPLANATION OF QUANTITATIVE MODELS

Comparison in Project Management. The need for automatically generated explanations of quantitative models became apparent during our previous work on an intelligent project management system called CALLISTO, the goal of which was to support the management of large engineering design or construction projects [Sathi86]. In order to plan, track, and evaluate the status of these projects, most companies use a collection of conventional spreadsheet and scheduling packages. These packages allow users to construct sets of quantitative variables and algebraic equations to represent the activities, resources, and processes of their businesses and the financial and temporal relations among them. The inputs to these models are estimates or measurable quantities representing conditions and events in the company (e.g., durations of activities, delivery dates and prices for materials, number and wage-rates of personnel). The results computed with the models correspond to important outcomes (e.g., projected completion dates, total expenses, resource needs).

Project modeling systems (PMS) are used not only to compute outputs from a single set of inputs. More commonly, they are used repeatedly to understand the interactions among numerous changing conditions and their consequences for important outcomes. Managers often need to compare the results generated from different input sets, such as:

- Estimates versus actual values (e.g., anticipated schedule dates versus actual progress),
- Data on performance over successive time periods (e.g., monthly profit projections), and
- Estimates based on different assumptions about the events that will occur in an organization (e.g., in scheduling construction projects, different estimates result from different assumptions about weather, productivity, materials availability, or technological choices).

Comparing the effects of different data sets on a model is a common, albeit time-consuming, activity because it helps managers determine project areas that may need attention. In addition, weekly comparisons are necessary because of the changeable nature of large projects, which managers must be able to analyze to determine causes of change. These situations result in managerial questions like:

- Why did Bill Smith's activities cost more than expected in the estimate?
- Why is the end date of the design approval activity later in this week's schedule, as compared to last week's?
- Why do John's estimates for total resource needs differ from Sue's?
- How did the change in the duration of the structural design activity affect the change in the start date of the frame assembly activity?

Questions like these are not easily answered using commercial project-modeling systems because no support is provided for comparing and understanding change. There is a clear need for a system that can automatically explain changes in model results in terms of the interaction of variables from which they are derived [Roth90a]. To illustrate this need, Figure 10.1 contains three miniature PMS models that are integrated here to compute project costs and schedules. Each model illustrates different aspects of the need for automatic explanation.

Financial Spreadsheet Model. The right side of the figure is a graph visualization of a fragment of a common spreadsheet budget. Nodes represent variables, which are computed from their immediate descendents in the graph. The algebraic equations linking variables are indicated by listing the operators beneath the variables. For example, *project-costs = activity-labor-costs + materials-costs + overhead-costs.* The important characteristics of this type of model for explaining change are that (1) the equations often involve non-linear relationships, (2) the model structure may often be non-tree-like (i.e., the same variable may occur in several equations), (3) there are no explicit semantics for understanding the meaning of the variables or equations, and (4) the model can be very large and, as a result, difficult to search to locate causes of change in each variable.

In order to support analysis of models like these, an explanation system must help determine significance, isolate common causes of changes, and support model navigation.

Alternative additive models. The upper left side of Figure 10.1 illustrates another type of model that is simpler algebraically but richer semantically than the previous one. This type of model exploits a strict hierarchical grouping of objects in a domain to aggregate some quantitative attribute. In this case, the objects are the activities necessary to complete a project, the attribute is their individual labor-costs, and the means by which activities are grouped and their costs aggregated is the organizational structure of a company. The vertical links represent group membership.

The semantics of activities, organizational entities, and the relations among them can be used to generate an additive model that aggregates cost (or any other activity quantity). There are many possible structures for grouping different objects in project management. For example, activities can be grouped and their quantities aggregated based on (1) the part-whole relations among the design components on which the activities work (using either spa-

FIGURE 10.1

THREE INTEGRATED MODELS

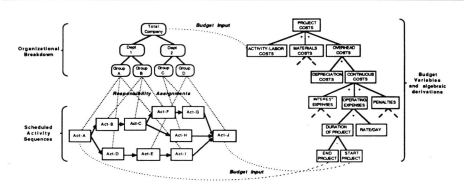

tial or functional design breakdowns), (2) a classification of resources the activities require, or (3) a classification of the activities themselves, based on the type of work they perform (e.g., in engineering projects: metal assembly, design, software debugging).

While the resulting hierarchical models are easier to analyze and search because of their additive properties, the semantics and uniformity of the variables provide the ability to summarize input changes on the basis of the groups that contain them. For example, managers use this type of model to ask whether most of the changes occurred among activities that are the responsibility of particular departments, or that work on some parts of a design, or that use certain types of materials. This task is made difficult by the large size of these models, the number of alternative hierarchical groupings, and the need to perform implicit statistical analyses to determine which model best localizes (within a particular group or variable) a significant portion of the changes. An explanation system must be able to perform tasks of hierarchical model selection and summarization.

Scheduling model. The third type of model, illustrated in the lower left of Figure 10.1 is an activity network used to generate schedules. While the organizational grouping of activities is used to aggregate costs or other quantities, the precedence relations in the activity network represent equations involving the start dates, durations, and end dates of the activities (specifically, an activity's start date = the maximum of the end dates of all prior activities, which are linked to it by a horizontal arrow; end date = start date + duration). The inputs to this model are the activity durations (or estimates) and the start date of the first activity. The outputs are all other start and end dates. In addition, there are a variety of derived quantities that give important information to managers about the interaction of activity values (e.g., project end date, slack, and criticality).

While the variables are uniform, the nonlinearities created by the *max* function of the start-date equation make it difficult to determine which duration changes were responsible for the change in a particular date. As with the other models, the occurrence of hundreds of activities or more makes this task tedious as well. Analysis must not proceed one activity at a time, but in terms of whole paths of activities. Furthermore, because activities can be grouped by their semantic properties, it is often useful for managers to find a single structure in the hierarchical model to classify the *causes of a change,* producing statements like, "The change in the end date of the project was due to changes in durations of activities that are the responsibility of Dept. 1 and Group D, and the activities that work on CPU design." This type of analysis provides some necessary information for determining the underlying problems responsible for changes in a model's inputs. An explanation system must be able to classify causes of change and group changes based on the unique algebraic properties of schedule paths.

Finally, it's important to note that these three model types are often integrated into a single analysis, which increases the difficulty of understanding a change in any one. The budget model in Figure 10.1, for example, contains a variable that computes expenses based on the duration of the project (operating expenses). Since the duration is computed from the project end date, it requires understanding why the schedule dates changed. Understanding schedule date changes may in turn require identifying the organizational groups in which they occur. Another analysis of the organizational breakdown may be necessary for understanding other variables in the budget model (e.g., activity-labor costs are computed from the organizational breakdown). The point is that answering a question like, "Why is our projection of project cost greater this week as compared to last week?" requires an analysis of all three model components.

To reiterate, explanatory capabilities were needed in this domain to help users understand the causes of change throughout quantitative models, including the ability to (1) isolate portions of models relevant to understanding changes and their interaction; (2) determine the significance of changes; (3) determine supportive quantitative facts that are useful for understanding change in a domain (e.g., properties like *slack* or *paths* in schedules); (4) describe important qualitative characteristics that identify, classify, and aggregate objects associated with variables that change; (5) compose texts that navigate through large models in a way appropriate to explanatory dialogues at computer terminals; and (6) design effective graphical displays that support explanation.

10.3 OVERVIEW OF SAGE APPROACH

The goal of this work was to develop an approach to the explanation of change in quantitative modeling systems. More generally, we are concerned with problems of composing texts and selecting and designing pictures and the problems of coordinating the two modes.

Figure 10.2 illustrates some rough architectural distinctions we have used to segment areas of study and simplify implementation. Boxes represent processes, and ovals represent data. The process of responding to a request for an explanation involves serial stages of *content selection* and *content expression*. This division between deciding what to say and how to say it has been useful in systems for text planning [McKeown85][1] and graphical design. The division allows consideration of the different ways that the same information can be expressed, depending on the goals and constraints of the discourse and graphical context, including: the type of communication (terminal dialogue or paper report), the goals expressed in a user's question, and the availability of graphics (i.e. whether content can be distributed across graphics and text).

---

[1] We acknowledge the difficulties in maintaining strict serial independence between these stages [Appelt81]. In fact, our approach to coordinating text and graphics required interaction between the two stages, allowing feedback to content selection for graphics to occur based on the quality of generated displays. In addition, some content selection occurs as part of text discourse composition, which must prune details based on pragmatics.

FIGURE 10.2
SAGE SYSTEM ARCHITECTURE

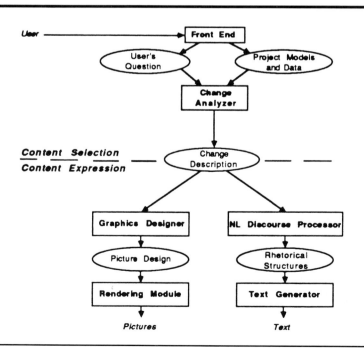

Our approach has been to extend and integrate four separate research areas within a single architecture. The starting point for our approach to content selection was work by [Kosy84] on ERGO, a system for supporting users of financial spreadsheets by identifying and explaining the causes of changes in results produced by these models. The models that ERGO explained contained no more semantics than what was represented by sets of variables in equations. Its contribution was a procedure called comparative analysis, which determines the significant causes of change within an equation. We needed to extend this approach to perform summarization, hierarchical model selection, and navigation through multiple equations at once. Extensions were also needed to exploit semantic relationships associated with variables and additional navigational knowledge for analyzing schedule models.

The design of components for content expression were influenced by the TEXT system [McKeown85], which organizes the content of descriptive texts about database structure using a model of expository prose, and by the BLAH system [Weiner80], which explains expert system conclusions using a discourse model derived from protocols of human justifications. In a similar manner, SAGE's multisentence texts are organized to reflect the structure of human explanations of causally related quantitative facts and descriptions of graphical presentations.

In addition, our work on content expression was influenced by APT [Mackinlay86], an approach to the presentation of quantitative information through the automatic design of graphical displays. Our goal was to develop capabilities not addressed in APT, including attention to users' information-seeking goals, awareness of many more data characteristics relevant to real databases (e.g., complex data types, missing data), and a larger repertoire of graphical design knowledge and techniques. We were also concerned with defining the capabilities required of a graphical system for coordinating it with textual presentation and application programs in general.

The components of SAGE are illustrated in Figure 10.2. Content selection (performed by a change analyzer) follows processing of a user's question and produces a change description: a set of frame-based assertions about the changes, their significance, the ways they combine and interact, the causal relations among them, and the qualitative attributes that serve to describe the objects that variables represent.

The information contained in the change description is expressed by separate text-discourse and graphics components. As Figure 10.2 suggests, our initial approach was to maintain parallel, independent text-discourse and picture-generation processes. This simplified the research tasks and allowed us to study the needs for coordination before making any architectural commitments or being concerned with distributing content across the two modes. Nonetheless, the essential operation of these components is similar in the coordinated architecture, and we postpone our discussion of these complexities until the last section.

We should also emphasize our focus on *strategic* rather than *tactical* processes [Thompson77]. For natural-language discourse, this means we are interested in decisions about the content and pragmatic structure of multi-sentence texts, and not with surface-level syntactic or lexical processing. Therefore, the text generator in Figure 10.2 was not a concern of our research and was developed in an ad-hoc manner for our application. Similarly for graphics, we are interested in picture-selection and design, not surface-level picture generation, so the rendering module was not developed in a general way.

The next four sections discuss content selection, textual and graphical expression, and our approach to coordination.

10.4 CONTENT SELECTION

The function of content selection: an analogy. The function of content selection is to determine from all information contained in a model which facts are relevant for understanding a change in a variable. It is analogous to a human speaker's attempts to understand a process prior to planning how to describe it to a listener. For example, in response to the question, "How can I get to Carnegie Hall?" one might first think about its location in an internal map of a city and some possible routes. This is a narrow partition of all possible locations and routes in a city. Further content selection might introduce results of brief mental analyses of typical traffic conditions along different routes and decisions about what would be visible landmarks (both based on the time of day). A speaker can think about this information independently of how it is to be expressed, although it is unlikely that expression follows selection in a strict serial fashion.

Analogously, our approach to content selection occurs in two stages. The first involves finding a narrow partition of all variables, data, equations, semantic relations, and attributes in a model that could potentially be related to the change in a variable (analogous to the set of possible routes and locations). This stage also reflects the focal points of a user's question. For example, different portions of a model would be relevant for answering questions like, "Why did X increase?" vs. "Why did X increase even though Y decreased?".

Our approach to this first stage of content selection is analogous to McKeown's partitioning of a *relevant knowledge pool* for descriptions of database structure and content. It is also related to the implicit content selection that occurs in diagnostic or other reasoning systems, which isolates from all input or derived facts those relevant for reaching a conclusion. In the latter case, selection has sometimes been based on the content's complexity and importance to a user [Swartout83].

The second stage of content selection involves analyses for deriving other quantitative facts about the interactions among changes in a model. These can further narrow the relevant partition or be used to clarify causal relationships (analogous to decisions about traffic conditions and landmarks). These include:

1. Measures of significance that further partition the relevant content (resulting in pruning of *insignificant* branches of a network of variables, equations, and related semantic attributes),

2. Information that describes the *net effect* of each variable's change when a nonlinear relationship exists (e.g., when $A = \mathrm{MAX}[B, C], B = 10$ and C changes from 5 to 15; the net effect of the change in C is only 5, since that is the amount by which A increased),

3. Information about the relationship between the direction of each variable's influence and that of other variables affecting a common target variable (i.e., whether the change in a variable exerted a force in the same direction or in an opposing or counteracting direction relative to others:) If $A = B + C + D$ and B and C decreased, but D increased, then D exerted a counteracting influence relative to B and C),

4. Derived quantities useful for qualifying some causal relationships (e.g., slack in activity schedules, measures of the uniformity of change among elements of a group of variables), and

5. Groupings or aggregations of changes that reflect underlying commonalities within the domain (e.g., total change in a path of activities, total change in a group of resources owned by one department).

The output of content selection consists of a set of frames and relations containing all the information mentioned above. In addition to the specific facts about changes, derived quantities, and qualitative attributes, the change description (CD) has a structure that parallels the model it characterizes and the pattern of causal relationships among relevant changes. Since each node in a CD corresponds to a change in a variable in a model, the CD can be viewed as an overlay and annotation of the model. Its structure is important for designing a presentation of the explanation, discussed in later sections.

An Illustration. Figure 10.3 illustrates these abstract categories with the results generated by content selection for a sample hierarchical, additive model of an organization, similar to the one in the upper left of Figure 10.1. The full model consists of cost variables representing each of the organizational groups in a company (in boxes) and activities for which they are responsible (in circles). In this case, a user asked about the change in total costs of Acme-Co (the topmost variable), so the entire model is initially selected as relevant. This was substantially pruned following the results of significance testing (e.g., the derivation of Advanced-Planning Center was pruned because it was not a significant cause of the Acme-Co change). Note that to conserve space some relevant branches are absent from the figure (e.g., the derivation of the Design Center and the Evaluation Center is only indicated with vertical links).

The important facts that would be contained in the CD for this model include:

FIGURE 10.3

THE RESULTS OF CONTENT SELECTION: A PARTITION OF A HIERARCHICAL-ADDITIVE MODEL.

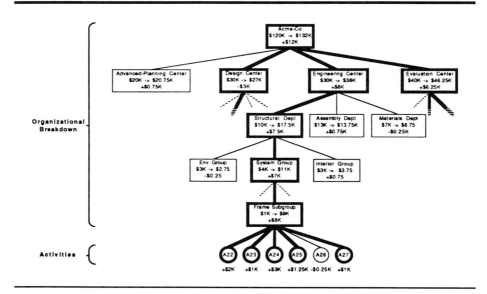

1. The significant components of change (indicated by bold nodes), their net effects at each level (net effect being the same as actual change because the model is additive),

2. The variables from which each significant variable was immediately computed (indicated by the links),

3. The semantic relationship underlying the computation of each variable (e.g., Engineering Center cost is based on the *has-organizational-part* relation to the center's departments; Frame Subgroup cost is based on the *has-responsibility-for* relation to specific activities),

4. Semantic attributes that identify each variable (e.g., for identifying activities and groups),

5. The values of all relevant variables in the two contexts (indicated in text within each node),

6. Whether the direction of each cause is counter to or consistent with the main effect (e.g., Engineering Center costs increased but were counteracted by a decrease in Design Center costs), and

7. The complexity of each equation (in this CD, the equations are all simple because the model is additive and the variables are homogeneous, all representing the costs).

The mechanisms by which this information is extracted from the input data and models includes a domain-independent component that determines the significant causes of a change in a variable in terms of the variables from which it is computed in an equation, based on the ERGO system [Kosy84]. Additional procedures are applied to choose effective hierarchical groupings of change for additive models and to partition and isolate critical paths in schedules prior to performing significance testing [Roth88, Roth91a]. While the complexity and structure of models differ, the same representation is used to describe the causal relationships in different models. As a result, the CD serves as a language for describing causal relations in a variety of models that can be expressed by a text-discourse processor. This serves to maintain the independence of presentation components from application-specific tasks of content selection (e.g., schedule analysis).

Once the CD assertions are created, they are ready to be expressed by the graphics and text-discourse components discussed in the next two sections.

10.5 TEXT-DISCOURSE PROCESSING

The function of the discourse component is to select and order the assertions of the change description in a manner that reflects the goals of each question and the constraints on dialogue length imposed by interactions at computer terminals. Following the approach of [McKeown85], goal differences correspond to different question types, which are realized by applying different rhetorical models for explaining different aspects of quantitative relationships. In our approach, the output of content selection is a complete set of relationships needed for explaining changes in the variables of a model. This set, and the discourse sequences produced to express it, depended on the type of question. Questions varied along two dimensions.

The first reflected whether a user was interested in just identifying a causal relation to a change (e.g., "What were the causes of the change in X?") or in understanding the full causal mechanism or model behavior underlying a causal relationship (e.g., "What were the causes of the change in X and how did they produce the change?"). The difference is in the kinds and amount of information needed to describe the behavior of a model in producing an effect (e.g., the ways effects combine, are mediated, and are moderated by the properties of equations). Questions about mechanisms are generally asked subsequent to cause identification to clarify relationships.

The second question dimension reflects whether the focus of a question is single or multiple and reflects whether a user specifies just the effect to be explained, or whether the relation between two changes is questioned (e.g., "What was the effect of the change in X on the change in Y?" or "*How* did the change in X affect the change in Y?"). A special case of this question is one that [Kosy84] calls *violated presupposition* (e.g., "Why did X increase, even though Y decreased?").

In sum, there are four question types derived from the two dimensions: **cause identification** versus **mechanism identification** and **single focus** versus **double focus**. The choice of question types and the corresponding discourse models designed to answer them reflected the kinds of questions and goals that were most commonly found in managers' analyses of PMS data. They are also implicit goals in many explanatory texts occurring in financial reports and process model descriptions.

Rhetorical Models. Each question leads to the selection of a rhetorical model, which constrains the kinds and sequences of facts that can be expressed in a text. A rhetorical model consists of a sequence of required and optional rhetorical categories or predicates. These were developed from protocols of managers' presentations about schedules and budgets, informal experiments in which business students explained changes in models and judged the acceptability of our own explanations, and from newspaper articles and financial reports. Predicates provide a set of primitive categories that can classify most of the rhetorical functions served by facts within explanatory texts for quantitative models.

Each predicate can be instantiated by one or more assertions from the application (i.e., the CD). While the predicates and sequential restrictions are meant to be application-independent, instantiation functions are needed to extract facts from the CD or other hypothetical application for analyzing change. The following are a few representative predicates and examples of corresponding assertions:

- *Change*: "The cost of activity X increased \$200."
- *Cause-effect*: "A caused B," or "B was due to A" where A and B are changes.
- *Mediation*: "The effect of A on B was mediated by C, D, E, and F."
- *Counteraction*: "The effect of A on B was counteracted by C."
- *Reinforcement*: "The effect of B on A was reinforced by C" (e.g., when B alone is sufficient to account for A, but C would have affected A, had B not occurred).
- *Moderating Influence*: "The effect of the delay of activity X on activity Y was small because Y could not start until January 1 anyway."
- *Constituency*: "A consists of B, C, and D", where A, B, C, and D might be groups (e.g., departments in a center) or composite changes.
- *Dependency*: "$A = B + C$" or "Activity X can start when Activity Y is complete."
- *Identification*: "The activities that require computer terminals."
- *Attribution*: "The value of A in version 1 is 3" or "Activity X works on the CPU design."

In addition to specifying a set of predicates and instantiation conditions, each rhetorical model describes alternative, acceptable predicate sequences.

For example, the simplest rhetorical model, *cause identification*, consists of a statement of the main cause-effect relationship, any counteracting or reinforcing relationships, and the main dependency the causal relations are based on (e.g., an equation or semantic relationship). In addition, since most of these predicates involve mentioning variables, they can sometimes be identified further as attributes of objects or groups of objects using identification or constituency predicates. There are a few alternative predicate orders based on focus considerations to provide smoother transitions across facts. Finally, for each cause and counteractant of a change, this sequence can be instantiated again to express more detailed or distant causes (i.e., each cause can be explained as an effect).

This predicate sequence is ordered to preserve the distinction between primary causes and those changes or processes that qualify them. The order also tends to preserve the coherence of changes that are related by a single equation or dependency by postponing the expansion of any one change (e.g., if $A = X/Y + Z$, then all changes and characteristics of this part of the model relevant to A in the CD will be expressed prior to the causes of change in X, Y, and Z). The text in Figure 10.4 illustrates some of these properties for the CD illustrated in Figure 10.3.

The first three predicates to be instantiated from the CD from Figure 10.3 express the main causes, the counteracting effect of the Design Center and the semantic relationship that underlies the algebraic dependency among the variables in the explanation of Acme-Co. If this had been a spreadsheet model with no further semantics, an equation would have been expressed instead. The decision to express the dependency in sentence 1 rather than 3 was based on focus considerations: most of the centers are mentioned in the other sentences, so expressing all of them first establishes focus better.

Dialogue Decisions. In addition to the sequential properties described by rhetorical models, it is necessary to make decisions about the amount of detail and suitable *pause points* in the explanation dialogue. An important property of dialogues (compared to reports) is the ability of a user to influence the depth or direction of an explanation. Decisions about what to say next and how much to say should be under user control whenever possible, but not so much that it becomes burdensome. Our attempt at compromise is based on the degree of uncertainty about the direction in which an explanation should proceed: As more directions are possible, more opportunities for user input are provided. In the absence of user input, the system assumes responsibility for control.

The change description (CD) in Figure 10.3 and the corresponding sample text in Figure 10.4 illustrate decisions about when to pause for user input and which details to prune. The dotted lines after sentences 3 and 7 are pause points. The decision to pause after sentence 7 was made because there are at least four directions from which to choose: further elaboration of either Frame Subgroup, Evaluation Center, or Design Center into its components; and further clarification of how the change in Frame Subgroup

FIGURE 10.4
SAMPLE TEXT GENERATED FOR CONTENT IN FIGURE 10.3.

>"Why did Acme-Co costs change from estimate-1 to estimate-2?"

(1) The organizational-parts of Acme-Co consists of Advanced-Planning, Design, Engineering, and Evaluation Centers. [Constituency]

(2) The increase in Acme-Co costs (+ $12000) was due to increases in Engineering Center (+ $8000) and Evaluation Center (+ $6250). [Cause-effect]

(3) These increases were partially counteracted by a decrease in Design Center (- $ 3000). [Counteraction]

- -

(4) The change in Engineering Center was due to changes in most of the activities which are the responsibility-of Frame Subgroup (+ $8000). [Cause-effect; Identification]

(5) Frame Subgroup is an organizational-part-of System Group. [Constituency]

(6) System Group is an organizational-part-of Structural Department. [Constituency]

(7) Structural Department is an organizational-part-of Engineering Center. [Constituency]

- -

(8) The increase related to Evaluation Center was . . . . .

---

propagated to affect Engineering Center. In the absence of user input, the system must base its decisions on the structure of the rhetorical model, continuing to elaborate the primary causes, then the counteractants, and reflecting any importance distinctions indicated by the CD. In line 4 of the example, the system's decision was to continue discussing the largest cause of the change in Acme-Co.

Decisions to prune information, particularly in the intermediate stages of a causal sequence (e.g., explaining the change in Engineering Center directly in terms of Frame Subgroup), were based on:

1. The complexity of the dependencies (in this model, simple sums make it easy to see the relationship between distant changes),

2. The number of significant branches emanating from each node (in this case, only one at each level until the subgroup is reached),

3. The number of nodes pruned (i.e., there is a limit on the size of jumps), and

4. Whether elaboration of a node would further distinguish causes from noncauses or merely enumerate its components (related to statistical judgments made by the Change Analyzer about whether a node adequately summarizes its components).

These four principles are application independent, although functions must be provided to realize them in each application.

In summary, the operation of the discourse processor is based on a definition of rhetorical categories underlying explanatory text, appropriate sequences in which they can occur, interface functions for instantiating the categories, and dialogue rules for determining pause points and levels of detail.

The output of the discourse processor is an ordered sequence of instantiated rhetorical predicates. These are input to a text generator, which uses templates and *smoothing functions* for sentence transitions, definite reference, and some forms of ellipsis to make the text less awkward. Our research is not concerned with the tactical issues of surface generation.

Evaluating SAGE's Texts. The text summaries generated by SAGE are relatively concise, structured descriptions that identify causes and relationships relevant for understanding important changes. These are especially useful when they isolate changes occurring among hundreds or thousands of activities that can be classified along five or more dimensions. In addition, the texts *identify* mechanisms influencing the relations between the causes and effects (e.g., the moderating influence of slack, the counteracting effects of increases and decreases, reinforcing effects).

The shortcomings of the texts are those of natural language in general. First, some information is not conveyed well textually. This includes hierarchical and other network dependencies like those expressed in (5) through (7) in Figure 10.4 (e.g., organizational relations or activity precedences). Relatedly, while a small number of quantitative facts can be expressed in text, there is no effective way to present them that allows search and comparison when many quantities need to be conveyed. Therefore, while all quantities in a model are ultimately relevant to understanding a change, these are not expressed in natural language.

Second, natural language is limited by the fact that users must devote full attention to each fact expressed. It is not possible to present many facts such that users can focus on only the interesting ones. As a result, a discourse processor must carefully select and elaborate a core of information to express (e.g., reflected in the decisions to pause after (3), to delay the expansion of Evaluation Center until (8), and not to further enumerate the activities that are the responsibility of Frame Subgroup after (7)).

We addressed these limitations by using graphical presentations to support text explanations, and by developing an approach for distributing information between the two modes effectively. These are discussed in the next two sections.

10.6 GRAPHICAL SUPPORT FOR EXPLANATIONS

Our approach to generating graphical presentations to support explanation was motivated by more general concerns for developing an application-independent graphics presentation system. The goal of such a system is to eliminate the need for end-users and application programmers to specify, design, and arrange a display each time output is needed for a program. Its function is to assume the graphics presentation responsibilities for other programs (in our case, the explanation system). The first part of this section describes SAGE's graphics system and especially the features that go beyond previous work. This is followed by discussion of the specific issues involved in using the graphics system to support the explanation system's presentation needs.

Overview of Automatic Graphics Presentation. Our work was based partly on related work on APT [Mackinlay86; Mackinlay91]. The project management domain and the need to support explanation dialogues required extending Mackinlay's approach to the *expressiveness* of graphical techniques and developing several new approaches for representing complex data structures and pictures, and for distinguishing different information-seeking goals. The latter included general-purpose goals needed for coordinating graphics with natural language.

Our attempt to maintain the generality and independence of the graphics system is illustrated in Figure 10.5. The architecture conveys the relation between an application program and a graphics system in a manner consistent with APT. To maintain graphics system independence, an application program must communicate in a general language both its *presentation needs* and a *characterization* of the data to be visualized. The graphics system must select and integrate *graphical techniques* that are expressive of the data characteristics and that satisfy the presentation goals. In SAGE, the application program is either the content selection part of the explanation system or a database query interface. The data consist of project models and a change description generated by the change analyzer.

The research goals suggested by this framework include:

■ Developing a complete set of characteristics to describe application data and using them to define the expressiveness of graphical techniques,

FIGURE 10.5
THE RELATION BETWEEN AN APPLICATION AND AN AUTOMATIC GRAPHICS SYSTEM.

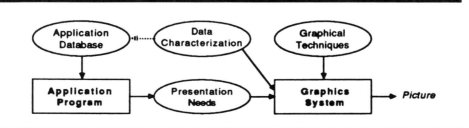

- Identifying and representing different information seeking goals, and
- Developing design representations and mechanisms for selecting and integrating graphical techniques to express data and satisfy informational goals.

Data Characterization. A detailed discussion of our research on data characterization is provided in [Roth90] and we only outline it here. Other related work is presented in [Norman89; McDermott90]. A driving force behind our definition of data characteristics was the ability to describe the expressiveness and relative effectiveness of different picture styles (as in APT).

Developing a general set of data characteristics required considering several dimensions. The first concerns properties of sets of data (e.g., activities, groups, resources, products), including the way they are ordered (i.e., quantitatively, ordinally, or nominally), whether they are measures of quantities or coordinates, and their *domain of membership* (i.e., whether they involve domains of time, space, temperature, mass, etc.).

Set ordering was the main expressiveness characteristic used in APT and was relevant for PMS data as well. The quantity-coordinate distinction (i.e., a distinction between ratio and interval scales) arose in SAGE because of the need to express dates and design locations in project management. Bar charts, gauges, and other techniques in which a graphical object varies quantitatively are inappropriate for conveying points in time or space because they imply an amount by convention. Therefore, point or plot charts, timelines, and other *coordinate*-based techniques were needed to express this data, and their appropriateness was defined based on this characteristic.

Domain of membership helped preserve stylistic conventions like expressing time along a horizontal axis (rather than vertical). It also helped partition information across pictures, when a single picture could not be synthesized for all information to be expressed.

Properties of Relational Structure. The second dimension along which information was characterized describes the way relations map from elements of one set to another. [Mackinlay86] distinguished relations having functional dependency as those for which each element of a domain maps to only one value in another domain. For example, the *cost* relation is a functional dependency, mapping from each activity in a set to exactly one dollar amount. In contrast, the *organizational-has-part* relation is not a functional dependency, since it maps from each organizational group to a variable number of subgroups (or none at all). The functional-dependency distinction helped determine the appropriateness of different techniques (e.g., networks do not require functional dependency, while bar charts do).

We refined and extended this distinction to handle a number of questions regarding the appropriateness of data-picture combinations not handled in APT. We defined three relational properties: *coverage*, *cardinality*, and *uniqueness*.

Relational Coverage conveys whether every element of a set can be mapped to at least one element of another. We distinguish several types of noncoverage, which occur when

1. Data are missing (e.g., some *activities* have missing *start-dates*, a realistic situation in most database applications).
2. A relation is not applicable to some elements (e.g., a relation called *cost-of-automatic-transmission*, which maps from *car-models* to *dollar-amounts*, won't apply to *car-models* without this option).
3. *No-value* is informative (e.g., some departments in a company may have no parts).

Cardinality expresses the number of elements to which a relation can map from an element of one set to those of another. Relations can be **single valued**, **fixed multiple valued** or **variably valued**. Examples are *activity start date* (single valued), *quality ratings by three inspectors* for a set of *product parts* (fixed multiple values), and *organizational parts for groups in a company*, (variably valued). Cardinality should not be confused with Mackinlay's concept of arity, in which multiple values refer to different *roles* in complex relations.

Uniqueness refers to whether a relation maps to a unique value(s) for each element of a set (i.e. whether it uniquely partitions a set). The *cost* relation is nonunique because two *activities* can map to the same *dollar-amount*. The *has-part* relation maps uniquely since each *organizational-entity* has a unique set of parts (i.e., groups in an organizational tree have only one parent department). The precedence relation among a set of activities does not map uniquely because several activities can have the same activity as a successor.

To summarize relational structure, we have made additional distinctions to further characterize relations that are functional dependencies, as well as those that are not. In the above terms, functional dependency implies **coverage** and **single-valued cardinality.**

Relationships Among Relations: Complex Data. There are several conventional graphical displays that do not express binary relations and therefore require a presentation system to have more knowledge of the semantics of data than provided in APT. For example, project management systems make use of Gantt charts, which are methods for expressing time intervals associated with activities or resources, as in Figure 10.6. A single bar along an axis of dates simultaneously expresses the start date, end date, and duration of an activity interval. Intervals are also important in other domains (e.g., the high, low, and closing quotes for daily stock market prices; minimum, maximum, and mean for statistical ranges; mean and error ranges for measurement data). Other complex relations are also common (e.g., location of design objects in a 2-D space; longitude, latitude).

These are examples of complex relations having three dependent values, each with a different role (e.g., beginning, end, and size of an interval).

FIGURE 10.6

AN INTERVAL CHART FOR EXPRESSING ACTIVITY START, END, AND DURATION.

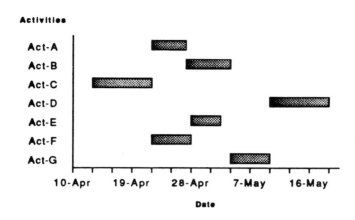

Mackinlay's approach to complex relations involved syntactically decomposing the dependent values into separate relations, thereby losing the relative roles of the different values and the ability to integrate them appropriately in a single picture. For example, decomposing an activity interval into three independent relations could result in the fragmented display of Figure 10.7.

Our approach to this problem is to develop a set of complex data types that can be used to define the roles played by groups of binary relations. We have also defined pictures that express these types (e.g., interval charts). During design, complex pictures are chosen for corresponding relations prior

FIGURE 10.7

FRAGMENTED DISPLAYS OF ACTIVITY START, END, AND DURATION.

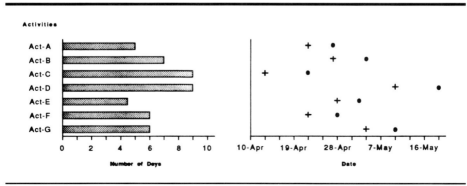

to considering individual primitive techniques. Additional decisions can be made based on characterizations of the individual roles within the complex relation (e.g., *start-date* and *end-date* relations, which can play the roles of beginning and end points of an interval, can still be characterized as mapping to coordinates in time with relational coverage, single-valued cardinality, and nonuniqueness.

Information Seeking Goals. One of the most important issues for graphical design not addressed in APT is the role of an application's or user's goals in viewing data. Differences in goals can greatly alter the effectiveness of graphical techniques or their combinations. Several information-seeking goals were brought out by the need to explain change and by typical graphical display variations in project management systems, although they are general in nature. Recently, [Casner90] has proposed an approach to graphical design with a large set of informational goals that include many of those which we found to be relevant in project management. SAGE was sensitive to goals that place emphasis on

- Accurate value lookup (which favors selection of text tables and makes stricter judgments about the acceptability of other techniques),
- Comparison of values *within*, but not *among* different relations, which results in evaluation criteria favoring separate pictures rather than a single *composite* for several relations (e.g., favoring single- rather than double-axis composition in Mackinlay's terms),
- Pairwise or *n*-wise comparison of relations for the same data set (which favors using the same technique to encode the relations and to position objects to be compared adjacently and in the same composite picture),
- Distributions of values for a relation, (e.g., where concern for the *number* of employees at each salary level and not for individual salaries requires graphics for frequency distributions),
- Functional correlations among attributes (e.g., observing the correlation between length of employment and salary for a set of employees as shown by scatter plot or other composite techniques for which two or more properties of a single mark convey different relations),
- Indexing needs for one or both data sets within a relation (which may lead to preferences for techniques that allow indexing by both data sets, or sorting of one set by the value associated with it in the other set), and
- Partitions of relations or sets into related groups (i.e., reflecting needs for connectedness of data, which influences the data's distribution within or across several pictures).

The last characteristic reflects two offsetting informational goals: the need to express as much information in a single display as possible and the need for selected partitions of sets or relations to each be easily and cohesively viewed. A graphics system needs to be able to determine how to distribute information across several displays and which information to reject if it is not possible to generate a presentation that honors the integrity of related data. This goal was fundamental to the problem of coordinating graphics with text and will be discussed in the next section.

In summary, we have developed a richer method by which applications or users can characterize their data and informational goals when communicating with the graphics system. Data characteristics and goals influence definitions of the expressiveness and relative effectiveness of techniques, the ways they can be combined, and the distribution of information within and across pictures.

Design Mechanisms. SAGE uses the notion of composition developed for APT to integrate primitive pictures involving single relations into complex pictures. In addition to the composition operators developed in APT (axis and mark composition), SAGE includes operators for

- Merging edges of displays (e.g., for synthesizing the leaves of a left-to-right tree and a vertical axis of a chart),
- Merging retinal techniques [Bertin83], textual techniques, or gauges with nodes of networks (for filling nodes with additional information),
- Merging node of networks (e.g., for building multirelation graphs),
- Merging the labels of objects with axis labels or text columns (e.g. for aligning graphical techniques tabularly).

The development of these synthesis methods required a somewhat different and more uniform view of the *functional components* of graphical techniques from that of APT [Roth91b]. Specifically, we view each technique as consisting of two types of graphical objects, those for encoding elements of data sets and those for encoding the *correspondence* between pairs of elements in two sets. Data sets are typically conveyed by graphical objects along axes or table columns, within keys, by nodes of networks, and by the labels of retinal techniques (e.g., size, color, length). Correspondence encodings are typically points, bars, links, lines, and spatial offsets. The existence of a graphical object functioning as a correspondence encoding conveys that a relation exists between at least one pair of elements across two sets. The particular elements of each set that are related are *indexed* by one or more properties of a correspondence encoding (e.g., its vertical and horizontal positions, shape, color). In this view, neither the correspondence object nor any property of it actually encodes a set element.

The notion of a correspondence encoding was not explicit in APT, and as a result the points, bars, and lines that express correspondence were sometimes viewed as encoding one or both sets in a picture. Thus, there were often two objects encoding a set element: what we call a correspondence object and a property of it (e.g., its position, color, shape).

Besides being a more accurate representation, the advantage to consistently maintaining this distinction across all techniques is that it provides a single guiding principle for technique composition: as the merging of graphical objects with *identical graphical functions* (i.e., the functions of encoding the sets versus encoding the correspondences between sets). Thus, it is possible to merge, in various combinations, the leaf nodes of trees, the axis elements of charts, and the labels of points because they all encode set elements. Similarly the labels of retinals can be merged with the labels of nodes.

Other advantages of this representation include the ability to select classes of compositions that support informational goals. For example, compositions that merge correspondence objects are more likely to support a goal of viewing the correlation between two relations than compositions that merge set encodings. They are less effective, however, at supporting pair-wise comparison of the two relations. Another advantage is that natural language captions or descriptions of pictures are more easily generated because of the refinement in the functional roles of these objects. Relatedly, a user can request help related to any object in a picture and have its role described unambiguously.

The search methods that select and compose graphical techniques are guided by user preferences, as well as by an implicit design goal favoring composed pictures, as was the case in APT (see [Mackinlay91] for a discussion of search in automatic design). However, we provided for the ability to weigh graphical effectiveness against the goal of composition, which allowed independent pictures if there was no way to compose them without sacrificing the effectiveness with which individual relations were conveyed. Search was guided by information-seeking goals and by the existence of complex relations, which affected the order in which candidate techniques and composition operators were considered. For example, textual techniques are considered first when the goal is to lookup values accurately. Text is considered last when the goal is to perform comparisons among quantities. Techniques that can present sorted objects are considered first when goals require users to search along some attribute (e.g., to locate a particular activity or those whose dates fall within an interval). When a user's goal is to explore correlations among attributes, SAGE attempts to design a presentation that represents these attributes as properties of a single graphical object. As a result, search is directed toward techniques and composition operators that achieve this goal [Roth91]. Finally, combinations of goals lead to compromise orderings of techniques.

The search component of SAGE is a relatively small and easily modified section of the system amenable to experiments for comparing mechanisms of design control. The reason for this is that components for selecting and synthesizing candidate techniques are independent of the search components which direct their operation. Also, data characteristics and graphical technique expressiveness and structure are represented declaratively, allowing addition and modification of these without changing search mechanisms.

Our comments thus far have addressed the design of the automatic graphics presentation component. We return now to the problem of quantitative model explanation and the role that this component played in SAGE.

Graphical Support for Explanation. As the architecture in Figure 10.2 indicates, content selection produced a frame-based description of changes and causal relations, which were then expressed by independent graphics and text components. The first function of the graphics system was to express the facts that support understanding of causal relationships in the models. These included the values of variables in each of the two contexts, their differences, the equations underlying the cause-effect relations and any semantic relationships corresponding to the equations, the significance of a variable for explaining change (a Boolean), and any semantic attributes for classifying or grouping variables.

The second function of the graphics system was to express this type of information for the entire partition of the model relevant to explaining a change. While text focused on navigating through causal relationships at each level in a model, graphics could provide a vehicle for rapidly searching and selectively attending to subsets of important information. Since both expressed information from the same models, our original view was that the text would serve to navigate through pictures as well. This turned out to be erroneous, at least in some situations, because of the lack of coordinated presentation design discussed in Section 10.7.

The information was extracted from the CD and provided to the graphics system using a general protocol called an info-spec. The same protocol was used by a database-query system and conveyed the relation names, data sets, and pairings, as well as directives regarding importance, technique preferences, and other information-seeking goals. Importance ordering varied with the question type: Questions emphasizing causal mechanisms resulted in higher importance being placed on semantic relations underlying the causal paths. Relations designated as more important were more likely to be expressed using the most effective techniques. Less important relations were expressed with less effective techniques, if necessary, to compose them with other relations.

The info-specs created by the explanation system included presentation goals of supporting the (1) *pairwise comparison* of the values of variables in the two contexts, (2) *accurate lookup* of these values, (3) *expression of differences* between the compared values, and (4) *proximity of pictures* expressing the significance relation and the value differences. The fourth goal was based on the fact that differences between values (and not the values themselves) were most relevant to determining significance and should occur in the same picture if it is necessary to partition the presentation into multiple pictures.

Figure 10.8 shows the picture generated for the CD described in Section 4 (Figure 10.3) and the text sequences associated with it. The picture is a five-way composition of techniques for relations of cost variables (in this case, organizational groupings of activities). The picture integrates five techniques: a set of *gauges* expressing cost differences, a *texture* technique (bold lines versus thin ones) for distinguishing significant from insignificant variables, two *textual* encodings of the actual costs in each budget version, and a *tree* representing the *has-part* relation among variables.

The design of this picture occurred in several steps. First, a bar chart was selected as the most effective technique for showing the changes, a

FIGURE 10.8
INDEPENDENT GENERATION OF PICTURE AND TEXT FOR EXPLANATION.

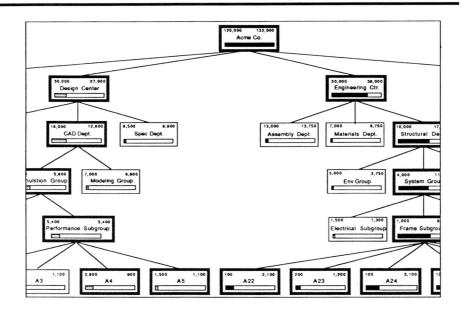

>"Why did Acme-Co costs change from estimate-1 to estimate-2?"

(1) The organizational-parts of Acme-Co consists of Advanced-Planning, Design, Engineering, and Evaluation Centers.

(2) The increase in Acme-Co costs (+ $12000) was due to increases in Engineering Center (+ $8000) and Evaluation Center (+ $6250).

(3) These increases were partially counteracted by a decrease in Design Center (- $ 3000).

- -

(4) The change in Engineering Center was due to changes in most of the activities which are the responsibility-of Frame Subgroup (+ $8000).

(5) Frame Subgroup is an organizational-part-of System Group.

(6) System Group is an organizational-part-of Structural Department.

(7) Structural Department is an organizational-part-of Engineering Center.

- -

(8) The increase related to Evaluation Center was . . . . .

background-highlighting technique for the *significant* relation, text tables for the cost values because of the goal of accuracy (the large range and continuous nature of the quantity made a bar chart less accurate), and a tree for the *has-part* relation. Attempts to compose these failed largely because the nodes of the tree could not be composed with an axis, since all variables would need to form an edge to be merged with the axis. A number of different techniques were tried for the other relations without producing a complete composition. The final set was reached without sacrificing the effectiveness of any one technique substantially.

In summary, our approach to graphical selection and design recognized the need to develop a graphical presentation tool. The starting point for this was the treatment by [Mackinlay86] of expressiveness, effectiveness, and composition for primitive graphical techniques. Supporting explanations suggested directions for further development, including data characterization, informational goals, improvements in picture representations, and additional composition methods.

The use of the graphics system often supported explanation adequately. However, the lack of coordination between the two modes led to some flaws. For example, the picture in Figure 10.8 is actually quite large and must be presented in a scrollable window. The size is due to the goal of conveying information from the entire partition of the project model that is relevant to understanding a change. As a result, all the changes discussed in each text segment are not easily integrated visually in the picture (e.g., not all of Acme's Centers can be seen at once, as they are described in the first paragraph of the text). The difficulty occurs because the sequential structure of the text discourse is not compatible with the spatial structure of the picture. This and other related problems are the result of the lack of coordination between the two modes and were the motivation for additional work described in Section 10.7.

10.7 AN APPROACH TO COORDINATION

When viewed in isolation, the graphics component adequately expressed the information that was input to it (i.e., all relevant facts in the Change Description). However, there were many cases in which a picture-text combination was confusing or noncomplementary due to a lack of coordination. The reasons for this problem are related to

- **Structural incompatibility:** a lack of correspondence between the sequential structure of information in text and the graphical structure of that information in a picture,
- **Lack of cohesion:** the inability of text to refer to the graphical representations of the application-domain objects that are being discussed
- **Redundancy:** the inability to exclude from text information that was better expressed by an accompanying picture and that needn't be re-emphasized.

Structural incompatibility comes from the fundamental difference in the way that pictures and text impose structure on facts. As described in the section on discourse processing, texts are structured according to the rhetorical conventions of explanation, which define coherent sequences and combinations, and by dialogue concerns, which further partition these sequences. Discourse processes produce an effective but inflexible traversal through the content being expressed.

In contrast to text's sequential structure, pictures impose structure on information by using spatial or other visual properties (e.g., contiguity, connectedness). The structure of a well-designed picture should flexibly support a user's information-seeking processes, including locating objects or facts, accessing additional attributes of objects, comparing quantities, and discovering relationships or patterns among them. In contrast, the purpose of text structure is partly to segment and focus attention on coherent clusters of ideas. Mutually supportive structures occur when (1) pictures support a user's information-seeking processes for clusters of facts conveyed *within* each of the discourse segments and (2) when the sequencing of ideas *across* discourse segments provides an effective way to explore a picture.

We discussed earlier how the picture in Figure 10.8 fails to support the first two segments of the sample text because it is difficult to locate and compare quantities for every center mentioned in sentences 1 and 2. It is confusing to view the picture after reading the first text segment because the picture structure is not well suited to viewing this smaller subset of facts. Figure 10.9, in contrast, presents only the information that supports both text segments and does so in a way that maintains the connectedness or integrity of the information corresponding to each text segment. The picture is also compatible with the transition between sentences 3 and 4, so that text effectively guides attention through the picture. This is due largely to the careful selection of a smaller number of facts but also to the way these facts are structured within the picture.

Structural incompatibility occurred in our application most often because the graphics component works unaware of the clustering of facts produced by the discourse component. Information relevant to one or two text segments is often distributed throughout one or more pictures. Even when the connectedness of information in each segment is preserved, however, the ordering of pictures must reflect the segment order as well. For example, jumping from one picture to a second and then back to the first is not a compatible partition of information for three text segments (even if the integrity of each segment is preserved within the pictures). Some degree of sequential access is assumed by readers.

More subtle forms of incompatibility occur when information is ordered within a picture inconsistently from the way it is sequenced in text. For example, text explanations often mention variables in order of the magnitude of their changes. However, these can correspond to alphabetically ordered axis elements or nodes ordered by their relation along a path in a network.

FIGURE 10.9
COORDINATED TEXT AND GRAPHICS DISPLAYS.

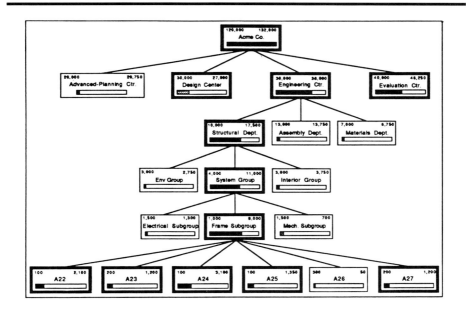

>"Why did Acme-Co costs change from estimate-1 to estimate-2?"

(1) The increase in Acme-Co costs was due to increases in Engineering Center and Evaluation Center, as shown by the gauges in Figure A.

(2) These increases were partially counteracted by a decrease in Design Center.

- -

(3) The change in Engineering Center was due to changes in most of the Frame Subgroup activities.

- -

(4) The increase related to Evaluation Center, shown in Figure . . . . .

Attempts to locate objects from text to graphics can be frustrating when these are inconsistently ordered.

Our approach to this problem is to provide guidance to graphics presentation from the results of a preliminary level of text-discourse processor. Prior discourse processing is necessary to determine an appropriate idea outline that sequentially partitions relevant content. In addition, a more sophisticated design approach was required in which information from different segments could be considered independently or as single merged sets. For example, if segment 1 expresses the durations of activities *A*, *B*, and *C* and segment 2 expresses the durations for *D*, *E*, and *F*, then the designer needs to consider separate pictures for each versus a single picture for the merged set *A* through *F*. The latter requires a general design goal to be communicated to the graphics system that requests all content be presented, but within the limits imposed by space and the need to maintain the integrity of data within each partition. This turned out to be a useful directive for graphical design for contexts other than coordination within explanation, because it enabled the system to flexibly eliminate information from presentations by weighing picture quality against information quantity. This capability required feedback to the design module from the rendering module, as well as measures of the integrity or connectedness of information in different pictures.

Cohesion is related to the need for sentences of a text to refer to the same objects or concepts to achieve a level of connectedness. For the problem of coordination, cohesion is related to whether texts can refer to graphical objects corresponding to the objects and attributes in an explanation. Also, texts can facilitate the effectiveness of pictures by explicitly directing attention to graphical objects (e.g., "The activities of Dept-X, located in the upper half of Figure *N*, accounted for 90% of the cost overruns.") and by clarifying graphical techniques and their relation to the facts being expressed (e.g., "The largest cost overruns are illustrated by the longest white bars in Figure *M*.").

In order to achieve these levels of coordination, the text-discourse processer needed to determine the facts that are expressed by a picture, the techniques used to convey them, and the spatial or structural characteristics of the graphical objects representing those facts. The discourse processor also needed rhetorical models for describing pictures. Just as there are rhetorical conventions for describing databases, justifying conclusions, describing apartments, and explaining quantitative models [McKeown85; Weiner80; Linde75; Kosy84], there are also conventions for describing and performing attention-directing functions for pictures.

Our first attempts at providing this capability extended the rhetorical models for explaining change to include predicates for referring to pictures and objects (e.g., "The change in *A* is due to changes in *B*, *C*, and *D*, which are shown by the gauges in Figure *N*.") and for summarizing information contained in pictures (e.g., "The changes that caused the increase in *C* are shown in Figure *M*."). We also divided text-discourse processing into two stages, the first for developing a partitioning or outline of facts by instantiating explanatory models. The second phase involved instantiating models that were hybrids for explanation and picture referencing. Operation of the second stage was very similar to the first and merely added references to pictures at appropriate points and dealt with redundancy issues.

Redundancy refers to the unnecessary repetition of information in text when facts have already been expressed effectively in pictures. In the cur-

rent application, this usually occurs when texts mention quantities, the semantic relationships underlying equations, or other facts that are the input
to graphics (as in sentences 1, 2, and 5 through 7 in the sample text). As was
the case for cohesion, solving this problem required graphical design to occur prior to the completion of text-discourse processing. Our solution simply
eliminated additional propositions if they were expressed in graphics. This
was implemented as conditional tests for some types of predicates that either
substituted a picture reference or eliminated their expression in text when
they were expressed graphically.

To summarize, we present an architecture in Figure 10.10 for coordinating discourse and graphics processing to deal with issues of structural
compatibility, cohesion, and redundancy. Achieving structural compatibility
required preliminary discourse processing to occur prior to graphical design
in order to segment content to be expressed, as well as additional graphical
design processes to deal with the informational goals implied by the segmen-
tation. The latter also involved considering the results of rendering during
graphical design so size and structural qualities could be considered. Graphical design had to precede a second phase of text-discourse processing so
that texts could refer to pictures and avoid excessive redundancy. Finally,
although not explicit in the figure, this architecture maintains the independence of the systems, even to the extent that information content passed
between them is done using the same general protocols that any explanation
would use to communicate with the graphics system.

FIGURE 10.10
ADDING COORDINATION TO THE SAGE ARCHITECTURE

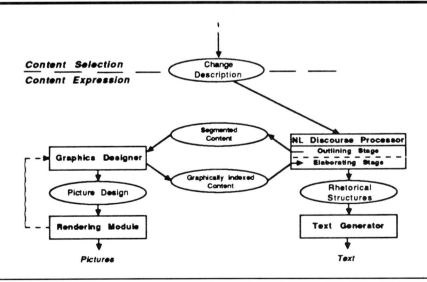

10.8 SUMMARY

We presented an approach to the explanation of change in quantitative models by expanding and integrating a combination of research approaches. The accomplishments include an approach to the analysis of change in a variety of quantitative model types, including those integrated with semantic networks or databases. We also developed general rhetorical models for quantitative explanation and mechanisms for using these to express analyses of change. Our work extended earlier work on automatic graphics presentation by developing a more complete set of data characteristics and picture styles and a more uniform representation of graphical displays. We also considered informational goals during design, including those necessary for coordination and, more generally, quantity-quality tradeoffs. Finally, we presented an approach to graphics and text coordination, outlined issues relevant for assessing compatibility of the two modes in presentations, and proposed some mechanisms within an architecture for achieving coordination.

REFERENCES

[Appelt81] Appelt, D. E. 1981. *Planning Natural-Language Utterances to Satisfy Multiple Goals*, PhD dissertation, Stanford University.

[Arens91] Arens, Y., Miller, L., and Sondheimer, N. *Presentation Design Using an Integrated Knowledge Base*. In present volume.

[Bertin83] Bertin, J. 1983. *Semiology of Graphics*, The University of Wisconsin Press.

[Casner90] Casner, S. M. 1990. *A Task-Analytic Approach to the Automated Design of Information Graphics*, PhD dissertation, University of Pittsburgh.

[Kosy84] Kosy, D. W. and Wise, B. P. 1984. Self-Explanatory Financial Planning Models. *Proceedings of AAAI-84*, August.

[Linde75] Linde, C. and Labov, W. 1975. Spatial Networks as a Site for the Study of Language. *Language*, 51, 924–939.

[Mackinlay86] Mackinlay, J. D. 1986. Automating the Design of Graphical Presentations of Relational Information. *ACM Transactions on Graphics*, 5 (2), April, 110–141.

[Mackinlay91] Mackinlay, J. D. 1991. Search Architectures for the Automatic Design of Graphical Presentations. In present volume.

[McDermott90] McDermott, J. 1990. Developing Software is like Talking to Eskimos about Snow. *Proceedings of AAAI-90*, Boston, July.

[McKeown85] McKeown, K. R. 1985. Discourse Strategies for Generating Natural-Language Text. *Artificial Intelligence*, 27, 1–41.

[Neal91] Neal, J. and Shapiro, S. 1991. Intelligent Multi-Media Interface Technology. In present volume.

[Norman89] Norman, D. A. 1989. Cognitive Artifacts. To be published in a book edited by John M. Carroll. Chapter prepared for the *Workshop on Cognitive Theory and Design in Human-Computer Interaction*, Chappaqua, NY.

[Roth88] Roth, S. F., Mesnard, X., and Mattis, J. A. 1988. Intelligent Analysis and Explanation of Project Schedules and Budgets. *Proceedings of the International Conference on CAD/CAM/CIM and Robotics: Contribution of Artificial Intelligence*, Bordeaux, France, March.

[Roth90] Roth, S. F. and Mattis, J. 1990. Data Characterization for Intelligent Graphics Presentation. *Proceedings of the CHI '90 Conference*, ACM, Seattle, April.

[Roth91a] Roth, S. F., and Hendrickson, C. 1991. Automated Explanation for Project Management Systems. *Journal of Computing in Civil Engineering, ASCE.*, April.

[Roth91b] Roth, S. F., and Mattis, J. 1991. Automating the Presentation of Information. In *Proceedings of the IEEE Conference on AI Applications*, Miami Beach, February.

[Sathi86] Sathi, A., Morton, E. and Roth, S. F. 1986. Callisto: An Intelligent Project Management System. *AI Magazine*, 7 (5), 34–52.

[Swartout83] Swartout, W. R. 1983. XPLAIN: A System for Creating and Explaining Expert Consulting Programs. *Artificial Intelligence*, 21, 285–325.

[Thompson77] Thompson, H. 1977. Strategy and tactics: a model for language production. *Papers from the 13th Regional Meeting*, Chicago Linguistic Society, University of Chicago.

[Weiner80] Weiner, J. L. 1980. BLAH, a system which explains its reasoning. *Artificial Intelligence*, 15, 19–48.

CHAPTER 11

PRESENTATION DESIGN USING AN INTEGRATED KNOWLEDGE BASE

YIGAL ARENS, LAWRENCE MILLER,
and **NORMAN SONDHEIMER**
USC/Information Sciences Institute

ABSTRACT

In spite of the development of user interface tool kits, construction and en-hancement of user interfaces for most computer applications remains time consuming and difficult. This is particularly true when the user interface systems must dynamically create displays. This chapter shows how artificial intelligence knowledge base and rule technology can be used to solve this problem.

A prototype model-driven user interface management system has been created using a hybrid knowledge representation system, KL-TWO, combin-ing a frame-based representation system, NIKL, with a propositional logic theorem prover, PENNI. NIKL is used to model the entities of the applica-

This research was supported by the Defense Advanced Research Projects Agency under Contract No. N0014-87-K-0130. Views and conclusions contained herein are the authors' and should not be interpreted as representing the official opinion or policy of DARPA, the U.S. Government, or any person or agency connected with them.

tion domain and the facilities of the user interface. Rules are written connecting the two models. These rules range from application specific to general rules of presentation. The situation to be displayed is asserted into the PENNI database. A *presentation designer* interprets this data using the domain model, chooses the appropriate rules to use in creating the display, and creates a description of the desired display in terms of the interface model. A system, *Integrated Interfaces,* using this design for a multimodal map graphics, natural-language, menu, and form interface has been created and applied to a database-reporting application.

11.1 INTRODUCTION

ISI is involved in user interface research aimed at bringing together multiple input and output modes in a way that handles mixed-mode input (commands, menus, forms, natural language), interacts with a diverse collection of underlying software utilities in a uniform way, and presents the results through a combination of output modes including natural-language text, maps, and other graphics, tables, and forms.

Our system, **Integrated Interfaces,** supports dynamic presentations, where displays are driven by the information that is available at the time they are produced. Determination of the best way to present information is made at run time when the actual data is available as opposed to being precompiled by the interface designer.

Much of Integrated Interfaces' ability to interact uniformly with the user and the underlying services and to build its presentations derives from the availability of a central knowledge base. This knowledge base integrates models of the application domain (Navy ships in the Pacific region, in the current demonstration version), the structure of visual displays and their graphical features, the underlying services (databases and expert systems), and interface functions. The emphasis in this paper is on a presentation designer that uses the knowledge base to produce multimodal output.

There has been a flurry of recent work in user interface management systems (we list several recent examples in the references). Existing work is characterized by an attempt to relieve the software designer of the burden of handcrafting an interface for each application. The work has generally focused on intelligently handling input. In our paper we deal with the other end of the pipeline—presentations.

The overall runtime architecture of the Integrated Interfaces system is given in Figure 11.1. Input is provided via the mouse and keyboard through forms and menus (produced by QFORMS). Output is provided via a combination of natural-language generation (produced by PENMAN), maps and graphics (produced by the Geographic Display Agent), and forms. Drivers have been written for each of these media, which translate from the language of the Integrated Interfaces rules (KL-TWO) to the input language they respectively require. QFORMS, PENMAN, and the GDA were all developed at ISI.

FIGURE 11.1
ARCHITECTURE OF INTEGRATED INTERFACES SYSTEM

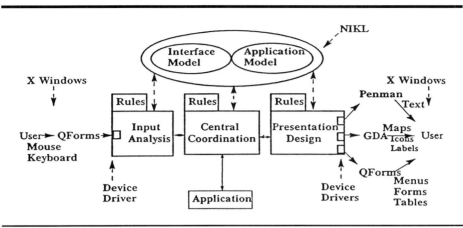

Presentations are put together by a **presentation designer.** The presentation designer decides what output mode or combinations of output modes to use for each piece of information. This involves recognition of the topic of the information, classification of the topic, a check of the user's preferences for presentation, and a coordinated delegation activity to assign tasks to the various output modes. This is done by rules that map between concepts and display modes.

In moving from an interface with a single-output device to an integrated multiple-output device interface output processing changes substantially. Even in single-mode systems, we find that some preparation is necessary beyond the mere determination of the contents of presentations. For example, an information retrieval system may use tables exclusively for the display of retrieved data. Such a system may still decide to split information between tables in a report to control the length of the tables before the final output is generated. In an integrated presentation system, such design activity grows considerably. The system must be able to decide what output mode to use for each piece of information.

The research issues that must be addressed in this context include determining what constitutes a good presentation of information, how to recognize information presentation situations, how to build knowledge that can be shared across several modalities, and how to choose the mode and form of output.

11.2 THE PROCESS OF PRESENTATION DESIGN

We call our method of developing and operating a user interface, **model-driven programming.** A model is a description of objects of the application and the interface and their classes, relationships among them, behaviors they can engage in, and the effects of such behaviors. Actions are associated with these classes. When new data (e. g., the existence of a new ship) is introduced into the system, it is classified, any implications that can be drawn from it are propagated, and actions associated with it are triggered—usually resulting in a potential change or addition to the display.

Presentation design is achieved by the application of a system of antecedent-consequent rules, the actions associated with certain objects. The rules are used to map types of information to appropriate types of presentations. Specifically, presentation design involves *realizing* the categories that a given piece of information fits within, that is, finding the classes to which the information belongs and thus the rules whose antecedents describe the information; *selecting* the most germane category for the information, that is, finding the most specific rules; and *redescribing* the information in appropriate textual and visual forms, that is, using the consequents of the rules to structure the presentation.

We cannot at this point claim that we have a complete theory of what constitutes a good presentation, since such a theory would have to explain aesthetic considerations involved in the preparation of presentations. While we cannot handle such considerations in general, we have been able to provide heuristics useful in certain situations. The Integrated Interfaces system contains rules that structure forms so that they contain what we consider appropriate amounts of information. Users whose aesthetic judgements differ from ours can modify these explicit rules to achieve different behavior. In this sense our system can be considered a presentation *shell*.

11.2.1. Example

The U.S. Navy's Pacific Fleet prepares a daily report on the situation and plans of the fleet. This report conveys current ship locations, courses, current activities, and the activities planned for ships in the near future. The person putting this situation report together has available for presentation a graphics system for ocean surface maps, a business graphics system for time tables, and methods for adding text to maps and tables.

Such a report could be presented in many ways: a map with lines showing each ship's course with a label at each point where the ship starts a new activity; or a map with points showing each ship's initial location and a timetable for each ship; or a map with points showing each ship's initial location and a label in English explaining its sailing plans. The Pacific Fleet uses the third form.

The Navy's report-generating activities can be described as following a process and rules similar to those encoded in our system. Information concerning ships is realized as belonging to certain known categories (e.g., the ship's planned activities). Rules for translating such information into a component of a report (e.g., an indication on a map or a textual description) are then examined, and a rule appropriate for the desired mode of presentation is selected. The information about the ships is then redescribed as part of the presentation being prepared.

A typical presentation generated by the Integrated Interfaces system is shown in Figure 11.2.

11.2.2. Design

Models

Our models characterize or define the categories of *entities* our user interface can deal with. One of the models identifies the categories of objects and actions in a common-sense view of the domain of our system. We indicate subclass relations present between categories, as well as relationships between objects and actions. For the Navy application we described above, we include the various categories of ships and sailing activities. We also include specific knowledge, such as that *tankers* are a type of *ship,* and that a *repair* activity involves a *disabled-ship*.

Another model describes the categories of objects and actions of the interface world. The objects here include windows, tables, maps, text strings, and icons. The actions here include creation, deletion, movement, and structure of displays.

A final model (not crucial for this discussion) describes the functions and data structures of the available application services. Included here are descriptions of underlying application software, and any database schemas.

When converting the interface to a new application, the existing interface model can be shared and need not be rewritten. Although some sharing may be possible with the application model, considerable work on a new application model will most probably be necessary. The interface designer will be aided, however, by the higher-level structures of the model containing abstract concepts such as "action," "event," and the like, which already exist and can be used to guide the design of a model for a new application.

Rules

The presentation rules are simple: They map objects from the application domain model into objects in the interface model. Hence, the entity that describes a daily status report may be mapped into a map. A position report may be mapped onto a point. A ship's planned future activities may be mapped onto a text string. These rules are arranged according to the class subsumption hierarchy of the models, so the rules applicable to all ships are further up the hierarchy than those applying only to tankers.

A system that constructs a visual display based entirely on an analysis of the details of the data to be presented [Mackinlay86] holds considerable appeal. However, in a domain as complex as ours, it is probably impossible to design such a presentation system. We thus allow both low-level rules that

FIGURE 11.2
SOUTH CHINA SEA SITUATION DISPLAY

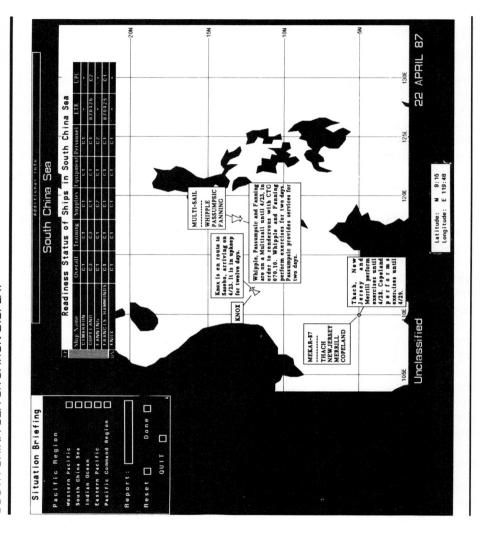

map details of the domain to details of the presentations, such as those that map the various types of ships to their icons, and high-level ones of wider scope that, given a particular type of presentation request, provide a script to be followed in fulfilling the request.

Rule Application

Presentation design can now be described as the task of recognizing the domain categories within which a request for information presentation falls, selection of the appropriate rules that apply to those categories, and mapping of the domain terms in the request into appropriate presentation terms.

The three phases that we refer to as *realization, selection,* and *redescription* are implemented in our system as described below. Realization relates the facts about instances to the abstract categories of the model. For example, the concrete facts about *Sprite,* a ship with a malfunctioning radar, must lead to the realization that it is a *disabled-ship* (assuming *disabled-ship* is defined in the domain model). Selection works by allowing for the appropriate mapping rules to be chosen, allowing for additivity. Selection also ensures that all aspects of the demand for presentation are met by some rule. Redescription applies the rules, mapping each aspect of a common-sense view of a presentation into an equivalent presentation form.

The forms produced by rule application are not actually the commands to the output subsystems (i.e., the map graphics system, text generator, and the business forms system). Instead, they are interpretable by *device drivers* that control these systems. This design allows the forms produced by the rules to serve as a model for the contents of the screen. Although we do not currently do so, user input activity on the screen could be interpreted with this screen model serving as a context. So, our design has the additional advantage of allowing, in principle, the use of the same knowledge base and many of the same inference mechanisms for analysis and presentation design.

11.3 KNOWLEDGE REPRESENTATION TOOLS

Our implementation of presentation design depends on two knowledge representation systems: NIKL and KL-TWO. NIKL holds our models; KL-TWO automatically carries out realization. KL-TWO also holds the demands for presentation and receives the forms read by the device drivers. This section provides a brief introduction to these tools.

11.3.1. NIKL

NIKL [Kaczmarek86] is a network knowledge-base system descended from KL-ONE [Brachman85]. This type of system supports description of the entities that make up a domain. The central components of the notation are sets of concepts and roles organized in *is-a* hierarchies. These hierarchies iden-

FIGURE 11.3
FRAGMENT OF DOMAIN MODEL CONTAINING SHIP

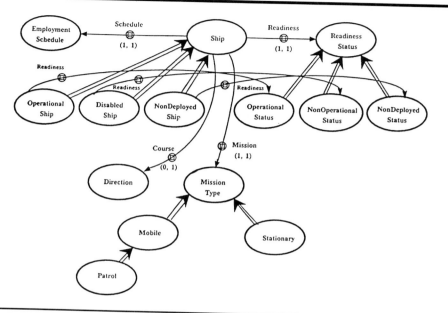

tify when membership in one category (or the holding of one relationship) entails membership in (or the holding of) another. The roles are associated with concepts (as *role restrictions*), and identify the relationships that can hold between individuals that belong to the categories. The role restrictions also hold number restrictions on the entities that fill these roles.

We have been experimenting with a naval assets model for the naval briefing application mentioned above. The model has a concept *disabled-ship* that is meant to identify ships that are unable to carry out their missions. A *disabled-ship is-a* type of *ship* distinguished from *ship* by having a role restriction *readiness* that relates *disabled-ship* to *nonoperational-status* (i.e., all ships with nonoperational status are disabled). All *ships* can have exactly one filler of the *readiness* role restriction. The concept of *nonoperational-status* is partly defined through the *is-a* relation to a concept *readiness-status*. This situation is shown graphically in Figure 11.3 in a notation used for KL-ONE knowledge bases.

In flavor, NIKL is a frame system with the concepts equivalent to frames and the role restrictions to slots. However, the NIKL representation has a formal semantics. We could translate our NIKL knowledge bases into predicate calculus expressions and use a theorem prover to make the same inferences; however, NIKL is optimized for the limited inferences it makes, and a general-purpose theorem prover would be less efficient.

11.3.2. KL-TWO

KL-TWO is a hybrid knowledge representation system that takes advantage of NIKL's formal semantics [Vilain85]. KL-TWO links a reasoner, PENNI, to NIKL. PENNI, an enhanced version of RUP [McAllester82], reasons using propositional logic. It is more restricted than systems that use first-order logic and a general-purpose theorem prover.

PENNI manages a database of propositions of the form (P_a) and $(Q_{a,b})$, where the forms are variable free. The first item in each ordered pair is the name of a concept in an associated NIKL network, and the first item in each ordered triple is the name of a role in the network. The assertion of any form (P_a) is a statement that the individual a is a thing described by the concept P. The assertion $(Q_{a,b})$ states that individuals a and b are related by the abstract relation described by Q.

NIKL adds to PENNI the ability to do taxonomic reasoning. Assume the NIKL database contains the concepts described above. Assume that we assert just the following three facts: (*Ship Sprite*), (*readiness Sprite C4*), and *nonoperational-Status C4*) (*C4* is a U.S. Navy readiness code). Using the knowledge base, PENNI is able to deduce that any *Ship* whose *readiness* is a *nonoperational-status* is a *disabled-ship*. So, if we ask if (*disabled-ship Sprite*) is true, KL-TWO will reply positively.

PENNI also provides a truth maintenance system that keeps track of the facts used to deduce others. When our rules are used to determine aspects of a presentation from facts about the world, the truth maintenance system records the dependencies between the domain and the presentation. For example, *readiness Sprite C4* triggers a rule that asserts *disabled-ship Sprite*. If *readiness Sprite C4* is retracted, PENNI's truth maintenance system will automatically retract the assertion that the Sprite is a disabled ship.

11.4 EXAMPLES

The power of presentation design is in its flexibility. The designer of a system does not specify rigidly in advance what form information will be requested from the user and how data and results will be displayed. Instead, our models contain descriptions of the types of information the application programs deal with and the types of graphical tools and instruments available. The rules for presentation enable the system to generate on demand displays appropriate for given needs. Here are some concrete examples.

11.4.1. Construction of a Visual Representation of an Object

Consider the knowledge about ships and about graphical instruments encoded in the NIKL models in Figures 11.3 and 11.4. Besides the aspects of Figure 11.3 already indicated, note that *ships* have *missions* and that *patrol* missions are a subclass of *mobile* missions. Note also that all *ships* have *sched-*

FIGURE 11.4
FRAGMENT OF INTERFACE MODEL CONTAINING GRAPHICAL-INSTRUMENT

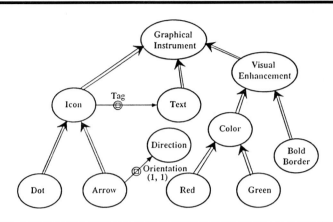

ules. Figure 11.4 describes some *graphical-instruments.* This includes *text* for language output, *icons* for maps and isolated forms, and *visual-enhancements* that could apply to icons and text. *Icons* have *text* as their *tag.* Several specific *icons* and *visual-enhancements* are included.

Let us assume that the user wishes to show ships engaged in a *mobile* mission with a special *icon,* and that the icon should be oriented in a direction identical to the ship's course. In addition, assume that *disabled-ships* are to be shown with *red* icons and that the *schedule* of a ship is to be shown in the natural-language *tag* of the *icon* representing it. A version of the rules that we would use to achieve this is shown in Figure 11.5.

FIGURE 11.5
SAMPLE PRESENTATION RULES

1. IF (operational-ship **x**) or (nondeployed-ship **x**)
      THEN (icon-color image (**x**) green)
2. IF (disabled-ship **x**)
      THEN (icon-color image (**x**) red)
3. IF (ship **x**) and (mission **x y**) and (course **y z**)
      THEN (orientation image (**x**) **z**)
4. IF (ship **x**) and (mission **x,y**) and
         (Mobile **y**) THEN (Icon-Type image(**x**) arrow)
5. IF (ship **x**) and (schedule **x,y**)
      THEN (tag image(**x**) textual-description(**y**))

The antecedent considers the categories of one or more individuals and their relationships, all in terms of the NIKL models. The consequents provide assertions about the graphic representation of objects for the PENNI database. These rules are asserted into PENNI so that the truth maintenance system may keep track of the dependencies between antecedent facts and their resultant consequents, as explained in the previous section.

The functions *image* and *textual-description* map the constants of the common sense world into constants of the visual and textual world, respectively. For example, rule 5 in Figure 11.5 states that if some individual **x** is a *ship* and another individual **y** is its *schedule,* then the *tag* of the image of **x** is the textual description of **y.** The textual description of **y** will be created by the invocation of our text generator.

To complete the example, suppose that the following set of facts was asserted into the PENNI database: (*ship Sprite*), (*readiness Sprite C4*), (*nonoperational-status C4*), (*mission Sprite X37*), (*patrol X37*), (*schedule Sprite U46*), (*course X37 220*), and (*employment-schedule U46*). Suppose further that the NIKL model defined *patrol* to be a subclass of *mobile* missions. Then realization would recognize the *Sprite* as a *disabled-Ship* and one engaged in a *mobile* mission on a course of 220 degrees. Selection would identify that rules 2, 3, 4 and 5 apply. Redescription would result in the addition to the PENNI database of the description of the image of the *Sprite* as a red arrow with an orientation of 220, and with a textual representation of its schedule as its label.

If any of the facts about *Sprite* are retracted, an automatic change in the description of its graphic image will occur.

11.4.2. Recognizing Special Cases

For many requests for information encountered in our domain, the presentation required is far more complex than the rules of the kind listed could provide. The construction of these complex presentations requires an evaluation of the coherence of the display. It would therefore be hopeless at this point to attempt writing rules for deriving an elaborate presentation entirely from low-level information about the objects to be described. Our approach provides us a partial solution to this problem.

The availability of models of the domain and of displays to our presentation designer allows it to recognize collections of data as representing information of a certain known type. The presentation designer can then make use of presentation techniques specialized for this type of data to provide the user with more appropriate displays.

For example, Figure 11.6 provides portions of our model that include the class *Pacific situation,* a display of data about ships and ports in the *Pacific region*, which includes certain specific information from the ships' employment schedule.

When provided with data about ships in the Pacific region and their employments, the presentation designer would classify the data in its model of

FIGURE 11.6
FRAGMENT OF DOMAIN MODEL INCLUDING SITUATION

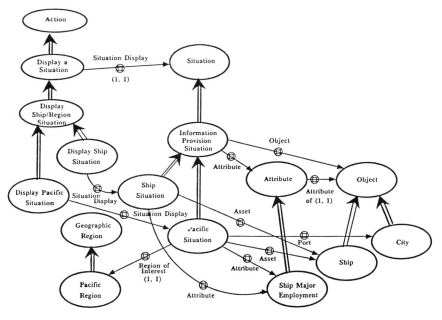

the domain. A spatial reasoner deduces the region containing all of the ships that would be included in the *Pacific region,* and the presentation designer recognizes that it has received a collection of data belonging to the class *Pacific situation.* Once the classification of the data is accomplished, the presentation designer will use specific presentation rules appropriate for displaying the information. In the domain we have considered there is a preferred way for presenting this information, to which we try to conform. This preferred presentation has developed in the Navy after years of handcrafted situation briefings. The specific presentation rules appropriate only for a situation briefing will combine the entities created by more general rules, of the kind described in the previous section, to produce the final presentation.

11.4.3. Generation of an Input Display

The presentation designer must also deal with the preparation of displays for soliciting information from the user. Here, again, the task and domain models are indispensable.

At some point the user may want to view data about ships in some region. In terms of our model (see Figure 11.6), that would mean *display a situation.* As it turns out, the presentation designer does not have any rules that can be used to redescribe this general request into a presentation, but there exist ways of satisfying more specific requests. For example, requests to have the *Pacific region* or any of its subregions displayed can be satisfied. As we see in Figure 11.6, the situation involves specific ships and ports, which may also be displayed.

The presentation designer collects all options the user can choose among to construct an executable request. The presentation designer then constructs a display form that will be used to present these options to the user. The result of this is a set of assertions in PENNI that the device driver for a separate forms-management package (Qforms [Kaczmarek84]) uses to prepare the input form.

The form below, presented to the user, allows the user to make one of several specific choices:

Pacific Regions:
    Western Pacific   ☐
    South China Sea   ☐
    Indian Ocean   ☐
    Easter Pacific   ☐
    Pacific Command Region   ☐
Ship: ─────────────────

It is instructive to examine precisely how this form is created. Specifically, how does the choice *Ship* become part of the form? It is not a Pacific region, but Navy personnel request that this possibility be supported.

We included in our model the concept *display-ship/region situation*. Since this has two subclasses of actions, namely *display ship situation* and *display regional situation* our system could have generated an intermediate two-item submenu, something like:

Situation in Pacific Region   ☐
Situation of Ship   ☐

We consider this unsatisfactory from a human-factor standpoint. We formulated a rule that if the choices on a proposed menu can be further subdivided, and if the number of choices is less than N, then the proposed menu should not be displayed. Instead, a more detailed form should be generated, based on the subchoices. Our prototype uses the value 3 for N, so in this case the rule causes the presentation designer to immediately generate the more specific form. A user is free to change the value of N in the rule, modifying the design of forms the system generates in situations such as this.

Note that the regions available were specified by name in the form, while ships were not; the user specifies a ship by typing on the form (Figure 11.2). This distinction in selection methods is a result of information about the cardinality of the relevant collections of objects—information encoded in our models. Since the number of possible choices for region is small, they are enumerated. However, the number of ships is large, so the user is provided with a way to specify a choice explicitly instead. Cardinality is information attached to concepts in the model and is specified at the time the model is created.

Generating interfaces by models and rules is time consuming and tedious, but it forces designers to think out every aspect of an interface. The decisions are not hidden in the code; they are explicit—observable and modifiable—in the rules and the model.

11.5 RELATED WORK

11.5.1. Related Work in Integrated Interfaces

The literature contains numerous examples of user interface management systems. However, we see our contribution as being our emphasis on *presentation design,* and very few systems are concerned with this aspect of the interface. Perhaps the best-known previous work dealing with this issue is that of [Mackinlay ([Mackinlay86] and Chapter 13 in this volume).

Much like part of our system, Mackinlay's *APT* uses information about characteristics of data it is provided to produce a graphical representation of that data. The differences between the two systems become clear when we consider the variety of data each deals with and the variety of presentations they produce. *APT* produces graphs of various kinds, and much of its effort goes into deciding which axes to choose and how to indicate the values along each axis. Data that can be dealt with is limited to what can be presented using such graphs. Consequently, Mackinlay has succeeded in producing a system that can generate graphical presentations automatically using only low-level information about the objects and their attributes.

Our system is expected to generate a much wider variety of displays, many that would require considerable design work even from an expert human graphic artist.[1] In addition, certain display layouts are often chosen simply to conform to pre-existing preferences of Navy personnel. Consequently, unlike Mackinlay we are required to provide for the possibility of following preset stereotypical instructions in certain cases. We must therefore devote considerable effort to recognizing which cases require these special displays.

A further significant difference between the systems is the complexity of the data we are required to present. In order to handle this range of data, we must represent it using a sophisticated knowledge-representation language, NIKL, a facility which Mackinlay finds unnecessary in APT. Both systems make use of sophisticated reasoning facilities.

Neal and Shapiro (see Chapter 2 in this volume) present a system with several superficial similarities to ours, due mostly to the choice of a simi-

---

[1] As in fact they do. Maps of the kind produced by our system take Navy personnel approximately four hours to produce every day.

lar domain and the common use of maps. However, the systems have emphases that differ considerably. Integrated Interfaces has devoted considerable effort to the integration of several different subsystems—the GDA, QFORMS, PENMAN—while Neal and Shapiro's only external system is the map-drawing one. Map-drawing itself is only a minor part of the functionality of the GDA. More significantly, Integrated Interfaces has a strong UIMS emphasis. We view our effort as an attempt to simplify the production of multimodal interfaces. Neal and Shapiro, on the other hand, have emphasized research into new integrated communication modalities, taking an intelligent systems approach.

It is interesting to compare the architecture of the Integrated Interfaces system to that proposed by Feiner (Chapter 12 in this volume). Our version of Feiner's *media experts* are external systems, integrated into the interface with the use of device drivers. All our models are written in a single knowledge-representation language, NIKL.

11.5.2. Coordinated Work at ISI

At ISI we have been working closely with the Services and Information Management for Decision Systems[2] (SIMS) project [Arens90; Pavlin88a; Pavlin 88b]. The goal of SIMS is to provide a wrapper around a diverse collection of underlying software. Input is transformed into a canonical representation, then passed to a planning agent that attempts to piece together the most appropriate subsystem, or combination of subsystems, to respond. If the response does not meet some a priori criteria, the request may be reiterated with other subsystems until it is satisfied. Finally, the output may be packaged in a form for the Integrated Interface's presentation planner.

11.6 CURRENT STATUS

A demonstration version of the Integrated Interfaces system is now available at ISI. The current version models the domain of Navy ships in the Pacific Ocean. A user may use the system to access information about ships' locations, tasks, readiness status, and more. The resulting information is displayed using combinations of maps, menus, tables, and natural-language output (Figure 11.2).

The system is written in Common Lisp and runs in the X-windows environment under UNIX on HP 9000 Model 350 workstations. Displays are presented on a Renaissance color graphics monitor. The map graphic modality is supported by ISI's Graphics Display Agent. Menus and forms are created using QFORMS [Kaczmarek84]. Natural-language output is produced by ISI's Penman system [Sondheimer86].

[2] Formerly called the Single Interface to Multiple Systems

11.7 FUTURE WORK

We believe our approach to the problem of presentation design is a viable one. Indeed, as illustrated in the examples of the previous section, we are using it to generate various interesting displays. However, there are still several problems that remain to be solved. Below we list three structures that we plan to add to our system.

- *User model:* enhances the presentation designer by allowing it to tailor presentations to individual user preferences. For example, it would enable the system to label only ports and regions unfamiliar to a user, thereby reducing screen clutter.
- *Dialogue model:* allows the presentations to be more closely tailored to specific users' requests. Currently, the presentation designer is simply provided with data to display. It is not aware of the purpose of the display.
- *Screen model:* the screen display is more than a bitmap; it is viewed by a user as containing icons and text that have real-world denotations. The interface's internal description of the display must be rich enough to allow a user to alternate between references to screen entities and their denotations. A screen model will make such relationships explicit.

11.8 CONCLUSIONS

We have realized the process of presentation design in a system that utilizes natural language, graphics, menus, and forms. Specifically, the Integrated Interfaces system can create maps containing icons with string tags and natural-language descriptions attached to them. It can further combine such maps with forms and tables presenting additional, related information. In addition, the system is capable of dynamically creating menus for choosing among alternative actions and of creating more complicated forms for specifying desired information.

To support this activity, we have constructed application models describing concepts in an important real-world domain—the naval situation briefing. We have implemented rules that enable the creation of different types of integrated multimodal output displays based on the Navy's current manual practices. We have represented large enough portions of both the general and application-specific domains to demonstrate that a model-driven presentation design approach is potentially useful in real-world situations.

In achieving this result, we have done more than produce a system for constructing and controlling multimodal application interfaces. We have shown that what would otherwise appear to be distinct communication mechanisms (viz., graphics, natural language, tables, etc.) can be treated as part of an integrated whole, all relating to a common level of meaning representation. We have further shown that the decisions on the use of the appropriate mode can be represented straightforwardly by explicit rules relating information to be presented to the method of presentation. We believe that this work can serve as the basis of a comprehensive theory of multimodal communication.

Acknowledgments

We wish to acknowledge the crucial help provided by others working on the Integrated Interface project. Stu Shapiro helped in developing the general framework of the system and contributed to its implementation. Paul Raveling has developed the graphical interface and continues to maintain the GDA. Chin Chee has ported QFORMS and PENMAN to the HP workstation and is responsible for coordinating the various parts of the system. Jim Geller has contributed to the implementation of the spatial reasoner.

The final form of this paper was enhanced by many useful comments provided by an anonymous reviewer.

References

[Arens90] Arens, Y. 1990. Services and Information Management for Decision Support. *AISIG-90: Proceedings of the Annual AI Systems in Government Conference.* George Washington University, Washington, DC, May 7–11.

[Brachman85] Brachman, R. J., and Schmolze, J. G. 1985. An Overview of the KL-ONE Knowledge Representation System. *Cognitive Science,* 9(2), 171–216.

[Feiner88] Feiner, S. 1988. An Architecture for Knowledge-Based Graphical Interfaces. *Proceedings, Architectures for Intelligent Interfaces: Elements and Prototypes,* Monterey, CA, March, pp. 129–140. Also available as Chapter 12 in present volume.

[Kaczmarek84] Kaczmarek, T. 1984. *CUE Forms Description,* ISI Internal Report, USC/ISI, Marina del Rey, CA.

[Kaczmarek86] Kaczmarek, T., Bates, R. and Robins, G. 1986. Recent Developments in NIKL. *Proceedings, AAAI '86,* Philadelphia, PA, pp. 978–985.

[Mackinlay86] Mackinlay, J. D. 1986. *Automatic Design of Graphical Presentations.* Ph.D. thesis, Department of Computer Science, Stanford University, Stanford, CA.

[McAllester82] McAllester, D. A. 1982. *Reasoning Utility Package User's Manual,* Massachusetts Institute of Technology, AI Memo 667, Cambridge, MA, April.

[Neal88] Neal, J. G., and Shapiro, S. 1988. Intelligent Multi-Media Interface Technology. *Proceedings, Architectures for Intelligent Interfaces: Elements and Prototypes,* Monterey, CA, March, pp. 69–91. Also available as Chapter 2 in present volume.

[Pavlin88a] Pavlin, J. and Bates, R. L. 1988. SIMS: Single Interface to Multiple Systems. Invited paper presented at *Tenth International Computer Symposium,* University of Dubrovnik, Yugoslavia. Also available as ISI Research Report ISI/RR-88-200.

[Pavlin88b] Pavlin, J. and Bates, R. L. 1988. SIMS: A Uniform Environment for Planning and Performing User's Tasks. *Proceedings of First International Conference on Industrial and Engineering Applications of AI and Expert Systems,* Tullahoma, TN, pp. 195–200.

[Sondheimer86] Sondheimer, N. K. and Nebel, B. 1986. A Logical-Form and Knowledge-Base Design For Natural Language Generation. *Proceedings, AAAI '86,* Philadelphia, pp. 612–618.

[Vilain85] Vilain, M. 1985. The Restricted Language Architecture of a Hybrid Representation System. *Proceedings of the Ninth International Joint Conference on Artificial Intelligence,* Los Angeles, pp. 547–551.

An Architecture for Knowledge-Based Graphical Interfaces

STEVEN FEINER

Department of Computer Science
Columbia University

ABSTRACT

A strawman conceptual architecture is proposed for knowledge-based systems that design their own graphical interfaces. The architecture is conceived of partly as an elaboration of the Seeheim model for user interfaces but differs from it in several fundamental ways. The Seeheim model describes a class of fully realized, modular interfaces without addressing how the interface itself is created. In contrast, we explicitly provide for an initial phase in which the system creates its user interface. Application domain-specific knowledge is used to influence interface design and to determine both the content and style of the information presented. Unlike the Seeheim model, we also suggest that media independence is not always desirable in the architecture's early stages.

Two testbed systems that we have developed are discussed in terms of the proposed architecture. APEX designs and renders sequences of pictures that illustrate how to perform simple actions in a world of 3D objects. GRIDS lays out displays containing text and pictures with which it is provided. Each emphasizes different components of the architecture.

12.1 INTRODUCTION

A growing number of experimental interface-design systems are being developed that allow system designers to specify the syntax and appearance of an interface. Such systems often use a graphical editor to create a representation of the display or dialogue [Newman68; Hanau80; Feiner82; Buxton83; Olsen83; Green85; Myers86]. These systems, if well-designed themselves, can make it possible for the designer to construct an interface faster and more comfortably than through conventional programming. If the system supports a tool box of reusable interface primitives, this can further encourage interface consistency and can eliminate the part of design time that would have been spent crafting the low-level primitives. By making the job of creating and editing interfaces more pleasant, these systems encourage rapid design iterations and foster a willingness to experiment, potentially resulting in the creation of a better product.

For all the benefits such systems provide, the look, feel, and effectiveness of an interface produced using one of them are still the result of a human designer's choice of a dialogue model and display layout. Thus, the resulting interface is only as good as the individual designer knows how to make it. The development of automated design assistants provides a first step toward augmenting, rather than merely harnessing, the designer's abilities. For example, DESIGNER [Hollan87] monitors the user of a graphical display layout editor and suggests design improvements, while Peridot [Myers86] infers patterns and relationships in the design of user-interface interaction techniques.

Even in the hands of a skilled designer, these systems still do not address a number of important problems. At the crux of many of these is the issue of customization. A static collection of predesigned parameterized displays and dialogues will not suffice if both the information to be presented and the users to be supported are sufficiently diverse. Even if only a single user is to use the system, his or her needs may change over the course of one or more sessions, as may the nature of the information to be presented. Moreover, the need for timely, often immediate, presentations rules out the use of human-mediated design to solve problems as they arise. If the system is to provide high-quality, customized presentations on the fly, it must be able to design them on its own.

Representative research into the automated creation of graphical presentations includes the design of command-and-control displays [Zdybel81], the graphical display of database retrieval requests [Friedell84], the design of pictures that show how to perform physical tasks [Feiner85a], the synthesis of charts and graphs [Mackinlay86], and much of the work described in this volume. Inspired by the diversity of issues raised by these and related projects, this paper discusses a strawman architecture for knowledge-based systems that design their own interfaces. Brief descriptions are then provided of two research projects whose architectures emphasize different aspects of the model.

12.2 AN INTERFACE ARCHITECTURE

As a point of departure, consider the Seeheim model for user interfaces, developed at the Seeheim Workshop on User Interface Management Systems [Pfaff85,Green85]. As shown in Figure 12.1, the Seeheim model consists of three components that mediate between an application and its user: the application interface component, the dialogue control component, and the presentation component. All communicate by sending and receiving tokens. The *application interface component* represents those data structures and routines of the application that are relevant to the user interface. The *dialogue control component* oversees the user-application dialogue. It is responsible for converting the tokens generated by the application interface component into tokens for the presentation component and vice versa. Typical conversion schemata are specified by recursive transition networks, context free grammars, or event handlers that are triggered by the arrival of tokens from the application interface component and presentation component. The *presentation component* manages the display and interaction devices, determining the exact appearance of the display in response to the tokens it receives. It contains the interface's only dependencies on the media and devices that it uses.

To a first approximation, the Seeheim model appears to be a good general paradigm for a well-modularized graphical interface, as evidenced by implementations such as [Green85]. In part, this is because it purposely does not say much about how each component is constructed or implemented. In contrast, the architecture shown in calloutFigure 12.2 is designed to be both an elaboration of the Seeheim model and a generalization of the model for generating graphical explanations described in [Feiner85b]. It is intended to address some of the issues raised by knowledge-based, rather than hardwired, dialogue and by the synthesis of mixed-media displays by the system itself.

Although the architecture is depicted here as a pipeline, the linear structure is meant only to show the major flow of information through the system, not to rule out additional interconnections. The individual components might be better thought of as communicating agents rather than just pipeline stages. A number of knowledge sources that have not been shown in Figure 12.2 should also be accessible to the interface components. These include models of the user, the current situation, and the display and interaction hardware, as well as a history of the current and previous sessions. In addition, a rich

FIGURE 12.1
THE SEEHEIM USER INTERFACE ARCHITECTURE

FIGURE 12.2
AN ARCHITECTURE FOR KNOWLEDGE-BASED GRAPHICAL INTERFACES

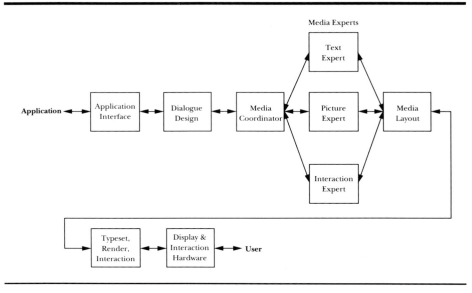

variety of application-specific knowledge will be needed. For example, knowledge of the objects processed by the application and of the actions performed on them is essential for creating the pictures and text.

The proposed architecture comprises seven major components. An *application interface* presents a set of goals that the interface is to accomplish to the *dialogue design component*, which plans how to communicate information to and obtain information from the user to satisfy these goals. The parts of the high-level dialogue created by the dialogue design component are presented to a *media coordinator* that oversees the coordinated generation of material by a set of *media experts*. Each media expert handles a specific medium, such as text, graphics, or interaction. A *media layout component* lays out the interface's displays, determining the size and position of the generated material. Low-level typesetting, rendering, and interaction management is provided by *typesetting*, *rendering*, and *interaction* components, which interface to the final, device-dependent *display and interaction hardware component*.

Information flows through the components continually as the user interacts with the system. When the system is started up for the first time, however, an initial interface-design phase is carried out, producing a set of interface design rules that will govern the interface. The interface design rules are based on knowledge of the user, application, kind of information to be presented, situation, and hardware. They determine a uniform "look and feel" that will be enforced by all of the components.

This architecture shares several emphases in common with other projects discussed in this volume [Arens91; Hollan91; Neal91; Roth91]: synthesis of material in different media; separation of the determination of what to say from how to say it; and reliance on a multiplicity of knowledge sources, including information about graphic design, the application, the user, and the capabilities of the interface hardware. We treat all media as being on an equal footing, as do Integrated Interfaces [Arens91] and CUBRICON [Neal91]; in contrast, SAGE [Roth91] orders material in the sequence in which it will be output as text, before it is presented to its graphics component. In the remainder of this section we provide a rough sketch of our conceptual architecture and discuss some of its implications.

12.2.1. Application Interface

As in the Seeheim model, the application, through an *application interface component*, generates information to be presented to the user, determines the high-level interaction capabilities that the user should have, and processes information obtained from the user. The information communicated to and from the application is, in general, intended to be higher-level than assumed by the Seeheim model. The application interface component may be thought of as presenting a set of goals that the rest of the interface must accomplish, ultimately by providing information to or obtaining information from the user. For example, a goal presented to the interface of a maintenance-and-repair technician's assistant may be to explain how to fix a particular piece of equipment. In a CAD system, a goal may be to offer the user the ability to enter, store, display, modify, and analyze certain kinds of designs.

12.2.2. Dialogue Design

The dialogue control component of the Seeheim model embodies the interface's control structure, created when the interface was designed. It contains implicit application knowledge insofar as it is a product of an interface designer who shaped it to satisfy the application's needs. In contrast, the *dialogue design component* itself plans how to accomplish the application interface's goals. It must therefore have explicit access to relevant application knowledge in addition to knowledge of the user and the circumstances under which the material is to be presented. One approach is to have the dialogue design component request each piece of application knowledge individually from the application interface. Alternatively, the application interface may turn over permission to the relevant parts of its databases so that the rest of the interface may access them directly.

  The Seeheim model assumes that dialogue control is accomplished in a media-independent fashion. If this is to be the case here, the dialogue design component would define the material to be presented as fully as possible without knowing what modalities will be available or preferred. This would entail specifying only that certain information must be communicated and specifying the relationships among the information, along with some constraints on the temporal order in which things should be said, drawn, or otherwise presented.

In the context of a traditional handcrafted interface, media independence is a wise approach because it enables the system to be reused for a variety of users and display systems. The Seeheim model achieves this by enforcing a clean division between the media-independent dialogue control component and the media-dependent presentation component. If the interface is fashioned on the fly by the system itself, however, the ability to recreate the interface when the user or equipment changes eliminates the need to reuse it. In this case, the contrast between the ease with which information can be presented using one medium or device and the difficulty of presenting it using another could be a worthwhile influence on the presentation's basic information content, timing, and order. For example, assume the dialogue design component knows that the user has limited, regularly scheduled access to the computational power needed to support a demanding interactive graphical simulation. The dialogue design component might change the sequence in which material is presented in order to accommodate the schedule. The alternative could be a presentation that followed the normally preferred order but that was longer and harder to understand because the simulation could not be used. Consider, as another example, a situation in which a technician is to be guided through a repair that requires her undivided visual attention when it is performed. The instructions may be provided twice. First, both pictures and text may be used to familiarize her with the task before it is begun. Then, while the task is actually being performed, she may receive only spoken verbal instructions. The instructions presented the first time around may emphasize the visual appearance of objects that can only be described verbally the second time. Thus, the content of the information to be communicated, as well as its form, may change between presentations.

12.2.3. Media Coordinator and Media Experts

The conceptual dialogue that has been generated thus far is next presented to the *media coordinator component*, which manages a set of *media experts* with expertise at generating text, pictures, and virtual interaction devices.[1] The media coordinator decides the appropriate medium to use for communicating each piece of information and determines how to coordinate the presentation of information in different media. Each media expert is given some subset of the high-level information to be communicated and decides how to present it through its own medium. For example, a *picture expert* would determine the objects to depict; select the viewing parameters, rendering styles, and lighting models; and specify the use of graphic annotations, such as callouts and

---

[1] A presentation might also include sound, smell, animation, and other kinds of information, each of which has its own unique design problems. An explanation of how to troubleshoot a motor, for example, would do well to provide the user with examples of how a variety of malfunctions sound and smell.

leader lines. Together these attributes constitute an explicit description of each picture that can later be handed off to conventional graphics software that will render the image. Similarly, a *text expert* would not only create the wording of the actual surface text; it would also provide information such as emphasis and paragraphing, needed later to determine appropriate typographic treatment. An *interaction expert* would determine how information is to be obtained from the user, choosing interaction devices and techniques that are best suited for the user and task.

Although pictures and text, for example, could be designed separately, albeit from the same underlying knowledge base, having the media coordinator oversee their joint generation can produce a more effective presentation. Two advantages are worth noting:

- Text and pictures can *complement* each other. It has long been argued that pictures are well-suited for the communication of concrete information and actions, while text is better for communicating abstract concepts [Gibson54]. The summation of cues between the textual and pictorial media can also improve the effectiveness of a presentation [Severin67]. As well, some things may simply be more easily and compactly expressed through one modality than another. For example, a picture may often better communicate an object's complex shape or condition, and do it in less space, than would a textual description. (e.g., "Replace the brake lining if it looks like this:" [picture of a worn brake lining]).

- Text and pictures can *reference* each other. For example, a textual description and a picture could refer to each other by means of a leader line drawn from the text to the object's depiction. Alternatively, related textual and pictorial material may be highlighted in unison (e.g., through changes in color or intensity). If information about the positions of the objects in the picture's projection is made available to the text expert, it may also be possible to refer directly to parts of the picture (e.g., "the cabinet at the lower left").

Instead of isolating interaction capabilities in a separate set of menus or dials on the display, they could be combined with otherwise passive pictorial or textual material. For example, the user might be able to query the meaning of a word or manipulate an object by pointing to it, or use the bars in a graph that display an array of values as input sliders to set those values. To do this, the interaction expert must be able to instrument the text and graphics to allow users to interact with it. This requires that the interaction expert know what material is being created by the other experts and that, ideally, its needs should be taken into account by them.

The parts of the dialogue being processed can now be thought of as a collection of specifications of pictures, text, and virtual interaction devices, coupled with information about their relationships. This material must next be structured into a coherent display.

12.2.4. Media Layout

The material created by the media experts is laid out on the display by a *media layout component*. This part of the system relies on human factors and graphic design expertise to determine the size and position of each item, based on its relationships to others. The media layout component produces descriptions of fully laid out displays to be sent on to the final components.

The decisions made in designing a picture or piece of text should not be independent of the devices used to present it or the absolute size of the display area that it can be allocated. In the case of a picture, these factors will determine the size and therefore the legibility of specific features that the picture contains. For example, a picture of an object that is satisfactory for a viewer at a given distance may, when displayed at its intended size and resolution, be ineffective if reduced by scaling. In this case, the single small image might be better replaced by a pair of equivalent combined area in which one image shows the approximate location of the object, while the other shows the object with full detail and less context—an example of a "successive locator" picture [Army78].

The picture expert could generate each picture along with a range of acceptable cropped sizes, allowing the media layout component to adjust the picture's size and aspect ratio to fit. Alternatively, rough layout might be done first, and the resulting range of acceptable sizes could then be used to constrain the media experts. Thus, the creation and layout process may be an iterative one involving substantial give and take among the media coordinator, media experts, and media layout component.

12.2.5. Rendering, Typesetting, Interaction, and Display

The rendering of images, setting of type, and specification of interactive behavior would be done by *rendering*, *typesetting*, and *interaction* components that use conventional graphics, typographic, and interaction-handling software to process explicit descriptions of pictures, marked-up text, and interaction capabilities provided by the media layout component. These would then be presented using a device-dependent *display and interaction hardware component*.

Information about the size or color of a picture's objects after rendering is needed by the picture expert, yet can only be obtained by doing at least part of the renderer's job. Although obtaining this information does not require using the same algorithms as the actual renderer, it will be necessary to take into account the viewing specification, object geometry, shading algorithms, and the like. Similarly, knowing how much space a text block will occupy involves some part of the work needed to set it, although the actual typesetting need not be done. One implementation strategy is to make these otherwise internal capabilities of the rendering and typesetting software accessible to the picture and text experts.

12.2.6. Input

Thus far we have concentrated on output. User input follows the reverse route through the system. Consider what happens when a user tries to refer to part of the information being displayed by pointing at it. The determination of exactly what is being referenced is context dependent and often has an easy solution only when the syntax rigorously constrains the possibilities [Sutherland66; Montalvo86]. Several projects are currently investigating disambiguation of combined pointing and verbal input [Moore90; Neal91; Wahlster91]. In the architecture described here, many possibilities for interpreting a selection are available, recapitulating in reverse the process by which the information was displayed.

The user's pointing gesture is first captured by the display-and-interaction hardware component, which determines the specific position touched. Next, the rendering, typesetting, and interaction software can determine the hierarchy of the text, picture, or interaction device objects that contain the selection. Each of the other components has access to different knowledge and expertise needed to interpret the user's action further. The media layout component could relate the objects to the display format, and thus to the rationale for determining an object's position and size relative to that of the other material. The media experts would be able to evaluate what the selection means in terms of the information that they have been assigned to present (e.g., whether an object's color was chosen to represent the object's actual color or to highlight the object). The dialogue design component can provide the context in which the selected information is presented, whereas the application interface can relate the selection back to the original high-level goal being achieved.

As mentioned previously, the overall linear pipeline structure is not intended to preclude the possibility of additional interconnections between components. There is also no reason, for example, why a virtual interaction device could not directly manipulate some object in the application when touched, an optimization that would eliminate the overhead of multilayered interpretation.

12.3 PHASES OF INTERFACE DESIGN

Traditional interfaces are designed, implemented, and then used repetitively. This partitioning between design and use promotes consistency among sessions, as the single program that embodies the interface is used to format all its displays each time the interface is run. Furthermore, if each of the interface's displays is based on the same coherent approach to design, the displays may also be mutually consistent. In both cases, two phases can be identified: development (of a program or of a design methodology) and use (to present the same parameterized display over many sessions or to generate many different displays that reflect the same design approach).

A two-phase approach is applicable here, as well. Rather than designing each part of the interface independently, an initial high-level, system-wide design phase may first set the ground rules to be obeyed later in the design of specific parts of the interface. Decisions made during this phase will be based on knowledge about who will be using the system, the tasks they will be performing, and the display-and-interaction hardware that will be available. The results of this phase will partially determine the information that the application intends to impart to the user and the kinds of interaction it expects from the user in return. A simple, small application may be able to provide a complete and detailed description of all its possible interactions, while a rich, flexible application would be able to provide only approximations and estimates. These expectations could be propagated through the interface to each component, where they would then be used to derive *interface design rules*. The interface design rules would govern the design and layout of the actual material presented by the system during the second phase. Generating interface design rules first, instead of treating each of the system's design problems separately as it is encountered, helps make for a consistent interface. Nevertheless, the rules may need to be altered over the life of an application to reflect changes in the application, user, situation, and even hardware.

Consider how some of these design rules may be applied to the output of the text expert. As mentioned above, the text expert does not decide on low-level typographic specifics; instead it provides information indicating, for example, that a word is to be emphasized, that a string is a heading, or that a series of sentences is intended as a list of points. The text expert is then much like the user of a declarative formatting system with markup tags, such as Scribe [Reid80], whose users are not supposed to make typographic decisions. As in Scribe, the typographic decisions would be embodied in the design rules, which could be created in advance by the media coordinator and media layout components. Similarly, the line style of a leader line in a picture would be specified in advance by the design rules, rather than on the fly by the picture expert.

12.4 CASE STUDIES

In this section we discuss two experimental systems whose architectures address the interface model discussed above. Although both of these systems were designed with this interface model in mind, each emphasizes different components of the model.

12.4.1. APEX

APEX (Automated Pictorial EXplanations) creates sequences of pictures intended to show a viewer how to perform simple actions in a world of 3D objects [Feiner85b; Feiner85a; Feiner87]. Our emphasis in developing APEX was on the design and generation of the individual pictures, so most of the stages in APEX's pipeline, other than the picture expert, are fairly simple. APEX depicts actions performed by a problem solver that serves as its application. The problem solver has expertise about a particular maintenance and repair domain and can develop a plan for fixing a piece of broken equipment that involves rigid body transformations (translation and rotation) of its parts. The dialogue design component is presented with the goal of depicting the highest-level task performed by the problem solver. It accomplishes this by traversing in chronological order the subtask tree created by the problem solver, passing each subtask in turn to the media coordinator. APEX's media coordinator selects for further processing only those subtasks that APEX can depict directly. These are the lowest-level tasks that translate or rotate objects.

Because APEX was designed to generate only pictures, it has a single media expert (a picture expert) that is presented with the tasks selected by the media coordinator. A trivial media layout component is provided that formats one picture per display. Input is not supported. Thus, the rest of the pipeline contains only the rendering software and display hardware needed to scan-convert and display the pictures. APEX is written in LISP and interfaces to problem solvers written in Frail and Micro-NASL [Charniak83], and rendering software written in C.

APEX's picture expert produces one picture for each subtask with which it is presented. It has full access to all the information used by the problem solver: the descriptions of the objects and of the actions in which they participate. Rather than simply passing the existing environment of objects to the rendering software, APEX instead builds a new environment based on the old. This process of transforming one environment into another has as its goal the creation of an environment whose picture will be more effective at communicating desired information than a picture of the original environment. Although the new environment is based on the original environment, objects may be selectively included, excluded, or even created from scratch. For example, an object may be left out if it is not related to the task to be illustrated, resulting in a simpler, less cluttered picture.

APEX supports rules for determining automatically the objects to be added to the new environment, the style and level of detail with which they should be rendered, the method by which the action itself should be indicated, and the picture's camera specification. We refer to this process of building a new environment to create a more effective picture and outfitting it with viewing and rendering information as *depiction* [Feiner87].

Depicting Objects and Actions

APEX starts with a new environment that is initially empty and adds the following kinds of objects, which it selects by processing the objects and actions in the original environment.

Frame objects. Each of APEX's pictures is designed to show a particular action being performed. A picture crystallizes around a small set of objects that directly participate in the action. We call these the picture's *frame objects*, since they are specified by the action frame being depicted.

Context objects. Next, APEX adds objects that will provide context for those objects that are already included. The objects in APEX's world form a hierarchy. Context objects are selected by traveling up the hierarchy, starting with each object that was originally included in the picture. Objects encountered are added to the picture up until the first object with which the user is already known to be familiar.

Landmark objects. Although the context objects are helpful, they are often not sufficient to help locate the frame objects and may themselves be difficult to recognize. Therefore, APEX searches for *landmark* objects that could serve as a reference in locating those objects that have been included in the picture thus far. It does this by examining the objects that are near the important objects and selecting those that have significantly different appearance, as determined by their shape, size, or the material from which they are made.

Similar objects. APEX searches the environment for nearby objects that are similar in appearance to those already included. These are added to the picture to help eliminate the possibility that the viewer will confuse them with the objects included so far.

Supplementary objects. Additional objects are added in order to ensure that the picture looks correct. For example, objects that physically support objects already in the picture are added so that the supported objects don't seem to be floating unsupported.

Meta-objects. In order to show the action being performed in a picture and to help distinguish the objects affected, APEX creates additional objects that are added to the picture. These *meta-objects,* which do not correspond directly to objects in the original environment, are arrows that are used to show translational and rotational motion. At the same time, the position of the arrow also indicates the object being moved.

Depicting Properties

As APEX adds an object to the environment it also determines a set of properties that will affect the picture to be generated: camera specification, rendering style, and level of detail.

Camera specification. The picture's camera specification is modified for each added object to determine how much of the object should be visible. APEX's rules force frame objects, context objects, landmarks, similar objects, and meta-objects to be entirely visible, so the camera specification is adjusted accordingly. Supplementary objects, on the other hand, either cause no change in the camera specification or may cause relatively small changes that enable some portion of them to be visible.

Rendering style. APEX selects the rendering style used for each object. Currently only two styles are employed. The first, the *regular* rendering style, causes objects to be depicted with their actual material properties. This style is used for frame objects, context objects, and meta-objects. A *subdued* rendering style is assigned to all other objects that are added to the picture to indicate that they are less important. APEX realizes a subdued style by blending the object's material properties (which determine its rendered color) with the properties of its parent.

Level of detail. APEX determines the level of detail to be used in rendering an object. Only enough detail is used to depict the subparts that are relevant to the action being illustrated and to disambiguate an object from others that are similar in appearance to it. APEX's objects are represented as hierarchies in which only the leaves are physical objects with properties such as material, size, and shape. Internal nodes of the hierarchy are assemblies of leaf and internal nodes that contain only transformations. Therefore, merely enabling or disabling the display of particular leaves will not, in general, suffice to remove details from a parent object. For example, an object composed of many small leaf objects, such as a wall built of bricks, cannot be depicted with less detail by removing the bricks.

Part of our work on APEX was devoted to developing geometric algorithms that process the object hierarchy bottom-up, associating with each internal node an automatically generated approximation of its children. Leaf nodes are treated as their own approximations. There are two benefits that result from this approach. First, in the search for similar and landmark objects, different parts of the same object can be examined at different levels of detail. Initially, only the top-level approximations of two objects are compared. Objects are compared at successively lower levels of detail only when significant differences have not yet been revealed. Second, the results of comparing an object with others can be used to determine how much detail is needed when rendering each of its parts. Suppose we wish to provide only enough detail to indicate the differences between an object and those with which it was compared previously. This can be accomplished by traversing the object's tree from the root down, displaying a node's approximation (and returning from its branch) only if no difference was found previously when comparing any descendant of that node. Otherwise, additional detail is needed and the node's children are traversed.

Examples

Figure 12.3 is a picture of a sonar system designed by APEX to show the viewer that they are to open the drawer of the center cabinet by pulling on its middle handle. The drawer and its handle are included first since they are the frame objects directly specified by the action frame for opening. The cabinet was included to serve as context for the drawer, which is part of it. The small cabinet on the rear wall was added as a landmark and the floor was included as a supplementary (supporting) object. The large cabinets on both sides were added because of their similarity to the center cabinet, while the drawer's top and bottom handles were included because of their similarity to the middle handle. Just enough detail was used in depicting objects to disambiguate

FIGURE 12.3
APEX: OPENING THE CENTER CABINET'S DRAWER

them from those objects that were decided to be similar to them. The middle handle, drawer, and center cabinet are rendered in a regular style, while the rest of the environment is rendered in a subdued style. Finally, a meta-object arrow was added to show that the drawer is to be pulled out.

Figure 12.4 is created for the same viewer and is intended to be shown after Figure 12.3. At this point, the drawer has already been swung around to gain access to a pair of side panels. This picture shows that the panel at the top of the cabinet is to be opened. The panel and its handle are the frame objects that directly participate in the action and are rendered in a regular style. The bottom panel is added because it is similar to the top panel, but is not shown in as much detail. (APEX's automated approximation technique includes the selective suppression of certain kinds of small objects, such as the bottom panel's handle [Feiner87].) The drawer and cabinet are now presumed to be familiar to the user, because they were disambiguated from similar objects in the environment when they were presented in Figure 12.3. Therefore, APEX doesn't include the context, similar, and landmark objects that were shown in Figure 12.3. The top and bottom rails on which the drawer slides are included because they support the drawer, and the cabinet and floor are included as supplementary objects.

Pictures pass through three different representations in APEX. While a picture is being designed by the picture expert, it is stored as a frame, with slots for the objects, viewing specification, and stylistic information. The design process involves filling in these slots, in many cases with references to other frames, such as those of the objects being depicted. Although the first format itself is media independent, its contents are created using rules

FIGURE 12.4
APEX: OPENING THE TOP PANEL

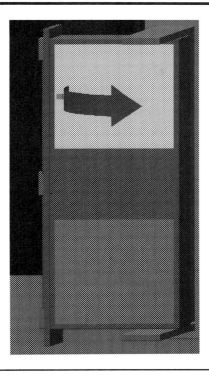

specifically oriented toward picture generation. For example, supplementary objects, such as the floor in Figures 12.3 and 12.4, are added to the representation because they physically support another object that was previously included and would be visible given the viewing specification. While the picture would look strange without these supporting objects, they would probably not be mentioned for this reason alone in an equivalent textual explanation. The second, media-specific picture representation is generated by the picture expert after the picture's design has been completed. It is a self-contained picture description that contains only the graphical information needed to render the image: object geometry and surface material, lighting, and viewing specification. The third representation is the pixel-array image file generated by the rendering software and hardware.

12.4.2. GRIDS

GRIDS (GRaphical Interface Design System) is a testbed that we designed to investigate problems in the automated layout of text, pictures, and virtual interaction devices [Feiner88]. The current version of GRIDS is written using the CLIPS production system language [Culbert88] and C++. It emphasizes the media layout component, augmented with simple versions of the rendering, typesetting, and display components.

GRIDS designs its displays guided by the concept of a design grid. A design grid [Hurlburt78; Müller-Brockmann81] is a set of typically horizontal and vertical lines, coupled with rules for their use, that is developed to constrain the size and position of objects on each page of a publication. A well-designed grid can at once establish a unique look for the presentation, enforce an effective layout, and ensure consistency among a sequence of displays. Computer-based grids, encoded by human designers, have been used by [Friedell84] and [Beach85].

The lines of a design grid delimit a set of rectangular grid *fields*. The fields are separated vertically and horizontally by equal-sized spaces, while the entire array of fields is surrounded by top, bottom, left, and right margins. Objects are sized and positioned on the grid so that they are aligned with the grid lines, with each object spanning an integral number of grid fields in its height and width.

Interface Design

GRIDS develops a grid that will be used to lay out its displays during a preliminary interface design phase. Before the actual material to be presented is made available to the system, a grid is first derived from information about the expected contents of typical presentations, the user, and the display hardware. For example, the size of the display and the user's distance from it determine the minimum legible type size that can be used and the minimum size at which objects must be depicted. The information about the expected contents of the presentation includes the approximate number of pictures, blocks of body text, and text heads that will used in each display, and their expected range of sizes. In a full implementation, this information would be developed through interaction among all components from the application interface down to and including the media layout component. In the current version of GRIDS, it is hand-encoded as input to the media layout component. This information helps determine the size of the grid's fields, margins, and inter-field spaces.

An important part of the information provided as input is a *prototype display grammar* that describes the classes of objects that will be included in the actual displays and their relationships. The specific objects that will be presented in a particular display are instances of the general classes of objects that are the grammar's terminals. The objects that the system currently supports are pictures, body text blocks, and headings. These objects may be further specialized by designating limits on their expected size and content. The grammar specifies relationships among these objects, currently restricted to hierarchical grouping in ordered and unordered sets. For example, the grammar may state that a particular kind of picture is related to a block of text that serves as its caption.

These relationships, along with the generated grid and the information on which its geometry is based, are used to derive a parameterized *proto-type display layout* whose elements are constrained in size and position by the grid. This process currently uses a simple bottom-up, generate-and-test strategy that lays out grouped material in rows and columns, with a pref-erence for alternating rows and columns between adjacent levels of the hi-erarchy. The prototype display layout is a set of assertions that guide the firing of the rules that control the layout of the material contained in the actual displays. At this point the preliminary interface design phase has been completed.

FIGURE 12.5
A GRIDS LAYOUT. (A) WITH THE DESIGN GRID. (B) AS PRESENTED TO THE USER

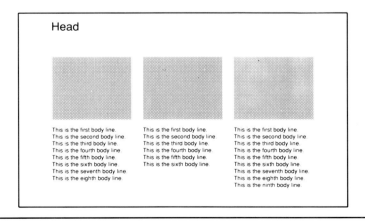

Media Layout

As the contents of each actual display are generated by the media experts (their output is hand-encoded in the current system), they are forwarded to the media layout component. The media layout component uses the proto-type display layout to determine the size and position of each item to be laid out. The current system uses rendering and typesetting components that display only halftone blocks for pictures and numbered lines for text. Figure 12.5a shows a GRIDS layout with its design grid superimposed. Figure 12.5b shows the same layout without the grid, as it would be presented to the user.

By generating a grid first and using it to produce multiple layouts, we gain one of the important advantages of grid-based design: consistency [Müller-Brockmann81]. Each display to be laid out is not optimized as an individual design problem but bears a visual relationship to the other displays that rely on the same grid. The limited selection of sizes and positions used within a single display also helps establish intradisplay consistency. Furthermore, once the prototype layout has been designed, the approach is efficient, since each display is not crafted separately, but rather reuses a common, shared design.

12.5 CONCLUSIONS

We have presented a conceptual architecture for knowledge-based graphical interfaces, based in part on the Seeheim user interface model. The dialogue control and presentation components of the Seeheim model were expanded into a dialogue design component, a set of media experts that create specifications for parts of the presentation, a component that coordinates the experts, one that lays out the presentation, and others that support rendering, typesetting, and the creation of virtual interaction devices. We stressed the desirability of an initial high-level interface-design phase, during which the general format and layout of the interface would be determined automatically, based on the system's estimates of the kind of material to be presented, the user, and the display hardware. We believe that if an initial interface-design phase is supported, then the current pragmatic arguments in favor of designing media-independent and user-independent dialogues will yield to the advantages of customizing the interface at all levels to cater to the specific user and interaction hardware.

Two research projects were evaluated in terms of the model: the APEX picture generation system and the GRIDS graphical interface design system. APEX has an output-only pipeline whose development concentrated on its picture expert. Although its pictures are stored in a media-independent representation while they are being designed, the information that they contain is predictably tailored to the kind of pictures that APEX creates. GRIDS provides a testbed for exploring some of the problems of laying out presentations whose pictures and text are designed separately. It emphasizes the two-part process of first generating interface design rules for an application and then using them to create a presentation. This helps ensure consistency across the many displays that GRIDS designs as part of a presentation.

In more recent work, Feiner and McKeown have developed COMET (COordinated Multimedia Explanation Testbed), a system that designs multimedia explanations that combine interactively generated text and 3D graphics to explain maintenance and repair tasks in response to user queries [Feiner90]. COMET emphasizes fine-grained media coordination among independent media experts. It relies on the knowledge-based picture generation facilities of IBIS (Intent-Based Illustration System) [Seligmann89], which supports a range of pictorial styles and can generate composite pictures that include hierarchically nested subpictures.

ACKNOWLEDGMENTS

Cliff Beshers and Dorée Seligmann provided valuable feedback on the ideas discussed in this paper. Mary Jones helped critique some of GRIDS's first layouts. The Hewlett-Packard Company, through its AI University Grants Program, generously donated the equipment on which GRIDS is being developed. The author's current work is sponsored in part by DARPA Contract N00039-84-C-0165 and New York State Center for Advanced Technology Contract NYSSTF-CAT(89)-5. APEX was developed at Brown University, where it was funded in part by ONR Contract N00014-78-C-0396, NSF Grant INT-7302268-A03, and an IBM graduate fellowship.

REFERENCES

[Arens91] Arens, Y., Miller, L., and Sondheimer, N. 1991. Presentation Design Using an Integrated Knowledge Base. In present volume.

[Army78] Department of the Army. 1978. *Technical Manual Writing Handbook.* Technical Report, Department of the Army, Lexington, KY, MIL-HDBK-63038-1 (TM).

[Beach85] Beach, R. 1985. *Setting Tables and Illustrations with Style.* Ph.D. thesis, Dept. of Computer Science, University of Waterloo, Ontario, May. Also available as Xerox PARC Report CSL-85-3.

[Buxton83] Buxton, B. 1983. Toward a Comprehensive User Interface Management Sustem. *Computer Graphics,* 17(3), 35–42.

[Charniak83] Charniak, E., Gavin, M., and Hendler, J. 1983. *The Frail/Nasl Reference Manual.* Technical Report, Dept. of Computer Science, Brown Univ., Providence, RI, CS Tech. Report CS-83-06.

[Culbert88] Culbert, C. 1988. *Clips Reference Manual.* Technical Report, Artificial Intelligence Section, NASA/Lyndon B. Johnson Space Center, TX.

[Feiner82] Feiner, S., Nagy, S., and van Dam, A., 1982. An Experimental System for Creating and Presenting Interactive Graphical Documents. *ACM Trans. on Graphics,* 1(1), 59–77.

[Feiner85a] Feiner, S. 1985. Apex: An Experiment in the Automated Creation of Pictorial Explanations. *IEEE Computer Graphics and Applications,* 5(11), 29–38.

[Feiner85b] Feiner, S. 1985. Research Issues in Generating Graphical Explanations. *Proceedings Graphics Interface '85,* Montreal, p. 117–123.

[Feiner87] Feiner, S. 1987. *Computer Generation of Pictorial Explanations.* Ph.D. thesis, Dept. of Computer Science, Brown Univ., Providence, RI. Also available as CS. Tech. Rep. CS-87-30.

[Feiner88] Feiner, S. 1988. A Grid-based Approach to Automating Display Layout. *Proceedings Graphics Interface '88,* Edmonton, Canada, p. 192–197.

[Feiner90] Feiner, S., and McKeown, K., 1990. Coordinating Text and Graphics in Explanation Generation. *Proceedings AAAI-90,* Boston, MA, July 29–August 3, pp. 442–449.

[Friedell84] Friedell, M. 1984. Automatic Synthesis of Graphical Object Descriptions. *Computer Graphics,* 18(3). 53–62.

[Gibson54] Gibson, J. 1954. A Theory of Pictorial Perception. *Audio-Visual Communication Review,* 1, 3–23.

[Green85] Green, M. 1985. The University of Alberta User Interface Management System. *Computer Graphics,* 19(3). 205–213.

[Hanau80] Hanau, P., and Lenorovitz, D. 1980. Prototyping and Simulation Tools for User/Computer Dialogue Design. *Computer Graphics,* 14(3). pp. 271–278.

[Hollan86] Hollan, J., Hutchins, E., McCandless, T., Rosenstein, M., and Weitzman, L. 1987. Graphical Interfaces for Simulation. In Rouse, W. (ed), Advances in Man-Machines Systems, volume 3. Greenwich, CT: Jai Press, pp. 129–163.

[Hollan91] Hollan, J., Miller, J., Rich, E., and Wilner, W. 1991. Knowledge Bases and Tools for Building Integrated Multimedia Intelligent Interfaces. In present volume.

[Hurlburt78] Hurlburt, A. 1978. The Grid. New York, NY: Van Nostrand Reinhold Co.

[Mackinlay86] Mackinlay, J. 1986. Automating the Design of Graphical Presentations of Relational Information. *ACM Trans. on Graphics,* 5(2), 110–141.

[Montalvo86] Montalvo, F. 1986. Diagram Understanding: Associating Symbolic Descriptions with Images. *Proceedings 1986 IEEE Comp. Soc. Workshop on Visual Languages,* Dallas, TX, June 25–27, pp. 4–11.

[Moore90] Moore, J., and Swartout, W. 1990. Pointing: A Way Toward Explanation Dialogue. *Proceedings of AAAI-90,* Boston, MA, July 29–Aug. 3, pp. 457–464.

[Müller-Brockman81] Müller-Brockman, J, 1981. *Grid Systems in Graphic Design.* Niederteufen, Switzerland: Verlag Arthur Niggli.

[Myers86] Myers, B., and Buton, B. 1986. Creating Highly-Interactive and Graphical User Interfaces by Demonstration. *Computer Graphics,* 20(4). 249–258.

[Neal91] Neal, J., and Shapiro, S. 1991. Intelligent Multi-Media Interface Technology. In present volume.

[Newman68] Newman, W., 1968. A System for Interactive Graphical Programming. In SJCC, Washington, DC: Thompson Books, pp. 47–54.

[Olsen83] Olsen, D., Jr., and Dempsey, E. 1983. Syngraph: A Graphical User Interface Generator. *Computer Graphics* 17(3), 43–50.

[Pfaff85] Pfaff, G. (ed.) 1985. *User Interface Management Systems.* Berlin: Springer-Verlag.

[Reid80] Reid, B. 1980. Scribe: *A Document Specification Language and its Compiler.* Ph.D. thesis, Computer Science Dept., Carnegie Mellon Univ., Pittsburgh, CMU-CS-81-100.

[Roth91] Roth, S., Mattis, J., and Mesnard, X. 1991. Graphics and Natural Language as Components of Automatic Explanation. In present volume.

[Seligmann89] Seligmann, D., and Feiner, S., 1989. Specifying Composite Illustrations with Communicative Goals. *Proceedings USIT '89 (ACM SIGGRAPH Symp. on User Interface Software and Technology),* Williamsburg, VA, November 13–15, pp. 1–9.

[Severin67] Severin, W. 1967. The Effectiveness of Relevant Pictures in Multiple Channel Communications. Audio-Visual Communication Review, 15, 386–401.

[Sutherland66] Sutherland, I. 1966. Computer Graphics: Ten Unsolved Problems. Datamation, May, pp. 22–27.

[Wahlster91] Wahlster, W. 1991. User and Discourse Model for Multimodal Communication. In present volume.

[Zdybel81] Zdybel, F., Greenfeld, N., Yonke, M., and Gibbons, J. 1981. An Information Presentation System. *Proceedings of IJCAI 81,* Vancouver, August 24–28, pp. 978–984.

CHAPTER 13

Search Architectures for the Automatic Design of Graphical Presentations

JOCK D. MACKINLAY
Xerox Palo Alto Research Center

ABSTRACT

One of the responsibilities of an intelligent interface is to design presentations of application information. An effective approach to this problem is to automatically search a space of possible designs. Since these design spaces are often large and complex, an important issue is how to control the search. This paper describes the search architecture used by the APT (A Presentation Tool) system for the automatic design of graphical presentations of relational information and discusses how it might be modified to handle more difficult design spaces.

3333 Coyote Hill Road, Palo Alto, CA 94304, (415) 494-4335, Mackinlay@Xerox.com

13.1 INTRODUCTION

Given the increasing importance of the user interface in successful computer applications, it has been suggested that artificial intelligence (AI) techniques should be incorporated into the user interface to form intelligent interfaces [Neches87; Rissland84]. Most research on intelligent interfaces has focused on natural-language communication, with only recent research focused on graphical communication. Natural-language communication immediately suggests an AI approach because it involves a dialogue among equals where each participant, including the computer, must have various "intelligent" capabilities, such as problem solving, expressive representations, and adaptability. Graphical user interfaces, on the other hand, can be developed without an AI approach by putting the computer in a supporting role of simulating an artificial, direct manipulation workspace, such as a desktop. However, such interfaces still involve communication. The computer "speaks" through graphical presentations and the human "speaks" through the manipulation of input devices. Furthermore, natural language and direct manipulation stand in a synergistic relationship to each other where the power of abstract natural-language description can be combined with the tangibility of virtual graphical workspaces [Cohen89]. Therefore, an important step to the development of intelligent interfaces is the development of knowledge-based techniques for graphical user interfaces that will make them participate more fully in their communication with humans.

This article describes research that is focused on the output side of graphical user interface communication, namely the automatic design of graphical presentations (such as bar charts, scatter plots, and connected graphs) of relational information [Mackinlay86a; Mackinlay86b]. The research developed of a prototype system called APT (A Presentation Tool), which was one of the first systems to use a search architecture to automatically explore a design space of graphical presentations. A search architecture is required because the design space is large and there are many different factors that enter into the choice of an· effective design. For example, the structural properties of the input information can vary in many ways. Each of these inputs can require a tailored combination of graphical techniques. User preferences can influence which of these graphical techniques should be used. Furthermore, the properties of the output medium can determine which of these graphical techniques can actually be used to render an image. For example, if a user is colorblind it is inappropriate to use color in a presentation design. However, if it is a monochrome display it is impossible to use color even if the user is not colorblind. Without a search architecture, the designer of the presentation tool would have to enumerate the relationships between every possible combination of design factors and the elements of the design space.

APT is based on a theory that describes graphical presentations as sentences that are compositions of primitive graphical techniques. The compositional property of this theory allows search architectures to be developed that generate and test alternatives in the design space of graphical presentations. The choice of a search architecture for automatic presentation influences the effectiveness of the search. APT, for example, uses a depth-first, backtracking architecture that assumes the design space can be explored systematically, one alternative design at a time. This assumption means that APT ignores various issues that are important for designing effective graphical presentations. In particular, this article considers three issues that were identified while APT was developed: (1) Conflicting evaluation criteria, such as user preferences, cannot easily be handled with depth-first search; (2) presentation rendering can discover design problems that can globally influence the search process; and (3) designing mixed-modality presentations requires coordination among the design subsystems for each modality. The discussion explains how prototypical AI search architectures can address these issues in automatic presentation and shows how systems developed since APT are starting to adopt such architectures.

13.2 A THEORY ABOUT GRAPHICAL PRESENTATIONS

The theory about graphical presentations that was used to develop APT's search architecture is based on the fundamental assumption that graphical presentations are sentences of graphical languages, which are similar to other formal languages in that they have precise syntactic and semantic definitions. A careful analysis of the properties of these definitions makes it possible to adapt AI techniques to the automatic presentation problem.

The analysis begins from the observation that most graphical presentations of relational information are based on a general vocabulary of graphical techniques. Figure 13.1 summarizes graphic designer Jacques Bertin's vocabulary of the graphical techniques commonly used to encode information in presentation graphics [Bertin83]. Graphical presentations use graphical marks, such as points, lines, and areas to encode information via their positional, temporal, and retinal properties. Retinal properties are so called because the retina of the eye is sensitive to them independent of the position of the object.

FIGURE 13.1
BERTIN'S GRAPHICAL OBJECTS AND GRAPHICAL RELATIONSHIPS

Marks:	points, lines, and areas
Positional:	1D, 2D, and 3D
Temporal:	animation
Retinal:	color, shape, size, saturation texture, and orientation

FIGURE 13.2
THE HORIZONTAL POSITION SENTENCE OF THE PRICE RELATION.

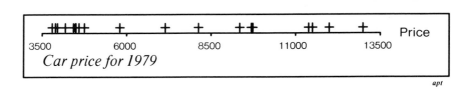

Bertin's graphical vocabulary is used to develop a compositional algebra for describing the space of possible designs. Typically, an algebra consists of a basis set and some composition operators. The basis set for APT's compositional algebra is a set of primitive graphical languages, where each language captures a single graphical technique for encoding information. For example, positioning points on a horizontal axis (see Figure 13.2) is one of the primitive languages used by APT. The composition operators of the algebra compose two graphical presentations when they both encode some of their information the same way. For example, a scatter plot is the composition of horizontal and vertical axes when the points encode the same information (see Figure 13.3).

Given the ability to describe the design space, the next problem is to develop criteria for evaluating alternative designs. Furthermore, APT could not simply generate the entire design space and then use the evaluation criteria, because the design space is large and many designs are possible for a given input. Therefore it is useful to be able to apply the evaluation criteria during the generation process. Two types of criteria were developed: expressiveness and effectiveness.

An expressiveness criterion, which is derived from a precise language definition, is associated with each primitive graphical language. A graphical language can be used to present some information when it can express exactly the input information, that is, all the information and only the information. Expressing additional information is potentially dangerous because it may not be correct. Of course, if the additional information is correct, the graphical presentation might actually be the appropriate one to use, which can only be determined with an expressiveness criterion that identifies what the additional information is.

Effectiveness criteria can be based on many different, potentially conflicting factors. A significant simplifying assumption for the APT research was to use only criteria that evaluated how accurately people perceive the design. APT's effectiveness criteria were based on the observation that a graphical language uses specific graphical techniques to encode information [Cleveland80]. When interpreting a graphical sentence, a person is confronted with perceptual tasks that correspond to these graphical encoding techniques.

FIGURE 13.3
THE SCATTERPLOT COMPOSITION OF THE PRICE AND MILEAGE
RELATIONS. IMAGINE THE PRICE PLOT FLIPPED ONTO THE VERTICAL AXIS
AND A HORIZONTAL MILEAGE PLOT FOR THE SAME CARS. THEY CAN BE
COMPOSED BY MERGING THEIR POINTS, AND THIS SCATTER PLOT IS THE
RESULT.

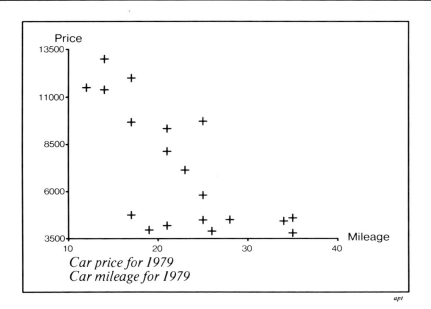

Car price for 1979
Car mileage for 1979

Since some perceptual tasks are accomplished more accurately than others,
the effectiveness criteria can be based on the comparison of the perceptual
tasks required by alternative graphical languages.

These evaluation criteria placed only a partial ordering on APT's infinite
design space. An additional principle was used to create a lexicographic, total ordering. This principle was to require that more important information
be presented more effectively. Thus, any two presentations of the same information can be compared by using the importance ordering to order the
comparison of their perceptual tasks.

13.3 APT'S SEARCH ARCHITECTURE

Figure 13.4 describes the basic model for combining an application and a presentation tool. A graphical design synthesized by a presentation tool represents
the basic structure and meaning of a graphical presentation. The rendering
process fills in the details that are required to form the final image.

FIGURE 13.4
MODEL COMBINING APPLICATION AND PRESENTATION TOOL.

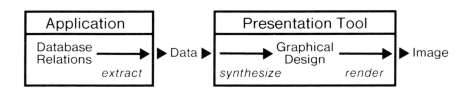

All AI search architectures are based on two fundamental activities: generate and test [Barry81]. They differ in the details about how they control the generation and when testing is done. The search architecture used by APT's synthesis algorithm folds the testing into the generation process. APT's synthesis algorithm is based on the following three operations:

1. *Partitioning.* The information to be presented is divided into partitions that satisfy the expressiveness criteria of at least one of the primitive languages. The importance ordering is used to determine the partitioning order: More important information gets partitioned first.
2. *Selection.* Given a partition, use the evaluation criteria to select a primitive language in which a design is created.
3. *Composition.* Composition operators are used to compose individual designs into a unified presentation of all the information.

APT's synthesis algorithm is a recursive application of these three operations in a depth-first, backtracking search architecture (see Figure 13.5). When the information cannot be presented directly by a primitive design, the information is divided into two partitions. If a partition matches the ex-

FIGURE 13.5
APT's SEARCH ARCHITECTURE. DOTTED LINES INDICATE DECISIONS
REVERSED BY BACKTRACKING. THE RELEVANT EVALUATION CRITERIA
ARE LISTED BELOW EACH STEP.

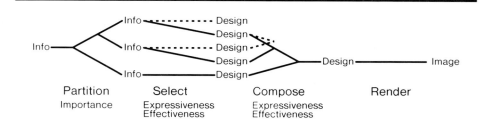

pressiveness criteria of at least one primitive graphical language, the most effective graphical language is selected for that partition. Otherwise, it is recursively partitioned. Once presentations are found for both partitions, a composition operator is used to compose them together. Backtracking occurs when partitions cannot be matched to primitive graphical languages or when two presentations cannot be composed together. This algorithm is guaranteed to generate the most effective design for a given input because the effectiveness criteria place a total ordering on the design space.

13.4 ISSUE: OTHER EVALUATION CRITERIA

In general, there can be many different evaluation criteria. For example, the APT criteria do not evaluate when a design satisfies a user's preference, when it has visual impact, or when it can be rendered in a cost-effective manner. Furthermore, such additional considerations can conflict with each other. For example, graphical presentations that have visual impact are often difficult to interpret accurately [Huff54]. When these additional criteria are codified, APT's search architecture will have to be changed. Two problems are considered here: partial ordering and global evaluation.

APT is based on the fact that the design space is totally ordered by its evaluation criteria. If the design space is only partially ordered, it is not possible to proceed in a simple depth-first manner. For example, if the importance ordering principle was removed from APT evaluation criteria, alternative partitions would have to be considered in a breadth-first manner to ensure that the most effective design was found. The most common breadth-first algorithm is A^*, which will find an optimal answer if the evaluation function meets an admissibility criteria [Barr81]. The problem with this approach is that APT's evaluation criteria are not numeric and it is not clear how they can be combined to form an admissible evaluation function. A more exploratory approach is to utilize the intuition embodied in the beam search algorithm that was used in the HARPY speech understanding system [Barr81], which is to consider a set of candidate solutions during the search. Adapting this approach to the presentation problem leads to the following architecture (see Figure 13.6): Generate a finite set of candidate designs using the composition algebra and the expressiveness criteria; order and prune the set with multiple phases of evaluation criteria; and render the design at the top of the order. The advantage of this architecture is that it does not restrict how the evaluation criteria must be combined. Furthermore, it will be easy to see the effect of a specific evaluation criteria on the ordering of the candidates.

Researchers at Lockheed use a phased architecture for their presentation system [Gargan88]. Their system is divided into two basic phases: modality selection and technique selection. Both major phases are divided into three subphases: expressiveness, effectiveness and adaption (which involves the evaluation of user preferences). The first two of these are based on the

FIGURE 13.6
BEAM SEARCH ARCHITECTURE. THE COMPOSITION ALGEBRA IS USED
TO GENERATE CANDIDATE DESIGNS AND EFFECTIVENESS CRITERIA ARE
USED TO ORDER AND PRUNE THE CANDIDATES. THE TOP DESIGN AT THE
END OF THE TESTING STEP IS RENDERED.

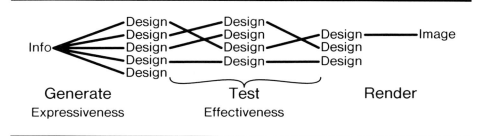

APT research. The three subphases sort and re-sort choices of modalities or techniques for the various pieces of information.

APT's effectiveness criteria have the useful property that they can be evaluated locally during selection and composition. This property means that they can be folded into the generation process for use every time a primitive language is selected or a composition is considered. However, additional criteria may require global evaluation. For example, user preferences can include opinions about composite designs, which would mean generating compositions before testing them. Thus, global evaluation criteria are another reason for adopting the beam search architecture shown in Figure 13.6, which divides the search into generation and test steps.

13.5 ISSUE: A BREAKDOWN IN THE LINEAR ARCHITECTURE

The linear architecture given in Figure 13.4 does not deal effectively with design problems that are found during the rendering process. For example, the rendering process may find that a pie chart slice is too thin to be visible at a given resolution. These problems were avoided in APT by elevating rendering tests into the synthesis algorithm. For example, the expressiveness criteria for a pie chart could be augmented with a test that identified information with small values. There are two major problems with the existing approach. First, it can be difficult to elevate rendering tests; they often require rendering-level information. Second, the current linear architecture does not allow for any feedback from rendering to design synthesis. For example, if the pie slice is too thin, the corresponding bar chart design should be rejected during the subsequent search because it would also have the same visibility problems.

There are two related solutions to this problem. The first solution would be to allow feedback information to be passed from the rendering step back

FIGURE 13.7
RENDERING FEEDBACK.

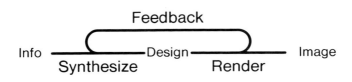

to the synthesis step (see Figure 13.7). This solution raises the open problem about what the feedback information should be. However, it is clear from the APT experience that this feedback will be similar to the representations already required: descriptions of the information to be presented, such as the small values example given above, and descriptions of rendering constraints, such as an indication that there is only a limited amount of space for the presentation.

The second solution deals with the problem of utilizing this feedback information. The idea is to combine the synthesis and rendering steps in a dependency-directed, backtracking search architecture [Doyle79], so that the rendering feedback is directly available to the search of the design space. Dependency-directed backtracking keeps track of the dependencies among search decisions. When backtracking is required, the decisions that forced the backtracking can be noted and reversed. The noting of these decisions means that the subsequent search can avoid remaking the same decisions. For example, when the small pie slice is discovered, the system can reverse the decision to use designs that may not work for small values, such as the bar chart design. This would mean that the bar chart design would not be considered in the subsequent search. The open problem for this solution is how to keep the resulting system from running too slowly.

13.6 ISSUE: MIXED-MODALITY PRESENTATIONS

An important extension to APT would be to design mixed-modality presentations, such as combinations of text and graphics. The fundamental problem associated with this goal is dealing with the interactions between the various modalities. It will not be as simple as combining expert systems that design presentations for each modality. Decisions made while designing the presentation of one modality may affect design decisions for other modalities. Consider using a natural-language generation system and a graphical presentation tool to automatically design presentations that combine text and graphics. In fact, Roth, Mattis, and Mesnard describe such an effort (see Chapter 10 in this volume). Sometimes decisions made by the presentation tool can be important to the natural-language system. For example, the presentation tool might discover that it needs to exchange the axes of a scatter plot to fit it into the page rectangle. This would mean that the text's references to "horizontal axis" would have to be changed to "vertical axis" and vice versa. On the other hand, decisions made by the natural-language system can be important to the presentation tool. For example, the natural-language system might decide to emphasize certain information, which would mean that the presentation tool should emphasize the corresponding graphical object. In fact, this is exactly what Roth, Mattis, and Mesnard discovered, which caused them to let the natural-language system design and generate input to the presentation system. However, as we have seen, these two systems can be locked in a deadly embrace, which requires more sophisticated forms of search control.

The existence of multiple expert presentation systems suggests the use of a blackboard architecture [Lesser77]. A blackboard architecture consists of a set of programs called *cooperating knowledge sources* that communicate through a shared data structure called a *blackboard*. Adapting this approach to the problem of automatic presentation requires a detailed analysis of the possible interactions between the individual expert systems. This analysis will determine the content of the blackboard. The APT experience suggests that the important information on the blackboard will be the mapping between presentations and the information they encode. This mapping will indicate the relationships between the various modalities of a mixed-modality presentation. For example, the blackboard might contain the fact that an object is to be emphasized and how that fact is manifested in the text and graphics of the presentation. Given such mappings on the blackboard, the relationships between the expert systems can be controlled.

Researchers at Columbia University have been developing a text-and-graphics presentation system that has a search architecture very similar to the blackboard architecture [Feiner90; Feiner91]. In their system, the "blackboard" is a logical form that can be processed by the various modules of their system. The architecture of their system includes a media coordinator that assigns information to a text generation module and/or a graphics generation module. These modules communicate via the shared logical form. Their output is recombined with a media layout module. This promising system begins to address the architectural issues identified by the APT research.

13.7 SUMMARY

As we have seen, automatic presentation raises many of the traditional issues surrounding the choice of an AI search architecture. The APT depth-first, backtracking architecture was based on a detailed analysis of graphical presentations. Expressiveness and effectiveness criteria were developed to control a search through a design space specified by a composition architecture.

A number of simplifying assumptions were made for this initial prototype. When these assumption are revisited, it is clear that more sophisticated search architectures will be required.

Automatic presentation is only one requirement for building intelligent interfaces. Recently, we have been developing a similar compositional theory for the input communication to graphical user interfaces [Card90; Mackinlay90]. Ultimately, intelligent interfaces should be able to communicate in a wide range of modalities and thus enhance the communication among humans and machines.

REFERENCES

[Bertin83] Bertin, J. 1983. *Semiology of Graphics.* Madison, WI: The University of Wisconsin Press. Translated by William J. Berg.

[Barr81] Barr, A., and Feigenbaum, E. A. (eds.) 1981. *The Handbook of Artificial Intelligence,* Volume 1. Los Altos, CA: Kaufmann.

[Card90] Card, S. K., Mackinlay, J. D., and Robertson, G. G. 1990. The Design Space of Input Devices. *Proceedings of CHI '90,* Seattle, WA, April, pp. 117–124.

[Cleveland80] Cleveland, W. S. 1980. *The Elements of Graphing Data.* Monterey, CA: Wadsworth Advanced Books and Software.

[Cohen89] Cohen, P. R., Dalrymple, M., Moran, D. B., Pereira, F. C. N., Sullivan, J. W., Gargan, R. A., Jr., Schlossberg, J. L., Tyler, S. W. 1989. Synergistic Use of Direct Manipulation and Natural Language. *Proceedings of CHI '89,* Austin, TX, April, New York, NY: ACM, pp. 227–233.

[Doyle79] Doyle, J. 1979. A Truth Maintenance System. *International Journal of Artificial Intelligence,* 12, 231–272.

[Feiner90] Feiner, S., and McKeown, K. R., 1990. Coordinating Text and Graphics in Explanation Generation. To appear in *Proceedings of AAAI' 90 National Conference on Artificial Intelligence,* Boston, MA, July–August, pp. 442–449.

[Feiner91] Feiner, S. 1991. An Architecture for Knowledge-Based Graphical Interfaces. In present volume.

[Gargan88] Gargan, R. A., Jr., Sullivan, J. W., and Tyler, S. W. 1988. Multimodal Response Planning: An Adaptive Rule Based Approach. *Proceedings of CHI '88,* Washington, DC, May, pp. 229–234.

[Huff54] Huff, D. 1954. *How to Lie With Statistics.* New York, NY: W. W. Norton.

[Lesser77] Lesser, V. R., and Erman, L. D. 1977. A Retrospective View of the Hearsay-II Architecture. *Proceedings of IJCAI-77,* pp. 790–800.

[Mackinlay86a] Mackinlay, J. D. 1986. *Automatic Design of Graphical Presentations.* Ph.D. thesis, Stanford University.

[Mackinlay86b] Mackinlay, J. D. 1986. Automating the Design of Graphical Presentations of Relational Information. *ACM Transactions on Graphics,* 5(2), 110–141.

[Mackinlay90] Mackinlay, J. D., Card, S. K., and Robertson, G. G. 1990. A Semantic Analysis of the Design Space of Input Devices. To appear in *Human-Computer Interaction,* Hillsdale, NJ: Lawrence Erlbaum.

[Neches87] Neches, R., Brown, J. S., Malone, T., Sondheimer, N., Williams, M. 1987. Intelligence in Interfaces. *Proceedings CHI+GI '87 Conference on Human Factors in Computer Graphics and Graphics Interfaces*, Toronto, April. Reading, MA: Addison-Wesley, pp. 267–269.

[Rissland84] Rissland, E. L. 1984. Ingredients of Intelligent User Models. *International Journal of Man-Machine Studies*, 21(4), 377–388.

[Roth91] Roth, S. F., Mattis, J., and Mesnard, X. 1991. Graphics and Natural Language as Components of Automatic Explanation. In present volume.

PART IV

KNOWLEDGE-BASED TOOLS
FOR INTERFACE DESIGN

CHAPTER 14

An INTRODUCTION TO HITS: HUMAN INTERFACE TOOL SUITE

JAMES HOLLAN*, **ELAINE RICH, WILLIAM HILL,
DAVID WROBLEWSKI, WAYNE WILNER,
KENT WITTENBURG, JONATHAN GRUDIN,**
and **MEMBERS OF THE HUMAN INTERFACE LABORATORY**

A tool is something that constrains some of the degrees of freedom of a medium in order to manipulate the other ones better, and the computer is no tool in that sense; it is the ultimate medium, because its content is other media. *Alan Kay, 1982, Testimony before House Subcommittee on Science, Research and Technology.*

ABSTRACT

This chapter introduces *HITS*, Human Interface Tool Suite, an integrated set of tools to support the construction and run-time execution of collaborative multimedia interfaces to high-functionality systems. HITS is a research prototype developed in the Human Interface Laboratory at MCC. We present the underlying research questions that motivated the project, describe the design rationale of building a set of interface construction tools around a

---

* James Hollan, Will Hill, Wayne Wilner, and Kent Wittenburg are now at Bell Communications Research.

common knowledge base, introduce the tools that comprise HITS, present an example application, and discuss the HITS blackboard run-time system.

14.1 INTRODUCTION

Computers are the most plastic medium yet invented for the representation and propagation of information. They can mimic the behaviors of other information media and manifest behaviors not possible in any other medium. They provide us with interactive representational media of potentially revolutionary consequence. To realize the communicative potential of these new computationally-based representational systems we must understand how to exploit this ultimate medium to the fullest extent, so we can provide collaborative support for the solution of complex problems. This requires understanding how to construct collaborative multimedia interfaces to high-functionality systems.

A multimedia interface is one that supports more than one medium through which users and computers communicate. Such an interface might support gestures, graphics, menus, natural-language, sketching, speech, touch, and video. A collaborative interface is one that exploits knowledge about tasks, applications, interfaces, and users in ways that help users accomplish tasks effectively. Collaborative use context as an aid to interpreting ambiguous inputs correctly, phrase outputs in ways sensitive to users' situations, and provide advice on efficient ways to accomplish users' goals. To act collaboratively, an interface must be integrated. Events and objects in one part of the interface must be accessible to the other parts so that tasks can be split between interface components as appropriate and still function with users in a collaborative and integrated fashion.

In this chapter, we introduce *HITS* (Human Interface Tool Suite), an integrated set of tools now under development in the Human Interface Laboratory at MCC. HITS supports both the construction and run-time execution of collaborative multimedia interfaces. Rather than documenting HITS as a user or reference manual would, this chapter explains the ideas that motivate the HITS research programme.[1] The first section shows how our research programme leads us to concern ourselves with (1) the role of tools in supporting the complete interface design cycle, (2) the role knowledge plays in the development of such tools and their integration, (3) a flexible run-time execution scheme that supports multimodal interaction, and (4) a new metaphor, the notion of a *tool chain* that mediates the way we think about interfaces and the tools used to construct them. The next section summarizes a set of research questions that we are addressing with HITS. The third section, Building Interfaces with HITS, presents the suite's anchor tools, characterizing in turn tools for graphics, gestures, natural language, and collaborative aspects of interface design. The fourth section, An Example Application, exemplifies integration of

---

[1] We use the term *research programme* to reflect our agreement with [Lakatos78] concerning the nature of scientific research.

FIGURE 14.1
COPIER CONTROL PANEL SKETCH INTERFACE SCENARIO

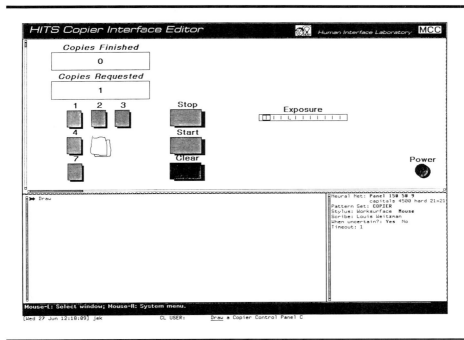

HITS interface technologies in a knowledge editor application that includes knowledge-based displays, graphical views, collaborative angels, and natural-language. The fifth section, the HITS Blackboard, presents the innovative run-time architecture that makes possible the hallmark integration that is characteristic of HITS designed interfaces. The final section provides a summary.

Before beginning a discussion of the HITS research programme, we should explore an example of the kind of interface that HITS is intended to produce. Consider the scenario depicted in Figure 14.1. Sitting at a desk, a designer of copier interfaces sketches a prototype copier control panel. The designer sketches directly on the desk, which has a flat interactive worksurface incorporated into it. Shown in the figure is the state of the interface just after the user has drawn another drop-shadow key and just before the system recognizes the sketch, turns it into another dynamic icon and positions it. During the evolution of the control panel design, the system offers access to comments and suggestions concerning graphic design principles relevant to the developing interface. The user employs natural-language phrases to describe and associate the components of the iconic interface with an underlying simulation model. Then, by touching the the control panel, the user specifies the number of copies to be made and activates the simulation by pressing the recently created *Start Button*. This scenario currently runs on an experimental interactive worksurface[2] in our laboratory. HITS tools used to construct this demonstration[3] and described in this chapter include neural nets constructed using our Gesture Editor, icons designed with our Icon Behavior Editor and configured with our Graphics Editor, collaborative advice constructed using our Advisory System and made available via Advice Angels, linguistic mappings made using Luke, and natural-language understanding employing Lucy, our natural-language system.

14.2 HITS RESEARCH PROGRAMME

HITS is a research project being pursued in the Human Interface Laboratory at MCC. The lab's purpose is to develop the scientific and technological foundations for principled and efficient construction of collaborative user-centered interfaces. This mission requires balance and interaction between the laboratory's scientific and technological efforts. Science done in isolation can lead to irrelevance, to the development of toy systems, and to clever ideas that have no practical impact. Technological applications in the absence of sound theory can lead to clever gadgets, perhaps important for a particular job, but unlikely to generalize to new situations. A central tenet for the Human Interface Laboratory is the crucial importance of coupling scientific and technological efforts. Productive tension between the two contributes to a balanced research portfolio and advances our long-range human interface research programme.

To coordinate our efforts and to focus the laboratory on a project that takes full advantage of the resources and facilities of MCC, we coordinate research within the laboratory around the construction of an integrated interface design environment. We envision the tools we are building as evolving from an integrated set of human interface tools (HITS) toward a general user interface design environment (GUIDE) with increasing amounts of intelligent support for the overall process of interface design. HITS and its evolution into GUIDE are experimental vehicles for grounding, motivating, and coordinating our scientific and technological efforts. They are intended to serve as prototypes supporting the rapid implementation, exploration, and demonstration of new human interface concepts.

Our work is motivated by the belief that the advancement of interface design necessitates understanding how to build collaborative interfaces. Collaborative interfaces increase peoples' productivity in computer-supported tasks by allowing them to work closer to their conceptions of tasks and by freeing them from irrelevant computer-oriented details. Advanced forms of col-

---

[2] The interactive worksurface is a horizontally mounted plasma display bonded with a high-resolution transparent digitizer and incorporating infrared touch sensitivity.

[3] A video tape of this demonstration is available.

FIGURE 14.2
TOOLS THROUGHOUT THE INTERFACE BUILDING PROCESS

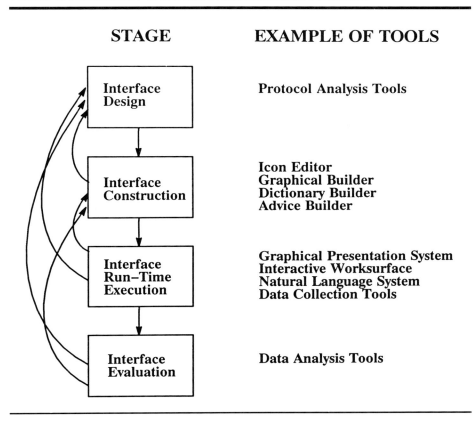

laborative assistance will make computer-mediated applications increasingly accessible to a heterogeneous set of users and provide interfaces that allow richer exploitation of the powerful computational platforms of the future. For interfaces to be cooperative and adaptive, they must have representations of applications, languages of interaction, users, and users' tasks. Thus, a substantial portion of interfaces to future knowledge-based and other high-functionality systems will themselves be knowledge-based.

A complete set of tools for building collaborative interfaces must support all phases of the interface design and construction process: design, implementation, run-time execution, and evaluation. Figure 14.2 shows these stages and suggests examples of tools that might be provided at each stage. Like many software design activities, interface design and construction involve iterative processes that rarely proceed in the linear fashion depicted in Figure 14.2. The delineation of phases is intended primarily as an aid to exposition and description of HITS.

14.2.1. Tools Throughout the Interface Building Process

Tools that address the first stage, design, require information about how people conceptualize the tasks supported by the interface, and how particular interfaces address those conceptualizations. [Norman86] refers to these two sides of the interface as the *User's Model* and the *System Image*. One way of understanding the human side of interfaces is to conduct protocol studies of people performing the tasks involved. Unfortunately, although such protocols can provide valuable insights, collecting the data and analyzing them is very difficult. Thus, protocol analysis tools are appropriate components of HITS.[4]

The implementation stage requires a set of tools that corresponds to the various facets of the interface. For example, building the graphical parts of the interface requires tools for the construction both of graphical objects and their dynamic behaviors, for their association with underlying applications, and for their integration into a complete interface. Building the natural-language part of the interface requires tools to support the construction of a dictionary that links words to representations of objects in applications as well as tools to facilitate construction of syntax, semantics, discourse, and pragmatics components. Building an advisory system requires tools that support the definition of advisory strategies, the construction of systems capable of planning in specific application domains, and the methods for delivering advice and support to users.

The use of the completed interface requires run-time support for the various components of the interface. For example, the graphical part of the interface requires a presentation system that converts representations of graphical objects into device level commands to draw objects and reflect appropriate dynamic state changes. If gestures are to be exploited as an input modality, then a system that recognizes and interprets them must be available at run-time. Natural-language interaction requires a system that maps from natural-language statements into an appropriate formal language (and back, if natural-language generation is used). An advisory system requires systems that can execute the available advisory strategies to collaborate with users in accomplishing their tasks.

Interface evaluation requires data about the use of the interface. This stage can be facilitated by incorporating data collection facilities into the run-time system and by providing data analysis tools. In addition, the tools and interfaces that comprise HITS need to record the appropriate data about their use to permit evaluations of HITS itself.

The final significant aspect of these tools is their linkage to earlier stages in the interface definition process. Tools for interface construction should be able to check the implementer's actions against previously established design constraints. The actions taken during the use and evaluation of an interface can be similarly associated with the design and construction stages that make

---

[4] Protocol analysis tools also have the potential of providing important support for the competitive argumentation [VanLehn82] that underlies productive understandings of user tasks.

these actions possible. This eases the task of finding the parts of the design or implementation that need to be modified during redesign or reimplementation. These linkages, and the resulting power that they provide, are possible only if tools are developed as related parts of an integrated environment. HITS employs a state-of-the-art knowledge-representation language, CYCL, [Lenat88] to provide the basis for integrated development and run-time environments.

14.2.2. The Role of Knowledge in HITS

The need for an underlying knowledge representation system follows directly from three important premises underlying the design of HITS:

- *Integrated multimedia interfaces:* If we want an integrated multimedia interface, as opposed to an interface that happens to allow multiple forms of input and output, then the various modalities in the interface must be able to communicate with each other. For example, to support the scenario we described above, it must be possible for the icons that were created with the graphical interface to be accessible to the natural-language system. This will happen naturally if all the interface components share a single formalism in which all accessible objects are represented in a unified way. For reasons that will become clear as we continue, we believe that a knowledge-representation language is an appropriate formalism for this purpose.
- *Collaborative interfaces:* If we want a collaborative interface, then we must provide the relevant knowledge to support reasoning about user actions. For example, if we want to give effective advice to users, then the advisory system must have access to knowledge about how to produce effective advice. If we want to be able to interpret ambiguous input then we need knowledge about what it makes sense to say in a given context. Thus, in addition to the dynamic knowledge about interface objects, a collaborative interface must exploit a more static knowledge base about interfaces in general.
- *Interfaces to knowledge-based and high-functionality applications:* The most important use for the kind of interface we are describing is to support application programs that have a great enough range of functionality that simpler interface structures are inadequate to provide effective access to the complete system. We expect next generation systems to have precisely this property. Thus, we are focusing on knowledge-based and other high-functionality applications. This means that, just as a HITS-based interface has access to the interface-specific knowledge we have just described, it has access to some useful domain knowledge, that it and the application program with which it is communicating share.

The theme that emerges from these premises is the key role that knowledge plays, both in the tools that compose HITS and in the interfaces that

FIGURE 14.3

AN INTEGRATED KNOWLEDGE BASE

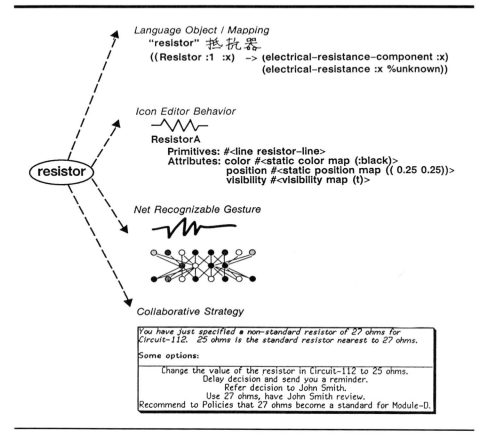

the tools are used to construct. To be effective, this knowledge must be both integrated, to support communication among interface components and between the interface and the application, and modular, to simplify the addition specific information that supports particular applications and their interfaces. Let's first consider the issue of integration.

Figure 14.3 shows a fragment of the shared knowledge base of an application and an interface. This integrated knowledge base, which might occur in an electronic CAD system, contains the concept of a resistor. Associated with that concept can be any number of basic facts (not shown in the figure) about resistors and about how resistors can be used in electronic circuits. These facts are then available both to the CAD application program and to the interface. So, for example, the fact that a resistor is a rigid physical object may be used both by the CAD system in enforcing design rules that prohibit multiple physical objects from being in the same place at once, and by the graphical display component of the interface in deciding on a screen layout that effectively displays a circuit. Similarly, both the CAD system and the advisory system can use knowledge about basic electronic properties of the resistor, such as Ohm's law.

In addition to knowledge that can be used by both the application and the interface, the integrated knowledge base must also contain representations that describe the view of a resistor from the perspective of each of the various interface components. Several examples of this are shown in Figure 14.3:

■ To support a natural-language interface, we need to know the words that can be used to refer to a resistor. In the figure, we show this for English and Japanese. We also need to know that resistors are often referred to by a number that quantifies the amount of electrical resistance (e.g., 10K) instead of by a word. People often use numbers to refer to electrical parts, and the magnitude of the number is frequently sufficient information for others to know whether they mean resistors, capacitors, or some other type of component.

■ To support flexible graphical interfaces, we need to know standard symbology. Two standard symbols for resistor are a number followed by a capital Greek letter omega, Ω, and a zigzag of about seven line-segments. Users expect to refer to such symbols rather than to the word *resistor* or pictures of physical resistors. The size, color, and orientation of such symbols as shown in an interface are likely to differ from the size, color, and orientation of resistors in the knowledge base. On the other hand, the position of such symbols may reflect the position of resistors in some larger context.

■ To support collaboration, we need knowledge not only about how this system allows users to manipulate resistors, but also about how people think about resistors: the different ways they conceptualize them, the kinds of problems that can arise in the use of resistors in circuit design, and the possible misconceptions about roles and properties of resistors.

Returning now to the issue of modularity of knowledge in HITS, it becomes useful to look again at Figure 14.2 and consider knowledge from the point of view of when it is created and used. This reveals two categories of knowledge. The first is knowledge that supports interface design and implementation (Boxes one, two, and four in the figure). It is, of course, possible to construct from scratch an interface of the sort we are considering by relying only on one's intuitions and experience as a source of good design principles and by hand-coding all of the necessary interface components. But the cost of constructing such an interface can be reduced and the quality of the resulting interface increased if relevant knowledge bases are contained within HITS and are exploited by the interface builder at interface construction time. A key theme of HITS is to make an increasing amount of this knowledge available to tool users. Examples of the kinds of knowledge that can be useful here are:

- *Presentation knowledge:* how to depict information in context and to provide context sensitive manipulation methods.
- *Graphical knowledge:* descriptions of icons, their behaviors, and graphical constraints.
- *Gesture and sketch recognition knowledge:* mechanisms that allow the system to recognize gestures and sketch-based forms of interaction.
- *Natural-language knowledge:* rules that describe the syntax of a language and rules that describe systematic relationships between words in the language and concepts in a knowledge base.
- *Design knowledge:* depictions of design knowledge of various types of interface techniques, such as graphical design principles.
- *Advising knowledge:* general facts about effective advisory strategies and more specific facts about the interfaces constructed with HITS tools.
- *Data analysis knowledge:* general knowledge of statistical and descriptive procedures for analyzing data, as well as more specific knowledge about how different kinds of data might be used to evaluate interfaces implemented with HITS.

Because most of this knowledge is about interfaces, rather than about specific applications, it is portable across application domains. The generality of this knowledge means that one key emphasis in building HITS is on the capture and representation of this application-independent knowledge within the HITS knowledge base.

Continuing with the perspective of when interface knowledge is created and used, a second category can be identified. It contains knowledge that supports the run-time use of an interface (the third box in Figure 14.2). Some of this knowledge is domain-independent, some is not. This knowledge can be further subdivided on the basis of when it is created. Static knowledge must be available at run-time but can be created any time prior to then. The domain-independent parts of this knowledge can be provided as part of HITS. For the domain-dependent parts, HITS contains tools to assist in knowledge acquisition. Dynamic knowledge about a particular user and a particular user-system interaction must be created at run-time by the interface run-time system. HITS provides run-time modules that create this knowledge using representations that are consistent with the other knowledge bases that HITS provides and supports.

One way to summarize this overview of knowledge in HITS is to say that HITS supports an integrated knowledge base. The knowledge itself covers a broad range of topics, all of which impinge in significant ways on the design and use of a flexible interface. In addition, the role played by HITS with respect to the acquisition of this knowledge must be tailored to the generality of the knowledge itself. General, domain-independent knowledge is represented once and provided as part of HITS. Specific, domain-dependent knowledge cannot be provided in this way. So the focus in HITS is on the construction of effective tools to support knowledge base development.

We will now step backwards through each of the first three stages[5] of Figure 14.2 and describe in more detail the knowledge and the tools that HITS contributes.

14.2.3. Supporting the Run-Time Execution of the Interface

The heart of HITS is a run-time system that supports collaborative multimedia interfaces. Components of HITS support the construction of this run-time system. We will first talk about the characteristics we require of run-time systems and then, in succeeding sections, describe the HITS component tools that make such systems possible.

A HITS-based run-time system has two parts: a set of modules that perform actions in the interface and a set of knowledge bases that those modules rely on. The processing modules and their associated knowledge bases must be separable enough that they can be used relatively independently, because not all interfaces will require all of the interface modalities that HITS supports. Some interfaces may not need natural-language, for example; others may not need graphics. But it must also be possible to integrate components so that a single, coherent interface can be presented to an end user. As we mentioned earlier, this integration is accomplished in HITS by tying all the components to a common knowledge-representation system.

The kernel of the HITS-supplied run-time system is a dialogue manager that handles both the user's input and the system's output. This dialogue manager performs low-level handling of input and output and routes what it sees to appropriate components of the run-time interface system. It also builds a history of the interaction, and makes this history available to those interface components that need it. It is important not only that this discourse history capture events in all the modalities within the interface, but either that it be implemented as a single integrated history or that separate discourse histories be able to communicate. Examples of ways in which discourse history are used include the following:

- *Understanding English sentences.* Suppose the user says, "I just created a new icon. Now I want to copy it." To interpret the word *it* correctly requires that there be a history at least as long as this two sentence dialogue, since *it* must be recognized as referring to the icon that was mentioned in the previous sentence. Now suppose that the user simply says, "Copy the last icon I created." Assume that the user has been creating icons using the direct manipulation capabilities of a sketching interface like the one in the copier example. Now, to identify correctly the referent of the phrase "the last icon I created," requires a dialogue model that also

[5] Specialized HITS tools to support the fourth state in Figure 14.2 have not been developed yet.

contains a record of the user's actions within the sketching system. These kinds of actions emphasize the need for a dialogue model that captures multiple interaction techniques.

- *Understanding gestures.* Suppose a user indicates with a gesture, perhaps a shake of a stylus or a finger, that the system has incorrectly identified a portion of a sketch. To respond appropriately to this it is necessary to have a model not only of the user's actions but also of the system's actions.

- *Generating appropriate advice.* Suppose a user asks, "What went wrong?" In order to answer such a question, it is necessary to be able to look at the last several interaction events and to explain the actions that the system took.

- *User modeling.* This dialogue model should provide advisory strategies with information about the commands that are and are not understood by the user, based on the user's patterns of usage. In addition to user modeling the history should also support clarifying actions for which multiple interpretations might exist, such as whether a request to delete associated with a mouse click is meant to refer to a single icon or a larger configuration of objects.

- *Critiquing and evaluating tool use.* The discourse history can be used to detect inefficient use of tools, either by the system (leading to coaching or critiquing), or by human protocol analysts.

14.2.4. Supporting Interface Construction

The only parts of an interface run-time system that HITS can provide directly are those that are domain-independent. Domain-dependent structures must be built for each new application interface, so the best support HITS can provide is a suite of tools that enable the efficient implementation of those structures.[6] Each tool in HITS is designed to support the construction of one facet of the interface. Just as the run-time systems in HITS must be both modular and integrated, so too must the construction-time tools. HITS uses the same approach here as it did in the structure of its run-time support; it ties all the tools together through a single knowledge-representation system. By doing this, we facilitate the construction of the sort of unified representation of application and interface knowledge demonstrated in the copier control panel example.

The fundamental notion behind all the HITS construction tools is that interface manifestations of objects are conceptually tied to the representation of those same objects in the application knowledge base in ways such as those shown in Figure 14.3. This suggests that the way to support building interface knowledge is to couple that process with the process of building the application knowledge base. There are several ways that this can be done:

---

[6] We do envision that portions of new application interfaces will frequently be derived from copying and tailoring components from existing applications that are similar. See also the discussion of *tool chains* following.

- Support the explicit statement of interface knowledge by the interface builder. This approach, in turn, has two facets, both of which are currently used in HITS:
  - —Build interface entities and allow the tool to build the associated application objects. This approach is illustrated by Pogo, a system described following for building graphical objects.
  - —Build application knowledge base objects and allow the tool to build the associated interface entities. This approach is illustrated by Luke, another system that is described below.

- Support the implicit acquisition of interface knowledge (knowledge is acquired as a task is being performed). This approach is illustrated by a neural net approach to the recognition of gestures, another system that will be described later in this section.

- Support users of HITS by providing design expertise that may complement their own knowledge and assist them in maintaining interface consistency. This approach is illustrated by Designer [Hollan87], a system for critiquing graphical views based on representations of graphical design principles.

If we consider this close coupling of the tasks of building an application knowledge base and of building corresponding interface knowledge bases, and if we also acknowledge the important role that application knowledge can play in a collaborative interface, it becomes tempting to view the entire knowledge base construction problem as an interface building issue. Thus, one approach we could take would be to include in HITS a general purpose knowledge editor, and then both the application and the interface knowledge could be built at once. Because of this and because of the importance of knowledge editing to the design of HITS, we are building HITS around a general facility for editing knowledge bases. A user of HITS can employ that system directly to create representations of interface knowledge. In addition, we are augmenting that system in several ways that are described below. One goal of these additions is to facilitate the creation of the kinds of interface mappings shown in Figure 14.3.

14.2.5. Supporting Interface Design

Fundamental to the design of effective interfaces is understanding the cognitive tasks that will be supported. This means that one must understand the particular tasks that users will employ an interface to accomplish, as well as the larger setting within which those tasks are situated. In an important sense an interface is a reification of the designer's view of users' tasks and associated task settings. To take a *user-centered* approach to interface design means taking a deep look at users' real tasks, related tasks, and the larger personal and organizational contexts in which the tasks are situated.

Understanding users' tasks means having a detailed model of them and of users' conception of them at a level that permits an effective instantiation of interfaces to support them. A key technique to assist in constructing the detailed models required is the analysis of protocols collected from users of systems or from the performance of tasks that interfaces are being designed to support. The importance of protocols and the current lack of facilities to assist with their analyses motivates us to include a set of protocol collection and analysis tools within HITS. The view of protocol analysis being taken is that it is a form of competitive argumentation [VanLehn82] in which one wants to provide structure to an annotation of a protocol. Tools are required to support maintaining multiple theories about the protocol [Pitman85], viewing of the analysis at multiple levels, and retrieving annotated segments that match flexible retrieval specifications.

Another aspect of supporting interface design is providing design expertise that complements that of users of HITS. An underlying premise is that each of the tools should incorporate representations about their own use and about types of expertise that users might find useful. For example, as mentioned above, the tool to help one form mapping rules between words in a natural-language portion of an interface to concepts in a knowledge base has a representation of lexical semantics that permits it to offer alternative mapping rules as well as assist users in maintaining mapping consistency in a large knowledge base. As another example, graphical tools can be augmented with the ability to provide critiques according to graphic design principles. In all of these cases, the ability to support design is facilitated by our commitment to an underlying integrated knowledge base.

14.2.6. Supporting Interface Evaluation

The discourse history built from the sequence of events pooled across interface modalities can serve as a powerful data base for evaluating the use of HITS and the use of interfaces built with HITS, and can also serve the run-time functions described elsewhere in this chapter. In addition to a history recorded by the system at run-time, protocols of user-system interaction may be recorded simultaneously by external means (such as video or audio taping). Other data may be generated following an interaction, either by automated analysis programs or by a human protocol analyst.

Although the design of our protocol collection and analysis system is in early stages, the evolutionary nature of the HITS tool chain, described below, requires a flexible and extensible approach to the handling of user-system interactions. Prior to run-time, the user of the protocol collection system may indicate which data is to be converted to the common format used by the facility and preserved permanently, where the run-time system would otherwise discard it. For example, the record of the lowest-level user actions—mouse or stylus movements, button and key presses—are of less interest to the run-time system than the higher-level actions they initiate. But at times this level of information is needed to understand user actions or misunderstandings, and under certain circumstances this level of *raw input* might be directed back into the system to *replay* a user session.

In examining an interaction, a protocol analyst may view, search, anno-
tate, and categorize the collected data, perhaps carrying out statistical analyses
and constructing alternative models of the interaction. Such analyses may aid
in evaluating use of a tool or interface or may provide knowledge of user
tasks and common misunderstandings that will contribute to the construction
of critiquing, advising, and user modeling systems.

14.2.7. Supporting Collaboration:
Tool Chains and Collaboration Profiles

In addition to supporting the sequence of processes that must occur in the design of a particular interface, HITS supports the idea of a *tool chain* in which
general tools can be used to craft more specific ones that can in turn be used
to produce tools or to create specific application interfaces. The idea of a tool
chain is a powerful one because it enables collections of activities to be done
once for entire families of applications rather than requiring them to be duplicated for every member of the family. So, for example, a HITS user might
use HITS to produce a new set of tools $HITS_{phys-sys}$, that is specialized for
building interfaces to programs that simulate physical systems. This new tool
set differs from HITS in that it contains a set of graphical icons that have been
designed to display parameters of such simulations, appropriate words (such as
momentum, mass, density, etc.) in its natural-language lexicon, and knowledge
about how to display complex simulations effectively using successively deeper
levels of detail. Now another tool developer can use $HITS_{phys-sys}$ to create an
even more specialized set of tools, $HITS_{auto}$, for building interfaces to simulations of automobiles. This new tool set has been further augmented with icons
and lexical entries for cars and their components. Now additional users can use
$HITS_{auto}$ to create interfaces to various automobile simulation programs.

It is easy to see how the notion of tool chains can be applied to any
application domain. For example, the basic HITS tools could be used to
create a set of specially tailored tools for constructing interfaces for new automated teller functions (e.g., loan applications). One might first create a
general $HITS_{Banking}$ containing a knowledge base of information appropriate to banking applications and a set of interface components that manifest
the specific interface *look and feel* required by a given corporation. Notice that
at each link in the tool chain, we empower users with less interface design
and system-level knowledge with the ability to participate in the interface construction process. The tool chain notion fits well with our view of interface
design as a multi-person and multidisciplinary activity. Linkage of the tools
also provides mechanisms to collect data about usage and to permit the tools
and the interfaces they are used to construct to be more readily modified in
principled ways.

Another idea supported by HITS is the notion of a *collaboration profile*.
Each user of HITS can have a profile that influences the form of interaction
with the system. This starts with a default profile and will evolve over time
via modifications that the user makes to it as well as modifications the system

makes as a result of the history of the user's interactions. It serves both as a user modeling component and as a communication mechanism between the user and system about the style of interactions with HITS.

14.3 HITS RESEARCH QUESTIONS

Limitations of current interfaces are the major impediments to fully exploiting computation in the conceptualization and solution of complex problems. We take as premises that the two major courses of interface development in the future will be toward much more collaborative and adaptive interfaces, interfaces in which tasks are more effectively shared between users and computational systems, and toward interfaces that provide facile access to much more functionality than is present in current systems. Interfaces of the future will not only provide collaborative support to individual users of high-functionality systems, but will also facilitate collaboration between individuals. These premises lead us to focus our research on the development of flexible, natural, multimodal interfaces, interfaces that approximate the ease and richness of person to person communication, and on how such interfaces can be effectively developed. This in turn has led us to HITS and the construction of an integrated environment for interface design.

The research issues that we are addressing with HITS derive primarily from our interest in understanding how to develop collaborative interfaces to high-functionality systems. There are a host of specific research questions associated with each of the disciplines underlying our work that must must be answered if we are to be able to provide principled support for the design and implementation of integrated interfaces. Here we focus on those research questions that span the disciplines represented by the HITS effort. These include a core set of common issues that all interface modalities need to address. For example, to support collaboration the interface must make sense out of often highly ambiguous input data, whether the input data is a phrase in natural-language or a gesture on our interactive worksurface. Similarly, the interface must present information in context sensitive ways that can be readily interpreted by users. Underlying these simple descriptions of collaborative interfaces are a set of difficult research issues. We are addressing a number of these in our research programme.

14.3.1. Multiple Active Interface Agents

We must support multiple active interface agents if the the interface is to be collaborative.

- We need to support n-way communication among the agents, one of which is the user, some of which are application programs, and some of which are the various interface agents. It is this issue that has primarily motivated our development of a flexible blackboard-based control structure for HITS.

- We need to support genuine mixed initiative dialogues. This is why we are concerned with a uniform treatment in the HITS blackboard of both input and output interactions and why the issue of processes and control is centrally important.

- We need to provide users with a coherent view of the various internal agents' individual communications. Although we might implement interfaces as a collection of independent agents, it must also be possible for the user to perceive the entire system as an integrated whole. Thus, we need to investigate strategies for managing coherent conversations.

- If we are going to support integrated multimodal interfaces then we need to allow the modalities to interact at multiple levels of granularity (as opposed just to, say, complete commands). This is another major motivation for the use of a blackboard structure. It is also an important motivation for the use of a common knowledge base. Each of these devices provides integration capability at several levels of granularity.

- We need a shared discourse history across agents if they are going to act in a coordinated way.

14.3.2. Tools for Effective User-Centered Interfaces

To understand our research agenda it is important to note that we are not just trying to build effective user-centered interfaces. We are trying to build a set of tools that will enable effective user-centered interfaces to be readily built. This has a number of implications. First, we need an ontology of interfaces and knowledge about interfaces. If we only wanted one interface, we would not need to make this explicit. Having it in the heads of the human designers would be good enough. But to provide powerful design tools and to enable less skillful designer to build more effective interfaces, this knowledge must be explicit. Second, modularity becomes very important so that the right pieces selected from the building blocks provided by the general tool suite can be mixed and matched for each new interface. Third, we need to support the evolution of tool chains of more specialized HITS with specialized HITS knowledge bases and libraries.

14.3.3. Knowledge-Based Tools and Interfaces

Because of the importance of knowledge in both our tools and the interfaces that those tools help build, we cannot avoid dealing with questions of how large knowledge bases can be built and maintained. Thus, we must worry about supporting individuals in the knowledge-base construction task. Our choice of a knowledge editor (HKE) as a demonstration platform for our work is motivated in large part by this concern. We must also consider supporting groups of people doing this task together. We need to support *co-representing communities*, which may span disciplines and experience levels.

14.3.4. Future Research Positioning

In addition to the research topics that we are addressing in our work on the individual modalities supported by HITS, there are a host of research questions that HITS will enable us to consider in the future. These include the following:

- Given that all of this technology is intended to make possible the construction of new kinds of interfaces, how can they be used? How can we use this technology to build interfaces that help people get their jobs done? Which interface modalities support which kinds of communications? What is the best general way to support the interleaving of modalities?

- How can we provide efficient implementations of the general architecture that we are formulating? For example, how do we structure and index the blackboard and how do we specify control within the blackboard?

- What building blocks should go into the general tool set? For example, are there parsers for common kinds of languages if the word *languages* is broadly construed to include gestures? Are there knowledge sources for common ways of structuring dialogues? Are there domain-independent forms of advice?

- How can the individual modalities provide leverage for each other? For example, how might knowledge about current discourse context be used to influence the interpretation of a sketch?

- What real advantages does an integrated knowledge base provide?

14.4 BUILDING INTERFACES WITH HITS

HITS consists of an integrated suite of tools. In this section we present a selective overview of the tools oriented towards characterizing their functionality and the knowledge that they rely on and provide. In subsequent sections we describe a detailed application of HITS for knowledge editing and then explain the HITS blackboard system. The underlying knowledge base and blackboard system are the keys to the integration of HITS.

14.4.1. Building Graphical Interfaces

The most effective graphical and direct manipulation interfaces [Hutchins86] are typically highly specialized to particular applications. Their appearance and functionality are peculiar to specific domains. Consequently, graphical interfaces should be built by people who have expert understanding of what people who use a particular application require, perhaps in conjunction with graphics design specialists. Rarely are such experts programmers, although they currently need programming skills in order to implement new interfaces. This is made even more difficult because interactive

FIGURE 14.4
ICON EDITOR

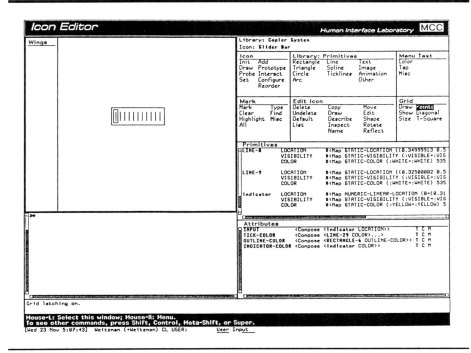

graphical interfaces are very complex programs to write. Our solution is to provide libraries of simple graphical components, methods of building complex graphics by composing simpler components, and techniques for coupling graphical behavior of components in an interface to numerical behavior of state variables in an application. Menu-driven editors write code for pieces of interactive graphical interfaces using the items people choose from the libraries.

Building Graphical Interfaces: Icon Editor

The individual boxes, buttons, borders, and backgrounds that make up a graphical interface[7] are built by a tool called the Icon Editor, depicted in Figure 14.4. We use the term *icon* in a very broad sense. All elementary objects that may appear in an interface are collectively called icons, and the purpose of a session with the Icon Editor is to implement or refine these icons. Once entered in the knowledge base by the Icon Editor, an

---

[7] We currently make use of the Symbolics window and presentation systems to provide some low-level capabilities. A portion of these facilities are also represented within the HITS knowledge base. Implementation of windows and menus are done using the normal Symbolics tools.

icon is ready to be instantiated in interfaces. Each icon has three kinds of characteristics:

- *Structure* the parts an icon has and the way they are connected
- *Appearance* the view one sees when an icon is presented
- *Behavior* the way an icon acts to show state or to respond to user actions.

An icon's structure is defined to be either a primitive icon or, recursively, an assembly of icons. Primitive icons are those that are predefined in the knowledge base. They range from the typical set of graphical primitives (such as line, box, ellipse, and character string) to an *ad hoc* collection of more sophisticated icons (such as dial, graph, column, help button, camera, window, and constraint) whose potential usefulness is anticipated. Primitives can be combined into hierarchical assemblies, theoretically forming arbitrarily sophisticated icons. Because graphical interfaces are highly specialized, we expect that the most frequently used icons (including both visual and behavioral characteristics) will not be stock primitives, but custom-built. One feature that helps with customization is recursion: every assemblage of icons is usable as a component in more complex icons. In addition, we expect custom libraries of icons to continue to grow and be reused across interface applications.

Components of icons do not necessarily correspond to part-whole relationships found among application objects. For example, the interface entity for a resistor may contain a list of colors (that may indicate current through the resistor) while the application entity for a resistor may not have color at all.[8] The appearance of an icon is separated into abstract and concrete aspects. Abstract aspects specify relationships between the components of an icon; for example, that the title of a window lies along the top edge, is centered, uses 12-point boldface Helvetica, and sits in a rectangle whose height is 1/20th of the height of the view. These relationships hold regardless of the medium through which an icon is displayed. Concrete aspects specify details that pertain to a particular medium, for example, the color of the line segments that make up the resistor and the list of coordinate points that comprise the segments. While abstract aspects are always present in the knowledge base, concrete aspects may be known only to a process that renders icons on a particular device.

An icon's behavior includes changing its visibility, color, texture, intensity, 3-D position, sound, or shape. One very simple behavior makes an icon visible whenever a boolean is true and invisible when it is false. Another

---

[8] The ability to provide interface manifestations of important conceptual properties can be quite powerful. In the Steamer system [Hollan84] for example, one of the most salient aspects of the interface was the ability to depict the causal topology of a propulsion plant by showing flow rates in the pipes that connected components. Nowhere in the underlying high fidelity simulation were these flows directly represented. Still they could be readily computed and used to augment the visual display in ways that were very revealing to users.

behavior makes an icon's size directly proportional to the value of a single variable. Changes may be singular or may cycle through a fixed sequence, as in multiple frame or color table animation. A more complicated behavior cycles segments of an icon through colors, as in a movie marquee, as long as a function of various states and events returns a value within a certain range. An icon's behavior is simply chosen from a menu. Behavior can be associated with any part of an icon. A user of the Icon Editor can compose new behaviors readily from a stock of primitives. Should one wish novel behavior that cannot be composed from the primitives provided, such as having an icon wrap itself around a sphere, or blow up, or wave like a flag, there is no way to obtain it short of writing code. While the general problem of describing arbitrary behavior remains unsolved, the Icon Editor provides a powerful set of stock behaviors and ways of composing them. Once a behavior has been described, it is stored in the behavior slot of an interface entity.

Building Graphical Interfaces: Graphics Editor

An entire interface's appearance is built by a tool (Figure 14.5) called the Graphics Editor [Hollan87]. One uses it to instantiate elementary objects or

FIGURE 14.5
GRAPHICS EDITOR

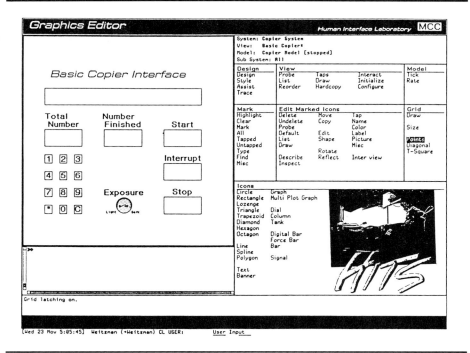

icons, place them in scenes, and arrange their activity. Most of its capabilities are similar to those of conventional object-oriented graphics editors, the details of which should be familiar to the reader. Its main difference is that its output is a single interface entity that is entered into the knowledge base. That entity and its components are thus available for inspection and reasoning when an application runs under that interface.

The coupling of an application and a graphical interface must be highly flexible. Users are never satisfied with a fixed number of views of a sophisticated application. The most important function of the Graphics Editor is to couple an application and an interface, a process called *tapping*. A tap is an object that associates an icon with behavioral functions. Icons may evaluate their behavioral function whenever a variable is changed, or at regular intervals, or by a user's command, or according to a complicated function of events and states. Maps are specified in the same way as behaviors. A number of standard maps are provided; a user selects one or composes simpler ones into a more complex map and tailors its parameters to fit a specific application. This approach minimizes the burden on application entities; each entity need only respond to a probe message. Interface entities are responsible for probing specific application entities at suitable times. This tends to concentrate the details of coordinating an interface in the interface, rather than spreading them throughout the application. Such a balance seems well suited to animated interfaces, where sometimes a riot of events in the application signifies only that an application's variables are sitting within nominal ranges. Also, it makes it easier to attach different interface perspectives to a single application, since an application is unaffected by the coming and going of entities in the interface.

Building Graphical Interfaces: Pogo

We use a tool called Pogo[9] (Figure 14.6) to create an architecture for 3-D graphical interaction by designing a hierarchical set of classes, attributes, and methods. Pogo has four jobs; one abstract, one declarative, one concrete, and one procedural. Its abstract job is to divide graphics into a hierarchy of concepts that can represent displayable objects for any application. Its declarative job is to represent graphical relationships and operations as rules in a knowledge base. Its concrete job is to translate graphical abstractions into tangible objects, frames of reference, and resolutions peculiar to various media. Its procedural job is to program the issuing of commands that render graphical abstractions onto various devices.

For every graphical component of an interface constructed with HITS, there is an object in the HITS knowledge base. Every graphical view has a

---

[9] At present Pogo is less completely integrated into HITS than the other tools discussed in this chapter. Pogo represents one direction we expect future graphics systems to take, and full utilization will require more sophisticated graphics hardware than is available on our present research platform. The Icon Editor and Graphics Editor exploit traditional bitblt types of graphics. Although Pogo is organized around the notion of display drivers and can be used on conventional hardware, it is best used with display-list graphic hardware.

FIGURE 14.6
POGO

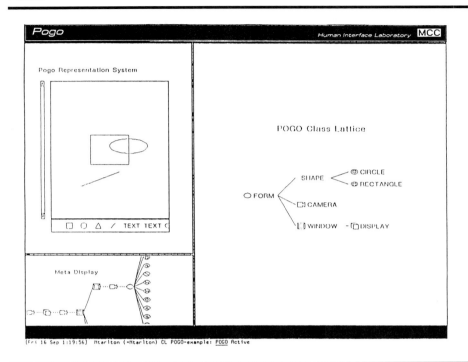

root component that corresponds to the entire view, as well as a set of other components that correspond to pieces of the view. A view can be presented on any device by simply handing its root to a driver for that device. Each device driver is responsible for making optimizations that allow views to be presented efficiently. Device drivers themselves are objects in the knowledge base.[10] For each medium, one builds device drivers that interpret abstract entities. That way, only device drivers contain hardware-dependent library calls, but there is a performance penalty.

One uses Pogo to enter declarative specifications of graphical primitives into a knowledge base. Graphical abstractions should cover a range of complexity, from bottom level primitives, such as line, to intermediate-level primitives, such as window, to top level primitives, whose names are

---

[10] Workstations today are in an awkward phase after the time when information was mostly textual and before the time when fast implementations of a flexible, well-thought-out, widely accepted, graphical standard are commonplace. We would like to use a graphical standard but the only routines that are acceptably fast come from proprietary libraries. Earlier work in multimedia led to the conclusion that interfaces need to be built out of abstract entities whose semantics are independent of media.

always controversial. It is in the attributes and methods of top level abstractions that one settles fundamental issues such as 2-D versus 3-D, real time versus non–real time, device independence, and coercion. Prior systems that were based on procedural primitives (drawing commands) and concrete primitives (pixels) were judged too complicated, too hardware-dependent, and too application-specific. Primitives should cover a spectrum of specialization. General-purpose primitives such as polygons and strings of text are needed by all applications. Special purpose primitives are needed both to give initial applications a head-start and to provide detailed examples for other applications to mimic.

The greatest benefit of representing all graphical information in a knowledge base is that all parts of the system are equally well informed about what the user can see. The application itself, the advisory system, the display device, and the interface all share the same entity. They do not have to build and maintain their own model of what is on the screen. Changes brought by one part are known to all other parts.

The greatest disadvantage of having all graphical information in the knowledge base is that a lot of sophisticated engineering has to be done to balance the competing needs for rapid interaction and semantically meaningful feedback. For meaningful feedback, every interaction should reach from I/O devices all the way to the knowledge base. For high performance, every trivial interaction should be handled entirely within I/O devices.

14.4.2. Building Gestural Interfaces

Freehand input presents a recognition problem analogous to that of continuous speech. The user's hands are in almost continuous motion, and what the system wants to receive is not a fast stream of coordinates but a slow trickle of very high-level interface entities. If the user sketches a graphical symbol that signifies a resistor, the device should encode the stream of gestures into the interface entity that represents a graphic for a resistor with the same position, size, and orientation that was sketched. This has motivated a tool called the Gesture Editor that trains a neural net to recognize users' sketches and gestures. After a neural net [Rumelhart86] has learned to recognize them its weights are entered into the knowledge base, to be retrieved whenever users want to draw icons in that vocabulary.

Building Gestural Interfaces: Interactive Worksurface

The Interactive Worksurface is a system that can recognize and interpret notations and sketches that are drawn freehand. It consists of a large, horizontal, 72 bpi plasma panel coupled with a 1000 bpi digitizer and a 16 bpi touch sensor. As an output device, it functions as a raster device compatible with SunViews, X11, and the Symbolics window system. As an input device, the digitizing stylus sends 200 coordinate pairs per second over a VME-bus to software on a host computer that converts them to strokes, thence to a normalized bitmap, which is input to a neural net. The net classifies the pattern and posts an object representing the sketch on the blackboard of the HITS run-time system. Touch inputs are posted directly as coordinate pairs.

Building Gesture-based Interfaces: Gesture Editor

The Gesture Editor (Figure 14.7) is a tool for collecting, editing, labeling, and transforming training samples for neural networks. It was built to ease the task of creating and handling the large training sets required for building effective networks. Originally designed to collect and edit hand notation gestures for a stylus-based digitizer such as that employed in the Interactive Worksurface, it has been expanded to process scanned image samples and to generate artificial patterns as well. Samples are presented via a filmstrip metaphor. The editor contains a neural net simulator and can output pattern files for use by the Rumelhart-McClelland simulator [Rumelhart86]. Network specification is simpler and learning is faster than in the Rumelhart-McClelland simulator.

Numerous facilities are supported by the Gesture Editor. These include facilities for switching between different coding schemes for inputs (e.g., size of array, dots vs. strokes) and outputs (e.g., conversions from feature

FIGURE 14.7
GESTURE EDITOR

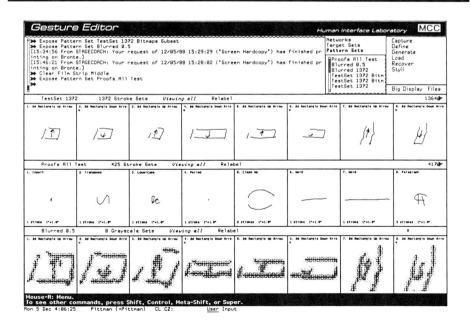

codes to category codes), for capturing stroke images from commonly available digitizers, for using a network to label images as they are captured, and for mapping schemes to assign image labels to specific neural network output patterns. In addition, the Gesture Editor provides a facility for random variation of images that can be used when training a network, so that on each pass through an image set a slightly different image is produced to feed to the network. Several sources of random variation are available, including rotation, aspect ratio stretch, stroke stretching and shrinking, and bitmap noise (pixel lossage and trashing). This facility is similar in purpose to the training-with-noise facility of the Rumelhart-McClelland simulator, but is much more sophisticated. It can be used both with the internal neural network simulator and with the pattern file generator. The Gesture Editor, like all HITS tools, can also be used interactively on the IWS.

14.4.3. Building Natural-Language Interfaces

Natural-language understanding and generation by computer requires complex programs. For a computer to use language as humans do requires a large body of knowledge about the world in general, knowledge about particular domains, knowledge about general discourse conventions and the particular discourse at hand, as well as knowledge about the sentence structure and words of a language and their mappings to representations in some internal store such as a knowledge base. The computational state of the art in natural-language processing falls far short of general human discourse, but nevertheless limited forms of natural-language can be usefully employed in the interfaces to restricted application domains.

The main rationale for use of natural-language in an interface is that natural-language provides the best means available for users to refer to sets of objects whose makeup is not fixed and finite, whose unique references are typically not known (or remembered) by a user, or whose reference by other modalities might be awkward or time consuming or both. For example, consider a computer model of something like a copier shown schematically in Figure 14.8.

As such a complex model evolves over time, typically involving many people, the need grows for some commonly understood language by which users can refer to concepts in the knowledge base. There seems to be nothing as suitable as a natural-language like English in such cases. Unique names given to entities in a knowledge base are likely to be unpredictable and hard to remember. In knowledge editing and retrieval applications, the usefulness of graphical navigational techniques goes down in proportion to the size and complexity of the knowledge base. In many other kinds of applications, users may need to refer to knowledge concepts without being conscious of them. Such is the case in the copier interface design scenario described in the outset of this chapter, in which a user taps an icon to the concept in a copier simulation model denoted by the English phrase "the start button." Phrases

FIGURE 14.8
A COMPLEX REFERENCE DOMAIN

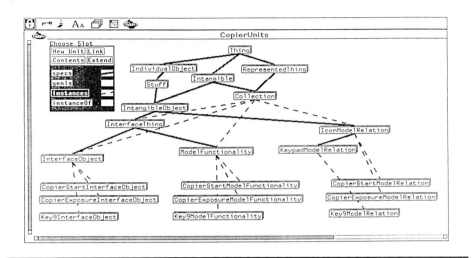

that would have worked equally well include, "a button to start the machine," "the start function," "starting the copier," and so on.

A complete natural-language system includes the ability both to understand input from the user and to generate appropriate responses in natural-languages. Because almost all of our effort up to this point has been devoted to the understanding side of such a system, we will focus our discussion here on this side of the problem.

Figure 14.9 shows a schematic diagram of a natural-language understanding system. The ovals represent the necessary knowledge sources. The rectangles represent the processes that use the knowledge. The domain-independent HITS run-time system supplies all the rectangles in the figure. Thus, HITS supplies the standard operational components of an natural-language understanding system, for example, a parser, a semantic interpreter, an anaphora resolver, and a pragmatic processor.

Unfortunately, HITS cannot go quite so far in specifying all the necessary knowledge in a domain-independent way. It can go a long way toward providing the top oval, since syntactic knowledge varies relatively little as a function of the domain that is being described. The bottom oval must, of course, be redone for each application, but we make the assumption that the natural-language system will use the same domain knowledge base that the application program itself uses. The middle oval must be created especially for each new natural-language interface. To do this, HITS provides a tool, Lucy, that will be described following.

FIGURE 14.9

A NATURAL-LANGUAGE UNDERSTANDING SYSTEM

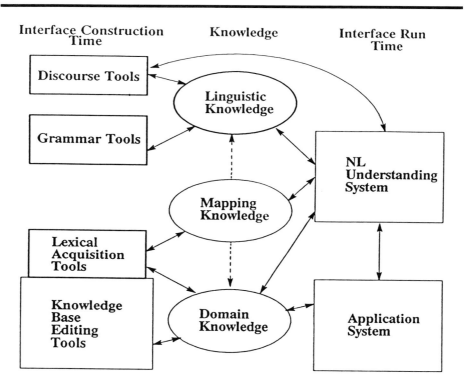

Building Natural-Language Interfaces: Lucy

Lucy is the English-understanding component of HITS. It is comprised of a set of tools for incorporating partial or full use of natural-language into an interface. Lucy is integrated with other HITS tools in such a way that the use of natural-language can be combined with other interface modalities such as graphics, sketching, pointing, menus, and command languages in the interface. Designers can then mix and match according to the needs of each particular interface being built.

The major components of Lucy are:

- a discourse and dialogue management module
- a semantic mapping module
- morphological and syntax modules
- an English grammar and core lexicon

The HITS run-time system, described later, integrates the processes involving these knowledge sources, as well as others in the interface, through a central blackboard. During analysis, the blackboard allows for flexible interleaving of knowledge sources. This design for system architecture has been the result of several years of research on natural-language understanding systems in which other approaches to the control problem have been tried and rejected.

As we saw in Figure 14.9, three kinds of knowledge are necessary to support a natural-language understanding system. We will briefly discuss the support HITS provides for the acquisition of each of them.

Linguistic knowledge (the top oval) is mostly portable from one domain to another. Although the words we use vary as a function of what we are talking about, there is little variation in the syntactic rules that govern the use of those words Thus, HITS provides a syntactic grammar for each language that it covers. But HITS also provides a set of grammar development tools. Interface designers (and perhaps even users) will probably want to do some extensions and customization of the grammar and discourse components as each new Lucy-based interface comes into being. Interface designers will certainly need to do testing. And further, such tools would, of course, be useful should HITS users want to write grammars for languages other than English. The major tool for grammar development is Lucy Lab, shown in Figure 14.10.

FIGURE 14.10
LUCY LAB SCREEN

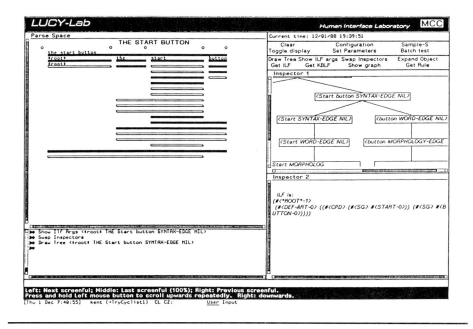

FIGURE 14.11

DISCOURSE LAB SCREEN

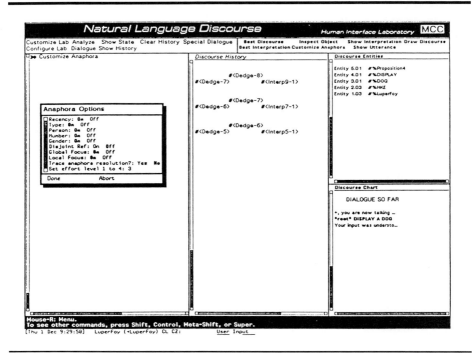

It is an interactive environment used to examine the state of an analysis by inspecting and stepping through a graphical display of the underlying rule firings in a chart/blackboard. Off-line testing of a corpus of input strings is available through a batch test facility.

Discourse Lab (Figure 14.11) is an analogous set of interactive debugging and development tools for inspecting the state and processes of the discourse component. An example where Discourse Lab would be used is in the development of an interface component to understand a pronoun such as *it*. As pronouns come into the dialogue, the discourse history needs to be consulted to assign a meaning to the pronoun. Lucy makes the best guess consistent with heuristics and the known constraints. Sometimes, however, insufficient information is available for Lucy to determine the user's meaning. In such cases the user is engaged in a clarification dialogue that in turn is added to the history of the interaction.

Domain knowledge (the bottom oval) must mostly be redone for each new domain (although there may even be portable parts of this [Lenat88]). The premise that underlies the HITS approach to natural-language understanding is that the natural-language system will not have its own domain

FIGURE 14.12
A LAYERED TOOL FOR KNOWLEDGE BASE CONSTRUCTION

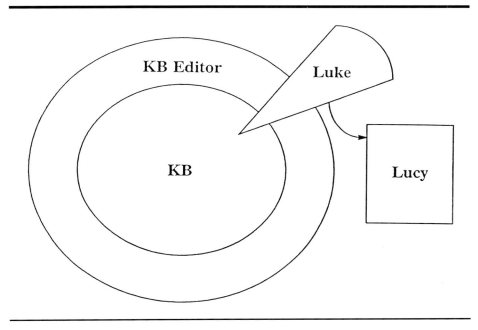

knowledge. Instead it will use the domain knowledge that the application program exploits. Thus the creation of the knowledge in this bottom oval is not specifically an interface creation problem. It can be done using the standard knowledge base tools upon which HITS is built.

Building Natural-Language Interfaces: Luke

Mapping knowledge (the third oval) is the main bottleneck in building a natural-language interface for a new application program. HITS provides a tool called Luke to help to overcome this problem. Luke facilitates the creation of the semantic mapping rules that are needed by a natural-language system when it maps from words in a language to and concepts in a knowledge base. The key idea behind the design of Luke is that, because these mappings are conceptually linked to the knowledge base objects to which they refer, the right time to build the mappings is roughly the same time that the knowledge base objects themselves are being created. Thus, Luke is implemented as a set of hooks into the most basic knowledge base editor on which HITS is built. The architecture of Luke is shown in Figure 14.12. Whenever a knowledge base object is created, the Luke command, *Associate Word*, can be invoked to associate one or more words with the new object. These words can be defined to map to the object itself or to some path that goes through the knowledge base and that refers to the new object. Luke incorporates a general model of lexical semantics so that it can, in many cases, guess the correct form for the semantic mapping rules that define a new word. It then displays its guess to the user, who can easily edit the new rules before they are actually stored.

Luke is a colloquial name for an extension to the HITS Knowledge Editor (HKE) that enables editing and maintaining lexical knowledge. Lexicon-building tools are crucial for making natural-language processing an integral part of the interface designer's tool kit, yet such interface designers cannot be expected to be experts in natural-language processing. Luke attempts to bridge this gap by representing and acquiring lexical knowledge in the same manner as any other knowledge representation task. Thus any user of HKE has almost all the requisite skills to build lexicons for the run-time Lucy natural-language system.

Luke provides a set of special display and editing methods for units representing *open class* English words: those that can gain new entries over the course of everyday usage, such as nouns, verbs, and adjectives. The *closed class* words such as articles and pronouns are automatically entered in the lexicon from the start. HKE users define new words by invoking one of a small number of commands. For example, *Associate Noun* defines a particular noun to semantically denote a set of units in the knowledge base, as well as defining that noun's syntactic properties, such as whether it has mass or count properties, its pluralization, and so on.

As a result of one of these special commands, several new units are created representing orthographic, syntactic, and semantic aspects of the word. These can be inspected in the same way as any other unit, although they have special display methods and so may appear slightly different than ordinary units. These units are processed by a special *lexicon compiler*, that produces a compact indexed run-time structure for the Lucy parser. As soon as acquisition of lexical units is completed, Luke compiles the new word sense and makes it available in the natural-language lexicon.

Unfortunately, word definitions are as likely to need modification over time as programs. The definitions of words can be debugged in HKE since the Lucy parser is an integral part of the HKE interface. After a new word is defined, it instantly becomes available for use in the HKE interface itself. Thus in one command, the user can define the noun *bear* to mean some instance of the class #%Bears and then in the next command make use of it by issuing the command:

        :Inspect Unit "a brown bear in Wisconsin"

instead of

        :Inspect Unit #%BrownBear76235

and expect the noun phrase to be parsed and analyzed correctly (assuming, of course, that *Wisconsin* and *brown* and *in* had been previously defined as words in a similar manner.) In this way Luke brings the same immediacy to lexical acquisition that has proven itself in the world of exploratory programming.

14.4.4. Building Collaborative Interfaces

Our approach to the acquisition of knowledge to support collaboration and advice follows the same two step approach described above. First, it should be possible to derive some of it from a declarative representation of the application. Ideally, this representation *is* the definition of the application, and not a *post hoc* representational depiction of the application developed independently of the application. There are several kinds of knowledge that could be constructed in this way:

■ *Static application representations.* Any implementation of an application contains definitions of the components of the application: the numbers and kinds of inputs and outputs each of these procedures has, constraints on the data that are accepted and produced by these procedures, and so on. In present-day applications, this information is all buried inside the application in unanalyzable procedural code. If these components were implemented in an inspectable, declarative form, it would be possible to derive advisory knowledge structures characterizing these aspects of the application's procedures (or, better still, to use these knowledge structures as the basis of advisory reasoning). This is rather low-level, abstract knowledge about the application, but it is important information nevertheless.

■ *Knowledge about basic interface capabilities from advisory-laden components.* A powerful interface development environment should make building blocks available to interface designers that can be combined to yield working interfaces. We envision these building blocks as supporting basic interface operations; for object-oriented graphical interfaces, these operations would include the creation and deletion of screen icons and techniques for drawing links between these icons. In addition, these building blocks would contain knowledge structures capable of informing an advisor about how the operations can be applied correctly (and incorrectly) in an application. For instance, a building block for drawing links between screen objects should contain the interface level code that portrays the creation and deletion of these links on the graphics display, and the application level code that implements the functional interconnection between the application elements connected by the link. This component should also contain knowledge relevant to the linking of objects: how users create and delete links, how links affect application programs, and how link manipulation can be misunderstood (i.e., there are invalid ways of drawing links and invalid models of how links support information transfer between application elements). The point of this approach is to define this knowledge once, and to have it be inherited by any application advisor that utilizes this link-drawing building block.

■ *Guided acquisition of advisory knowledge.* A final important classification of advisory knowledge is the knowledge that is highly application-specific. As noted above, a representation of the number of inputs to a statistical procedure could be derived from a declarative representation of that procedure, but that same representation could not support the derivation of knowledge about the role that this procedure plays in the application, the reason that one would want to compute such a statistic, or the use for the statistic if it existed. Because of its application specificity, it is also unlikely that this knowledge could be inherited from some other application in the way that knowledge about linking might be inherited from an intelligent interface tool kit. The only way to get this knowledge into the system is to encode it through standard knowledge acquisition techniques.

Two aspects of HITS facilitate the task of representation of knowledge to support collaboration and advising. The first is a knowledge base rich in knowledge about interface topics. This provides a strong foundation for representing application-specific knowledge. This is operationally no different from normal knowledge acquisition procedures; the power comes from the accumulation and richness of the knowledge available, and the shorter conceptual distance between the concept to be represented and the concepts already present in the knowledge base. The second aspect is a set of techniques for guiding the knowledge acquisition process. Just as Luke prompts the user who enters knowledge for semantic mapping rules corresponding to concepts being entered into the HITS lexicon, a similar set of techniques can prompt the user for the advisory knowledge discussed earlier: the common models and misconceptions of these concepts. Together, these features serve to structure, and thereby ease, the knowledge-representation task.

As was the case with our approach to natural-language understanding, our approach to collaboration and advising draws on several types of knowledge. THEMIS [Hill88a; Masson88], which handles user queries and supplies advisory strategies for their solution is composed of a procedural component and a set of knowledge bases to which the component refers. Some of the knowledge bases contain domain-independent knowledge; this knowledge is also provided as part of HITS. As an example, many of the advisory strategies that are exploited by THEMIS are very general (e.g., the strategy for describing a plan is very general, even though the content of a particular plan is, of course, tied to a problem domain.) Some of the required knowledge is necessarily domain-dependent. What HITS can provide for these domain-specific knowledge bases is a set of tools to aid in their construction.

Building Collaborative Interfaces: Conversation Tool

A number of recent empirical studies have pointed out problems inherent in both human-human and human-computer communication [Hill88b; Suchman87]. Consequently, exploring techniques for dealing with communication problems has become a focus of our research in advising. We search for ways advice seekers can take a more active role in the advisory interaction, such as allowing them to redirect the course of the interchange, to follow up on parts of it, or to suspend the interaction and resume it at a later time. In short, we seek to move toward a *collaborative* interaction, in which the advisory system and the user share the ability to direct the interaction [Terveen88]. The HITS Conversation Tool is an experimental interface built on this foundation. It supports collaboration design by making it easy for designers to obtain relevant information about existing collaborations and allowing them to begin from any piece of advice and pursue not one, but many alternative conversational avenues.

There are several ways for collaboration designers to initiate an advisory interaction. By indicating the knowledge structure they are interested in, they can set the advisory focus to relevant strategies. The collaboration designer can then seek advice by pointing at the focus unit and the relevant strategies associated with it. In addition, two important types of advice-seeking, obtaining descriptions and obtaining instructions, can be initiated.

When an advisory interaction is completed, the structure of the interchange is shown on the display. Collaboration designers can follow up on any piece of advice by clicking on it. This brings up a menu of further advice available from that point. The possibilities for further advice include getting an elaboration of the instruction, receiving an explanation of any of the concepts referred to, and being shown the actual knowledge base objects that were referred to.

Collaboration designers also may redirect the interaction dynamically. When advice is being given, they may indicate trouble. The system responds by asking them to describe which of its communications caused the trouble and then to choose from the further advice that is available. After this clarification subdialogue has been completed, the collaboration designer may resume the interrupted interaction.

14.5 AN EXAMPLE APPLICATION: THE HITS KNOWLEDGE EDITOR

The HITS Knowledge Editor (HKE, shown in Figure 14.13) is an example application of HITS in the domain of CYC knowledge base editing. Our purpose in building HKE is twofold. First, HKE provides a working example of the use of HITS. Second, HKE is a research vehicle for understanding the demands that the knowledge editing task places on interfaces. As a knowledge editor, HKE supports browsing and editing of the CYC knowledge base. This is a substantial application because:

- **Complexity of the Knowledge Base** The CYC knowledge base is large (approximately 30000 units) and complex (20 inference methods, thousands of classes of objects) Users need effective methods of visualizing the knowledge base's structure, contents, and inference processes with-

FIGURE 14.13
HKE SCREEN

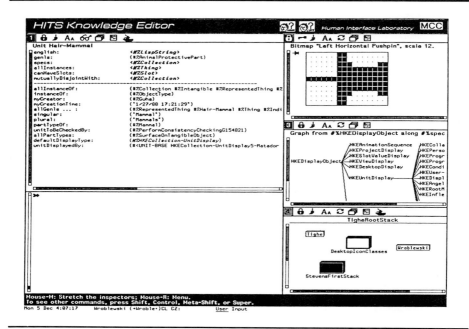

out being overwhelmed with information. Users who enter knowledge into CYC must not only enter information but must also ensure that the knowledge is coordinated with that being entered simultaneously by many other users.

■ **Complexity of Knowledge Editing** Knowledge editing is not a single task. It consists of the multiple complex tasks that are involved in deciding how to conceptualize and represent the important aspects of domain knowledge for various types of applications. The representational difficulty varies with the type of domain being represented and the amount of epistemologically primitive representations required to tie the domain into the CYC knowledge base. This can vary from having to make deep epistemological decisions to being able to exploit the copying and editing of already existing closely related representations.

14.5.1. HKE Is Implemented with HITS

As an example HITS application, HKE makes use of most of the components of HITS in its implementation. For instance, to handle user input HKE uses the HITS blackboard (discussed later), and to collaborate with users it exploits a representation of itself and the task of knowledge editing. When a user types a command or clicks the mouse, the knowledge base is consulted about how to handle the command or mouse gesture, and appropriate routines to respond to the user action are invoked.

HKE allows graphical views to be created and attached to portions of the knowledge base in order to browse or document its structure. For instance, suppose one were creating a portion of the knowledge base concerning the distribution, scheduling, and maintenance a set of computer workstations. Although the requisite units for the workstations need to be created, the user entering of this knowledge has the tools available to make a graphical view of the building floorplan, with icons for various workstation types, and so on. Subsequently, other users who are entering knowledge may choose to browse that part of the knowledge base via this graphical representation rather than the default tabular method.

HKE integrates natural-language processing in its interface. At any point in the HKE command set where a unit's name may be typed, HKE also allows the Lucy natural-language parser to intervene and parse the user input as a noun phrase. Conversely, the user may associate nouns, verbs, adjectives, prepositions, and so on, with units and relations in the knowledge base as a method of semantically defining English words for later use. Thus, in exactly the same manner as with the previous graphical methods of documenting the workstation knowledge base, one may document or browse that section of the knowledge base by describing in English the units desired.

HKE uses a flexible *advice angel* mechanism to detect possible user errors and report them. This is done in conjunction with a personal agenda for each user. When one of HKE's angels detects a possible task for the user and presents it, the user has the option of ignoring it, dealing with it immediately, or scheduling it on his or her agenda for later consideration. The personal agenda mechanism helps avoid intrusive error messages while retaining the advantages of having an automated assistant to help.

14.5.2. HKE Is Represented in CYC

As an example HITS application, major portions of HKE itself have been represented in CYC. For example, most of the HKE state information is stored in the knowledge base. This gives a powerful computationally reflective ability to HKE and other HITS tools. In addition, information, such as the user's current tasks, personal agenda, and so on, is stored in the knowledge base and remembered by HKE from one session to the next, even if the user switches machines or reboots.

One major advantage of representing this knowledge editor in the representation language it edits is that HKE can be customized by the user in exactly the same way that any other knowledge is edited. For instance, a user can customize the display of the standard inspector menu icons by editing the units that represent those icons. This provides an interesting and useful interface-prototyping environment, where effective ways to visualize information can be developed *concurrently* with the information structures themselves. Of course, the abilities of users to have access to this kind of facility can be modified, and specialized variants of the HKE can be implemented as part of a tool chain of HKE editors.

14.6 THE HITS BLACKBOARD

One key to enabling collaborative multimodal interfaces like HKE is a run-time architecture that permits the flexible intermixing of multiple modes of interaction and the maintenance of overall dialogue and subdialogue histories. The HITS Blackboard serves this important integrating function. It provides:

- support for modular design of knowledge sources
- a problem solving mechanism
- a communication medium for HITS knowledge sources
- a common mode-independent format for sharing information between knowledge sources
- support for fine-grained integration of the problem-solving actions of the knowledge sources
- a priority-based agenda control structure for scheduling the possible actions of the knowledge sources
- a goal-oriented control structure for organizing the proposed actions of the knowledge sources

14.6.1. The Basic Blackboard

The basic action of the blackboard is to schedule actions proposed by the knowledge sources. Every time an entry is posted on the blackboard, all the knowledge sources have an opportunity to examine the new posting and propose new actions for the blackboard to schedule. The scheduler component of the blackboard chooses from the proposed actions and executes one. The others normally remain on the agenda and are reconsidered at a later time. These actions typically operate on the new posting (possibly in addition to older postings) and produce additional new postings. The knowledge sources then have an opportunity to look at this new posting and the process repeats.

The blackboard processing cycle starts when some external process injects a *primitive event* onto the blackboard. This triggers the knowledge sources and the blackboard cycle takes over. A primitive event may represent a user action (e.g., keyboard input, a mouse click, or other gesture) or it may represent an event request from a knowledge source (e.g., to ask the user for some information, to tell the user something, or to perform any of a wide variety of other potential system actions).

A number of different perspectives help to illuminate the blackboard's operation. These include viewing the blackboard as priority queues or as goal trees. From the perspective of a priority queue, when a knowledge source proposes an action, it associates a priority or score with the action. The higher the priority, the more likely this action is to help solve the current goal. Priorities can be used to direct the search of the solution space in a propitious order. In a given search we may be searching for the best solution to our problem, or we may merely be searching for a good solution. If we are looking for the best solution, then we may have to explore the entire solution space. In the latter case the heuristic ordering may allow us to avoid searching portions of the solution space (based on knowledge gained earlier in the search).

In general, computation on the blackboard proceeds from bottom to top, with the knowledge sources reacting opportunistically to the appearance of events. However, without some organizational structure this type of computation can frequently become expensive and unproductive. In the HITS blackboard, information is structured and maintained as a goal tree. The goal tree serves several important functions: it provides a place to state which problem each knowledge source is trying to solve, to associate methods for recognizing adequate solutions when they appear, to store heuristic information about how to efficiently organize the computation, and to describe how knowledge sources relate to one another in terms of priority, sequencing, and dependency.

The goal tree is primarily an and/or tree of goals in which subbranches are allowed to be ordered or unordered. In the case of an ordered-or subtree, goal solutions are attempted sequentially until one succeeds or all goals fail. In the ordered-and subtree the goal solutions are attempted sequentially until one fails or all succeed. These ordered subtree types allow the specification of order dependencies between particular computations taking place on the blackboard. Unordered subtrees have the same satisfaction conditions except processing is allowed to proceed in parallel.

Each knowledge source that proposes to perform an action must indicate which goal in the goal tree the action is intended to help solve. This action is then scheduled on a locally controlled agenda. During each cycle of the blackboard, the goal tree is searched for an unsolved goal with actions scheduled to be performed. The action is then performed and the result is reported back to the goal. The goal decides whether the action was sufficient for solution. If so, the goal is marked as solved and its supergoal is notified. This is the first method of goal satisfaction. The goal is directly achieved as a result of executing an action scheduled on the goal itself. The supergoal can now either accept this solution and move on or reject the solution and instruct the subgoal to try again. The second method of goal satisfaction is through the satisfaction of associated subgoals. This is treated in the same manner as direct satisfaction and the supergoal is notified.

14.6.2. Use of the Blackboard within HITS

The blackboard is used within HITS in the performance of two major tasks: parsing and interpretation of information received from the users interaction with the system, and communication between system components.

As an example let's consider what follows from a user initiating the command *Tap Icon* to relate the visual behavior of an icon to an object in the knowledge base. The command string is broken down by the command processor into the type of command being performed and the arguments specified. These constituents are then placed on the blackboard as depicted in Figure 14.14. Several knowledge sources are activated by the appearance of

FIGURE 14.14
HITS BLACKBOARD EXAMPLE

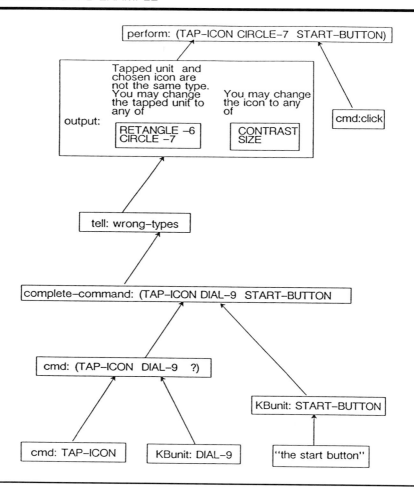

this information. One knowledge source is responsible for recognizing the type of action and linking it to its knowledge base equivalent. Others are responsible for determining the correctness of the arguments to the command and building partial command descriptions. Note that some operations simply add information to an existing blackboard description (elaboration), and others create a new description from existing descriptions (composition). Once all the arguments have been interpreted and accepted, a description is built that contains enough information to perform the action. Unless some other knowledge source intervenes, this action is performed, and the resulting effects are described and placed back on the blackboard.

The modularity provided by the blackboard architecture allows multiple mechanisms to operate on information during interpretation. In the preceding example a knowledge source that simply checks the arguments for validity is successful in resolving the first argument. In many cases, however, this simple checking mechanism will be unable to resolve the argument. The second argument in the above command has been entered using the natural-language phrase "the start button." This requires the activation of knowledge sources to handle the natural-language input. Figure 14.15 shows the information placed on the blackboard by Lucy during the process of resolving this argument.

The public aspect of the blackboard allows other HITS knowledge sources to look at and influence the information appearing on the blackboard. A knowledge source can react to the information appearing on the blackboard passively (as a monitor of user activity), constructively (deriving new information to place back onto the blackboard), or destructively (blocking information on the blackboard from being processing by other knowledge sources). One knowledge source within HITS which reacts in all these ways is the advisor. In the *Tap Icon* example, the user has attempted to tap a dial icon (a continuous type icon) to a discrete value. The advisor notices this discrepancy when the information appears on the blackboard in the form of an executable command. The advisor then supplies several options: attempt to proceed as is, select a discrete icon, or select a continuous tap variable. If either of the latter two options are taken then the current executable command is blocked and a new description is constructed and allowed to proceed.

Figure 14.16 shows the HITS Blackboard Goal Tree. At a high level the goal tree is a specification of the goals of the system while interacting with the user. Knowledge sources for interpretation of user input operate under the Interpret goal, their relative order and dependencies are determined by the subtree type of their supergoal. Knowledge sources that react to user input (e.g., advisory functions and applications) operate under the Respond goal. In the *Tap Icon* example, the successful interpretation of the command causes the application to schedule the performance of the action on the State-Change goal. The advisor also reacts to the command by scheduling some advice for the Advice goal. Since the Advice goal precedes the Respond goal in the goal tree the advice gets a chance to run first, thereby allowing it to block the scheduled performance of the command if necessary.

FIGURE 14.15
LUCY BLACKBOARD PROCESSING

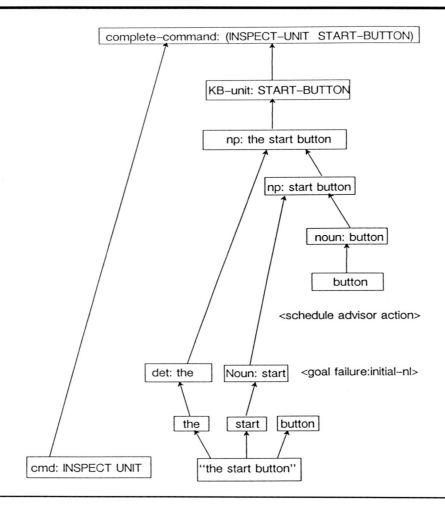

14.7 SUMMARY

In this chapter, we have explained the ideas motivating our research program and introduced HITS, an integrated set of tools for building collaborative multimedia interfaces. The most important difference between HITS and the User Interface Management Systems (UIMS) to which it might be compared is the emphasis on the role of knowledge representation. HITS provides an integrated knowledge base that covers a broad range of topics, all

FIGURE 14.16
HITS BLACKBOARD GOAL TREE

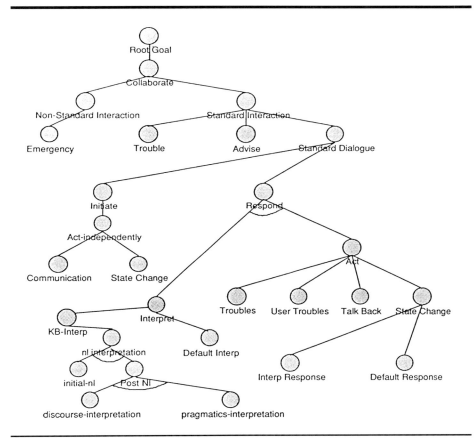

of which impinge in significant ways on the design of collaborative multimedia interfaces. General domain-independent knowledge is represented once and provided as part of HITS. HITS tools assist users in the construction of domain-dependent knowledge. We have assumed that application programs for which HITS-based interfaces are being built are themselves knowledge-based systems and that applications and interfaces are being designed and built together. This contrasts with other UIMS systems in which the application is viewed as a black box by the interface and any relevant parts of it must be modeled explicitly. In HITS, we attempt to avoid duplicating the representation of the application in the interface.

Throughout the chapter we have emphasized the knowledge-based parts of the interface. Thus, although such standard interface capabilities as properly presented menus, scrolling windows, and simple command interpreters are clearly important, we have focused on the more knowledge intensive aspects of interface design: understanding natural language and gestures, generating advice, modeling users and their tasks, and critiquing graphical design. Because HITS is a set of integrated knowledge-based tools focused on design knowledge and semantic mappings between interfaces and knowledge bases, it might be better characterized as what [Foley88] terms a UIDE, User Interface Design Environment, and in fact we envision HITS evolving into a General User Interface Design Environment, GUIDE.

Another unique aspect of HITS is its emphasis on allowing multiple input and output modalities (pointing, sketching, touch, natural-language, graphics, video) to be employed in an integrated fashion by users. This permits interaction with HITS-designed interfaces in the ways most natural for the tasks at hand, and allows us to explore new research questions about how users exploit this freedom to mix modalities in ways best suited for a particular task.

Acknowledgments

The design and construction of HITS is a project of the Human Interface Laboratory at MCC. All of the members of the laboratory are involved in its design and implementation. We want to acknowledge their efforts, ideas, and assistance and thank them for making it such an intellectually exciting activity. This chapter is based on a presentation given at a workshop on Architectures for Intelligent Interfaces [Hollan91].

Members of the MCC Human Interface Laboratory

Chinatsu Aone, Anthony Aristar, Jim Barnett, Bill Bohrer, Rich Cohen, Jonathan Grudin, Will Hill, Jim Hollan, Megumi Kameyama, Janet Kilgore, Carol Kroll, Bill Kuhlman, Susann Luper-Foy, Gale Martin, Paul Martin, Tim McCandless, Jean McKendree, Linda Marshall, Jim Miller, Martha Morgan, Maria Nasr, Michael O'Leary, Jay Pittman, Steve Poltrock, Mosfeq Rashid, Mark Rosenstein, Supoj Sutanthavibul, Mark Tarlton, Nong Tarlton, Loren Terveen, Steven Tighe, C. Unnikrishnan, Louis Weitzman, Wayne Wilner, Kent Wittenburg, Dave Wroblewski, and Ken Zink.

References

[Foley88] Foley, J. 1988. *personal communication.*

[Hill88a] Hill, W. C. 1988. *Advice Seeking, Giving, and Following at a Graphical Computer Interface.* Ph.D. Thesis, Northwestern University.

[Hill88b] Hill, W. C., and Miller, J.R. 1988. Justified Advice. In *CHI '88 Conference on Human Factors in Computing Systems.*

[Hollan84] Hollan, J. D., Hutchins, E. L., and Weitzman, L. 1984. Steamer: An Interactive Inspectable Simulation-Based Training System. *AI Magazine* 5 (2), 15–27.

[Hollan87] Hollan, J. D., Hutchins, E. L., McCandless, T. P., Rosenstein, M. B., and Weitzman, L. 1987. Graphical Interfaces for Simulation. In Rouse, W. ed., *Advances in Man-Machine Systems Research.* Connecticut: JAI Press, pp. 129–163.

[Hollan91] Hollan, J. D., Rich, E., Miller, J. R., and Wilner, W. 1991. Knowledge Bases and Tools for Building Intergrated Multimedia Intelligent Interfaces. In present volume.

[Hutchins86] Hutchins, E. L., Hollan, J. D., and Norman, D. A. 1986. In Norman, D. A., and Draper, S. W. (eds.) 1986. *User Centered System Design: New Perspectives on Human-Computer Interaction.* Hillsdale, NJ: Lawrence Erlbaum Associates, pp. 87–124.

[Lakatos78] Lakatos, I. 1978. *The Methodology of Scientific Research Programmes,* Cambridge: Cambridge University Press.

[Lenat87] Lenat, D. B., and Feigenbaum, E. A. 1987. On the Thresholds of Knowledge. In *Proceedings of IJCAI '87.*

[Lenat88] Lenat, D., Guha, R. V., and Wallace, D. V. 1988. *The CycL Representation Language.* Technical Report, MCC Artificial Intelligence Laboratory.

[Masson88] Masson, M., Hill, W. C., Guidon R., and Conner, J. 1988. Misconceived Misconceptions. In *Proceedings of the User Centered System Design CHI '88 Conference on Human Factors in Computing Systems.* pp. 151–156.

[Norman86] Norman, D. A., Draper, S. W. (eds.) 1986. "Cognitive Engineering." Hillsdale, NJ: Lawrence Erlbaum Associates, pp. 32–61. *User Centered System Design.*

[Pitman85] Pitman, K. M. 1985. *CREF: An Editing Facility for Managing Structured Text.* Technical Report, MIT A.I. Memo 829.

[Rumelhart86] Rumelhart, D. E., McClelland, J. L., and the PDP Research Group. 1986. *Parallel Distributed Processing.* Cambridge, MA: MIT Press.

[Suchman87] Suchman, L. 1987. *Plans and Situated Actions: The Problem of Human Machine Communication.* Cambridge: Cambridge University Press.

[Terveen88] Terveen, L. 1988. *Making Interaction Accountable.* Technical Report, MCC Human Interface Laboratory.

[VanLehn89] VanLehn, K., Brown, J. S., and Greeno, J. 1982. *Competitive Argumentation in Computational Theories of Cognition.* Technical Report, Xerox CIS-14.

CHAPTER 15

U IDE—AN INTELLIGENT USER INTERFACE DESIGN ENVIRONMENT

JAMES FOLEY, WON CHUL KIM,
SRDJAN KOVACEVIC, *and* **KEVIN MURRAY**
Department of Electrical Engineering and Computer Science
George Washington University

ABSTRACT

The user-computer interface is frequently the major impediment to successful use of interactive computer graphics systems. Design of the interface is often thought of as art rather than science, and suffers from lack of formalism, models, tools, and methodical design approaches. Slowly, the design process is becoming more structured, and more formal tools are becoming available.

This chapter describes an intelligent User Interface Design Environment (UIDE), a knowledge-based system to assist in user interface design, evaluation, and implementation. UIDE goes beyond the capabilities of the typical User Interface Management System and provides a higher-level conceptual design tool that facilitates the iterative design process of specification, generation, and evaluation.

At the heart of UIDE is a representation of the conceptual design of a user interface. This design includes: the class hierarchy of objects that exist in the system, properties of the objects, actions that can be performed on the objects, units of information required by the actions, and pre- and post-conditions for the actions. The conceptual design and related information is used to: check the interface design for consistency and completeness; transform the knowledge base, and hence the user interface it represents into a different but functionally equivalent interface; evaluate the interface design with respect to speed of use; serve as input to a Simple User Interface Management System (SUIMS) that implements the user interface; automatically generate intelligent run-time help to the end user; and produce a printed description of the design.

15.1 INTRODUCTION

We are developing UIDE, the User Interface Design Environment, a system whose long-term objective is the near-automatic generation of user interfaces for interactive programs. UIDE provides a set of tools for designing, analyzing, and implementing user-computer interfaces, in the same spirit that computer-aided software engineering (CASE) tools integrate various steps in the design process. UIDE is structured around a representation of a user-computer system that is at a higher level of abstraction than has been used in most user interface software. The representation is stored as schemata in a knowledge base implemented in ART (Automated Reasoning Tool), an expert system shell [Inference87].

UIDE is the next logical step in a progression of user interface development software that began many years ago with the concept of using finite-state machines or other language-oriented formalisms to specify and manage interaction sequences. This approach led to the general field of User Interface Management Systems, abbreviated as UIMS. Over the past ten years a number of increasingly sophisticated research prototypes [Buxton83; Green85a; Green86; Haye85; Hill86; Hudson88; Hudson89; Hurley89; Koivunen88; Myer90; Olsen84; Olsen86; Singh89; Smith88; Wellner89] and commercial UIMSs have evolved. A typical UIMS permits the user interface designer to specify screen organizations, icons, and menus; create help and error messages; select from alternative interaction techniques such as command language, static menus, or pop-up menus; specify user action sequences; and specify the names of application procedures to be called by the UIMS when a command and its parameters have been interactively input by a user. The run-time component of a UIMS is layered between the application and the user.

UIMSs are enjoying increasing success because they increase programmer productivity (up to 50% of the code in interactive programs is often user interface code [Sutton78]); speed up the development process; facilitate iterative refinement of a user interface as experience is gained with its use; and allow user interface designers, who often are not programmers, to work directly with interactive design tools. There is ample evidence that various forms of UIMS technology are valuable in leveraging designer and/or programmer productivity: systems such as Apollo's Dialogue [Schulert85], Apple's MacApp [Schmucker86], NASA's Transportable Application Environment (TAE-Plus) [Miller88], and Interactive Design Environment's RAPID/USE [Wasserman85] have reaped many benefits for their users.

Several UIMSs and other user interface tools allow the designer to interactively create and modify user interface elements, such as menus and dialogue boxes, much as one works with a drawing program. This is usually preferable to first writing textual specifications that must later be interpreted or compiled to create the interfaces. Systems and tools in this category include SmethersBarnes' Prototyper [Cossey89], Myers' Peridot [Myers90], Cardelli's dialogue editor [Cardelli88], Sun's GUIDE [Sun90], Visual Edge's UIMX [UIMX90], and NeXT's Interface Builder [NeXT90].

There has been increasing recognition that the classic UIMS, while useful, has a number of deficiencies. First, it does not go nearly far enough in facilitating the overall cycle of user interface design, implementation, testing, and deployment. Second, the focus on control flow and screen design neglects other key elements of user interfaces such as context-sensitive menus, direct manipulation of interactively created objects, intelligent and context-sensitive help, macros, and undo. Third, the level of abstraction used by current UIMSs is too low, forcing the designer to deal with too many details—too many trees, not enough forest. Because of this, making a design change for some of the higher-level concepts of an interface requires many changes throughout the specification. For instance, changing from a prefix command syntax to a postfix syntax with a current selected-object paradigm (a la Macintosh) is quite difficult if one is dealing with state diagrams or BNF. This actually orients the current UIMSs more toward the implementation rather than the design task. What is really needed is something akin to the CASE approach, providing a set of integrated tools that help at various stages of the design process.

Several new research directions have developed in the past few years; they have provided the foundation upon which UIDE is built. The first is the integration of a data model into the UIMS, to complement and balance the past emphasis on control models. The second is a move toward higher levels of abstraction in the specification. The third is the development of intelligent help systems. The fourth is the inclusion of intelligent design tools.

A user interface can be partitioned into control and data models. The control model concerns actions, parameters, and sequences of user actions needed to input control information. The data model concerns the types, properties, and relations of application-specific objects created by the application: for example, words, sentences, and paragraphs in a word processing application. UIMSs have historically focused on the control model, in part because finite-state machines and BNF could be used as formal specification tools. However, if the UIMS is to mediate between the user and the application for direct manipulation interfaces [Shneiderman82; Shneiderman83], it is necessary for the UIMS to have some knowledge of the objects that can be manipulated. Hudson recognized the need for a data model as part of the UIMS [Hudson86; Hudson87; Hudson88]; more recently, the Serpent UIMS [Bass88; SEI88] and CREASE [Hurley89] have also included a data model.

Most UIMSs provide user interface specification at the lexical and syntactic levels of keystroke and mouse click sequences, parameter order, and menu and screen organization. This very fine-grained specification can be quite tedious to use. Higher-level issues, such as the types of information required by each command, types of objects commands can operate on, relationships between different kinds of objects, and conditions under which various commands are available, have often been ignored. The first step toward higher levels of abstraction can be found in COUSIN [Hayes83; Hayes84], which automatically generates a menu and form fill-in user interface from a specification of commands and their parameters' data types. Green [Green85b] uses pre- and postconditions to specify the semantics of user commands. Olsen, in his MIKE [Olsen86; Olsen88] system, declares commands and parameters, also generating a user interface in a fashion similar to COUSIN, but allowing some direct manipulation. In Mickey [Olsen89], Olsen uses extended Pascal declaration constructs to generate the menu definitions, dialogue box layouts, and window type definitions. Szekely [Szekely89; Szekely90] describes how the construction of intelligent interface can be facilitated by classifying the concepts that users and programs communicate, and separating the user interface from the program's functionality.

In recent years intelligent help systems have been developed for a variety of applications, with help systems for UNIX becoming a particular favorite [Chin90; Kemke87]. The classical example is the UNIX consultant, which contains a knowledge base about UNIX and gives user advice, either actively or on request. This is a very valuable capability, but the fact that help is grafted onto the application program after the fact introduces some limitations. It is in general hard for the help system to know the state of the application, making context-specific help difficult or inaccurate. If the application program is changed, then the help knowledge base must also be changed. And of course, the builder of the knowledge base might introduce errors due to an incomplete understanding of the application.

Intelligent design tools embody a set of rules and apply those rules to automatically create (hopefully) good designs, or to critique a design component. The design component might be a graphic, such as a page layout [Feiner90], a data chart [Mackinlay90; Gargan88], a graphic view [Weitzman86], a color selection [Meier88], interaction techniques selection [Bleser90], a demonstration of the best way to do something [Feiner87; Feiner90; Sukaviriya88; Sukaviriya90], an explanation of some information [Roth90], or menu and dialogue box organization [Kim90].

The User Interface Design Environment begins to integrate these previously disparate themes. Figure 15.1 shows the overall architecture of UIDE.

FIGURE 15.1
THE OVERALL ORGANIZATION OF UIDE. DASHED LINES ENCLOSE
ELEMENTS OF UIDE THAT HAVE NOT YET BEEN IMPLEMENTED

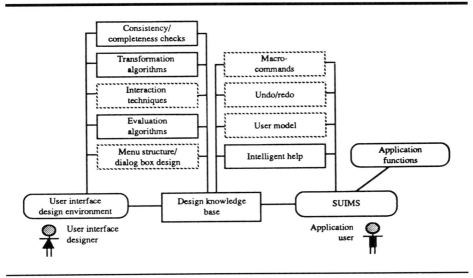

At the heart of the system is a knowledge base representation of the conceptual design of a user interface, consisting of:

■ The class hierarchy of objects that exist in the system (only single inheritance is currently supported)
■ Properties of the objects
■ Actions that can be performed on the objects
■ Units of information required by the actions
■ Pre and postconditions for the actions

Figure 15.1 also shows various ways in which the design knowledge base can be used to:

■ Check the design for consistency and completeness
■ Transform the knowledge base, and hence the user interface it represents, into a different but functionally equivalent interface via a set of transformation algorithms
■ Evaluate the "goodness" of the interface design
■ Design menu structures and dialogue box layouts
■ Choose appropriate interaction techniques
■ Automatically generate intelligent run-time help to the end-user

- Maintain a model of user knowledge about the application, for use with the intelligent help facility
- Implement macros and an undo/redo capability
- Provide input to SUIMS, a simple UIMS, which implements the user interface

Our basic tenet, reflected in the architecture, is that the design knowledge base is central. One of our goals is to continue to develop new ways to use the design knowledge base, and in the process, to continually extend the knowledge base so that we can come closer and closer to our goal of automatic generation of user interfaces. In this chapter we focus on the structure of the knowledge base, how it is acquired, and some of its many uses.

15.2 THE USER INTERFACE DESIGN KNOWLEDGE BASE

The user interface design is represented internally as instances of seven ART schemata [Inference87], or frames. The most important slots and the relationships between the seven schemata are shown in Figure 15.2. In the following text, schema names are given in **boldface,** and slot names are given in *italic*. For each of the seven schemata there exists a description slot, which the user interface designer can use to provide a meaningful response to a run-time help request.

The data model used in UIDE is a single inheritance class hierarchy of objects. It is represented by instances of the **Object Schema**, which define the classes of objects known to the user interface design. The relations *has subclass* and *is subclass of* are used to define the application's object hierarchy. *Actions on object* is a relation linking an **Object Schema** instance to the **Action Schema** instances for those actions that can be applied to the object class. *Attributes of object* is a relation linking an **Object Schema** instance to an **Attribute Schema** instance for each of the object's attributes. Both the *actions on object* and the *attributes of object* are inherited down the object hierarchy.

For each attribute that an object inherits from its superclass, the system creates a copy of the superclass' **Attribute Schema** instance, and also forms a separate hierarchy of **Attribute Schema** instances analogous to the object hierarchy. The *current value* slot (which keeps the run-time specified attribute value for the object) and the *default value* slot (which keeps the optional initial default for each object's attribute) are inherited down the attribute hierarchy. Each attribute of an object points to an instance of the **Attribute Type Schema**, which records the attribute's *data type* as being integer, real, subrange, enumerated, or the like, and provides other information that is specific to the data type.

Action information is inherited down the object hierarchy, but unlike the **Attribute Schema** instances, only a single instance of the **Action Schema** for each action defined in the user interface is represented in the knowledge base.

FIGURE 15.2

SCHEMATA AND THEIR MAJOR RELATIONS.

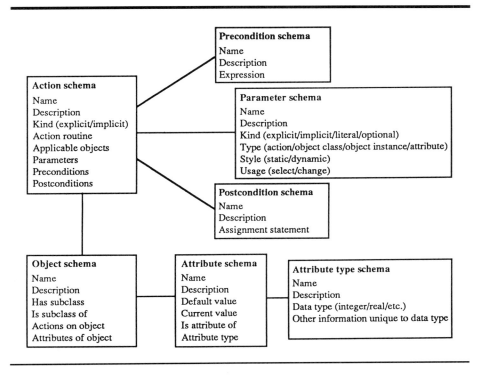

The three relation slots *parameters, preconditions,* and *postconditions* refer to schema instances that further describe the action. *Applicable objects* is a relation that links an **Action Schema** instance to all of the objects to which this action can be applied. The *origination object* slot links an **Action Schema** instance to the object at the highest level in the object hierarchy that can have control of the action, whereas the *control object* slot links an **Action Schema** instance to the object that actually has the control of the action. The control object is the same as the origination object, or is a subclass of the origination object if the action is specialized down the object hierarchy. The *action routine* name provides the link to the run-time action routine that actually carries out the action. The interface to the action routines is discussed in Section 15.

For each action there is a **Parameter Schema** instance for each parameter or unit of information required by the action. The *parameter kind* slot describes how the parameter is given its value with keywords explicit, implicit, optional, and literal. Explicit means the value must be obtained from the user when the action is invoked. If the parameter is given a value with a separate command (such as, a set_attribute_fill command for the fill attribute), the *parameter kind* is implicit, while a parameter that has a default value is optional. Such a parameter need not be specified when the user invokes an action. Literal indicates a parameter with a specific value, such as fill-type black. The *parameter type* slot indicates whether the parameter information is an action, an object class, an object instance, or an attribute. If the parameter is to be continuously evaluated and feedback is needed to reflect each change, *parameter style* slot is dynamic; if continuous feedback is not needed, *parameter style* slot is static.

A **Precondition Schema** exists for each action. Preconditions are predicates that must be true in order for an action to be enabled and thus available to the user for selection. Context variables are used in the preconditions. Preconditions focus on semantic dependencies, not on syntactic-level sequencing. The actual *expression* of the precondition is represented in a form that can be conveniently evaluated at run-time, to determine whether the precondition is true or false. Preconditions are used at run-time to enable commands, to explain why a command is disabled, and (in a future implementation) to back-chain to commands that will satisfy the unsatisfied preconditions.

A **Postcondition Schema** is instantiated for each action. A postcondition is one or more statements that assign values to the variables used in the preconditions following the execution of the action with which they are associated. The *assignment statement* is represented in a form which can be conveniently evaluated at run-time. Postconditions are used at run-time to change state context, to explain partial semantics of commands, and (in a future implementation) to back-chain to provide help.

Pre- and postconditions specify just enough of the application's semantics to allow context-sensitivity in presenting menus, to give context-sensitive help, and for the very limited encapsulation of the semantics that is necessary for the transformations. The information currently encoded and used in the pre- and postconditions include the following:

- the number of objects of a particular object class that are in existence. A creation command increments this number as a postcondition; a deletion command decrements the number.
- the number of objects of different object classes that have been selected as belonging to the currently selected set (discussed in Section 15.4).
- the existence of a currently selected command (discussed in Section 15.4).
- the existence of a value for a parameter.
- any context variables established by the interface designer.

A detailed discussion of the schemata slots can be found in [FOLE88].

To simplify definition of a user interface design, we have recently added the concept of generic action classifications, such as create object, delete object, copy object, modify object attributes, and change object relationships (such as set membership). Associated with each category of actions are a unique set of predefined pre- and postconditions: thus automatic definition of pre- and postconditions is possible during knowledge base specification. Generic action classes and their pre- and postconditions are shown in Figure 15.3. As we identify more generic commands, we will also strive to maximize the functionality of the generic command and action classes, in order to minimize the design work needed to get a meaningful prototypic interface underway.

Externally, the design knowledge base is represented in the Interface Definition Language (IDL), which was developed to present the conceptual design of the user interface in a structured and readable way. IDL will be used here to present user interface design examples. Figures 15.4 and 15.5 show the IDL representation of the knowledge base for SimpleDraw, a subset of a MacDraw-like application, which is used as the sample application throughout this chapter. As seen in the figure, IDL is a fairly high-level specification. IDL cannot in general be used to completely specify the semantics

FIGURE 15.3
GENERIC ACTION CLASSES AND THEIR PRE- AND POSTCONDITIONS.
VARIABLE OBJECTS IN PRE- AND POSTCONDITIONS ARE IN ITALIC

pre-condition: true
   creation action
post-condition: number (*object*) = number (*object*) + 1

pre-condition: number (*object*) > 0
   deletion action & instance action
post-condition: number (*object*) = number (*object*) − 1

pre-condition: number (*object*) > 0
   deletion action & class action
post-condition: number (*object*) = 0

pre-condition: number (*object*) > 0
   attribute—modify action
post-condition: none

pre-condition: number (*object*) > 0
   cut action
post-condition: number (*object*) = number (*object*) − 1
post-condition: number (clipboard, *object*) = number (clipboard, *object*) + 1

pre-condition: number (*object*) > 0
   copy action
post-condition: number (clipboard, *object*) = number (clipboard, *object*) + 1

pre-condition: number (clipboard, *object*) > 0
   paste action
post-condition: number (*object*) = number (*object*) + number (clipboard, *object*)

FIGURE 15.4
IDL REPRESENTATION OF OBJECT HIERARCHY AND ATTRIBUTE TYPES FOR
THE SIMPLE DRAWING APPLICATION EXAMPLE. SET (N, M) IS USED TO GIVE
THE CARDINALITY FOR THE CHOICES FROM THE SET OF ENUMERATED
VALUES THAT FOLLOWS. THE ATTRIBUTE MUST HAVE A MINIMUM OF N
AND A MAXIMUM OF M VALUES CHOSEN FROM THE SET. IF CARDINALITY
IS UNSPECIFIED AT DESIGN TIME, IT IS DENOTED BY A DOT, AS IN SET(2,.)

{Attribute types: Max_Size, Max_X, and Max_Y are designer defined constants.}

string	:	set(1, .) of (a..z, A..Z, 0..9, !, @, #, ...)
font	:	set(1, 1) of (Chicago, Geneva, Toronto, Monaco, ...)
fill	:	set(1, 1) of (white, gray, black)
scale	:	range [0..Max_Size] of integer
thickness	:	set (1, 1) of (0..10)
angle	:	range [0..360] of integer
position	:	range [x:(0..Max_X), y:(0..Max_Y)] of integer

{A portion of object class hierarchy: *italics* represent inherited actions or attributes}

general-object
        superclasses : ()
        subclasses : (line, shape, text)
        actions : (cut, copy, paste, move, rotate, delete, delete_all)
        attributes : (position, angle)
texts
        superclasses : (general-object)
        subclasses : ()
        actions : (*cut, copy, paste, move, rotate, delete, delete_all*, create_text, change_font)
        attributes : (*position, angle*, font, string)

of an application, and hence does not obviate the need for programming the application semantics.

Logical Dependency Rules

The design knowledge base is initially defined and then constantly updated explicitly by the designer as well as automatically by the different modules of UIDE. Maintaining the correctness and integrity of the design knowledge base in such an environment is difficult. We have begun to utilize ART's powerful logical dependencies capability to aid the designer in maintaining a knowledge base with current design information, excising unneeded and old information.

Logical dependencies indicate the continuous dependence of some facts on other facts in the knowledge base. This is different from the simpler

FIGURE 15.4 (Cont.)

shape
        superclasses : (general-object)
        subclasses : (triangle, square)
        actions : (*cut, copy, paste, move, rotate, delete, delete_all*, create_shape, change_scale, change_fill)
        attributes : (*position, angle*, scale, fill)
square, triangle
        superclasses : (shape)
        subclasses : ()
        actions : (*cut, copy, paste, move, rotate, delete, delete_all, change_scale, change_fill*)
        attributes : (*position, angle, scale, fill*)
lines
        superclasses : (general-object)
        subclasses : (free-line, poly-line)
        actions : (*cut, copy, paste, move, rotate, delete, delete_all*, change_thickness)
        attributes : (*position, angle*, thickness)
simple-line
        superclasses : (lines)
        subclasses : ()
        actions : (*cut, copy, paste, move, rotate, delete, delete_all, change_thickness*)
        attributes : (*position, angle, thickness*, points: set (2,2) of *position*)
poly-line
        superclasses : (lines)
        subclasses : ()
        actions : (*cut, copy, paste, move, rotate, delete, delete_all, change_thickness*)
        attributes : (*position, angle, thickness*, points: set(2,.) of *position*)

and more common if-then reasoning that involves one-shot logic: *if* the conditions of a rule are true, *then* take the action indicated by the rule. Logical dependencies continually monitor a set of conditions which, if modified, alter the conclusions that are derived: *while* conditions of the rule remain in the database *then* maintain the action indicated by the rule. The central idea in logical dependencies is the automatic removal of facts from the knowledge base because they logically depend on other facts that were removed [Inference87].

Logical dependency rules are used during knowledge base specification to automatically create the pre- and postconditions associated with each action category, and to check completeness and consistency of the knowledge base. The use of logical dependency rules is discussed in the following section and in Section 15.4 where they are used to maintain the design in a predictable, reproducible, and consistent state.

FIGURE 15.5
EXAMPLE ACTIONS IN IDL REPRESENTATION FOR THE SIMPLEDRAW
APPLICATION.

pre-condition: number (general_object) > 0
 cut(obj_type: general_object)
post-condition: number (general_object) = number (general_object) − 1
post-condition: number (clipboard, general_object) = number (clipboard,
 general_object) + 1

pre-condition: number (general_object) > 0
 copy(obj_type: general_object)
post-condition: number (clipboard, general_object) = number (clipboard,
 general_object) + 1

pre-condition: number (clipboard, general_object) > 0
 paste(anchor_pt: position **optional**)
post-condition: number (general_object) = number (general_object) + number
 (clipboard, general_object)

pre-condition: true
 create_shape(anchor_pt: position, fill_style: fill, orientation: angle, obj_type:
 shape_class)
post-condition: number (shape) = number (shape) + 1

pre-condition: number (general_object) > 0
 rotate_general_object(obj_type: general_object, orientation: angle)
post-condition: none

pre-condition: number (general_object) > 0
 delete_general_object(obj_type: general_object)
post-condition: number (general_object) = number (general_object) − 1

pre-condition: number (shape) > 0
 change_fill(obj_type: shape, fill_style: fill)
post-condition: none

15.3 DESIGN SPECIFICATION INTERFACE

The major steps in the design process are building the design knowledge base,
checking it for completeness, and analyzing it for consistency. In essence, the
design specification interface can be thought of as a knowledge-acquisition.
It was built using SunView windows and is connected to ART. The interface
was developed to avoid forcing the designer to learn IDL syntax rules. Any
element of the design can be specified at any time, allowing the designer to
move freely from one part of a design specification to another. While this
strategy increases the possibility of an incomplete design, we do not want to
force the designer into a particular specification sequence.

The interface consists of three windows, which are the Main, Report, and Object Hierarchy windows. The designer can define, view, modify, and delete the seven UIDE schema types, discussed in Section 15.2, in the Main Window (Figure 15.6). Using direct manipulation of graphical representations of objects and assisted by the inheritance mechanisms provided in ART, the designer can rapidly define an object hierarchy in the Object Hierarchy Window (Figure 15.7). The system provides messages to the designer, lists UIDE schemata, displays the design knowledge base in IDL (Figure 15.8) and provides Consistency and Completeness reports in the Report Window (Figure 15.9).

FIGURE 15.6
THE MAIN WINDOW (THE ACTION **MOVE**).

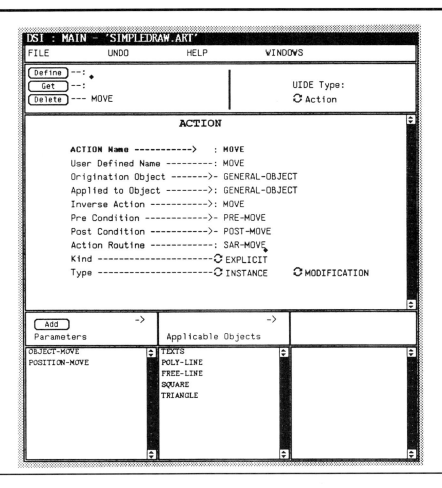

FIGURE 15.7
THE OBJECT HIERARCHY WINDOW (THE SIMPLEDRAW DESIGN
IN DEVELOPMENT)

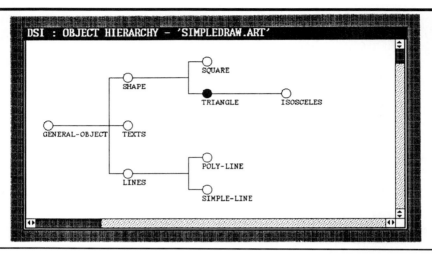

To further explain the interface, we briefly describe some of the steps a designer would use in defining SimpleDraw. It is worth noting that because of the free-form specification, almost all of the steps in the following example could have been performed in a different order.

We start by defining the object **general-object**, which will form the root of the object hierarchy. New objects are inserted via direct manipulation in the Object Hierarchy Window by selecting a class and providing a name for the new subclass. Pressing the mouse menu button over an object produces a pop-up menu with three options; *Insert Subclass* (new), *Delete Class* (only enabled if the object is a leaf node), and *Move Class* (from one superclass to another). Figure 15.7 shows the SimpleDraw object hierarchy with the object **triangle** selected. Information about the selected object is displayed in the Main Window (not shown).

Actions are defined in the Main Window. The newly defined action or predefined actions can be attached to an object via the *origination object* value. Figure 15.6 shows the action **move** with **general-object** as the value of *origination object* slot. Alternatively, we can add the action **move** to **general-object** using the link command (not shown).

Pre- and postconditions are automatically defined when actions are classified in one of the generic action categories. For instance, if an action is defined as a deletion of an object instance, the postcondition that decrements the number of object instances is associated with the action. These definitions are based on combinations shown in Figure 15.3 in Section 15.2.

FIGURE 15.8
THE REPORT WINDOW (AND ACTION SHOWN IN IDL).

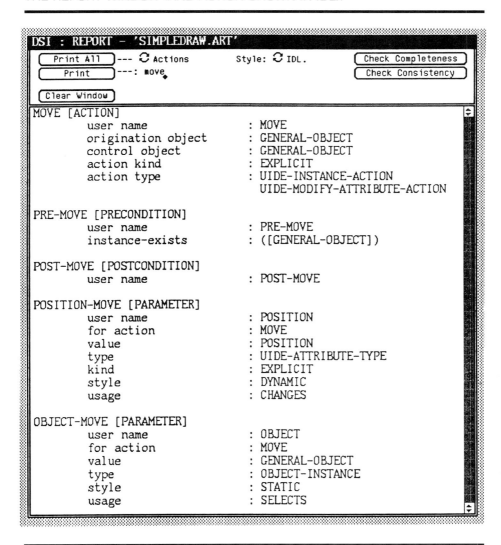

```
DSI : REPORT - 'SIMPLEDRAW.ART'
  [ Print All  ]--- ⟳ Actions        Style: ⟳ IDL.          [ Check Completeness ]
  [ Print      ]---: move▪                                  [ Check Consistency  ]
  [ Clear Window ]

MOVE [ACTION]
        user name                   : MOVE
        origination object          : GENERAL-OBJECT
        control object              : GENERAL-OBJECT
        action kind                 : EXPLICIT
        action type                 : UIDE-INSTANCE-ACTION
                                      UIDE-MODIFY-ATTRIBUTE-ACTION

PRE-MOVE [PRECONDITION]
        user name                   : PRE-MOVE
        instance-exists             : ([GENERAL-OBJECT])

POST-MOVE [POSTCONDITION]
        user name                   : POST-MOVE

POSITION-MOVE [PARAMETER]
        user name                   : POSITION
        for action                  : MOVE
        value                       : POSITION
        type                        : UIDE-ATTRIBUTE-TYPE
        kind                        : EXPLICIT
        style                       : DYNAMIC
        usage                       : CHANGES

OBJECT-MOVE [PARAMETER]
        user name                   : OBJECT
        for action                  : MOVE
        value                       : GENERAL-OBJECT
        type                        : OBJECT-INSTANCE
        style                       : STATIC
        usage                       : SELECTS
```

We now have objects, actions, and pre- and postconditions partially defined. Parameters, attributes, and attribute types are defined in a similar manner to defining actions and objects.

At any point the design can be saved for future use. Our experience is that the time to specify a simple design is reduced from hours using a text

FIGURE 15.9

THE REPORT WINDOW (A CONSISTENCY REPORT)

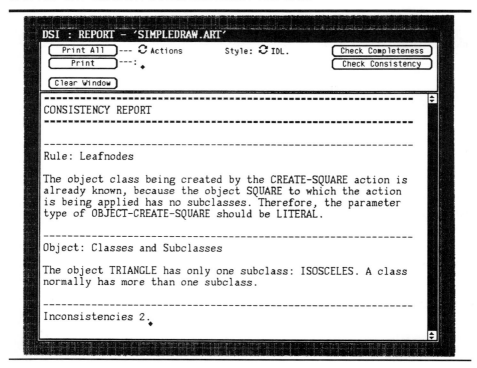

editor, to minutes using the design specification interface. At this point in the design specification, we can request a check for completeness or an analysis of consistency. Figure 15.8 shows the result of a request to print an action in IDL and Figure 15.9 shows an example report in response to a request for design consistency.

Completeness and Consistency

Checking for completeness and analyzing the consistency of the design knowledge base are two major components of the design specification tool. *Completeness* checks verify that all schemata in the knowledge base contain enough information for the transformation system to operate and for SUIMS, the Simple UIMS (Section 15.5), to implement the interface. *Consistency* checks examine the overall design knowledge base, advising the designer of potential inconsistencies.

There is an important difference between completeness and consistency checks. An incomplete design cannot be used by the transformation algorithms (Section 15.4), so completeness must be checked before a transformation algorithm can be applied. If a transformation algorithm were applied to an incomplete design knowledge base, it would fail in a manner similar to compilation failure of a Pascal program with incomplete declarations. However, in contrast, an inconsistent design can be transformed, and may be exactly what the designer intends. Consider as an example a design with two subclasses of shape, square and triangle. In most applications it would be inconsistent to have a rotate_square action without having a comparable rotate_triangle action, but this is not incomplete. Of course, a design that is complete and hence can be transformed may not work as intended, just as a program that successfully compiles may not run as expected.

We have developed a small rule base for analyzing a design's completeness and consistency. The designer must attend to the violations recognized by the completeness rules; otherwise the knowledge base cannot be reliably transformed or used by SUIMS. The designer is informed of consistency rule violations, but is not forced to correct the violation(s). The designer may have a reason, not known to UIDE, for the design choice. Descriptions of some of the completeness and consistency rules we have developed are listed.

Completeness Rules

- Proper class hierarchy: The object class hierarchy graph must be a tree, starting at the root class. There can be neither cycles nor nodes with in-degree greater than one (assuming our current single inheritance model).
- Complete information: Required information for each schema must be present.
- Preconditions must be set: A variable that is used in a precondition must be given a value by some postcondition.

Consistency Rules

- Postcondition variables: A variable that is set in a postcondition should be used in some precondition(s).
- Classes and subclasses: the object class will normally have more than one subclass.
- Comparable actions: Subclasses of the same object class will normally have the same actions. If triangles can be rotated, it is likely that squares should also be able to be rotated.
- Inverse actions: Actions typically have inverse actions. (Delete is the inverse of both create and duplicate.) The inverse can sometimes be identified by examining postconditions: if none can be identified, the designer is notified.
- Leaf node creation actions: An object being created by an action is already known if the object is a leaf node. Therefore the parameter type should be literal, not explicit or implicit.

Completeness checks are necessary because the "freestyle" form of definition, in which the designer can work in whatever sequence seems most natural, can readily lead to missing information. Many opportunities for incompleteness violations have been programmed out of the interface to prevent the designer from making mistakes that would have to be corrected later.

Figure 15.9 shows a report generated after the SimpleDraw design knowledge base has been analyzed for consistency. The consistency report tells the designer that the class triangle has only one subclass, isosceles. Also the object being created by the create_square action is already known, because the object to which the action is being applied has no subclasses. Therefore the parameter type should be literal, not explicit or implicit.

Additional completeness and consistency rules can be added to the rule base with minimal effort, providing the opportunity to expand the range of checks. Rules are created by an experienced UIDE developer/programmer and are written in ART/Lisp code. The rules rely heavily on pattern matching of the schemata in the design knowledge base. Figure 15.10 shows a rule in pseudo-ART/Lisp.

15.4 USER INTERFACE TRANSFORMATION ALGORITHMS

A user interface designer typically develops and evaluates a number of alternative conceptual designs. Some of the alternatives will be slight variations of one another, while other designs will be quite different. UIDE can automatically generate alternative conceptual designs that are slight variations of one another. This is done via *transformations* that are applied to the user interface knowledge base and are in the spirit of correctness-preserving program transformations, although we have not attempted to prove that the transformations preserve the functionality of the user interface design. Each transformation automatically creates a new user interface design with the same functionality as the original, but with a slightly different user view of the functionality. This automatic generation of alternatives can save considerable effort, by allowing the designer to quickly apply and test different design paradigms.

Several generic design paradigms have been implemented as transformation algorithms. The transformations include factoring (sometimes also called orthogonalization), special cases of which are the creation of a currently selected object (CSO), a currently selected command, and a currently selected attribute value; establishing a currently selected set (CSS) as a generalization of the CSO concept; establishing initial default values; specializing and generalizing commands based on object hierarchies; and modifying the scope of certain types of commands. The transformations are discussed in depth in [Foley87].

In this section, the currently selected set transformation is discussed in detail to illustrate the general concept of transformations. The effect of a

FIGURE 15.10
CONSISTENCY RULE FOR CREATION ACTIONS OF LEAF NODE OBJECTS.
WORDS BEGINNING WITH A ? ARE VARIABLES.

(**defrule** CONSISTENCY-LEAFNODE-CREATION-ACTIONS

    {If the following is true.}

    {Pattern match to find all actions that are user-defined-actions
    and creation-actions}
    {and for which objects and parameters have already been
    defined.}
    (**schema** ?Action
          (*instance-of*   user-defined-action)
          (*instance-of*   creation-action)
          (*control-object*   ?Object)
          (*has-parameters*   ?Parameter)
)

    {For all the parameters of the actions found by the above pattern match,
    find the}
    {parameter for which the parameter type is object-class and the parameter-kind
    is explicit}
    {or implicit and the parameter value is the same as the control object
    of the action.}
    (**schema** ?Parameter
          (*instance-of*   UIDE-parameter)
          (*parameter-type*   object-class)
          (*parameter-value*   ?Object)
          (*parameter-kind*   explicit OR implicit)
)

    {And the controlling object is a leaf node. (The absence of any subclasses.)}
    (**schema** ? Object
        (**NOT** (*has-subclasses*   ?))
)

⇒

    {Then}

    (**printout** *print-window* t
        "The object being created by the ?Action action is already known, because
        the object ?Object to which the action is being applied has no subclasses.
        Therefore the parameter type of ?Parameter should be literal not explicit or
        implicit."
)
)

transformation on the knowledge base will be illustrated on the set of actions from the example of Figure 15.4.

The currently selected set (CSS) transformation *factors* a specified class of objects out of the actions that operate on that object class. This means in general that the object(s) will no longer be selected by the user when the action is invoked, but will instead be given in advance of the action, and might be used by several actions. More specifically, a CSS is comprised of selected objects that can be operated on by a succession of actions. The user selects the set of objects, and each subsequent action requested by the user is applied to each member of the CSS. The CSS transformation adds to the design knowledge base actions to add an object to the CSS, remove an object from the CSS, and clear the CSS. The action to add an object to the CSS has a postcondition that increases by one the size of the CSS, and decreases by one the size of the remaining, nonselected set of objects (called the NSS). A precondition, requiring that the CSS be non empty, is added to actions that operate on instances of the object class that has been factored.

Figure 15.11 shows the set of actions that are added when the previous example of Figure 15.4 is transformed to have a CSS. Figure 15.12 shows the additional preconditions and postconditions that are added, and also the keyword **implicit** is added to the factored object instance parameter in each of these actions. Our definition of CSS is that a newly created object becomes the CSS, and that any other objects that were in the CSS are now rejected. Hence a postcondition is added to all actions that create a new instance of the class, asserting that the CSS has size one. Actions that delete an object of the class being factored have an additional postcondition asserting that the CSS is empty, because the deletion applies to the CSS, leaving it empty.

The CSS transformation allows several different CSSs, one for each type of object known to the system. This is a common necessity in CAD systems, where a selected point and a selected circle are used to draw a line through the point, tangent to the circle. Given several CSSs, we also need to add preconditions involving the type of the selected objects. For instance, a command that creates a tangent to two circles must have as a precondition that the CSS contains exactly two circles, while a command to create a plane through three points should have as a precondition that the CSS contains three points.

Other transformations work similarly, and are not described here in as much detail. In each case, schemata for actions, parameters, preconditions, and postconditions are added, removed, or modified. The class hierarchy specialization transformation adds specialized actions in place of a general action. For instance, create_triangle and create_square actions could replace the create_shape action seen in the previous examples. Class hierarchy generalization does the opposite. Attribute value specialization adds specialized actions for each value of an enumerated attribute. If the fill type in our drawing example can be black, gray, or white, then create_general_object could be replaced with create_general_object_black, create_general_object_gray, and create_general_object_white. Attribute value generalization does the opposite.

FIGURE 15.11

THE SYSTEM-DEFINED ACTIONS FOR SIMPLE DRAW APPLICATION AFTER BEING TRANSFORMED TO HAVE A CSS. NSS IS THE SET OF NON-SELECTED OBJECTS; CSS IS THE SET OF SELECTED OBJECTS. CSS AND NSS ARE DISJOINT, AND TOGETHER INCLUDE ALL OBJECTS. FOUR SYSTEM DEFINED ACTIONS – SELECT_GENERAL_OBJECT, ADD_TO_CSS_GENERAL_OBJECT, RE-MOVE_FROM_CSS_GENERAL_OBJECT, AND CLEAR_CSS_GENERAL_OBJECT – ARE CREATED BY THE "IF-THEN" PROCEDURAL RULES OF CSS TRANSFOR-MATION ALGORITHM. "+" INDICATES NEW INFORMATION THAT IS ADDED OR UPDATED BY THE TRANSFORMATION.

---

    initial: number(general_object) = 0
    initial: number(CSS, general_object) = 0 {Currently Selected Set is initially empty.}
    initial: number(NSS, general_object) = 0 {Non-Selected Set is initially empty.}

+ **pre-condition:** number(NSS, general_object) > 0
+   select_general_object(obj_type: general_object)
+ **post-condition:** number(NSS, general_object) = number(NSS, general_object)
+   + number(CSS, general_object)
+ **post-condition:** number(CSS, general_object) = 1

+ **pre-condition:** number(NSS, general_object) > 0
+   add_to_CSS_general_object(obj_type: general_object)
+ **post-condition:** number(CSS, general_object) = number(CSS, general_object) + 1
+ **post-condition:** number(NSS, general_object) = number(NSS, general_object) − 1

+ **pre-condition:** number(CSS, general_object) > 0
+   remove_from_CSS_general_object(obj_type: general_object)
+ **post-condition:** number(CSS, general_object) = number(CSS, general_object) − 1
+ **post-condition:** number(NSS, general_object) = number(NSS, general_object) + 1

+ **pre-condition:** number(CSS, general_object) > 0
+   clear_CSS_general_object()
+ **post-condition:** number(NSS, general_object) = number(NSS, general_object)
+   + number(CSS, general_object)
+ {All currently selected general_object become non selected shapes.}
+ **post-condition:** number(CSS, general_object) = 0

The Currently Selected Command (CSC) transformation adds a set_command action with a postcondition asserting that the command has been selected. The actual action has a precondition added requiring that the command be selected. The object naming transformation adds a name parameter to the parameter list of the action that creates an object, and adds an action to change an object's name.

The transformations are implemented with ART rules that instantiate, modify, or delete instances of the seven types of schemata shown in Figure 15.2. To facilitate maintaining the knowledge base's consistency and integrity,

FIGURE 15.12
THE SUBSET OF USER-DEFINED ACTIONS OF SIMPLEDRAW APPLICATION
AFTER BEING TRANSFORMED TO HAVE A CSS. PRE AND POSTCONDITION
VALUES AND PARAMETER-KIND INFORMATION IN DEFINITIONS OF AP-
PLICATION ACTION DEFINITIONS ARE MAINTAINED BY THE "WHILE-THEN"
LOGICAL DEPENDENCY RULES OF CSS TRANSFORMATION ALGORITHM.

      pre-condition: number(CSS, general_object) > 0
      pre-condition: number (general_object) > 0
+   cut(obj_type: general_object **implicit**)
+ post-condition: number(general_object) = number(general_object) −
      number(CSS, general_object)
      {Cut decreases the total number of general_objects in CSS.}
+ post-condition: number(clipboard, general_object)
             = number (clipboard, general_object) + number
                (CSS, general_object)
      {Cut increases the total number of general_objects in clipboard}
+ post-condition: number(CSS, general_object) = 0
      {CSS of general_object becomes 0.}

+ pre-condition: number(CSS, general_object) > 0
      pre-condition: number (general_object) > 0
+   copy(obj_type: general_object **implicit**)
+ post-condition: number (clipboard, general_object)
             = number (clipboard, general_object) + number
                (CSS, general_object)

      pre-condition: number (clipboard, general_object) > 0
        paste(anchor_pt: position **optional**)
      post-condition: number (general_object) = number (general_object) +
      number(clipboard, general_object)
+ post-condition: number(NSS, general_object) = number(NSS, general_object) +
      number(CSS, general_object)
      {Existing CSS of general_object, if any, is deselected, thus adding
      to the NSS of general_object.}

a combination of "if-then" procedural rules and "while-then" logical dependency rules are used to implement the transformation algorithms. Logical
dependencies indicate the interdependence of some facts on others in the
knowledge base; this logical primitive in ART helps to maintain the correctness of the knowledge base, especially when many transformations interact.
"If-then" rules are used in transformations that create or delete system-defined actions, for example, select_general_object, add_to_CSS_general_object,
remove_from_CSS_general_object, and clear_CSS_general_object as shown in
Figure 15.11. "While-then" logical dependency rules are used in transforma-

FIGURE 15.12 (Cont.)

+ post-condition: number(CSS, shape) = number (clipboard, general_object)
   {Size of the CSS shape after paste action is the size of the clipboard.}

   pre-condition: true
       create_shape(anchor_pt: position, fill_style: fill, orientation: angle,
       obj_type: shape_class)
   post-condition: number(shape) = number(shape) + 1
+ post-condition: number(NSS, shape) = number(NSS, shape) + number
   (CSS, shape)
   {When a shape is created, the existing CSS of shape, if any, is deselected,
   thus adding to the NSS of shape.}
+ post-condition: number(CSS, shape) = 1
   {Size of the CSS of shape after creation action is 1: the newly-created shape.}

+ pre-condition: number(CSS, shape) > 0
   pre-condition: number(general_object) > 0
+   rotate_general_object(obj_type: general_object **implicit**, orientation: angle)
   post-condition: none

+ pre-condition: number(CSS, general_object) > 0
   pre-condition: number(general_object) > 0
+   delete_general_object(obj_type: general_object **implicit**)
   post-condition: number(general_object) = number(general_object) − 1
+ post-condition: number(general_object) = number(general_object) −
   number(CSS, general_object)
   {Deletion decreases the total number of general_objects in CSS.}
+ post-condition: number(CSS, general_object) = 0
   {Size of the CSS of general_object becomes 0.}

+ pre-condition: number(CSS, shape) > 0
   pre-condition: number(shape) > 0
+   change_fill(obj_type: shape **implicit**, fill_style: fill)
   post-condition: none

---

tions to add, modify, and delete precondition, postcondition, and parameter-
kind slot values. Figure 15.12 illustrates the results of the CSS transformation
algorithm being applied to update these slots.

   Applying a transformation includes setting a status variable that asserts
that the current knowledge base is in a certain state or paradigm. Logical dependency rules maintain that state or paradigm throughout the design session, even if the designer opts for additional application action descriptions.
Figure 15.13 shows three actions being added to the current base after the
CSS transformation has been already applied. Preconditions, postconditions,

FIGURE 15.13
ADDITIONAL ACTIONS BEING ADDED AFTER CSS TRANSFORMATION HAS BEEN
APPLIED. PRECONDITIONS, POSTCONDITIONS, AND PARAMETER-KIND VALUES
ARE AUTOMATICALLY UPDATED BY LOGICAL DEPENDENCY RULES.

+   **pre-condition:** number(NSS, general_object) > 0
     {Automatically added by logical dependency rule.}
     pre-condition: number(general_object) > 0
+   move_general_object(obj_type: general_object **implicit**)
     {Parameter-kind automatically updated by logical dependency rule.}
     post-condition: none

     pre-condition: none
          create_text(obj_type: text_class)
     post-condition: number(text) = number(text) + 1
+   **post-condition:** number(NSS, text) = number(NSS, text) + number(CSS, text)
     {Automatically added. The existing CSS of text, if any, is deselected, thus adding to
          the NSS of text.}
+   **post-condition:** number (CSS, text) = 1
     {Automatically added. Size of the CSS of text after creation action is 1:
          the newly-created text.}

+   **pre-condition:** number(CSS, text) > 0
     {Automatically added by logical dependency rule.}
     pre-condition: number(text) > 0
+   change_font(obj_type: text **implicit**)
     {Parameter-kind automatically updated by logical dependency rule.}
     post-condition: none

---

and parameter-kind values are automatically updated by logical dependency
rules to maintain the knowledge base in the CSS paradigm. This capability
supports incremental design.

Canonical Form

All interfaces that can be created by applying arbitrary sequences of transformations form an equivalence class of interfaces. Each such equivalence class
is represented by its *canonical form*, which is a unique member of the equivalence class. While we have no proof, we believe that the canonical form is one
in which all actions are generalized (pushed up) to the highest possible level
of abstraction; all parameters are explicit; no defaults exist; and all modes,
both action and object, are removed. Proof of this conjecture, and developing
an algorithm that can find a sequence (which is non-unique) of transformations to take any member of the equivalence class into the canonical form are
open research problems. The canonical form has the most compact represen-

tation of the various alternatives and would be useful for defining a standard interface between a UIMS and the semantic modules that implement the functionality of an interface.

15.5 SIMPLE USER INTERFACE MANAGEMENT SYSTEM (SUIMS)

SUIMS supports the design process by allowing a designer to explore different user interfaces to an application, with minimal additional effort involved. The transformation algorithms allow the designer to create a variety of functionally equivalent user interface designs for an application. Whenever a transformation is applied and a design is changed, SUIMS can produce a corresponding user interface. Further refinements of the automatically generated interface are possible; SUIMS provides support for such fine tuning.

Two distinct levels of interface functionality are possible. The prototyping level operates without any application-specific action routines. It allows commands and parameters to be entered, and executes two classes of actions:

- those added by transformations, such as: add_to_CSS_general_object, remove_from_CSS_general_object, clear_CSS_general_object;
- the generic actions of Section 15.2, to the extent that they modify instantiations of data objects. The graphical representations of the objects are not displayed, but objects can be selected (e.g. for the purpose of executing a command operating on it) using a name that is automatically assigned to it.

The second level is full functionality. Here, the application's semantic action routines have to be provided, but only for application actions given in the initial design.

At both levels, a set of standard actions (e.g. help, quit) are available. Postconditions are handled by generic action routines that operate on SUIMS internal variables and object representations. This important use of postconditions is possible because SUIMS is in charge of the application objects.

A set of standard actions is automatically provided by SUIMS and need not be specified in the design description. This set currently includes cancel (the input of parameters for the current command), quit, and some forms of help actions. Undo/redo will be added in the future.

SUIMS started as the Small UIMS. Now it is no longer small, but it is still, and we hope will remain, very simple to use, hence the current name of Simple UIMS. As it grows and uses more knowledge, we hope that it will become more sophisticated, the Smart UIMS. Figure 15.14 illustrates SUIMS in use.

SUIMS uses both the design knowledge base and an additional SUIMS knowledge base that describes the run-time context for both SUIMS and

FIGURE 15.14

THIS FIGURE SHOWS SUIMS EXECUTING THE SIMPLEDRAW APPLICATION, WITH THE SIZE ATTRIBUTE FACTORED OUT.

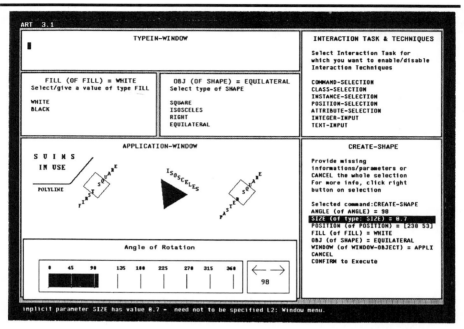

The running version uses a richer knowledge base—with more subclasses (equilateral isosceles, and right are subclasses of triangle) and a WINDOW parameter (if we have more than one application window; otherwise it has default value of the existing one)—than in other examples used in the chapter. The application window contains object instances. Text strings shown are object instances of class texts and are used to comment on other objects. The TYPEIN window is used for textual input. The currently selected action is create_shape, and values for all of its parameters are provided, as shown in the CREATE-SHAPE menu window. A parameter SIZE (shown in reverse video) has been selected, and additional information for it is given at the bottom of the screen, explaining that its value is provided by the system (because the attribute SIZE is factored out). POSITION was selected by pointing in the application window (therefore, no textual input in the command window is present). FILL and OBJ are selected from the menus displayed at the middle-left part of the screen. ANGLE is selected using gauge shown in the lower-left part of the screen. Confirmation is requested, although it is possible to provide new values for parameters as long as neither CANCEL nor CONFIRM have been selected. It is also possible to change selected interaction techniques using the menu in the top-right corner, or to rearrange the screen layout.

the application, environment characteristics, and dialogue objects. The pre- and postconditions, together with the object class hierarchy and the actions described in the design knowledge base, are used to control the dialogue with the user.

The key issues to be discussed in the rest of this section are the SUIMS knowledge base and dialogue control, interaction tasks and techniques, screen layout presentation and the internal interface between SUIMS and the semantic action routines.

SUIMS Knowledge Base

Three salient parts of the additional knowledge that SUIMS needs are the run-time context, environment characteristics, and dialogue objects.

The first part, the run-time context, comprises three kinds of information that are distinguishable based on what part of the system is in charge of the information, and what parts have access to it:

■ SAR context—information maintained by and accessible to the application only, that is, its Semantic Action Routines (SAR);

■ SUIMS context—information maintained by and accessible to SUIMS only; and

■ Application context—information shared by both SUIMS and the application.

The SUIMS KB (knowledge base) must have the latter two, while the first kind is optional. For example, SUIMS can generate and emulate a prototype without having semantic action routines, in which case the SAR context is not present. The SAR context is described in the discussion of the internal interface between SUIMS and semantic action routines.

The application context consists of the application database that includes the application object instances. In contrast, the design KB contains descriptions of the corresponding object classes. SUIMS creates, deletes, and can modify object instances. The application (i.e., the semantic action routines) also has access to object instances so it can use all of the information stored therein. Furthermore, the application can modify this information.

The SUIMS context includes information about the application that is not accessible to the application, as well as information reflecting the SUIMS internal status. For instance, the application-related part of the SUIMS context includes the current values of factored attributes and information about the subsets partitioning the set of all object instances, such as the nonselected set (NSS), the currently selected set (CSS), and clipboard. The SUIMS internal status is defined by state variables that control the current dialogue style (verbose or terse dialogue), whether command confirmation is required, what is currently being processed (e.g. preconditions, postconditions, action parameters), whether user actions are being recorded, and so on.

The second part of the SUIMS KB describes the run-time environment. Though it may be incorporated as a part of the SUIMS context, we model it separately because it does not depend on any particular application and it may be reused in numerous applications. The run-time environment consists of the available I/O devices, types of windows, and interaction tasks and techniques that are supported. This is what Lantz [Lantz87] calls the "workstation agent." ART currently provides SUIMS the basic workstation elements.

Interactions in SUIMS take place via dialogue objects, definitions of which make up the third part of the SUIMS KB. Examples of dialogue objects are utterances (generated by external events, e.g. a user's actions), outgoing messages, menus, and windows. This idea of interactions via dialogue objects is similar to the approach used in [Sibert86].

Dialogue Control

The definition of an action specifies all the units of information and context needed to carry out the action. Hence there is no need for an explicit dialogue specification. SUIMS uses pre- and postconditions to define the current context and to determine enabled actions. SUIMS is nearly syntax-free, putting minimal constraints on the sequence of parameters specified for an action. The only ordering imposed is that a command must be selected before its parameters, except for parameters that have been factored out by a transformation algorithm and hence can be set globally. The user can change parameter values of a command as long as the command has not been performed or canceled. When all necessary parameters have been provided, SUIMS either performs the command or, if confirmation mode is on, waits for the user to explicitly confirm that all parameters have desired values. Confirmation provides more equality in the treatment of parameters, by giving the user the opportunity to modify the last parameter value entered as well as the ones previously entered. It also allows proper handling of parameter defaults and a variable number of parameters. The designer chooses whether confirmation mode is on.

SUIMS cycles through the following steps.

- Establish and update the screen layout
- Check all preconditions and recognize enabled actions
- Accept an action selected by the user
- Process each parameter according to its kind (explicit, implicit, etc.)
- Accept parameter values in arbitrary order, using any of the enabled interaction techniques
- Confirm an action implicitly (if all necessary information is provided), confirm explicitly (if required), or cancel an action
- Execute the action
- Evaluate postconditions

SUIMS does not necessarily perform every step in each cycle. Postconditions will be evaluated only if the selected action is not canceled; the screen layout is updated only when required by changes made to the knowledge base. Only preconditions whose status may have been changed because of postcondition changes are actually evaluated.

Interaction Tasks and Techniques: Interaction Techniques are defined in the SUIMS knowledge base for carrying out seven different interaction tasks: command_selection, class_selection, instance_selection, attribute_selection, position_selection, text_input, and integer_input. For instance, we have implemented pointing, name type-in, and menu selection for the instance_selection interaction task. An interaction technique is available and can be used for some interaction task if all interaction devices it requires are supported and available. Available interaction techniques can further be enabled or disabled; a designer can change these settings depending on the desired interaction style. There are no restrictions on the number of interaction techniques enabled for each interaction task. Of course, if none are enabled, the interaction task cannot be performed. If more than one technique is enabled, the user can choose which one to use.

Internal Interface to Semantic Action Routines

SUIMS is basically an external control UIMS: it is in charge of invoking the application's Semantic Action Routines (SARs). SARs can modify the SUIMS knowledge base which in turn controls SUIMS, so there is also an element of shared control. SARs are optional, and SUIMS can prototype the application user interface without them.

Parameters associated with an action can be static or dynamic. Dynamic parameters are continually evaluated and fed back to the user to reflect each change in the parameter value. For example, while dragging an object using direct manipulation, every change in mouse position is reflected in the object placement. Another example where a dynamic parameter might be used is rotation of an object using a gauge (slider); as the user moves the gauge, the object would be rotated accordingly. However, the feedback for intermediate parameter values is not necessarily the same as for the final parameter value. For instance, the intermediate feedback for dragging might be an outline of the object being moved, while the final feedback would be a fine drawing of the object. The intermediate values are passed continuously by SUIMS to the SARs.

If continuous feedback is not required, a parameter is declared static. For example, if the rotation action is invoked and the angle of rotation is declared as a static parameter, then the angle attribute of the selected object is updated only after a final value of the angle is provided. Only then is this information passed from SUIMS to the SAR.

The characteristics of the internal interface between SUIMS and SARs depend on the way in which SARs are invoked and information is passed between SUIMS and SARs, and the amount of knowledge SUIMS has about an application's semantics. SUIMS links to the semantic action routines using active value slots in the action schemata; the action routines are encapsulated as methods, and are invoked automatically by ART whenever SUIMS changes relevant slot values. Different types of active values are used for static and dynamic parameters. A dynamic parameter is implemented using two slots: one for intermediate values and another for the final value of the parameter. A static parameter needs only one slot—for its final value.

Application object instances are instantiated by SUIMS whenever an action that creates an object is invoked by the user. SUIMS maintains the attribute values for each object, and also makes them available to the application's semantic action routines. Thus these object instances are the application context shared between SUIMS and the application. If the CSS transformation has been applied, SUIMS records which objects are members of the CSS and NSS (Section 15.4). CSS and NSS are defined as objects. While it is possible to handle an action operating on the CSS by sending an appropriate message to the CSS object, which then broadcasts the message to all its members, we have designed SUIMS to query the CSS object for its members and then broadcast directly to the members.

SUIMS has enough information to create or delete objects. It uses pre- and postconditions in addition to the action classification to find out whether creation, deletion, or modification is required. An action parameter is related to a corresponding object attribute using the action and the object descriptions in the conceptual KB. Such reasoning is also used to generate help messages (see next section). Currently, we support limited attribute modification, because we assume "replacement" usage of a parameter (an attribute value of an object being modified is replaced with the parameter value).

The semantic action routines can be written as ART rules, Lisp, C, or any other language that can be linked to Common Lisp on the Sun. They can use data from the application context, shared with SUIMS, or they can maintain the SAR context, as their own data base. If the SAR context is used, it is the responsibility of the SARs to keep it updated.

Screen Layout Presentations

Managing the screen presentation involves two subtasks: screen layout control and content control. The screen layout consists of a set of windows. Each window is an object with its characteristics defined by a set of attributes. The attributes currently supported are: name, size, position, type (graphical, text, or menu), content, and visibility (visible or hidden). A window may contain application objects' instances, in which case we call it an application window. There may be one or more application windows. In the current implementation, contents of application windows are controlled by the application's semantic action routines. Contents of all other windows are controlled by SUIMS. The screen layout of all windows is controlled by SUIMS.

The screen layout is controlled by two sets of information in the SUIMS knowledge base, initial settings and changes. Initial settings are used when a window is first created to define its size and position. Once the window is created, SUIMS maintains all of the size and position changes, even if the window is temporarily made invisible. This allows the designer to interactively rearrange screen layouts to modify the existing or initial layout. Such changes become a permanent part of the design of a user interface.

15.6 HELP

UIDE's help system uses the conceptual-design and SUIMS run-time knowledge bases to generate context-sensitive help messages. Two kinds of help are provided: explanation of why a command is disabled, and explanation of what a command does (i.e., the command's semantics).

Our approach to providing intelligent help differs significantly from the traditional one. Most help systems are grafted onto an interface after the fact. The traditional intelligent help development cycle can be illustrated as in Figure 15.15a. It starts with the design and implementation of a user interface. Once the user interface is developed, the knowledge about it is extracted and help using that knowledge is added onto the system. The context-sensitivity of such help is constrained to the preexisting hooks in a user interface.

FIGURE 15.15
INTELLIGENT HELP DEVELOPMENT

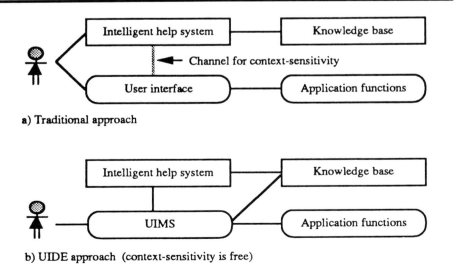

a) Traditional approach

b) UIDE approach (context-sensitivity is free)

The user interface might have to be modified to provide for these hooks. In addition, the help KB must be updated whenever the interface changes.

Figure 15.15*b* shows our approach to the intelligent help development cycle. We start with a KB representing the conceptual design. The same KB is used to implement a user interface, and help that is integrated into the user interface. If the KB is updated, the help changes automatically corresponding to changes in the user interface. The KB reflects the full context of both SUIMS and the application, so help is context-sensitive as well.

The help system has a set of rules that operate on the KB. It uses pre- and postconditions, together with action and object descriptions and their relationships, to generate help explanations. Each type of entity is managed by a group of rules. There are a finite number of pre- and postcondition types that may occur in any design. For each set of rules handling pre- and postconditions in SUIMS there is a corresponding set of rules in the help system. The correspondence of rules is not necessarily "one-to-one," but it is important that semantics be preserved; the help system must assign the same meaning as is interpreted by SUIMS.

Depending on the kind of explanation and its complexity, the actual text of a message is generated in several stages. For example, explaining why a command is disabled takes two stages, while explaining what a command does takes three. In either case, the starting points are predefined text elements associated with certain categories in the KB that are assembled into larger constructs. The wording of messages generated in this manner is not always the best possible, as can be seen from the examples. The messages can be improved and made more natural language-like by adding a sophisticated natural-language synthesizer. The messages generated by the help system can, if desired, be modified by the designer once the final design has been developed.

The explanation of why a command is disabled is based on the unsatisfied preconditions for that command. For example, assume the design of Figure 15.4, with no object instances yet created. If the user selects the rotate_general_object command, SUIMS responds with "rotate_general_object — Sorry, but this command is now disabled." If the user then requests an explanation, SUIMS responds "Command rotate_general_object is disabled because there is no general_object." If the angle attribute has been factored out, and a value for angle has not been provided yet, the explanation would be "Command rotate_general_object is disabled because there is no general_object, and angle of general_object has not been set."

The explanation of what a command does is based on the command semantics as represented by the command's postconditions. Because our postconditions do not completely encode a command's semantics, the semantics are in general only partially explained. Typical explanations, constructed from the knowledge base, indicate whether the command creates, deletes, or modifies an object, what object class and/or attributes are affected, and other consequences such as deselecting all previously selected objects.

Rules that generate command descriptions use knowledge about actions, action parameters, action postconditions, application objects, object attributes, and their relationships. The reasoning process involves answering four main questions, each associated with specific units of information in the knowledge base:

- Is the action type Create, Delete, or Modify, and what is created, deleted, or modified? This is an action's primary effect, and is inferred from the action's postconditions and parameters or from action classification.
- Are there other consequences that will affect the current context and the state of the knowledge base? This is a secondary effect, and is inferred from postconditions. An example is selecting or deselecting one or more object instances.
- How do command parameters affect object attributes? This is inferred from the description of the action parameters, the objects on which the action operates, and the attributes of these objects. Each command parameter can be distinguished according to its usage: whether its value serves as a selection criteria, or is used to change the corresponding object attribute.
- What is the appropriate message to be generated? The answer is based on all the relevant information.

Let's consider the reasoning process involved in determining an action's type (its primary effect). Whether an action creates or deletes an object or just modifies an existing object can be deduced by keeping track of the object counts, with the number of objects in each class (e.g. square, triangle, shape) and the number in the two sets (CSS, NSS) that partition these classes. If postconditions explicitly state a change in the number of objects, then it is easy to deduce the action type. The rules are:

- number(square) = number(square) + 1 => creates square
- number(square) = number(square) − 1 => deletes square
- [not delete] AND [not create] AND [some attribute modified] => modifies attribute...

If direct counts are not used, indirect reasoning is used, based on cumulative changes in all subsets partitioning the object class. In the following example, CSS and NSS of shapes partition the shape class, and the number of instances in the shape class is equal to the sum of the number of instances in CSS and NSS of shapes:

- number(NSS, shape) = number(NSS, shape) + number(CSS, shape) deselect previously selected objects number(CSS, shape) = 1 => creates new instance

FIGURE 15.16
THE DESCRIPTION GENERATED BY THE HELP SYSTEM.

HELP for create_shape:

The create_shape command has 4 parameters: (ANCHOR_PT, FILL_STYLE, ORIENTATION, OBJ_TYPE).

The create_shape command will:
- Create an instance of the subclass of "shape", determined by parameter OBJ, which is one of:
("square" "isosceles" "right" "equilateral").

In addition:
- Previously selected shape objects are deselected.
- The new instance becomes the currently selected object.
- ORIENTATION becomes the angle attribute of the newly created shape.
- ANCHOR_PT becomes the position attribute of the newly created shape.
- FILL_STYLE becomes the fill attribute of the newly created shape.

- number(CSS, shape) = 0
number(NSS, shape) does not change
=> deletes number(CSS, shape) instances

The alternative to this approach is to use the recently introduced concept of generic command types (delete, create, cut, copy, paste...) instead of just pre- and postconditions. This would require a different line of reasoning. The exact reasoning process to be used also depends on the classification we want to offer to the end user: whether we want just to restate the initial definition, or to give an interpretation of what the system does internally.

Figure 15.16 shows a help description assuming a design with object "shape" factored out to form a CSS. The help system is useful to the designer as well as to the user because the help messages represent the system's understanding of the designer's intent. The system can be thought of as being a "cautious assistant" to the designer who, when asked to do something, paraphrases and restates the task to make sure it is understood. This is a direct consequence of the requirements that each pre- and postcondition as well as other entities be interpreted in the same way SUIMS interprets them. If something is not understood, a warning is given. For example, the designer is notified of a nonsupported postcondition.

15.7 SPEED-OF-USE EVALUATION

The Card, Moran, and Newell keystroke model [Card83] predicts how much time a skilled user who makes no mistakes will take to perform a short task using a given design and set of interaction techniques, ignoring perceptual acquisition times. The model can be used to compare functionally equivalent designs having different interface paradigms or dialogue styles, in order to find the "fastest to use" design alternative. For example, the predicted times for one script vary from 64 seconds with mouse-based interaction techniques to 114 seconds with keyboard-based interaction techniques [Foley89]. When a CSS transformation is applied to the interface and hence to the scenarios, these numbers become 46 and 89 seconds, respectively.

The model defines the time needed to execute a task as the sum of the times needed to carry out primitive operators: T(Execute) = K(Keystrokes) + P(Pointing at screen objects) + H(Homing on devices) + D(Drawing) + M(Mental preparation).

The knowledge needed to perform a keystroke analysis is listed here.

- A definition of the interaction techniques used to input each type of information, and the keystroke model primitives (Keystrokes, Pointing, Homing, Drawing, and Mental Preparation) used for each technique. For UIDE techniques, this is built-in.
- A set of task scenarios, expressed as sequences of the commands from the untransformed (that is, canonical form) user interface definition.
- Transformation algorithms on the task scenarios, to express them in terms of a transformed design.
- The syntax of commands.
- Human performance data, for each of the keystroke model primitives.

The task scenarios can be created interactively, by example. The designer simply carries out a task, and the sequence of actions is recorded. It is also possible for the designer to define scenarios using a text editor. When transformations are applied, scenarios themselves are transformed automatically to conform to the set of actions in the current design.

A designer can study the effect of using any interaction technique simply by specifying its keystroke operators, first device used, and last device used.

The speed-of-use evaluation system is currently only partially integrated with UIDE. However, it uses the UIDE knowledge base. Transformation algorithms from UIDE are used for script transformations. A more thorough discussion of the speed-of-use evaluation system can be found in [Senay88].

15.8 FUTURE EXTENSIONS

The fun has just begun! There are many directions for future development of UIDE: we focus here on those that will make extensive use of the knowledge base, or will require restructuring and/or additions.

Help

The help system is being augmented in several ways. The first is to add descriptions for other kinds of meta-objects (i.e., types of schemata in the knowledge base) including composite objects and tasks (clusters of actions). Linking all meta-object descriptions will then allow building a help network through which the user can navigate. Links in the network would correspond to meta-object relationships, and one of the most useful being the part-whole relationship. This linked network will serve as the basis for a guided tour to be generated automatically from the knowledge base of the conceptual structure of an application. Work on automated guided tour generation is being completed as part of the dissertation research of our colleague Lucy Moran.

Another extension is to explain how to enable a disabled command, or how to achieve some specific goal based on the current state of the user interface. This requires back-chaining from the schema for the disabled command or desired goal to find other commands whose postconditions will enable the command in question. Several steps of back-chaining may be needed, and there may be multiple ways to enable the command. For instance, in the transformation example discussed in Section 15.4 to create a currently selected set, the rotate command could be enabled by selecting an object (so there is a CSS), creating an object (it becomes the CSS), or duplicating an object (the duplicate becomes the CSS).

Piyawadee Sukaviriya has developed a prototype system, which does this type of back-chaining and then shows the user what to do, in the context of a hierarchical directory manipulation with a direct-manipulation interface [Sukaviriya88]. The knowledge structures and back-chaining capability necessary for animated help have been generalized and integrated into UIDE [Sukaviriya90]. The major objectives are: (1) to systematically structure the information about both the application and its interface necessary to provide explanations of "how to" in the application; and (2) to embed the architecture (of which animation and the back-chaining mechanism are a part) that builds on this information to generate complete context-sensitive explanations in the existing UIDE architecture.

If there are multiple ways to enable a command, the help system has to decide which one to show or explain to the user. A user model that records usage of the various commands and object classes can choose an explanation based on maximizing the use of familiar commands and objects, or based on minimizing the time to carry out the sequence of commands.

Predicates

The current structure of the knowledge base is not suited to the back-chaining needed for these types of help. The preconditions are predicates, but the postconditions are assignment statements. This complicates the syntactic reasoning needed to do the back-chaining: the postconditions need to include predicates that can be used in the pattern-matching of syntactic reasoning. Every assignment affecting variables which are in turn involved in predicates needs to be replaced with predicates, as shown in the following example, which is a restructured example from Section 15.4 (the terms *precondition* and *postcondition* have been replaced by *pre-predicate* and *post-predicate*):

initial-predicate: number(general_object, 0)
pre-predicate: number(shape, X)
create_shape(anchor_pt: position, fill_style: fill, orientation:
angle, obj_type: shape_class)
post-predicate: delete-list: number(shape, X)
add-list: number(shape, increment(X, 1))

pre-predicate: number (general_object, X) AND gt(X, 0)
rotate_general_object(obj_type: general_object, orientation: angle)
post-predicate: none

pre-predicate: number(general_object, X) AND gt(X, 0)
delete_general_object(obj_type: general_object)
post-predicate: delete-list: number(general_object, X)
add-list: number(general_object, decrement(X, 1))

Our colleague Hikmet Senay is further developing this knowledge base organization and back-chaining [Senay89].

Automatic Menu and Dialogue Box Organization

Many interactive systems have menus from which commands and some parameters are entered, and associated dialogue boxes from which further parameter information is entered. In a classical user interface design environment, the designer organizes the commands and parameters into menus, menu hierarchies, and dialogue boxes based on an understanding of the logical relationships between commands and parameters. We will do the same, based on the logical relationships between commands and parameters represented in the UIDE knowledge base. Some criteria that might be used to organize commands into multiple menus are commands that

■ Create/delete various objects
■ Operate on a class of objects
■ Modify attributes
■ Operate on default (initial) values
■ Operate on relations

Attributes that have been factored (made global) can also be accessed as menu commands. For instance, a command to set a text font might be one of several commands in a menu, or the actual enumerated values of the text font might be given as different menu entries. Alternatively, the text font attribute might be combined with other text attributes in a dialogue box, in which any of the attributes can be set.

There are many alternative ways to organize and present the same underlying information. Won Chul Kim is developing the design tool called DON [Kim90] that assists the designer in organizing the information, selecting appropriate interface object classes and their attributes, and placing selected interface objects in a dialogue box or a menu in a meaningful, logical, and consistent manner. Various knowledge components needed for an effective user interface presentation design are integrated into the UIDE knowledge base. Useful and reusable knowledge about the organization of interface objects is identified and encapsulated in the form of design rules. We expect that the knowledge found in the extended UIDE knowledge base will also be useful for automatically laying out menus and dialogue boxes, in a fashion comparable to the work of Mackinlay [Mackinlay86; Mackinlay90]. The major objectives are to allow designers to: (1) specify high-level style and organization preferences, (2) customize low-level interface object attributes, and (3) control the usage of design rules by explicitly stating organization rules and enabling the designer to modify associated priorities.

Visual design rules would be used to reinforce the underlying logical relationships between elements of the dialogue box. For example, Figure 15.17 shows a dialogue box for the user task of specifying alignment of objects in a graphics editor. Part (a) is the dialogue box without application of the visual design principle of grouping like items together: there is difficulty in understanding which sets of alternatives are grouped together. Part (b) is an improved version of the dialogue box, and (c) is further improved. Any of these designs could be generated from the design knowledge base. In part (d) we see use of knowledge about the spatial relationships implied by the two sets of mutually-exclusive alternatives: this knowledge is not currently represented in UIDE, but can be trivially added.

Interface Objects as Application Objects

A modification underway is to treat user interface objects such as windows and menus in the same way as application objects, so that actions on them can be represented in exactly the same way. This will in turn facilitate using the precondition mechanism to control the visibility and enabling of these user interface objects: a precondition, when true, will cause the object to become visible; when false, the object will become invisible.

FIGURE 15.17

FOUR DIFFERENT DIALOGUE BOXES FOR SPECIFYING ALIGNMENT OF OBJECTS IN A GRAPHICS EDITOR

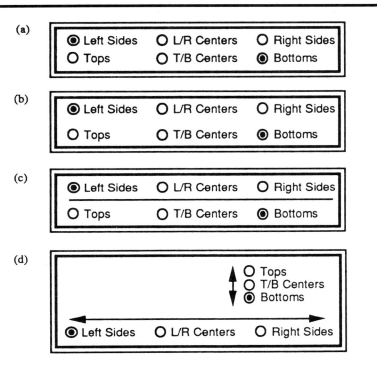

More Sophisticated Transformations

Our basic motivation for developing user interface transformations is that each transformation represents an alternative for the user interface designer to explore. Even if a designer did not have UIDE to automatically apply the transformation to a design, having a catalog of design alternatives would be very useful. Furthermore, describing a transformation as a set of rules formalizes the alternatives and removes ambiguity about their meaning.

While the transformations we have thus far implemented are useful, they only scratch the surface of what is possible. For instance, several important variations of the currently selected object (CSO) transformation became apparent as we defined the CSO transformation rules. As now defined, a newly created object becomes the CSO. However, another possibility is for the CSO, which existed prior to the creation, to remain as the CSO when an object is created. Also as now defined, if the CSO is deleted, there is no CSO. Still another possibility is for a different object to become the CSO: either the previous CSO, or the most recently created object, or the most recently created object of the same type as the deleted object, or the object closest to the deleted object.

The currently selected set (CSS) transformation, as now defined, adds three commands: add object to the CSS, remove object from the CSS, clear all objects from the CSS. These are not the only possible commands for manipulating a set of objects. Others are: add multiple objects to the CSS, remove multiple objects from the CSS, remove all objects from the CSS and add another object to the CSS, and remove all objects from the CSS and add multiple other objects to the CSS.

The knowledge base transformation mechanism provides a useful way to precisely specify these and other alternatives; future versions of UIDE will give the designer a choice of these various alternatives.

The fundamental research issue here involves continuing to develop both the set of user interface transformations and the knowledge representations needed to allow the transformations to be realized. Developing a collection of user interface transformations that have known properties and that can be applied by user interface designers to improve an interface has a high potentiality for improving user interface design. The transformations regularize and formalize existing knowledge about design alternatives, and create a logical framework in which new alternatives can be discovered.

Dialogue Model

Based on experience with UIDE and its SUIMS component, Srdjan Kovacevic is developing a new model of human-computer dialogues, which views a user interface as a composition of primitives organized in a specific way; selection of primitives and the way they are organized are driven by application semantics and a desired dialogue style. With the compositional model in place, we plan to further expand the range of UIDE transformations by providing both a richer set of low-level transformations for fine-grain control and high-level transformations for creating different dialogue styles or their combinations.

Optimum Design by Applying Transformations

An "automatic design" optimization algorithm searches the space of design alternatives provided by the set of user interface transformations to minimize the time required to execute a set of task scenarios. This optimum design would be a reasonable starting point for further refinement, *if* the designer's objective is to minimize task times.

The search space is quite large. We have already implemented eight transformations, and some of the transformations can be applied selectively to different object classes or object attributes. Hence an exhaustive search is inappropriate. Fortunately the search space can be pruned. First, some combinations of transformations don't make sense. Second, examination of the scenarios can show whether there is any potential payoff in applying a transformation. For instance, unless the scenario includes several operations applied to the same object, the CSO transformation will not affect speed of use.

Top-Down versus Bottom-Up Design

The current UIDE design specification approach emphasizes a top-down design methodology. However, some user interface designers prefer to work in more of a bottom-up fashion, typically with storyboard-like screen sketches showing various sequences of user interactions. We want to allow this design approach by building a system that will interrogate the designer about various elements in the storyboards in order to elicit the information needed for the knowledge base.

15.9 SUMMARY

UIDE is an evolving system, whose capabilities are continually being developed. The most fundamental notion in UIDE is its higher-level representation of a user interface design. The ways in which we use this representation have the potential to decrease the time needed to develop a user interface. However, the current representation is not sufficiently robust, and is being further refined to represent relationships other than the class hierarchy, and various dependencies between objects.

Our fundamental research objective is to identify knowledge, logical relations, and rules used by interface designers, and to embody them in UIDE as a way of further automating the design process. In so doing, we recognize that some rules are subjective and are open to disagreement among experts. Our objective is *not* to reconcile such disagreements, but rather to create a framework in which rules, both those for which there is a strong theoretical, experimental, or experiential base as well as those that are subjective, can be applied by UIDE. The key is to represent the knowledge needed for the rules.

The UIDE project represents new user interface design tool approaches in the following areas:

- Formal definition of the logical structure of the user interface, as embodied in the knowledge base.
- Further enhancement of systematic and methodical design of dialogues, by identifying and formalizing (as transformations) design alternatives.
- Development of a general, application-independent framework for providing intelligent, context-sensitive help.

■ Provision of an integrated suite of tools driven from the same knowledge base, to support design, prototyping, evaluation, and run-time needs of a user interface.

Our operational prototype demonstrates the viability of providing the user interface designer with user interface specification tools at a higher level of abstraction than those of past UIMSs. The notion of an integrated knowledge base which provides support both to the designer at design time and to the user at run-time has the potential of leading to better user interface designs. To test the utility of the UIDE approach, we need to develop more substantial applications, study how practicing designers work with UIDE, and test the effectiveness of interfaces created with UIDE.

ACKNOWLEDGMENTS

The Graphics and User Interface Research Group at GWU provided an intellectual environment supporting this work. We are grateful to John Sibert, Piyawadee Sukaviriya, Hikmet Senay, and Lucy Moran for their discussions concerning some of these ideas, and to Christina Gibbs who helped develop an earlier version of UIDE. Financial support was provided by National Science Foundation grants DMC-8420529 and IRI-8813179, Inference Corporation, Software Productivity Consortium, Siemens Corporation, and the Department of EE & CS Industrial Liaison Program.

REFERENCES

[Bass88] Bass, L., Hardy, E., Hoyt, K., Little, M., Seacord, R. 1988. *Introduction to the Serpent User Interface Management System,* Software Engineering Institute, Carnegie-Mellon University, Pittsburgh, PA, March 1988.

[Bleser90] Bleser, T., and Sibert, J. 1990. Toto: A Tool for Selecting Interaction Techniques. In *Proceedings of the ACM SIGGRAPH Symposium on User Interface Software and Technology,* Snowbird, UT, October 1990.

[Buxton83] Buxton, W. 1983. Toward a Comprehensive User Interface Management System. *Computer Graphics: SIGGRAPH'83 Conference Proceedings,* 17(3), 35–42.

[Card83] Card, S., Moran, T., and Newell, A. 1983.*The Psychology of Human-Computer Interaction,* Hillsdale, NJ: L. Erlbaum Associates.

[Cardelli88] Cardelli, L. 1988. Building User Interfaces by Direct Manipulation. In *Proceedings of the ACM SIGGRAPH on User Interface Software,* Banff, Canada, ACM, New York, pp. 152–166.

[Chin90] Chin, D. 1990. The UNIX Consultant as an Intelligent Agent. In Sullivan, J., and Tyler, S. (eds.), *Architectures for Intelligent Interfaces: Elements and Prototypes,* Reading, MA: Addison-Wesley.

[Cossey89] Cossey, G. 1989. *Prototyper*. Portland, OR: SmethersBarnes.

[Feiner87] Feiner, S. 1987. *Computer Generation of Pictorial Explanations,* Brown Univ., Dept. of Computer Science Technical Report CS-87-29.

[Feiner90] Feiner, S. 1990. An Architecture for Knowledge-Based Graphical Interfaces. In Sullivan, J., and Tyler, S. (eds.), *Architectures for Intelligent Interfaces: Elements and Prototypes*, Reading, MA: Addison-Wesley.

[Foley87] Foley, J., Gibbs, C., and Kim, W. 1987. Algorithms to Transform the Formal Specification of a User-Computer Interface. In *Proceedings INTERACT '87, 2nd IFIP Conference on Human-Computer Interaction,* Amsterdam: Elsevier Science Publishers, pp. 1001–1006.

[Foley88] Foley, J., Gibbs, C., Kim, W., and Kovacevic, S. 1988. A Knowledge-Based User Interface Management System. In *Proceedings of CHI '88 — 1988 SIGCHI Computer-Human Interaction Conference,* ACM, New York, pp. 67–72.

[Foley89] Foley, J., Kim, W., Kovacevic, S. and Murray, K. 1989. Defining Interfaces at a High Level of Abstraction, *IEEE Software,* 6(1), 25–32.

[Gargan88] Gargan, R., Sullivan, J. and Tyler, S. 1988. Multimodal Response Planning: An Adaptive Rule Based Approach. In *Proceedings of CHI '88 — 1988 SIGCHI Computer-Human Interaction Conference,* ACM, New York, pp. 229–234.

[Green85a] Green, M. 1985. *The Design of Graphical User Interfaces.* Technical Report CSRI-170, Computer Systems Research Institute, University of Toronto, Canada.

[Green85b] Green, M. 1985. The University of Alberta UIMS. In *Proceedings SIGGRAPH '85,* published in *Computer Graphics,* 19(3), 205–213.

[Green86] Green, M. 1986. A Survey of Three Dialogue Models. *Transactions on Graphics,* 5(3), 244–275.

[Hayes83] Hayes, P., and Szekely, P. 1983. Graceful Interaction through the COUSIN Command Interface. *International Journal of Man-Machine Studies,* 19(3), 285–305.

[Hayes84] Hayes, P. 1984. Executable Interface Definitions Using Form-Based Interface Abstractions. In Hartson, R.H. (ed.), *Advances in Computer-Human Interaction.* New Jersey: Ablex.

[Hayes85] Hayes, P., Szekely, P., and Lerner, R. 1985. Design Alternatives for User Interface Management Systems Based on Experience with COUSIN. In *Proceedings of CHI '85,* ACM, pp. 169–175.

[Hill86] Hill, R. 1986. Supporting Concurrency, Communications, and Synchronization in Human-Computer Interaction — The Sassafras UIMS. *ACM Transactions on Graphics,* 5(3), 179–210.

[Hudson86] Hudson, S., and King, R. 1986. A Generator of Direct Manipulation Office Systems. *ACM Transactions on Office Information Systems,* 4(2), 132–163.

[Hudson87] Hudson, S. 1987. UIMS Support for Direct Manipulation Interfaces. *ACM SIGGRAPH Workshop on Software Tools for User Interface Management,* published as *Computer Graphics,* 21(2), 120–124.

[Hudson88] Hudson, S., and King, R. 1988. Semantic Feedback in the Higgens UIMS. *IEEE Transactions on Software Engineering,* 14(8), 1188–1206.

[Hudson89] Hudson, S. 1989. Graphical Specification of Flexible User Interface Displays. In *Proceedings of the ACM SIGGRAPH Symposium on User Interface Software and Technology,* Williamsburg, VA, ACM, pp. 105–114.

[Hurley89] Hurley, D., and Sibert, J. 1989. Modeling User Interface-Application Interactions. *IEEE Software,* 6(1), 71–77.

[Inference87] Inference Corp. 1987. *ART Reference Manual.* Inference Corporation, Los Angeles, CA.

[Kemke87] Kemke, C. 1987. Representation of Domain Knowledge in an Intelligent Help System. In *Proceedings INTERACT '87, 2nd IFIP Conference on Human-Computer Interaction,* Amsterdam: Elsevier Science Publishers, pp. 215–220.

[Kim90] Kim, W., and Foley, J. 1990. DON: User Interface Presentation Design Assistant. In *Proceedings of the ACM SIGGRAPH Symposium on User Interface Software and Technology,* Snowbird, UT, October.

[Koivunen88] Koivunen, M., and Mäntylä, M. 1988. HutWindows: An Improved Architecture for a User Interface Management System. *CG&A,* 8(1), 43–52.

[Lantz87] Lantz, K. A., Tanner, P. P., Binding, C., Huang, K. T., and Dwelly, A. 1987. Reference Models, Window Systems, and Concurrency. *Computer Graphics,* 21(2), 87–97.

[Mackinlay86] Mackinlay, J. 1986. Automating the Design of Graphical Presentations of Relational Information. *ACM Transactions on Graphics,* 5(2), 110–141.

[Mackinlay90] Mackinlay, J. 1990. Search Architectures for the Automatic Design of Graphical Presentations. In Sullivan, J., and Tyler, S. (eds.), *Architectures for Intelligent Interfaces: Elements and Prototypes,* Reading, MA: Addison-Wesley.

[Meier88] Meier, B. 1988. ACE: A Color Expert system for User Interface Design. In *Proceedings of the ACM SIGGRAPH User Interface Software,* Banff, Canada, October, pp. 109–116.

[Miller88] Miller, P. and Szczur, M. 1988. Transportable Application Environment (TAE) Plus Experiences in 'Object'ively Modernizing a User Interface Environment. In *Proceedings OOPSLA '88,* pp. 58–70.

[Myers90] Myers, B. 1990. Using AI Techniques to Create User Interfaces by Example. In Sullivan, J. and Tyler, S. (eds.), *Architectures for Intelligent Interfaces: Elements and Prototypes,* Reading, MA: Addison-Wesley.

[NeXT90] NeXT, Inc. 1990. *Interface Builder,* Palo Alto, CA.

[Olsen84] Olsen, D., Buxton, W., Ehrich, R., Kasik, D., Rhyne, J., and Sibert, J. 1984. A Context for User Interface Management. *IEEE Computer Graphics and Applications,* 4(12), 33–42.

[Olsen86] Olsen, D. 1986. MIKE: The Menu Interaction Kontrol Environment. *Transactions on Graphics,* 5(4), 318–344.

[Olsen88] Olsen, D. and Dance, J. 1988. Macros by Example in a Graphical UIMS. *IEEE Computer Graphics and Applications,* 8(1), 68–78.

[Olsen89] Olsen, D. 1989. A Programming Language Basis for User Interface Management. In *Proceedings of CHI '89,* ACM, New York, pp. 171–176.

[Roth90] Roth, S., Mattis, J., Mesnard, X. 1990. Graphics and Natural Language as Components of Automatic Explanation. In Sullivan, J. and Tyler, S. (eds.), *Architectures for Intelligent Interfaces: Elements and Prototypes,* Reading, MA: Addison-Wesley.

[Schmucker86] Schmucker, K. 1986. MacApp: An Application Framework. *Byte* (Special Issue on Object-Oriented Programming), 11(8), 189–194.

[Schulert85] Schulert, A., Rogers, G., and Hamilton, J. 1985. ADM—A Dialog Manager. In *Proceedings of CHI '85,* ACM, pp. 177–183.

[SEI88] *SEI Serpent SADDLE User's Guide,* 1988. Software Engineering Institute, Carnegie-Mellon University, Pittsburgh, PA.

[Senay88] Senay, H., Moran, L., Sukaviriya, P., Foley, J., and Sibert, J. 1988. *Tools for Improving User-Computer Interfaces.* Report GWU-IIST-88-22, Dept. of EE & CS, George Washington University, Washington, DC 20052.

[Senay89] Senay, H., Sukaviriya, P. and Moran, L. 1989. Planning for Automatic Help Generation. In *Proceedings IFIP WG2.7 Working Conference,* Napa Valley, CA, August 21–25.

[Shneiderman82] Shneiderman, B. 1982. The Future of Interactive Systems and the Emergence of Direct Manipulation. *Behaviour Inform. Technology,* 1, 237–256.

[Shneiderman83] Shneiderman, B. 1983. Direct Manipulation: A Step Beyond Programming Languages. *IEEE Computer,* 16, 57–69.

[Sibert86] Sibert, J., Hurley, D., and Bleser, T. 1986. An Object-Oriented User Interface Management System. In *Proceedings SIGGRAPH '86,* published in *Computer Graphics* 20(3), 259–267.

[Singh89] Singh, G., and Green, M. 1989. Chisel: A System for Creating Highly Interactive Screen Layouts. In *Proceedings of the ACM SIGGRAPH Symposium on User Interface Software and Technology,* Williamsburg, VA, ACM, New York, pp. 86–94.

[Smith88] Smith, D. 1988. Building Interfaces Interactively. In *Proceeding of the ACM SIGGRAPH on User Interface Software,* Banff, Canada, ACM, New York, pp. 144–151.

[Sukaviriya88] Sukaviriya, P. 1988. Dynamic Construction of Animated Help from Application Context. In *Proceedings of the ACM SIGGRAPH on User Interface Software,* Banff, Canada, ACM, New York, pp. 190–202.

[Sukaviriya90] Sukaviriya, P., and Foley, J. 1990. Coupling a UI Framework with Automatic Generation of Context-Sensitive Animated Help. In *Proceedings of the ACM SIGGRAPH Symposium on User Interface Software and Technology,* Snowbird, UT, October 1990.

[Sun90] Sun Microsystems. 1990. Graphical User Interface Design Environment. Mountain View, CA. 1990.

[Sutton78] Sutton, J., and Sprague, R. 1978. A Survey of Business Applications. In *Proceedings American Institute for Decision Sciences 10th Annual Conference, Part II,* Atlanta, GA, 1978.

[Szekely89] Szekely, P. 1989. Standardizing the Interface Between Applications And UIMS's. In *Proceeding of the ACM SIGGRAPH Symposium on User Interface Software and Technology,* Williamsburg, VA, ACM, pp. 34–42.

[Szekely90] Szekely, P. 1990. Structuring Programs to Support Intelligent Interfaces. In Sullivan, J., and Tyler, S. (eds.), *Architectures for Intelligent Interfaces: Elements and Prototypes,* Reading, MA: Addison-Wesley.

[UIMX90] Visual Edge. 1990. UIMX, Montreal, Quebec, Canada.

[Wasserman85] Wasserman, A. 1985. Extending State Transition Diagrams for the Specification of Human-Computer Interaction. *IEEE Transactions on Software Engineering,* 11(8), 699–713.

[Weitzman86] Weitzman, L. 1986. *Designer: A Knowledge-based Graphic Design Assistant.* ICS Report 8609, Institute for Cognitive Science, University of California, San Diego, La Jolla, California 92093, July 1986.

[Wellner89] Wellner, P. 1989. Statemaster: A UIMS Based on Statecharts for Prototyping and Target Implementation. In *Proceedings of CHI '89,* ACM, New York, pp. 177–182.

CHAPTER 16

Using AI Techniques
to Create User Interfaces
by Example

BRAD A. MYERS
School of Computer Science*
Carnegie Mellon University

ABSTRACT

Creating user interfaces is a very difficult task. Existing tools to help create
user interfaces, called *User Interface Management Systems (UIMSs)*, have typically been very difficult to use and have not addressed the modern, highly-
interactive interfaces that are most desirable. Peridot, an experimental UIMS,
uses *Programming-by-Example* techniques to make the interface design task significantly easier. Peridot uses knowledge about the typical properties of user
interfaces to generalize from the user interface designer's specific examples
to create general-purpose parameterized programs. Peridot is a working prototype UIMS and has been successfully used by nonprogrammers to create
interaction techniques such as menus, scroll bars, buttons, sliders, and iconic
and title line window controls. In addition, it appears that, using Peridot,
expert users can create interfaces significantly faster than by coding the in-

*This work was performed while the author was at the University of Toronto.

terfaces by hand. Peridot created its own interface and can create most of the interaction techniques in the Macintosh Toolbox.

16.1 INTRODUCTION

Peridot is a new, experimental tool for creating graphical, highly interactive, direct manipulation style user interfaces. Peridot, which stands for *Programming* by *Example* for *Real-time Interface Design Obviating Typing*, uses Programming-by-Example, with plausible inferencing and other Artificial Intelligence (AI) techniques, to make the design task significantly easier than with previous user interface creation tools or with programming by hand.

Peridot is an actual working prototype implemented in Interlisp-D on a Xerox 1109 DandeTiger workstation. It has been used to create a number of working interfaces, and can create most kinds of menus, property sheets, light buttons, radio buttons, scroll bars, two-dimensional scroll boxes, percent-done progress indicators, graphical potentiometers, sliders, and iconic and title line controls for windows. These low-level parts of user interfaces are often called *Interaction Techniques*. Peridot can create almost all of the Apple Macintosh interface, as well as many new interfaces, such as those which use multiple input devices concurrently. Peridot also created its own user interface.

Peridot is very easy to use. The user interface designer draws a picture of the desired interface, and then demonstrates how the mouse should interact with this picture. This paper discusses how Programming-by-Example, plausible inferencing, condition-action rules, active values, and other AI techniques make Peridot's interface so easy to use. Previous papers about Peridot presented a general overview [Myers86a], described how the mouse is programmed [Myers87a; Myers87b], detailed the programming language aspects [Myers90a], and provided a detailed discussion of all aspects of Peridot [Myers88]. There is also a videotape available [Myers87c].

In this paper, the term *designer* is used for the the person creating user interfaces (and therefore using Peridot). *User* means the person using the interface created by the designer.

16.2 MOTIVATION

Creating a good user interface (UI) for a system is a difficult task, and the software to support the user interfaces is often large, complex, and difficult to debug and modify. The user interface for an application is usually a significant fraction of the code. One study found that the user interface portion was between 29 percent and 88 percent [Sutton78]. In Artificial Intelligence applications, an informal poll found it was about 50 percent, which is supported by observations of a number of specific AI projects, reporting 40 percent to 50 percent [Mittal86,Bobrow86]. Unfortunately, it is generally the case that as user interfaces become easier to use for the end user, they become more complex and harder to create for the UI designer. The easy to use *direct manipulation* style interfaces [Shneiderman83] popular with most modern systems are among the most difficult kinds to implement [Williams83].

In addition to the fact that user interfaces are difficult to create, there are no guidelines or design strategies that will ensure that the resulting interface will be learnable, easy to use, and user friendly. Consequently, the only reliable method for generating quality user interfaces is to test prototypes with actual end users and modify the design based on the users' comments [Anderson85]. As reported by [Sheil83], "Complex interactive interfaces usually require extensive empirical testing to determine whether they are really effective and considerable redesign to make them so." This methodology is called *iterative design* and has been used in the creation of some of the best current user interfaces: the Xerox Star [Bewley83], the Apple Lisa [Morgan83], and the Olympic Messaging system [Boies85].

To provide rapid prototyping and also to make the final user interfaces cheaper and easier to create, a number of *User Interface Management Systems* (UIMSs) [Olsen87a] have been created. Some of these have been successful. For example, the Apple MacApp UIMS has been reported to reduce development time by a factor of four or five [Schmucker86]. Unfortunately, UIMSs are not generally used, and most user interfaces are still created by hand without appropriate tools. Two reasons for this are that (1) current UIMSs are very hard to use [Olsen87b] and often require the user interface designer to learn a special purpose programminglike language, and (2) UIMSs typically are fairly limited in the types of interfaces that they can create with few able to create direct manipulation style interfaces [Myers87d]. The Peridot UIMS attempts to overcome these problems by specifically addressing direct manipulation interfaces, and by using Programming-by-Example as the specification technique.

16.3 RELATED WORK

A number of previous UIMSs have allowed the designer to use graphical techniques to specify parts of the interface. For example, Menulay [Buxton83], Trillium [Henderson86], and GRINS [Olsen85], support interactive placing techniques using the mouse (e.g., specifying where menus are located and what type of light button to place where). Some systems, such as Squeak [Cardelli85], allow interaction techniques to be specified textually, but no system that I am aware of attempts to allow the dynamics of the actual input devices and the interaction techniques themselves to be programmed in a graphical, nontextual manner.

In order to try a new approach to these problems, Peridot uses techniques from Visual Programming and Programming-by-Example [Myers86b]. *Visual*

Programming refers to any system that allows the specification of programs using graphics. An example is Rehearsal World [Gould84], which has been successful in making programs more visible and understandable and therefore easier to create by nonprogrammers. Rehearsal World allows teachers to use icons to create computer-based math instruction programs. *Programming-by-Example* systems attempt to infer programs from examples of the data that the program should process. Some systems that allow the programmer to develop programs by using examples do not use inferencing. For example, SmallStar [Halbert84] allows users to write programs for the Xerox Star office workstation by simply performing the normal commands and adding control flow afterwards on a textual transcript of the actions. One way Peridot uses inferencing is to guess these control structures automatically and avoid the necessity of using a written form for the program. The Tinker system [Lieberman82] lets the user choose example values for the inputs before starting to program, and the system executes the program on these examples as the code is typed in. Tinker requires that all of the code be specified in conventional Lisp, however.

An important component of Peridot is *constraints*, which are relationships among objects and data that must hold no matter how the objects are manipulated. There are two forms of constraints used in Peridot. *Graphical constraints* ensure that relationships among graphical objects (rectangles, circles, strings, etc.) always hold. Graphical constraints were first used in the Sketchpad drawing system [Sutherland63], and have been used in the Thinglab simulation system [Borning79] and a few recent drawing systems (e.g., Juno [Nelson85] and PED [Pavlidis85]). In Sketchpad, Thinglab, and Juno, the user must explicitly define all the constraints. In PED and Peridot, the constraints are guessed automatically.

The other kind of constraints used in Peridot are *data constraints* which ensure that a graphical object has a particular relationship to a data value. For example, the position of the indicator in a vertical scroll bar changes based on a variable that indicates what part of the file is visible in a window. Data constraints in Peridot are associated with active values, which are accessed and set like variables. Typically, a graphical object will be tied to an active value using a data constraint, so the object will immediately be updated when the active value changes. Active values also form the link between the application program and the user interface. The data constraints are very much like the binding of data to graphics in the Process Visualization System [Foley86], which was influenced by *triggers* and *alerters* in database management systems [Buneman79]. They are also similar to the *Control* values in GRINS [Olsen85] except that they are programmed by example rather than textually and can be executed immediately without waiting for compilation. Active values have been used previously in some Artificial Intelligence simulation and control environments (e.g., Knowledge Engineering Environment (KEE) [Ramamoorthy87] and LOOPS [Stefik86]).

16.4 OVERVIEW

With Peridot, the designer *demonstrates* what the user interface should look like and how the end user will interact with it. This approach frees designers from having to do any programming in the conventional sense and allows them to design the user interface in a very natural manner. The general strategy of Peridot is to allow the designer to draw the screen display that the end user will see, and to perform actions just as the end user would, such as moving a mouse, pressing a button, turning a knob, or toggling a switch. The results are immediately visible and executable on the screen and can be edited easily. The designer using Peridot can create parameterized procedures, like those found in interaction technique libraries such as the Apple Macintosh Toolbox. The designer gives examples of typical values for the parameters and Peridot automatically guesses (or *infers*) how they should be used in the general case. The procedures created by Peridot can be called from application programs and used as part of other user interfaces.

To the user interface designer, Peridot appears like a direct manipulation drawing package such as Apple's MacDraw, except that after each drawing operation, Peridot guesses the relationship of the new object to the existing objects.

Figure 16.1 gives an example of using Peridot to create a pop-up menu. For brevity, a number of steps have been left out; see [Myers88] or a videotape [Myers87c] for a complete description.

16.5 USES OF AI IN PERIDOT

Although Peridot was not designed as an AI system, it uses a large number of techniques normally classified as AI. These include Programming-By-Example, graphical constraints, plausible inferencing, and the use of active values with data constraints.

16.5.1. Example-Based Programming

Example-Based Programming (EBP) refers to all systems that allow the programmer to use examples of input and output data during the programming process [Myers86a]. When the systems try to infer the program from the examples, then they are called "Programming-*By*-Example" (PBE). Systems without inferencing are called "Programming-*With*-Example" (PWE). The Tinker system discussed above is an example of PWE because the user gives examples for input values but the system does not use inferencing.

Peridot uses Programming-by-Example to allow the designer to see the interface as it is being developed. Without example values for the parameters, there could be no direct, visual presentation of the interface. When the designer wants to use the value of a parameter in the interface, the display

FIGURE 16.1
A SEQUENCE OF FRAMES DURING THE CREATION OF A POP-UP MENU.

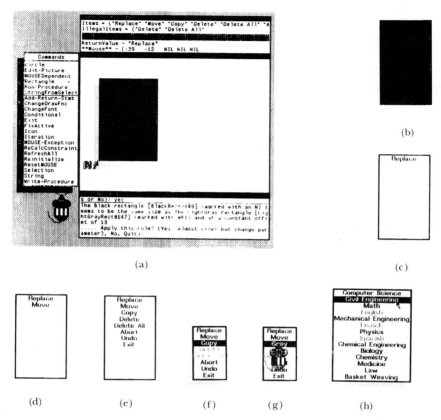

(a)

(b)

(c)

(d)

(e)

(f)

(g)

(h)

For full details, see [Myers88]. (a) shows the Peridot windows and command menu. The upper window contains the names of the parameters and active values used by *PopMenu* and example values for each. The center window contains the interface being created, and the bottom window contains the prompts and error messages from Peridot. In (a), a grey rectangle for the shadow has been drawn, followed by a black rectangle. Peridot has inferred that the black rectangle should be the same size as the grey rectangle but offset slightly. The designer confirms that this guess is correct, and the black rectangle is adjusted to be exactly the size of the grey one (b). Similarly, in (c), a white rectangle has been drawn in the black one, and a string centered at the top of the white rectangle. The designer drew these in approximately the correct position and Peridot adjusted them to be exact. The string is the first element of the parameter *Items*. The designer next places the second element of *Items* centered beneath the first one (d). Peridot now infers that an iteration is desired and calculates how to display the rest of the elements in a similar manner (e). Next, the designer modifies the rectangle to be the size of the strings (f) and declares that the parameter *IllegalItems* controls which elements should be grey. The XORed black rectangle should follow the mouse, so the designer moves the "simulated mouse" over it with the left button down (g). Now the menu is complete, and it can be used with a different set of parameter values (h).

of that value can simply be selected and used, as in Figure 16.1(c), where the first element of the parameter *Items* was selected, which is *Replace*. The picture shows the example value, but the generated code refers to the correct parameter.

16.5.2. The Use of Graphical Constraints

Many forms of interaction techniques must change appearance based on the values of the parameters supplied to them. For example, the pop-up menu of Figure 16.1 changes size based on the size of the text strings supplied. In order to support this, Peridot must know how the various graphical objects depend on each other. In Figure 16.1, the size of the white rectangle depends on the size of the strings, the size of the black rectangle depends on the size of the white one, and the size of the grey rectangle depends on the size of the black one. Therefore, they all change size appropriately when a different set of strings is used, as shown in Figure 16.1(h). These dependencies are implemented in Peridot as graphical constraints, and are maintained even when the objects are manipulated.

The constraints can be explicitly specified in a number of ways, or Peridot will automatically try to infer them.

16.5.3. Inferring Graphical Constraints Using Condition-Action Rules

In order to make it easier to specify what these graphical constraints are, Peridot incorporates a rule-based plausible inferencing system that attempts to guess the correct relationships as objects are drawn and edited. Because the rules specify very low level relationships (e.g., that a string should be centered inside a box), and Peridot only incorporates the relationships that are common in user interfaces, only a small number of rules are needed. Currently, Peridot uses about 50 rules.

These *condition-action* rules have a very simple form, with three parts. The *condition* part tests to see if the the object was drawn within a certain tolerance of the desired picture [Myers86b]. For example, in Figure 16.1(a), the black rectangle is approximately the same size as the grey rectangle. The *action* part of the rule adjusts the picture to follow the rule exactly (Figure 16.1(b)) and asserts a graphical constraint to ensure that the relationship will hold even if the objects are edited. The *message* part of the rule contains an English-language explanation of what the rule does, and is used for asking the designer whether to apply the rule.

Because any inferencing system will occasionally guess wrong, Peridot uses three strategies to ensure correct relationships. First, Peridot always asks the designer if guesses are correct. Second, the results of the inferences can be immediately seen and executed. Finally, the inferences can be undone if they are wrong.

In order to allow for human imprecision, some leeway must be given to the designer as to the placement and size of objects, so the initial drawings do not need to be drawn exactly. For example, the designer may want one box to be inside another box with a border of three pixels all around, but may actually draw it with a border of five on one side and two on another. Therefore, the tests in Peridot for whether to apply a particular rule have threshholds so that a rule will pass even if the drawing is not exact. A consequence is that the same drawing may pass more than one test. The *conflict resolution strategy* is needed to determine which rule to use. Peridot orders the tests based on restrictiveness (the most demanding tests are first) and based on the heuristically determined likelihood of their being appropriate. This ordering is changed based on the types of the objects being tested, since, for example, it is much more likely for a text string to be centered at the top of a box than for another box to be.

When the designer draws an object and a rule's test succeeds, Peridot queries the designer whether to apply the rule using the message that is attached to the rule. An example of this can be seen in the prompt window in Figure 16.1(a):

> The Black rectangle [BlackRect0149] (marked
> with an N) seems to be the same size as the
> LightGray rectangle [LightGray0147] (marked
> with WRT) and at a constant offset of 13.
> ...... Apply this rule?

If the system has guessed wrong, the designer answers "no", and the system will try to find a different rule that applies. If the system is correct, the designer may still want to modify parameters of the rule. For example, the system may decide that a box is inside another box with a border of 13 pixels all around, and the designer may decide to use 15 pixels instead. In this case the designer can answer "almost" and type in the new value. Of course, the designer can also answer "yes." It may be the case that no rule is found for the desired relationship. This can happen for two reasons. First, the designer has drawn the picture so sloppily that the appropriate rule's test does not pass. In this case, the designer will usually select the object and redraw it, but it is also possible to explicitly select the rule to apply. The other case is that there was no appropriate rule to apply because the desired relationship is not directly supported. In this case, there are a number of ways that the designer can explicitly specify the relationship [Myers88].

Most rules in Peridot relate a first object to a second existing object.[1] The designer can explicitly specify the objects to which the rules apply, but normally the relationships are inferred automatically when an object is created. In the case of relating a new object to an existing object, the (existing) object is found by searching through all the existing objects in a certain order: (1) the selected objects, (2) the previous object that was created just before the

---

[1] There are a small number of special rules that test a *group* of objects. This is necessary, for example, to make the size of a box depend on the sum of the sizes of all the items inside it, as in Figure 16-1(f).

new object, and (3) the objects in the vicinity of the new object. When objects are created from scratch, usually case (2) holds, so the number of tests the system must make is small. Peridot stops searching when an object and a rule are found that completely specify all of the positional and shape properties of the new object.

Occasionally some of an object's properties may depend on one object and other properties depend on a different object. For example, the highlight bar in a menu may have the same height and y value as a string, but the same width and x as a surrounding box (as in Figure 16.2). To handle this case, there are rules in Peridot that only constrain some of the properties of objects. These rules are marked as *incomplete* so that Peridot knows to try additional rules with other objects to handle the rest of the properties.

Peridot will infer relationships among objects no matter how they are created. Therefore, the same rules will be applied whether an object is created from scratch, by copying some other object, or by transforming an existing object. Since Peridot generalizes from the results of the operations, and not from the traces of the actions like many previous Programming-by-Example systems, it provides much more flexibility to the designers and allows user interfaces to be easily edited.

An unintended extra benefit of inferring graphical constraints is that they allow the designer to draw the picture quickly and sloppily and then have Peridot automatically *beautify* it by applying constraints. Since the constraints are executed incrementally, Peridot is more successful than batch beautifiers such as PED [Pavlidis85], and this beautifying seems to overcome the negative aspects of having to answer questions after each drawing operation.

16.5.4. Inferring Iterations

Peridot automatically infers the need for an iteration when the designer uses the first two elements of a list, as shown in Figure 16.1(c-e). This has two im-

FIGURE 16.2
THE GREY RECTANGLE IS THE SAME HEIGHT AND Y POSITION AS THE STRING LINE AND THE SAME WIDTH AND X POSITION AS THE WHITE RECTANGLE

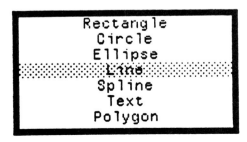

portant advantages. First, the designer does not have to place each element individually, which would be very tedious. Second, using an iteration allows Peridot to handle variable length lists. The menu of Figure 16.1, for example, will handle any list of strings for *Items*.

16.5.5. Inferring Iteration Variables vs. Constants

A complication with iterations is that multiple objects might be displayed for each cycle through the loop. For example, in Figure 16.3, the grey, black, and white rectangles are repeated for each cycle, along with the string.

When creating the iteration, Peridot must determine which properties of the objects are constant and which should change each time through the loop. For example, in Figure 16.3, the size of the boxes is constant, but the y position is incremented and the string text comes from subsequent elements of a list. Peridot uses very simple pattern matching to determine which properties change and how they change. This algorithm only works for simple, linear changes, but this seems to be all that is needed for most user interfaces.

16.5.6. The Use of Active Values with Data Constraints

Each part of a user interface that can change at run-time has an associated active value that controls the change, as shown in Figure 16.4. An active

FIGURE 16.3
EACH CYCLE THROUGH THE ITERATION DISPLAYS THREE RECTANGLES
AND A STRING

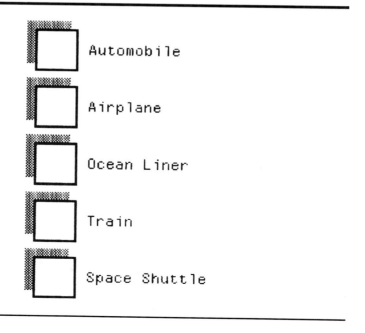

value can control the interface by showing which item in a list is selected (as *ReturnValue* does in Figure 16.1), it can be a number in a fixed range that controls an indicator (e.g., *PlaceInPicY* and *PlaceInPicX* which control the vertical and horizontal scroll bars in Figure 16.4); it can control an object that goes on and off (as *StopControl* does in Figure 16.4), and so on. The names and types for active values are specified by the designer when the interface is being created. The designer must also give example values for each active value. These example values are used to allow the system to infer how the active value controls the interface and whether single or multiple items can be selected. If the example value is a list of names, then Peridot guesses that the names are menu items. It guesses they can be selected, and that more than one selection is allowed. If the example value were a single name, then Peridot would infer that only one selection was allowed.

The designer can also attach filters to active values. One use for these is to provide application procedures to process the data and therefore provide *semantic feedback*. Some built-in filters handle clipping of the values to legal limits. This is used, for example, to keep the scroll bar indicators from going outside the active region. Another use for filters is to map the range of values into numbers meaningful to the application using linear interpolation. For example, the scroll bar active values use numbers in the range 0 to 100, which allows the application to be totally independent of the particular graphics used.

When the designer is running the user interface, the current values of the active values are continually updated in the upper Peridot window, and the graphical objects are updated appropriately. This makes the operation of the active values transparent and allows the designer to test to make sure that all dependencies are set up correctly.

16.5.7. Inferring Mouse Actions

Each input device is associated with an active value. This is sufficient to generate any kind of input device dependency because active values can be tied to graphics and each other. For example, to have a knob control the size of a box, the designer could simply specify a data constraint for the size of the box to the active value associated with the knob. If this was all that was provided, however, then handwritten code would be needed for each mouse action in the user interface. This is because most mouse actions should happen only under certain conditions. For example, the inverting black rectangle in Figure 16.1 follows the mouse, but only while the mouse button is held down over the strings.

Peridot therefore allows the designer to demonstrate how the mouse should work and infers the conditions. Unfortunately, the real mouse cannot be used for this demonstration because it is used for giving Peridot commands. Therefore, a *simulated mouse* is used, as shown in Figure 16.1(g). From the position of the simulated mouse, Peridot infers where the mouse should be for the interaction to happen. For example, the mouse might have to be

FIGURE 16.4

A COMPLEX INTERFACE CREATED ENTIRELY BY PERIDOT.

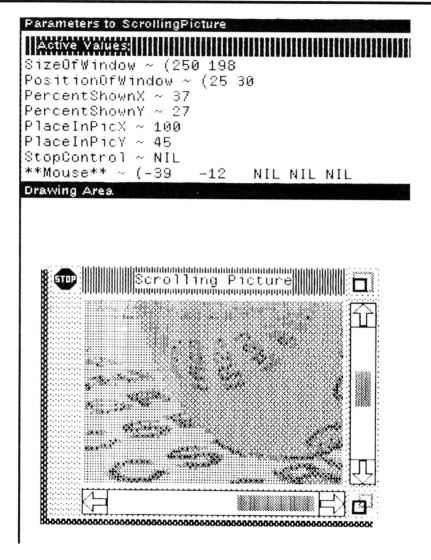

The user can move the window or change its size by pointing with the mouse at the icons in the right corners, and the picture can be scrolled either vertically or horizontally by pressing on the arrows or by moving the indicator boxes with the mouse. Each of the seven properties that can change is attached to a separate active value. An application procedure is called to display the picture and calculate what percentage of the picture is visible in the window, but all other manipulations are handled by Peridot and were defined by demonstration without programming.

over a menu item in Figure 16.1, or over one of the arrows in Figure 16.4. From the state and history of the user's presses of the simulated mouse's buttons, Peridot infers which button should be pressed for this interaction to happen, and whether single or multiple presses (e.g., double-clicks) are needed. The actions that the mouse can control include changing which item is selected (e.g., in a menu), moving freely or changing size (e.g., the window itself in Figure 16.4), or moving in a fixed range (e.g., in a scroll bar). These actions can happen continuously while the button is down or only once when it is pushed. Exception areas, where the action should not happen, can also be demonstrated. For example, the designer can specify that the grey strings in Figure 16.1(f) cannot be selected with the mouse, and then the inverting black rectangle will not appear over them.

16.6 EVALUATION

In order to evaluate how easy Peridot is to use, ten people used the system for about two hours each. Of these people, five were experienced programmers and five were nonprogrammers who had some experience using a mouse. The results of this experiment were very encouraging. After about $1\frac{1}{2}$ hours of guided use of Peridot, the subjects were able to create a menu of their own design unassisted. This demonstrates that nonprogrammers are able to create user interfaces using Peridot.

In addition, programmers will appreciate using Peridot to define graphical parts of user interfaces because it is so much faster and more natural than conventional programming. As a small, informal experiment, six expert programmers implemented a particular menu using their favorite hardware and software environments. Some wrote the menu by hand and others modified existing code. The results were that with Peridot, the time to create the menu ranged from 4 to 15 minutes, but programming took between 50 and 500 minutes [Meyers88]. Therefore, using Peridot appears to be significantly faster.

The range of Peridot is also very good. Peridot can create all of the interaction techniques in the Macintosh toolbox that do not involve text input (Peridot does not yet handle the keyboard). It can also create some entirely new user interfaces, such as those using two hands at the same time on different input devices. Peridot created its own user interface. The ideas in Peridot could be easily extended to handle the keyboard and other types of input devices.

16.7 IMPLICATIONS FOR FUTURE SYSTEMS

Peridot demonstrates that Programming-by-Example, graphical constraints, plausible inferencing, and active values with data constraints can be successfully integrated into practical, useful, and easy to use systems. Now the challenge is to find other areas where these techniques can be applied. An important criterion for an appropriate area seems to be that it be relatively small, so the system can know about many aspects of the examples and how to generalize from them.

Programming-by-Example seems to be a good way to provide programming capabilities to nonprogrammers. For instance, it may be possible to allow the creation of macros or shell scripts by example in a direct manipulation interface (as in SmallStar [Halbert84]). It also may be possible to use inferencing to help add the flow of control,—usually the most difficult part of the process.

An intriguing part of a UIMS where AI might be applied is the evaluation of the design of the user interface. To the extent that user interface design rules can be codified, the system might apply them to check how effective the interface is and to propose ways to improve it. These rules might come from graphics design, cognitive psychology, ergonomics, or other disciplines.

Although Peridot's specific techniques are successful, it will take further research to evaluate when it is acceptable to have a system that occasionally guesses wrong. In Peridot, this problem is alleviated by having the system confirm each guess and show the results of the inference immediately. A related issue is when this type of questioning is appropriate. In Peridot, it appears that the benefit of the automatic beautification of the picture makes the expense of confirming correct guesses and correcting the occasional incorrect guesses acceptable.

We are exploring these issues in our new research project, called Garnet [Myers90b], specifically as part of the Lapidary interface builder [Myers89].

16.8 CONCLUSIONS

Peridot demonstrates that the application of a number of Artificial Intelligence techniques to the user interface design task can be very successful. The novel use of demonstrational (Programming-by-Example) techniques makes a large class of previously hard to create user interfaces easy to design, implement and modify, even for nonprogrammers. In addition, since Peridot is a graphical tool, even expert programmers find that interaction techniques can be created significantly faster with it than by using conventional coding. The success of Peridot should be an inspiration for research into further ways to use AI in user interfaces.

ACKNOWLEDGMENTS

I want to thank Xerox Canada, Inc. for the donation of the Xerox workstations and Interlisp environment that made the development of Peridot possible. This research was also partially funded by the National Science and Engineering Research Council (NSERC) of Canada. The preparation of this paper was supported by the Defense Advanced Research Projects Agency (DOD), ARPA Order No. 4976 under contract F33615-87-C-1499, monitored by the Avionics Laboratory, Air Force Wright Aeronautical Laboratories, Aeronautical Systems Division (AFSC), Wright-Patterson AFB, OH 45433-6543. The views and conclusions contained in this document are those of the author and should not be interpreted as representing the official policies, either expressed or implied, of the Defense Advanced Research Projects Agency of the US Government.

I would like to also thank my advisor, Bill Buxton, for his support and good ideas. For help with this paper, I would like to thank Bernita Myers.

References

[Anderson85] Anderson, N. S., and Olson, J. R., (ed).) 1985. *Methods for Designing Software to Fit Human Needs and Capabilities.* Washington, D.C.; National Academy Press.

[Bewley83] Bewley, W. L., Roberts, T. L., Schroit, D., and Verplank, W. L. 1983. Human Factors Testing in the Design of Xerox's 8010 'Star' Office Workstation. In *Proceedings SIGCHI'83 Human Factors in Computing Systems,* Boston, Mass, December, pp. 72–77.

[Bobrow86] Bobrow, D. G., Mittal, S., and Stefik, M. J., 1986, Expert Systems: Perils and Promise. *Communications of the ACM,* 29(9), pp. 880–894.

[Boies85] Boies, S. J., Gould, J. D., Levy, S., Richards, J. T., and Schoonard, J. W., 1985. The 1984 Olympic Message System—A Case Study in System Design. *IBM Research Report* RC-11138.

[Borning79] Borning, A. 1979. *Thinglab—A Constraint-Oriented Simulation Laboratory,* Technical Report SSL-79-3, Xerox Palo Alto Research Center, July.

[Buneman79] Buneman, O. P., and Clemons, E. K., 1979. Efficiently Monitoring Relational Databases. *ACM Transactions on Database Systems,* 4(3) pp. 368–382.

[Buxton83] Buxton, W., Lamb, M. R., Sherman, D., and Smith, K. C., 1983. Towards a Comprehensive User Interface Management System. In *Proceedings SIGGRAPH'83 Computer Graphics,* Detroit, MI., July, pp. 35–42.

[Cardelli85] Cardelli, L., and Pike, R., 1985. Squeak: A Language for Communicating with Mice. In *Proceedings SIGGRAPH'85 Computer Graphics,* San Fransisco, CA, July, pp. 199–204.

[Foley86] Foley, J. D., and McMath, C. F., 1986. Dynamic Process Visualization. *IEEE Computer Graphics and Applications,* 6(2) 16–25, March.

[Gould84] Gould, L., and Finzer, W., 1984. *Programming by Rehearsal.* Technical Report SCL-84-1, Xerox Palo Alto Research Center, May.

[Halbert84] Halbert, D. C., 1984. *Programming by Example.* PhD thesis, Computer Science Division, Dept. of EE&CS, University of California, Berkeley, Also: Xerox Office Systems Division, Systems Development Department, TR OSD-T8402, December, 83 pages.

[Henderson86] Henderson, D. A., Jr., 1986. The Trillium User Interface Design Environment. In *Proceedings SIGCHI'86 Human Factors in Computing Systems*, Boston, MA, April, pp. 221–227.

[Liberman82] Lieberman, H., 1982. Constructing Graphical User Interfaces by Example In *Proceedings Graphics Interface'82*, Toronto, Ontario, May, pp. 295–302.

[Mittal86] Mittal, S. Dym, C. L., and Morjaria, M., 1986. Pride: An Expert System for the Design of Paper Handling Systems. *IEEE Computer*, 19(7), 102–114.

[Morgan83] Morgan, C., Williams, G., and Lemmons, P. 1983. An Interview with Wayne Rosing, Bruce Daniels, and Larry Tesler. *Byte*, 8(2), February, pp. 90–114.

[Myers86a] Myers, B. A., and Buxton, W., 1986. Creating Highly Interactive and Graphical User Interfaces by Demonstration. In *Proceedings SIGGRAPH'86 Computer Graphics*, Dallas, Texas, August, pp. 249–258.

[Myers86b] Myers, B. A., 1986. Visual Programming, Programming by Example, and Program Visualisation; A Taxonomy. In *Proceedings SIGCHI'86 Human Factors in Computing Systems*, Boston, MA, April, pp. 59–66.

[Myers87a] Myers, B. A., 1987. Creating Dynamic Interaction Techniques by Demonstration. In *Proceedings CHIGI '87 Human Factors in Computing Systems*, Toronto, Ont., Canada, April, pp. 271–278.

[Myers87b] Myers, B. A., 1987. Creating Interaction Techniques by Demonstration. *IEEE Computer Graphics and Applications*, 7(9), 51–60.

[Myers87c] Myers, B. A, 1987. Creating User Interfaces by Demonstration: The Peridot User Interface Management System. *SIGGRAPH Video Review*, 59 15-minute videotape.

[Myers87d] Myers, B. A., 1987. Gaining General Acceptance for UIMs. *Computer Graphics*, 21(2) 130–134.

[Meyers88] Myers, B. A., 1988. Creating User Interfaces by Demonstration. Academic Press, Boston MA.

[Myers89] Myers, B. A., Vander Zanden, B., and Dannenberg, R. B., 1989. Creating Graphical Objects by Demonstration. In *Proceedings of the ACM SIGGRAPH Symposium on User Interface Software and Technology*, Williamsburg, VA, November, pp. 95–104.

[Myers90a] Myers, B. A., 1990. Creating User Interfaces Using Programming-by-Example, Visual Programming and Constraints. *ACM Transactions on Programming Languages and Systems* 12(2), 143–177.

[Myers90b] Myers, B. A., Guise, D., Dannenberg, R. B., Vander Zanden, B., Kosbie, D., Marchal, P., Pervin, E., and Mickish, A. Garnet: Comprehensive Support for Graphical, Highly Interactive User Interfaces. IEEE Computer, 23(11), pp. 71–85.

[Nelson85] Nelson, G., 1985. Juno, a Constraint-Based Graphics System. In *Proceedings SIGGRAPH'85 Computer Graphics*, San Francisco, CA, July, pp. 235–243.

[Olsen85] Olsen, D. R., Jr., Dempsey, E. P., and Rogge, R., 1985. Input-Output Linkage in a User Interface Management System. In *Proceedings of SIGGRAPH'85 Computer Graphics*, San Fransisco, CA, July, pp. 225–234.

[Olsen87a] Olsen, D. R., Jr. (ed.) 1987. ACM SIGGRAPH Workshop on Software Tools for User Interface Management. *Computer Graphics*, 21(2), 71–147.

[Olsen87b] Olsen, D. R., Jr. 1987. Larger Issues in User Interface Management. *Computer Graphics*, 21(2), 134–137.

[Pavlidis85] Pavlidis, T., and Van Wyk, C. J., 1985. An Automatic Beautifier for Drawings and Illustrations. In *Proceedings of SIGGRAPH'85 Computer Graphics*, July, pp. 225–234.

[Ramamoorthy87] Ramamoorthy, C. V., Shekhar, S., and Garg, V. 1987. Software Development Support for AI Programs. *IEEE Computer*, 20(1) 30–40.

[Schmucker86] Schmucker, K. J. 1986. MacApp: An Application Framework. *Byte*, August, 189–193.

[Sheil83] Sheil, B. 1983. Power Tools for Programmers. *Datamation*, 29(2) 131–144.

[Shneiderman83] Shneiderman, B. 1983. Direct Manipulation: A Step Beyond Programming Languages. *IEEE Computer*, 16(8), pp. 57–69.

[Stefik86] Stefik, M., Bobrow, D. G., and Kahn, K. M. 1986. Integrating Access-Oriented Programming into a Multi-Paradigm Environment. *IEEE Software*, 3(1), 10–18.

[Sutherland63] Sutherland, I. E. 1963. SketchPad: A Man-Machine Graphical Communication System. In *Proceedings AFIPS Spring Joint Computer Conference*, pp. 329–346.

[Sutton78] Sutton, J. A., and Sprague, R. H., Jr. 1978. *A Study of Display Generation and Management in Interactive Business Applications*. Technical Report RJ2392, IBM Research Report, November.

[Williams83] Williams, G. 1983. The Lisa Computer System. *Byte Magazine*, 8(2), 33–50.

CHAPTER 17

Graphical KNOWLEDGE-BASED MODEL EDITORS

ALLEN CYPHER
Apple Computer

MARILYN STELZNER
IntelliCorp

17.1 INTRODUCTION

This paper discusses graphical interfaces to knowledge-based systems. We describe SimKit™, which is a general tool for building graphical model editors. We then present a variety of interfaces, several of which were built using SimKit. Based on these examples, we discuss the types of knowledge typically represented in knowledge-based systems and the appropriate graphical metaphors for presenting that knowledge.

AI has made significant advances in the design of graphical knowledge-based interfaces. One type of knowledge-based interface, the graphical model editor, extends the "toolkit notion of interfaces," exemplified by Bill Budge's

Pinball Construction Set [Budge85]. In these interfaces, "the desired operations are done simply by moving the appropriate icons onto the screen and connecting them together. Connecting the icons is the equivalent of writing a program. . . . There are no hidden operations, no syntax or command names to learn," [Hutchins86]. The end user can quickly, and with minimal training, build up a description of a complex structural model, run that model to observe its behavior, and then modify the structure if desired. The user of this class of interface never needs to be aware of the complexities of the internal representations that actually support the model.

AI has contributed flexible tools for building these interfaces, such as Impulse [Smith86], the Steamer graphics editor [Hollan86], and KEEpictures™ [IntelliCorp86], as well as representation techniques that facilitate mapping a complex domain model onto a graphical interface.

17.1.1. Graphical Interfaces to Knowledge-Based Systems

An increasingly important application of artificial intelligence techniques is in the domain of knowledge-based reasoning. Real-world problems like scheduling a factory are so complex that there are no efficient means of solving them algorithmically, and stand-alone expert systems do not have the flexibility to deal with the myriad exceptions and special cases that arise in real life. One approach to solving these problems is to build into the computer a model of the problem domain. A computerized "expert assistant" then reasons either by applying heuristics to the model or by simulating the effects of various possible actions on the model. Human problem solvers can then work together with the computer expert assistant to find reasonable solutions to their problems. The success of this collaboration between human and computer is made possible by a *graphical knowledge-based model*. By making the computer's model of the domain explicit, we achieve an interface that (1) allows the computer to present an accurate description of the current situation and the results of its simulations or heuristical analyses, and (2) allows the user to express details of the situation and decisions on how to proceed.

In this approach to interface design, the intelligence is embodied in the underlying knowledge-base, rather than in the interface itself. In contrast to Foley's approach (Chapter 15, this volume), which he characterizes as "intelligent interfaces to dumb systems," graphical knowledge-based models are "dumb (direct) interfaces to intelligent systems." The challenge for the interface designer in this approach is to assist in the *visualization* and *manipulation* of complex domains. That is, the essential features of objects in the domain and the essential relationships between those objects, should be evident and manipulable in the graphical display. This may be considered a passive technique for using intelligence to try to simplify the task mappings between the user's model and the system's model. Nonetheless, we will try to show that these interfaces are intelligent user interfaces because of the kinds and amount of knowledge that can be embedded in them.

17.2 SIMKIT: A GENERAL TOOL FOR BUILDING MODEL EDITORS

Having seen many efforts to build domain-specific model editors, we have implemented SimKit, a domain-independent set of tools for building graphical model editors. SimKit is currently being used to construct graphical model editors for a range of knowledge-based applications: from factory scheduling to design of automated control systems to fault analysis in nuclear power plants.

SimKit is a set of object-oriented tools implemented on top of the Knowledge Engineering Environment (KEE) system . Our objective in the design of SimKit was to build a set of tools that would help system developers build graphical model editors in any of a wide range of domains. The interface would facilitate graphical manipulation of objects and relationships between objects: each icon would represent an object in the domain. In the process of using the editor, the end user would build a knowledge base by moving icons onto the screen and connecting them together with arrows.

Once a model is constructed, it can be run so that the user may observe a graphical animation of the system's behavior. This implies that generic facilities for animating the graphical models must be provided. Animation may take a range of forms, including moving graphical objects on the screen, highlighting an object to reflect its state, or updating a gauge to indicate an object's state.

17.2.1. Design Considerations

Our basic design approach for SimKit was based on two distinctions: the distinction between a model and a library, and the distinction between a structural model and a behavioral model.

Models and Libraries

We use the term *model* to describe a particular configuration of objects and the relations between those objects. The term *library* is used to describe the generic classes of objects and the generic types of relationships that can exist in a model. Many different models can be constructed from the basic object classes and relations defined in a library. Libraries can be broad or narrow in their focus. For example, one library might deal with general queuing problems. That library might be specialized into a library for building manufacturing models, which in turn, might be specialized into one sublibrary for printed circuit board manufacture and another for sheet metal manufacture. A model, built using the printed circuit board library, might represent a particular factory located in the Santa Clara Valley. Figure 17.1 displays a model built with the sheet-metal manufacturing library.

When we apply these terms to graphical model editors, we see that models are constructed using a domain-specific editor. Because libraries define the

FIGURE 17.1
A SHEET-METAL FACTORY MODEL EDITOR BUILT IN SIMKIT

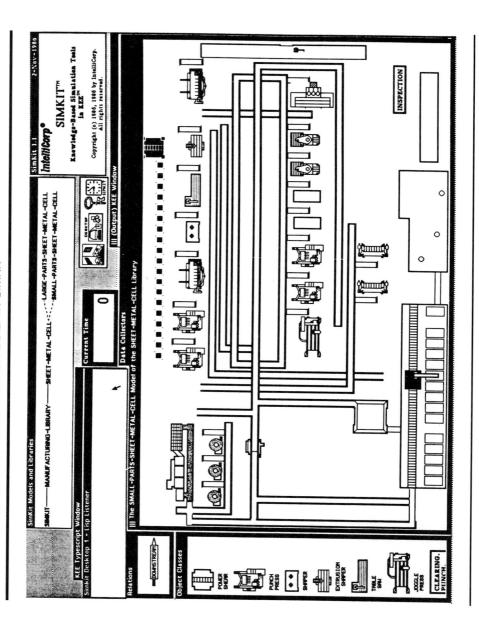

domain-specific objects that can appear in that editor, the process of building a domain-specific editor in SimKit is accomplished by building a library. SimKit can be thought of as a model editor shell into which the system developer adds domain knowledge. SimKit's facilities for constructing libraries require different skill levels from those for constructing models. Although library development requires programming skills, models may be built by nonprogrammers. This model-building task is frequently performed by people who are experts in the application domain.

Structural and Behavioral Models

The distinction between structural models and behavioral models is also inherent in the design of SimKit. Structural models define the objects and relationships between objects in the domain of interest. Behavioral models are typically "run" by some sort of simulation technique that allows system behavior to emerge from the interaction of the behaviors of its component objects. Individual object descriptions contain knowledge of how the object will react to specific changes in its state. Typically, this behavioral description includes constraints or simulation behavior.

In SimKit, object behaviors are defined in methods at the class level (i.e., in the library) and are inherited by members of the class in the model. When the model is run, the behavior of individual objects typically affects other related objects, and the global model behavior is the result of the interactions between objects.

The implementation approach to SimKit was heavily frame-based and object- oriented, both for the representation of domain objects, and for the implementation of SimKit tools. The major SimKit tools are each implemented as KEE knowledge bases. These knowledge bases are accessible to the kit builder, so that a high degree of extensibility may be maintained. For example, each type of relation that is defined in a library is represented by an object that has methods for asserting and retracting that relation. The developer can specify what classes of objects may legally participate in a relation, and the model editor will then prevent the user from connecting objects improperly by "wrapping" the assertion method for the appropriate relation, the library developer can implement side effects to asserting that relation.

The graphical requirements of the SimKit model editor led to the development of a general-purpose, object-oriented graphics package called KEE-pictures. KEEpictures provides viewports with built-in scrolling and zooming facilities, and various classes of mouse-sensitive pictures. Each object on the screen is represented by a frame with a large range of inherited attributes and behaviors. Pictures, for example, can be moved, shaped, opened, closed, highlighted, and edited. The functions invoked when a picture is moused are also methods, allowing the kit builder to change the pop-up menus available by mousing on icons. The frame for each object on the screen has slots for each of the graphical features of the object, such as length and position. Demons are attached to all of these slots, so that a change to the value of the position slot will cause the object to move to a new position on the screen. Likewise, if the user moves an object with the mouse, the change causes the appropriate slots in the frame to be updated.

17.2.2. Building Libraries and Models

A library builder, who is a programmer, creates icons to represent the various classes and subclasses which can appear in a model (for instance, a class of factory machines and a subclass of lathes) and writes Lisp methods to describe their behavior (for instance, a method which consults a table to determine how long it takes a lathe to produce a spindle).

The end user who sits down to build a model from this library is presented with icons for all of the object classes created by the library builder (Note the column of icons on the left side of Figure 17.1). The user clicks on an icon and drags it into the model editor window. This action causes the underlying system to create an instance of this class, and the instance inherits its behavior and initial slot values from its parent. The user then clicks on objects to connect them with lines, which represent relations. Queuing models, for instance, have a *downstream* relation that specifies how items may flow through the model.

Since all objects inherit default behavior, it is possible to run a simulation of a model as soon as it has been built. The library builder may have integrated an expert system into the simulation model for several reasons. One reason is that an expert system may be called to determine how the simulation should proceed. For instance, a factory model may use an expert system to decide which part a machine will work on next. Another reason is that sometimes the main system is an expert system that occasionally invokes a simulation in order to obtain information: a factory scheduler expert system might run several simulations and choose the one with the best results as the basis for its schedule.

17.2.3. Experiences with the Use of SimKit

SimKit currently has approximately one hundred users, who are building and using graphical model editors in a wide range of applications. Many of these editors are for queuing systems, because we provided a sample library for that type of system. The majority of these queuing systems are in manufacturing or telecommunications domains.

A fairly typical application is the control system editor built by Allen-Bradley [Nielsen87], a major vendor of factory control systems and controllers. The objective of this application is to allow a control system engineer to experiment with different design parameters for control systems. Parameters such as the number of levels in the control hierarchy of processors, the power of each processor in the hierarchy, the levels at which various types of data should be stored, and the level at which various types of control processing should be performed. With the model editor, the end user can build a model reflecting the control system hierarchy of processors and communications links. Special menus have been added to facilitate experimentation with other design parameters.

SimKit has also been used as a framework for qualitative modeling of continuous processes. In this class of application, object classes might include pipes, tanks, and valves, and system developers would be trying to answer questions, for example, about the effects of a specific valve malfunctioning or of a pipe breaking. Another class of SimKit users have used the graphics capabilities in a range of battle management applications. Their end goal is to develop AI planning systems, with a SimKit-based simulation demonstrating graphically the implications of various plans. Levitt and Kunz [Levitt85] have explored the application of knowledge-based techniques to the project management of large construction projects. The SimKit model editor was used to construct critical path networks of project activities and to indicate successor and predecessor relations between activities.

17.3 REPRESENTING KNOWLEDGE IN A GRAPHICAL MODEL

We now turn from SimKit to a more general investigation of how graphical interfaces can be effectively employed to represent an underlying model. We will focus on how spatial relationships can be exploited, because this is an area that SimKit has not yet covered, and it is the next natural extension to the current system. To use the terminology introduced in the following discussion, current SimKit models are *schematic*, and we want to extend them to be *spatial*. At IntelliCorp, we have built numerous spatial interfaces, but they have required extensive programming, and a point-and-click system for constructing them has not yet been built. So let us now consider how such an interface builder could be constructed.

The standard representation technique for knowledge-based systems is to use frames to represent objects. Objects belong to *classes*, the *properties* of objects are represented as values of slots in a frame, and objects inherit properties from their parent classes. Some example properties are: the board-wiring task duration is 5.3 minutes; the shaft length is 840 cm.; the compressor pressure is 6.4 atm. Slots are often used to specify *relations* between objects: part-whole (engine A is a part of car B); location (lathe4 is located in the main factory); next task (after drilling, this part must be deburred). Slots are also used to specify *constraints* between objects: pouring must be completed before framing can begin; lathes can turn only one part at a time.

17.3.1. Mapping to Graphical Features

To create a graphical model, the interface designer must map objects and their properties, relations, and constraints onto graphical features. The available graphical features are:

1. **Shape**—The class of an object is often mapped to a particular shape. For
    instance, for Trucks.
2. **Texture, color, shading**—A property with a limited number of values can
    be mapped to color or shading—All trucks not owned by your company
    are shown as *shaded*:
3. **Size**—The height, width of an object. Properties are often mapped to
    height or width. Truck capacity could map to *length*:
4. **Relative Position**—inside, above, contiguous, overlapping, each have dis-
    tinctive meanings and are appropriate for representing relations and con-
    straints. Truck contents could be mapped to *inside*: The size of
    the truck body could be used to constrain the number of objects that can
    legally fit inside.
5. **Animation**—Motion can be used to represent the value of a feature.
    Truck speed could be mapped to the speed of its motion across the screen.

In general, class *membership* maps to *shape*, *properties* map to *color, size and animation*, and *relations and constraints* map to *relative position*. Constraints are complex, and will be dealt with in greater detail in a later section.

A graphical interface for associating features of a domain with graphical features of the end user interface could be constructed by allowing the user to point to slots in a frame and then point to the corresponding graphical feature, such as the *length* of a box.

Numerous authors have developed taxonomies of graphical features. For comparison, see Bertin, referenced in (Chapter 13, this volume), the section "Building Graphical Interfaces" in (Chapter 14, this volume).

17.3.2. Example Interfaces

We are now going to examine several interfaces to expert systems and see how they map important features of the underlying domain to graphical features in the interface.

Control System

Allen-Bradley used SimKit to build a control system simulator [Nielsen87]. Figure 17.2 shows a display from their system. Their display utilizes the standard features of the SimKit model editor: icons represent the various classes of objects (computers), and lines connecting objects represent the relation of two computers being connected to each other on a communication network.

FIGURE 17.2
ALLEN-BRADLEY CONTROL SYSTEM SIMULATOR

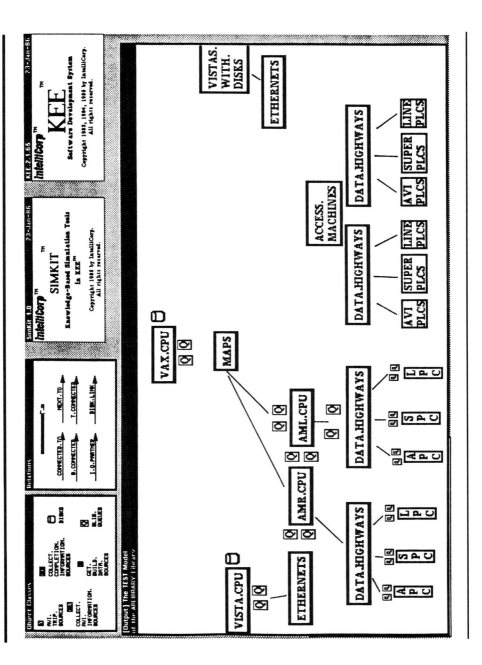

The model is used to analyze various possible configurations of computers in a network. When the simulation is running, a computer is highlighted (shown in reverse video) if it is busy processing a message from the network. Note that spatial features are not used, either to display features of an object, or to show relationships between objects, or to express constraints.

Sheet Metal Factory

Another interface built with the SimKit model editor was shown in Figure 17.1. This system simulates a sheet metal factory and is used to experiment with the scheduling of different process plans. Icons suggest the shape of the various machines, and conveyor belts show the possible paths for moving parts between machines. Animation shows parts moving from machine to machine on the belts. Although the layout of the machines corresponds to the actual arrangement on the factory floor, this information is not used by the underlying model—information on paths and distances between machines is stored internally, and is not derived from the layout—so once again there is no information in the model that is mapped to spatial features in the display.

Steamer

Figure 17.3 shows a screen from the Steamer system [Hollan86]. Steamer is used to teach the proper operation of a large steam engine. The display shows gauges, which display temperatures and pressures that the user may alter with the mouse, and valves, which the user may open and close, and pipes connecting the various components of the engine. Whenever the user makes an alteration by mousing on a gauge or valve, a mathematical model of the engine is invoked to calculate how this change affects the other parts of the system. For instance, closing a valve could cause a pressure buildup which would lead to temperature changes in distant parts of the system.

Flow through pipes is animated, so that rate of flow is mapped to speed of animation. Icons are used to distinguish certain classes of objects, such as valves. Salient properties are made visual and manipulable through the use of gauges and sliders. The spatial location of objects is unimportant—the layout is schematic and relationships between objects are shown by drawing lines (pipes) between them.

Spatial information is used at a micro level—within gauges—because the relative position of a needle in a gauge corresponds to the temperature or pressure reading of the associated real gauge. Sliders **120.0 rpm** also use spatial information at a micro level, but in a very indirect way, because a *property* of an underlying object (rpm) is being mapped to a graphical *object* (the slider). This is in contrast to the more direct cases in which a *property* of an underlying object (truck size) is mapped to a *property* of a graphical object (picture length). When we describe the boxes in the Gantt chart below, it is

FIGURE 17.3
STEAMER SCHEMATIC

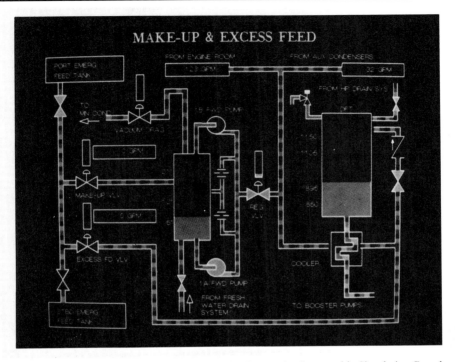

Reprinted by permission from "STEAMER: An Interactive Inspectable Simulation-Based Training System," by J. D. Hollan, E. L. Hutchins, and L. Weitzman, *AI Magazine*, Vol. 5, No. 2 (Summer), p. 18. © 1984, American Association for Artificial Intelligence.

interesting to note that they also use spatial information directly (mapping *length* of time to perform an operation to *length* of a box), although the picture itself is quite indirect and abstract (a box is used to represent that a drill is putting a hole into a piece of metal).

Bin Packing

Figure 17.4 shows an interface for a bin packer. In this problem, data for computer jobs is to be organized in an efficient order, subject to the hardware constraints of a particular computer.[1] The display in the upper right, *BINs for Current Task*, shows several items packed into four bins. Expert system

---

[1] The computer has only four registers—data must be assigned to bins so that each program can find all of its data in at most four bins. Since the data is shared by the programs, there are multiple conflicting constraints on the bin packing.

FIGURE 17.4

INTERFACE FOR A BIN-PACKING EXPERT SYSTEM

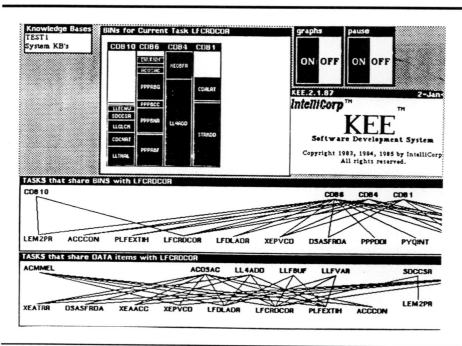

heuristics assigned the items to bins. However, users can modify this solution by directly manipulating data items; they simply mouse on a data item and move it into another bin. The expert system will then apply the relevant constraints to see whether the new solution is legal. In this interface, the item feature *size* is mapped to the spatial feature *height*. The relation "bin B *contains* item I" is mapped to the relative spatial graphical feature *inside-of*, so that the constraint "total size of contained objects ≤ size of bin" is visually apparent.

Gantt Chart

A Gantt chart (see Figure 17.5) is used to schedule factory floor operations. There is a line in the chart for each machine in the factory. The horizontal axis represents time, and boxes represent operations that machines perform in order to produce a part. Suppose a shaft is manufactured by first turning it on a lathe, then drilling a hole, and finally deburring it. There will be a box on the lathe line early in the day, a box on the drill line a bit later (i.e., to the right), and a third box on the debur line sometime in the afternoon. This interface uses an abstract representation: it does not use icons whose shapes

FIGURE 17.5

A GANTT CHART FOR SCHEDULING A FACTORY

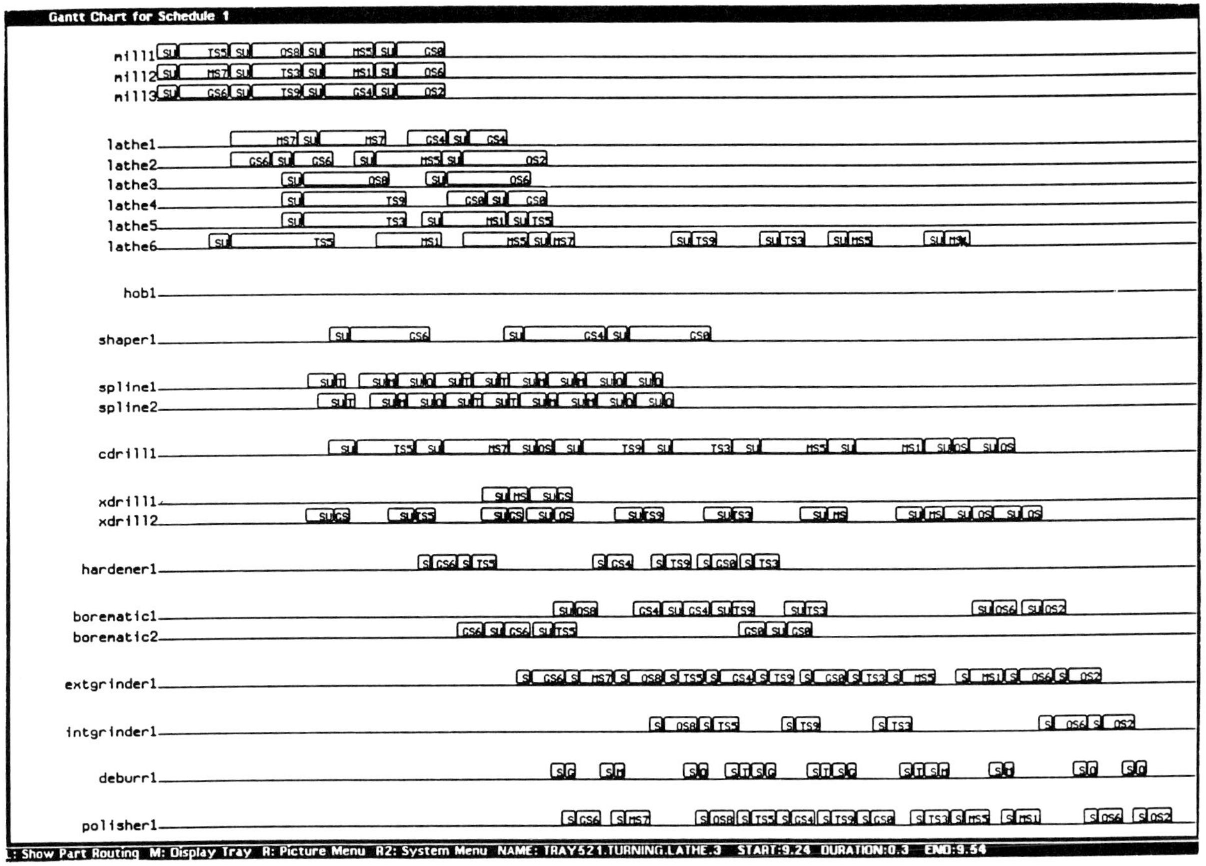

mimic the objects—instead, lines represent machines and boxes represent operations. Relative position is used extensively: The relation "Operation O is *performed by* Machine M" is mapped to "Box O *on* Line M." The relation "Operation O_1 *occurs after* Operation O_2" is mapped to "Box O_1 is *to the right of* Box O_2." As a consequence, the constraint "A machine can perform only *one operation at a time*" maps onto the relative position constraint "Operation boxes *cannot overlap*."

The schedule in the display was produced by expert system heuristics. The user can modify the schedule by direct manipulation—any box may be moved to a different time. The interface constrains the boxes to machines that can perform the operation specified at the new time, and other boxes slide over to satisfy the *cannot overlap* constraint.

17.3.3. Spatial Models and Constraints

A significant distinction between these models is that the control system, sheet metal, and Steamer interfaces are schematic, and the bin packing and Gantt chart interfaces are spatial. That is, the last two examples use the spatial location of objects to convey information about the models. At least intuitively, spatial displays seem to be very effective at communicating a large amount of complex information to the user. One reason for this is their effectiveness at representing constraints.

Graphical Constraints

The spatial models showed several ways of representing relational constraints graphically. Constraints are commonly associated with relations: "No more than six pallets inside a truck" is a constraint on the *contents* relation between pallets and trucks. Spatial models can exploit the fact that certain spatial relations provide a natural visual representation for related constraints. For example, the graphical relation *inside of* provides a natural visual representation for the *maximum* constraint: namely, the size of the enclosed objects can be chosen so that no more than the maximum number will fit into the container. Another example mentioned above is that *to the right of* provides a natural visual representation for *one at a time*: the Gantt chart shows the *occurs after* relation represented by *to the right of*, and consequently the *no temporal overlap* constraint shows up as *no spatial overlap*.

Maintaining Constraints

Given a graphical constraint, the model must implement some procedure for dealing with a violation of that constraint. It may do the following:

- Prohibit the violation
- Display the violation
- Resolve the violation

Prohibit: In the Gantt chart, the user can mouse on an operation and move it to a different machine. As the user moves the operation, its motion is constrained to the region of the chart that contains machines that are capable of performing that operation. Prohibiting is effective in this case, because violation of the constraint can be detected very quickly, and the appropriate feedback can be supplied in real time.

Display: In bin packing, the user may create a packing which violates the four-bins-per-program constraint for some program. If so, the system simply displays the infeasible solution. The constraints are very complex, and a display allows the user to browse around in order to understand the problem. This provides a "What if " facility that allows the user to try out a variety of alternatives and explore their consequences.

Resolve: In the Gantt chart, the user may place an operation so that it overlaps another operation. The model treats this action as a signal for conflict resolution. It invokes expert system heuristics to reschedule the conflicting operations so that the overlap is removed. In this case, constraint violation is a means for the user to communicate with the system. This is another example of a "What if " facility.

17.4 MODELS IN EXPERT SYSTEMS

The use of a model is essential to modern expert systems that employ "deep reasoning"—systems that consult a model of the domain to draw their conclusions, as opposed to some older expert systems that simply pieced together pre-packaged advice from an expert. Because a detailed model is available, it is natural to make this model visible to the user. In the examples of knowledge-based systems that we discussed in the preceding text, the picture on the screen is a *visualization* of the user's mental model of the problem.

17.4.1. Tightly Coupled Input and Output

SimKit shows a way in which end users can graphically create a model of the domain. Being able to simplify the problem of inputting a model is reason enough to use a graphical interface. But we are not finished, because we also need a way for the user to see the results of the expert system's decisions, and then, finally, we need a way for the user to modify those decisions. As the preceding examples illustrate, a graphical model or visualization of the user's domain is an ideal solution to both of these needs; so we have a sequence of input-output-input, performed completely through the common graphical knowledge-based model. By tightly coupling input and output, this model enhances user-computer communication. Two of the chapters in this book focus on output presentation only: (Chapter 11, this volume) and (Chapter 13, this volume). A natural next step would be for them to consider the addition of tightly coupled input and output.

A further advantage of a graphical model arises in simulation, because the user can continually monitor how the simulation is proceeding. In this way it is possible to watch a queue building up and to decide quickly that another machine needs to be added to the factory, without having to wait to analyze the statistics from an all-day mainframe simulation.

Many of the models built with SimKit are used to solve NP-Complete problems [Garey79]. Graphical knowledge-based models are essential in these domains because the constraints between objects are complex, and spatial representations are helpful in displaying those relationships.

Since analytic solutions are not possible, it is essential that experts have effective tools at their disposal. Such tools can help them visualize their particular instances of the problem, so that they can locate and exploit regularities and idiosyncrasies. Also, many heuristic methods for these problems are based on iterative improvement—this requires continual collaboration between the human expert and the computer expert system, and we have found that a common, interactive graphical model of the problem effectively promotes the communication to achieve this. Another characteristic of the interaction between user and computer in this sort of situation is that there is *mixed initiative*: Sometimes the user initiates action, by telling the computer to analyze a situation, and sometimes the computer takes the initiative and asks the user to make a decision. This is in contrast to traditional computer programs, in which the user types a series of commands, and traditional AI diagnosis systems, in which the computer poses a string of questions. In both the bin-packing and the Gantt chart expert systems described above, the system applies expert heuristics, and then the human expert can modify those solutions.

17.4.2. Agency

One of the main functions of a graphical knowledge-based model is to keep track of complex constraints for the user. For instance, consider again the behavior of the Gantt chart when the user relocates a box: Suppose a factory is running two hours late on a drilling operation. The user goes to the Gantt chart and moves the appropriate box. In the process, it overlaps some other boxes. By making this change to the chart, the user is actually giving the command "reschedule the factory to minimize late time, given that this drilling operation is two hours late." In order to accomplish this, the expert system may use its expert heuristics to suggest three possible approaches to rescheduling and then run simulations of each approach. It will then compare the results of the simulations and select the one that is most successful.

In any situation where complex, intelligent behavior of this sort is involved, we would do well to consider the concept of *agency*. An agent (a travel agent, for instance) is an assistant that can work with a limited amount of input information, plus a large amount of domain knowledge, and go off on its own to make significant decisions for the user. In the factory rescheduling example, your assistants go and investigate what they consider to be the three best scheduling alternatives. Because an agent is making numerous off-line decisions and may take considerable time to do so, the agent style of interface is in marked contrast to direct manipulation interfaces, which are founded on quick response and keeping the user visually informed about all that is happening [Hutchins86]. Our intelligent interfaces are trying to merge direct manipulation and agency, and the strain is apparent. Perhaps a solution to this tension is to make agents visible parts of the interface as well, so that a user can watch them leave to perform their tasks and then return later with results.

17.5 FUTURE DIRECTIONS

Visual knowledge-based models are the first step in a move towards custom environments. They apply well to situations in which users need assistance to visualize their problems, and in which tightly coupled input and output, via a shared graphical model, promote a collaborative style of interaction between user and computer. SimKit provides an environment that allows end users to construct their model worlds without having to program. Further steps are needed to allow these worlds to exploit spatial information—to move from schematic to spatial models—and to reduce the library builder's programming effort. This will be difficult because it involves *behavior*. Brad Myers' work in (Chapter 16, this volume) is an encouraging step in this direction. Also, Alan Borning's work on constraint languages offers another promising approach [Borning86]. Eventually, we can hope that systems of this sort will allow users to create graphical mental models for all of their personal tasks.

REFERENCES

[Borning86] Borning, A., and Duisberg, R. 1986. Constraint-Based Tools for Building User Interfaces, In *ACM Transactions on Graphics*, 5(4) October.

[Budge85] Budge, W. 1985. *PinBall Construction Set*. Electronic Arts, San Mateo, CA.

[Garey79] Garey, M., Johnson, D. 1979. *Computers and Intractability: A Guide to the Theory of NP-Completeness*, San Francisco, W. H. Freeman and Co.

[Hollan86] Hollan J. D., Hutchins, E. L., McCandless, T. P., Rosenstein, M., and Weitzman, L. 1986. *Graphical Interfaces for Simulation*, Technical Report 8603, Institute for Cognitive Science, University of California, San Diego, May.

[Hutchins86] Hutchins, E., Hollan, J., Norman, D. 1986. Direct Manipulation Interfaces. In Norman, D. and Draper, S. W. (eds.), *User Centered Design: New Perspectives on Human-Computer Interaction*. Hillsdale, NJ: Lawrence Erlbaum Associates, pp. 87–124.

[IntelliCorp86] IntelliCorp, 1986. KEEpictures Reference Manual.

[Levitt85] Levitt, R. E., Kunz, J. C. 1985.*Using Knowledge of Construction and Project Management for Automated Schedule Updating*, The American Society of Mechanical Engineers.

[Nielsen87] Nielsen, R. 1987. The Impacts of Using AI-based Techniques in a Control System Simulator, In *Proceedings Conference on AI and SImulation*, San Diego, CA. pp. 72–77.

[Smith86] Smith, R., Dinitz, R., Barth, P. 1986. *Impulse-86: A Substrate for Object-Oriented Interface Design*, In *OOPSLA '86 Conference Proceedings*, Portland, OR. pp. 167–176.

CHAPTER **18**

Backbord: An Implementation of Specification by Reformulation*

JOHN YEN[†],
ROBERT
NECHES,
MICHAEL
DEBELLIS[‡],
PEDRO
SZEKELY,
and
PETER
ABERG

USC/Information Sciences Institute

ABSTRACT

Specification by reformulation is a general interaction paradigm for helping users express themselves to computer systems in ways that achieve the users' intents. It is an abstraction of *retrieval by reformulation*, a paradigm used in previous systems for assisting users in formulating database queries. *Specification by reformulation* serves as a general foundation upon which domain-specific applications can be built. To illustrate its usage, we describe three services built within it: a database retrieval aid, a notes facility, and an electronic mail

*The research described in this paper was supported by The Defense Advanced Research Projects Agency (DARPA) under contract No. MDA903-86-C-0 178, and by the Air Force Logistics Command under contract No. F33600-87-C-7047. Views and conclusions contained in this paper are those of the authors, and should not be interpreted as representing the official opinion or policy of the sponsoring agencies.

† The author's current address is Department of Computer Science, Texas A&M University.
‡ The author's current address is Anderson Consulting, Chicago, IL.

421

interface to an on-line procurement system. Since these services share a large amount of code, it is desirable to develop a shell that captures the domain-independent components of the paradigm. We will thus describe an architecture for a *specification by reformulation shell*, which aids application builders in developing a set of cooperating tools within the paradigm. The paradigm, along with the specification by reformulation shell, represents an approach to building integrated user-support environments that benefits both application builders and end users.

18.1 INTRODUCTION

An integrated user-support environment is a set of modular software tools that can interact and smoothly pass partial results back and forth [Neches88]. It is similar to the concept of a tool-oriented programming environment such as UNIX. However, whereas a programming environment consists of tools that are used primarily by computer programmers, a user-support environment consists of cooperating higher-level tools that aid users in their day-to-day activities. Good programming environments are marked by close integration of their tools (for example, the ability to invoke an editor from a debugger in order to edit the source code of the function being examined in the debugger). Similarly, the tools of a user-support environment should be constructed in an open fashion so that they will naturally be able to work together.

In this chapter we will demonstrate a particular approach to constructing such environments that is under continuing development by the Integrated User-Support Environments group at USC/Information Sciences Institute. Our starting point is an interface paradigm called *retrieval by reformulation* [Tou82; Williams84], which has been used for knowledge-based database retrieval systems. We show how this paradigm can be generalized to a paradigm that we call *specification by reformulation*. By this we mean a paradigm of human/computer interaction in which the user develops, by successive approximations, a specification of the objects that a system is to manipulate and/or the behavior it is to evince. In this style of interaction, the system provides an environment that facilitates the refinement of the specification, largely by generating feedback for the user about the specification in its current form and by providing guidance about means for modifying that specification.

The implementation of the specification by reformulation paradigm consists of (1) a knowledge representation structure that represents the current specification, and (2) general functions that provide feedback and guidance on refinement of the specification. Once an environment for operating within the specification by reformulation paradigm has been implemented, it is relatively easy to build applications on top of it. Although such applications may seem to have little in common on the surface, at a higher level of abstraction they all utilize the same paradigm for accomplishing their various tasks. The one thing they have in common is that they all depend on the structure of a database or knowledge base to successfully complete their tasks. Constructing such systems benefits users via a consistent interface and cooperating tools, and benefits system builders via modularity and reusability of code.

In this chapter, we discuss the BACKBORD system, an implementation of the specification by reformulation paradigm.[1] BACKBORD illustrates how the paradigm can be applied to database query formulation, the creation and attachment of notes to a knowledge base, and the creation of mail messages. These particular example services are tools that must operate in an integrated fashion within an intelligent workstation for procurement of standard electronic parts [Neches88]. Since services such as these share a large amount of code, it is useful to have an architecture for a domain-independent *specification by reformulation shell* to facilitate their construction; this is described in Section 18.5. The first parts of this chapter are oriented toward the version of BACKBORD that represents our first implementation of the shell. We then discuss the goals and issues that we seek to address in the second version of the shell, now in progress, and report on the current status of the effort.

18.2 SPECIFICATION BY REFORMULATION

Specification by reformulation is an abstraction of retrieval by reformulation, a paradigm for assisting users in formulating database queries [Tou82; Williams84]. Retrieval by reformulation assists users who know what they are trying to retrieve but cannot construct a query to retrieve it, either because they do not understand the query language or because they lack knowledge about the structure of the database. The major techniques of the paradigm came from a psychological theory of human remembering [William81]. Stelzner and Williams [Stelzner86] developed the term *specification by reformulation* to refer to a generalization of the retrieval by reformulation paradigm used to develop knowledge base interfaces. By generalizing the retrieval by reformulation paradigm, we achieve a general paradigm, based on a psychological theory of human information retrieval, for interacting with large amounts of stored data.

18.2.1. Related Work

Previous systems such as RABBIT [Tou82; Williams84], ARGON [Patel-Schneider84], HELGON [Fischer89], and *Intelliscope*™ (a recent commercial product of Intellicorp) have used retrieval by reformulation to aid database users. Such systems consist of a query, a matching list, and an example. The

---

[1] BACKBORD stands for "Browsing Aid Complementing Knowledge Bases OR Databases."

query serves as the current context that the user has been able to establish and as a description of what is being searched for in the database. The *matching list* contains all database records that match the description used for the last retrieval. The *example* shows the detailed content of one of the matching records.

The idea is to provide interactive guidance on possible ways to reformulate the query. Using this guidance, users can modify the original query to better reflect their intent. For example, a user can select values from the example to further constrain the query. The refined query is then used for another retrieval. Reformulation and retrieval iterate until the user is satisfied with the retrieval results.

18.2.2. A General Interface Paradigm

Specification by reformulation provides a high-level tool for applications utilizing databases or knowledge bases. The paradigm consists of alternating between the following:

1. Creating/refining a specification for achieving a user's goals
2. Obtaining feedback on the effect of the current specification and guidance about how it can be modified

When satisfied with this process, the user can then execute actions that utilize the resultant specification.

In a retrieval-by-reformulation aid, *refinement* means modifying the query; *feedback* is obtained by retrieving against the query; *guidance* is obtained through menus indicating ways that contents of information fields in the display can be used to modify the query; and *actions* consist of tools for graphically displaying the retrieved data. By generalizing the notions of queries, retrievals, and examples to those of specifications, feedback, and guidance, we can address applications well beyond database browsing. We next describe an architecture for doing so, followed by some illustrative applications.

18.3 MODELING THE GENERIC ELEMENTS OF SPECIFICATION BY REFORMULATION

This section elaborates the paradigm and describes its implementation in BACKBORD. Since BACKBORD operates on LOOM knowledge bases, a few terms in the LOOM knowledge representation language must be introduced. (A more detailed description of the LOOM language is provided by [MacGregor87].) A LOOM knowledge base consists of *concepts* and *roles*, which correspond to frames and slots in frame-based systems. In this paper, all references to knowledge-base objects will appear in **boldface**. The most significant aspect of LOOM related to our concerns is the presence of an automatic *classifier* [Schmolze83], which utilizes the semantics of concept and role definitions to reason about where new concept descriptions fit with respect to preexisting concepts in a subsumption (*isa*) hierarchy.

18.3.1. Refinement: Search in a Description Space

Specification by reformulation involves a search through a space representing an abstraction hierarchy of descriptions. At any given time, the current specification can be thought of as a node in that space. Based on the node's location, the system helps users select operations to produce descriptions that are closer to expressing their intent. The specification consists of various roles. Each role has properties (information on possible values, restrictions on cardinality, etc.). Based on these properties, the specification can always be classified to determine its current position in the knowledge base. Based on its classification, certain things can be said about the specification in its current state (*feedback*). Based on the system's model of valid specifications, the system can make inferences about how the specification needs to be changed in order to classify into a valid place (*guidance*).

For an application to be suitable for the paradigm, it must be formulated so that successful completion can be viewed in terms of one or more concepts to be found or created in the knowledge base. Once formulated in this manner, execution of the application takes the form of searching through the space of possible descriptions until the correct one is found. Thus, an application developer's task is to provide BACKBORD with the following:

1. A taxonomy of the concepts in the application domain (e.g., a knowledge-base model of the information covered in a database)
2. Mappings from class concepts in the taxonomy to procedures for obtaining feedback (e.g., functions for converting a concept into a database query)
3. Associations between class concepts and actions applicable to members of that class (e.g., offering auto-dialing on data entries containing phone numbers)

With this information, the system can provide a general-purpose user interface for viewing specification descriptions, obtaining feedback and guidance, modifying the descriptions, and invoking actions upon resultant descriptions. The interface is customizable within certain parameters because an application developer specifies how feedback is generated from a description and what actions can be applied to it. However, the interface provides a framework in which application developers are freed from specifying much that would otherwise be required, and in which users see a high degree of consistency across individual tools.

FIGURE 18.1

A BACKBORD SCREEN FOR DATABASE BROWSING

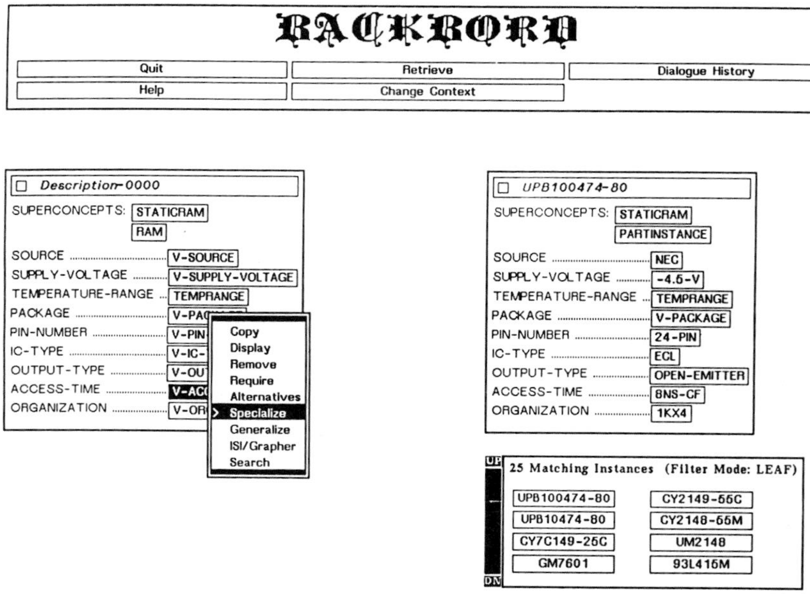

18.3.2. Guiding the User through the Search Space

Because of the general nature of the specification by reformulation paradigm, aids can be provided to help the user navigate through the space of possible descriptions, which can be used with little or no modification by specific applications.

In BACKBORD, the specification is represented by a structure with superconcepts, roles, and value restrictions for the roles. This is a LOOM concept[2] to be classified into the knowledge base. Figure 18.1 shows a BACKBORD screen used for browsing a database of standard electronic parts. The specification is displayed in a window called the description window. BACKBORD also has a scrollable window that contains all the objects that classify below the current specification (the window "Matching Instances" in Figure 18.1). The user can select any one of these to be displayed in detail in the "Example" window, which appears just above the "Matching Instances" window.

---

[2] In the version of BACKBORD used to implement the examples shown in this and the following section, the specification was actually a special structure that allowed disjunctive value restrictions and other facilities that were not available in LOOM at the time. In current versions of BACKBORD, the need for this has been eliminated, so the specification can be represented as a LOOM knowledge-base object. The full range of what can currently be expressed through BACKBORD is discussed in detail in Section 18.5.4.

The specification by reformulation paradigm as implemented in BACK-BORD consists of operations on the specification and matching objects. The underlying notion is that the specification and the matching objects serve as *memory joggers* that, by showing the user what kinds of things can be expressed, will help the user think of what should be expressed. The operations enable the user to act on those realizations.

Operations on the Specication

BACKBORD allows the user to modify the superconcepts and value restrictions of the specification. These modifications take advantage of the fact that all superconcepts and value restrictions are concepts in the knowledge base. All such concepts will henceforth be referred to as *specification concepts*. The operations provided for modifying specification concepts are as follows:

- **Generalize, Specialize,** and **Alternatives:** These options allow the user to replace a reference to a specification concept by a reference to one or more of its immediate parents, children, or siblings in the concept taxonomy. For example, in Figure 18.1, if one wanted to look only at electronic parts manufactured by NEC, one could *specialize* the value restriction of the *source* role on the specification (the window with the title "Description-0000") from **V-Source** (the concept representing all possible manufacturers) to **NEC**.
- **Examine Tree:** This invokes the ISI Grapher [Robins87] to give the user a graphical display of the knowledge base relative to the chosen specification concept. The user may then choose any concept from the graph to replace the specification concept.
- **Search:** The search option creates a recursive call to BACKBORD with the specification concept as the starting specification.

Operations on the Matching Objects

The matching objects are used as reminders for information that should be added to or excluded from the specification. One can modify or add a role or a superconcept to the specification by transferring the value from a matching object. One can also perform any of the operations described for specification concepts on a concept that serves as a value restriction or superconcept for a matching object.

18.4 EXAMPLE APPLICATIONS

Once we have implemented the specification by reformulation paradigm, building applications on top of it consists of developing customizations or extensions to the representation of the specification and/or the functions that implement feedback and guidance. The following are examples of applications in the BACKBORD system developed using this methodology.

18.4.1. The Mail Interface

ISI's FAST project [Neches88] provides price quotes and handles purchase requests for electronic parts via structured machine messages transmitted by computer mail. The BACKBORD mail interface to FAST (see Figure 18.2) helps the user construct messages for part quotations and orders.

In the mail interface, the specification represents a message being constructed by the user. The matching instances are examples of previously completed messages that can be used to help construct the current message. The steps necessary to build the mail interface using the specification by reformulation paradigm will be discussed next.

A Model of Legal Specications

New concepts describing the hierarchy of message types must be entered into the knowledge base. The concept (in this case **Message**) that should

FIGURE 18.2

THE BACKBORD MAIL INTERFACE, INVOKED FROM THE DATABASE
BROWSER

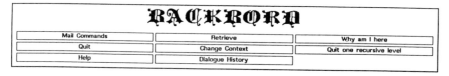

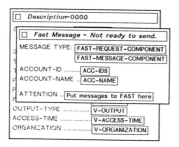

serve as the starting point when entering the mail interface must also be specified.

Feedback Procedures

The most important method of feedback is the retrieval of objects that classify under the specification. From these objects, the user can find a message or messages similar to the one being created. The default commands for manipulating examples allow the user to utilize information in the examples to modify the new message, by copying a field, for example.

In the mail interface, it is possible for the system to make further changes to the specification based on changes made by the user and on declarative representations of dependencies between roles of a **Message** concept. For example, in Figure 18.3, once the user has specified that the type of message is a **Request-for-Quote**, the system knows that such messages have a *Part-Id* role. As the value for that role, the system therefore uses the **Part** that the user was browsing when the mail interface was entered (in this case **UPB100474-80**). The instantiation of the *Part-Id* role causes further dependencies to be triggered, and the *Manufacturer* and *Description* roles are filled in by the system

FIGURE 18.3
A PARTIALLY COMPLETED MAIL MESSAGE

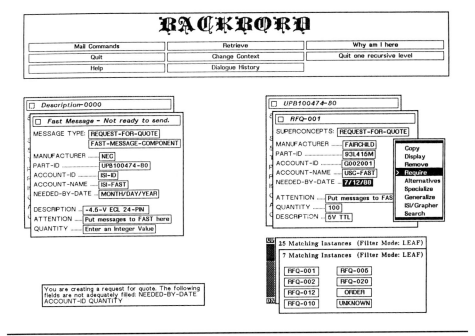

based on values computed from the filler for the *Part-Id* role (see [Harp88a] for more details on this mechanism).

Another type of feedback specific to the mail interface is the ability to compare the specification to valid message classes and advise the user on how to change the specification in order to classify it into a message type that is valid to send. For example, in Figure 18.3, the feedback message in the lower left-hand corner of the screen tells the user which fields of the message are not yet adequately filled. In Figure 18.4, the user has made the final changes needed in order to classify the specification as a message that is valid to send, so the system has displayed a feedback message informing the user that "All required message fields have been filled" and has added the menu item "Send the Message" to the options available when clicking on the specification.

Associations between Actions and Concepts

Associated with the mail interface concepts are the actions of sending and incorporating (receiving) mail messages. The primary effort for this application was to interface the LOOM mail concepts to the UNIX mail facility.

FIGURE 18.4
A COMPLETED MAIL MESSAGE

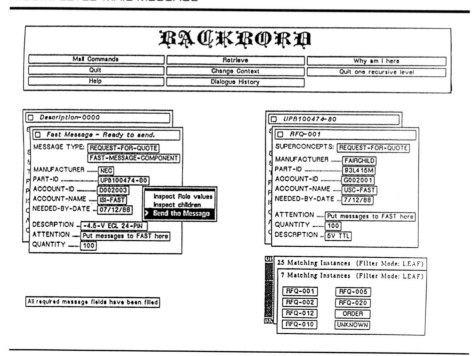

The interface converts concepts to messages and vice versa, and executes UNIX commands to send and incorporate mail via the Lisp workstation. All of this is transparent to the user.

18.4.2. Database Retrieval

When BACKBORD is used for database retrieval, the specification represents a query to the database. The matching objects represent database instances that would be retrieved using the current specification. The specification is refined by selecting roles and role values from the matching instances until only the desired instances are retrieved.

This is very similar to retrieval by reformulation systems such as AR-GON and RABBIT. The main difference between their database capabilities and BACKBORD's is that they work in a bottom-up fashion only. Although such systems create an internal knowledge-base representation for the data being retrieved, the user is never able to explicitly view the structure of that representation. The feedback in these systems comes only from the prompts provided by matching instances.

In addition to supporting this type of feedback, BACKBORD also makes possible a top-down manner of specification. The user is able to view the hierarchical representation of the database. In this way the user can modify the specification based on feedback from matching examples (bottom up) and by specializing the type of object that is being searched for (top down).

18.4.3. The Notes Interface—TINT

The Intelligent Note Taker (TINT) enables users to create notes, attach notes to knowledge-base objects, and retrieve notes relevant to an object. Notes are classified into a note taxonomy in the knowledge base. A detailed discussion of the notecard facilities can be found in [Harp88b].

For the note creation task, the specification represents a new note to be created. The procedure for creating a note is almost identical to that for creating a mail message. Just as in the mail interface, the user must decide the type of note to create and correctly instantiate the fields of the note. This can be accomplished by specifying the appropriate superconcept for the note specification and searching the database for field values. Feedback can be given when the note correctly classifies under a valid note type and default values can be filled in based on the context the user is in when he or she decides to attach the note.

18.5 A SPECIFICATION BY REFORMULATION SHELL

The three applications described in Section 18.4 share a large amount of code. This motivates us to develop a specification by reformulation shell as our next goal. Like an expert system shell, the specification by reformulation shell should capture domain-independent components of the paradigm, and it should allow the application builder to easily customize it to different applications by adding domain-dependent components.

A major difference between a specification by reformulation shell and an expert system shell is that the former supports building *a set of cooperating applications*, whereas the latter is normally aimed to support development of single applications. Hence, two major requirements on the design of the shell are that:

1. Building new applications on top of the shell should not interfere with existing applications.
2. Different applications built using a shell should cooperate easily by sharing information.

In this section we first identify major functional modules of the paradigm. Then we describe an architecture for the shell that dynamically determines the appropriate handlers for those functional modules. A discussion of the benefits offered by the shell follows. Finally, we give a progress report on the design and the implementation of the shell.

18.5.1. Major Functional Modules of the Paradigm

A functional module is a generic capability. In our scheme, the methods that realize these generic functions are called *handlers*. Each oval in Figure 18.5 represents a major functional module in the specification by reformulation paradigm.

- **Reformulation:** allow the user to modify the specification using operations such as those described in Section 18.3.2. Each reformulation alternative is a handler that is tied to a class of specification; some are tied to a particular kind of displayed feedback object as well. For example, in data retrieval, the option to REQUIRE a value is associated with anything that is an attribute value of a retrieved example item.
- **Generate Feedback Requirements:** transform the specification into a related specification, to be used in generating examples and/or other forms of feedback. Because it is so fundamental, we see a need to build in special hooks for a particular case of this: generating a query for retrieving examples by "massaging" the specification. Particularly when the specification represents a unique object, useful examples can be merely "similar" to the one being specified rather than strictly consistent with it. In the general case, the basis for feedback may also differ. For example, the feedback might be a drawing generated from a textual specification, where the graphical specification deliberately omits features that are represented in the textual specification. The main

FIGURE 18.5
MAJOR FUNCTIONAL MODULES OF THE PARADIGM

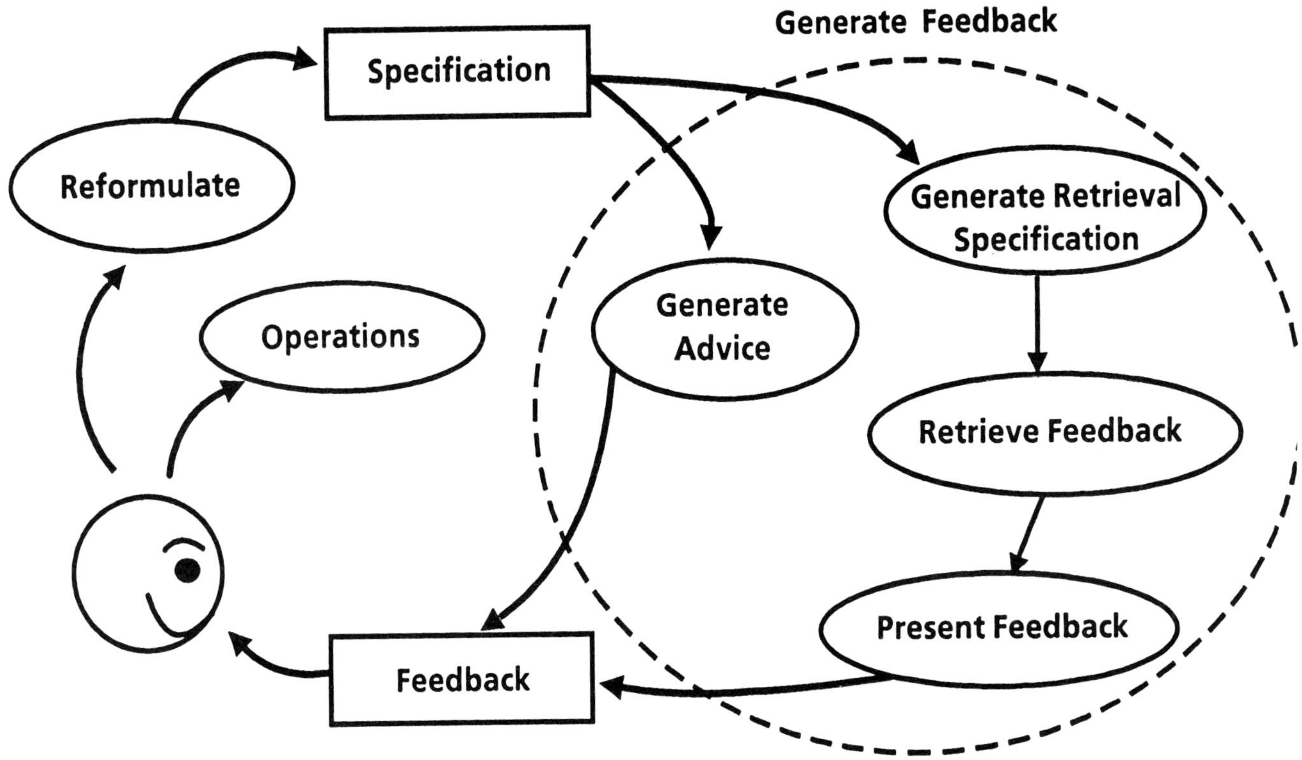

function of this module is, then, to generate an intermediate form of the specification suitable for generating useful memory joggers.

- **Generate Feedback:** evaluate the transformed specification to obtain a set of candidate information items for use as feedback. Again, special hooks are worthwhile to facilitate the case of retrieval, in which the original specification is recast as a query. In that case, there are default handlers that function to retrieve examples using that generated query. In the general case, handlers of this type take a feedback requirements specification as input and produce a set of one or more feedback instances as output.

- **Present Feedback:** determine what information about the feedback instances (e.g., retrieved examples) should be presented and how they should be presented. For example, suppose we have a database of items with a large number of attributes, but the user is interested in only a few attributes for an application; this class of handler would be used to filter the information so that only the attributes of interest to the user are presented. Feedback presentation handlers are defined in terms of the kinds of feedback instances they are prepared to handle. Each handler has associated methods for filtering the set of feedback instances, ordering the set, determining which attributes of the instances will be shown, and managing the display.

- **Generate Advice:** generate suggestions, annotations, and advice, based on the status of the current specification and the displayed feedback.

- **Operations:** allow the user to act on the specification and/or the presented feedback instances, in order to invoke external actions that take them as input (generating graphs from retrieved data, mailing a completed message template, etc.).

During execution, a specification by reformulation application consists of a set of *active handlers*, which serve as the methods that realize the major functional modules. The set of active handlers is determined by the current context of the system, which includes (1) the application that the user is engaged in; (2) the status of the current specification; and (3) the output of any relevant preceding handlers. As the system changes from one application to another, some of the active handlers are replaced by others. Moreover, as the specification changes, some inactive handlers may become active, and some active ones may become inactive. For example, when all the required fields of a message specification have been filled in, the operation handler for sending a mail message becomes active. As handlers become active and produce output, the kinds of objects they produce may cause the activation or deactivation of other handlers.

The major functional modules can be characterized in three aspects: (1) the number of active handlers it can have, (2) whether its handlers are domain-independent or domain-specific, and (3) whether its handlers are initiated by the user or initiated by the system.

1. **The number of a module's active handlers:** Some modules are restricted to exactly one active handler, whereas others may have any number of active handlers. For instance, the system may have only one active handler for generating its feedback requirements but could have any number of active handlers for generating various kinds of advice.

2. **Domain-independent handlers vs. domain-specific handlers:** The handlers of some modules remain the same for different applications, but those of other modules are often application-specific. For instance, the three applications we built share the same reformulation handler, but they have different handlers for advice generation and operations.

3. **User-initiated handlers vs. system-initiated handlers:** The handlers for reformulation, operations, and feedback requirements generation, are usually invoked by the user interactively. The handlers for generating feedback and for presenting examples are often initiated by the system. The handlers for the generate advice module could be initiated either by the system or by the user. For example, the mail interface informs the user about the fields remaining to be filled only upon user's request, yet it automatically informs the user about the completion of a message whenever that occurs.

18.5.2. An Architecture for Specification by Reformulation

An architecture for the specification by reformulation shell is shown in Figure 18.6. The shell provides a set of default handlers, which are handlers common to many applications. In addition, the shell allows the application builder to describe application-specific handlers. Moreover, the shell dynamically selects active handlers based on its knowledge about the user's task, the results of previously executed handlers, and the status of the specification. A central controller invokes active handlers and communicates with the user. The underlying mechanism for implementing the handler selector is classification-based programming [Yen88; Yen89], which is a production system architecture that is based on the classification capabilities of the KL-ONE family of knowledge representation systems.

We will illustrate the architecture using the following scenario of a user's interaction with the system. Suppose that the user invokes the mail interface from the database browser. The architecture changes the high-level user task from **Data-base-browsing** to **Mail-interface**. As the new user task is classified into the knowledge base, the system discovers that the active handlers for both the **Generate Feedback Requirements** and the **Present Feedback** modules need to be replaced. Once the set of active handlers for the mail interface has been set up, the user can start modifying the specification using various active reformulation handlers (e.g., the *specialize*, *generalize*, and *alternatives* options). When the user invokes a command for retrieving examples, the system will retrieve examples using three active handlers: one for generating the query, one for retrieving examples from a database of messages, and one

FIGURE 18.6
ARCHITECTURE FOR THE SPECIFICATION BY FORMULATION SHELL

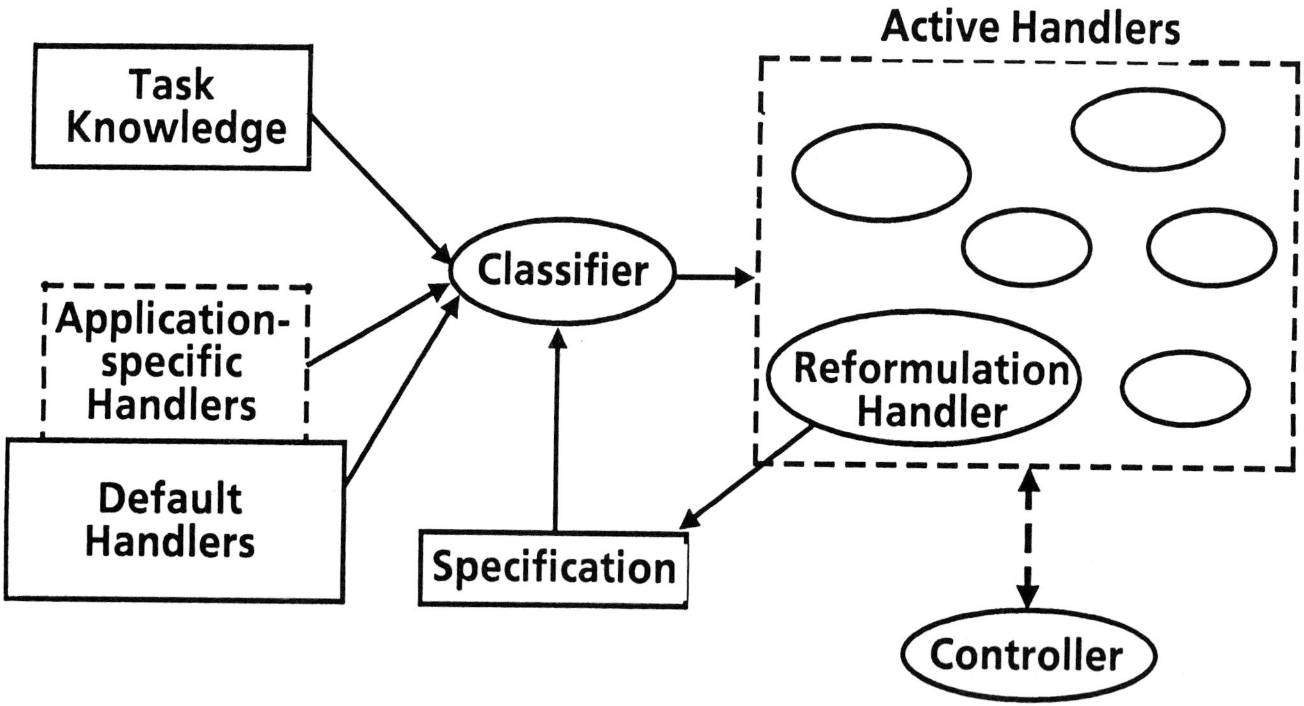

for filtering and displaying information about the retrieved messages. The handler for query generation that becomes active in this context differs from the default handler in that it ignores certain fields of the message specification in generating the query, in order to be able to retrieve example messages that are similar rather than strictly identical.

When all the required fields of the message have been filled out, the specification will be classified as a **Completed-message**. As a result, two handlers become active: an operation handler for sending mail messages, and an advice generation handler for informing the user about the completion of the message. The activation of the operation handler causes a menu item, "Send the Message," to be added to the list of operations that the user can apply to the specification. The newly activated advice generation handler displays the text "The message is ready to send" on the screen.

18.5.3. Benefits

The specification by reformulation shell offers several benefits to the system builders.

1. By maximizing the reusability of code, it reduces the effort necessary to develop a new application or modify an existing application within the paradigm. Different applications could share common handlers; moreover, all applications share the central handler controller, which characterizes the control flow among various modules in a specification by reformulation system. Sharing handlers and controllers reduces the amount of duplicated code. Hence, it is easier to maintain the system.

2. The shell facilitates developing a set of cooperating tools through a shared knowledge base. All applications built using a shell work on the same knowledge base; hence, an object created by one application is both visible and accessible to other applications. For example, a message created by the mail interface can be browsed by the database browser, and the notes interface can attach a note to the message as well.

3. The shell minimizes interference between different applications within one system. The shell achieves this level of separation by explicitly modeling the user's task for each application, modularizing the system in a standard fashion, and associating each task to only the relevant modules.

The shell enforces a consistent interface across different applications. Once the user learns the basic techniques for modifying a specification by copying values from examples and generalizing and specializing along the knowledge-base hierarchy, these techniques can be applied to many different domain applications. For example, in BACKBORD the mail interface (Figure 18.2) is very similar to the browsing interface (Figure 18.1). The operations for constructing a mail message or a note are also similar to those for constructing a query. All of the operations described in Section 18.3.2 can be used to construct a message or a note.

18.5.4. A Progress Report

The version of BACKBORD described in this chapter is our first implementation of the shell, on top of which we built the three applications discussed in Section 18.4. We are now partway through the second implementation. In this section, we describe the status of that implementation, dividing the discussion between what has been accomplished and what remains to be done.

As will be seen below, we are seeking to address two sets of issues in the reimplementation. The first set has to do with how to facilitate the embedding and integration of the specification by reformulation shell into knowledge-based applications programs. As of this writing, much of the work on those issues is complete, the primary exception being that we have introduced new functionality and are still experimenting with alternative approaches to minimizing the apparent complexity that this adds to the user interface. The second set of issues has to do with the generality of the shell and the completeness of our implementation of the architecture outlined in the preceding sections. Portions of the full architecture still remain as future work.

Current Status

It will not suffice for specification by reformulation systems to exist only as stand-alone services. To realize the fullest range of potential for the architecture outlined in this chapter, it is essential to address the software engineering issues of embedding the system within applications. Many of our recent efforts have focused on developing BACKBORD so that it is properly integrated with other components necessary to provide a comprehensive framework for building integrated user support environments [Harp90; Neches90].

In that framework, BACKBORD properly lies situated between the application programming system on the one hand and the user interface management system (UIMS) on the other. Thus, our efforts have had two primary thrusts. First, we have integrated BACKBORD with the LOOM knowledge-based programming language [MacGregor87]. This means that BACKBORD can serve as a front end to that language and that it can be available automatically as a front end to any services implemented in that language. Second, we have embedded BACKBORD within a fully functional UIMS called HUMANOID [Szekely90]. This integration means that user interfaces based on BACKBORD's specification by reformulation paradigm can be more readily customized and tuned for special needs. It also means that BACKBORD can be used recursively, to provide end users with an interface to the UIMS that helps them customize applications' user interfaces for themselves.

One of the key ideas that make the notion of a specification by reformulation shell viable is the ability to provide a default internal language for representing specifications. Within the BACKBORD system, the internal objects that capture the current state of a specification are referred to as descriptions.

In the first version of BACKBORD (which was built upon NIKL [Moser83] and later ported to LOOM [MacGregor87] without any redesign), representational limitations forced us to implement descriptions as extensions to the underlying representation language that had to be supported with special-purpose code. In the new version of BACKBORD, which is based on LOOM, these limitations are removed because LOOM is a far more expressive language. Descriptions are no longer special objects defined in the BACKBORD system. Rather, any concept in LOOM can be used as a description.

Hence, the expressive power of BACKBORD is now equal to the expressive power of the underlying knowledge representation system. In the old language, BACKBORD could help users create only specifications that could be expressed in terms of superconcepts and attribute value restrictions. In the new language, BACKBORD has the machinery to assist users with creating descriptions containing anything that can be expressed in LOOM's TBox and Abox languages (that is, both terminological definitions that describe classes of objects and assertional specifications that describe instances of those objects). Thus, users can evolve descriptions that refer to the following:

- **Superconcepts and value restrictions**, as in the first version of BACK-BORD. Thus, one could use BACKBORD to create a description of, say, a **Rolling-Vehicle** that references **Vehicle** as a superconcept and restricts a *mechanism* relation to the concept of *Wheels*.

- **Number restrictions**, which allow the user to create descriptions of objects for which some numeric predicate applies to a value restriction. This allows one, for example, to refine the description of a **Rolling-Vehicle** to describe a **Two-Wheeler** as a **Rolling-Vehicle** whose *mechanism* is *exactly two* **Wheels**.

- **The connectives And, Or, and Not,** with which it is possible to refine descriptions logically, for example, to describe **bicycles, motorcycles,** and **mopeds**, which are all **Two-Wheelers**, but differ with respect to being *human-powered, motor-driven,* or *both*.

- **The quantifiers Some and For-All**, which make it possible to specify a context for a description. This allows the user, for example, to refine the description of a **Vehicle** to describe a **Used-Vehicle** as a **Vehicle** such that *For-Some* **Person**, that **Person** *owns* the **Vehicle**.

- **Specific instances**, allowing the user to define descriptions that depend not just on other concepts, but on specific individuals. For example, the description of a **Japanese-Vehicle** must refer to the instance **Japan**, which is an instance of the concept of **Country**. (If only value restrictions were available, one would have to define first the concept of **Japan-Country** as a subconcept of **Country** whose only instance is **Japan**, and then use **Japan-Country** as a value restriction.)

- **Embedded descriptions**, which allow the use of descriptions within descriptions. For example, while defining the description of a **Disabled-**

Vehicle, one might need to refer to the description of a **Wheel-With-Low-Pressure-Tire**. If the concept of a **Wheel-With-Low-Pressure-Tire** does not exist in the knowledge base, **Disabled-Vehicle** can be described as a **Vehicle** with *at least one* **Wheel** such that the **Tire** on that **Wheel** has *pressure* **Low**. (Without embedded descriptions one would have to separately define and name the descriptions of both **Low-Pressure-Tire** and **Wheel-With-Low-Pressure-Tire**, and then use the latter description in the description of **Disabled-Vehicle**.)

Using concepts as descriptions has many benefits besides the increase in expressive power. For one, it facilitates the integration of BACKBORD with application programs that use LOOM. Since any concept used in an application can be used as a description, BACKBORD can be used to browse and operate on all the objects of an application. Since BACKBORD is an interactive tool with an easy-to-use interface, applications can provide BACKBORD's facilities to their end users as a convenient way to allow users to extend and customize the applications.

Using the underlying representation language to represent specifications while eliminating specially supported constructs is also a beneficial step because it makes BACKBORD useful as an application development tool. The first version, specifications could be created in BACKBORD that were not supported outside the interface; therefore, there was no guarantee that those specifications could be used elsewhere in an application. The current version provides the assurance that system builders can create all specifications (and only those specifications) that can be handled by an implementation language that is usable for the rest of their application. This means that BACKBORD can be used as an interactive tool to define the concepts needed in an application program, and that its powerful browsing facilities can be used in debugging the application.

We have recently begun to experiment with using BACKBORD as the basis of a knowledge-base development environment for LOOM. In that capacity, it can be used to view and find certain knowledge-base entities (concepts and instances). It can also be used to create and modify these entities. Work remains to extend it to knowledge-base entities such as relations, roles, rules, methods, and user-defined structures. Systems representing related work in this area are described in [Abrett97] and [Terveen90].

Although BACKBORD can be viewed as providing a valuable front end to a knowledge-based programming language such as LOOM, it is not intended to be a complete user interface. Furthermore, it needs a user interface itself. For these reasons, embedding BACKBORD in a user interface management system has been the second major thrust of our current work. The system into which it is being integrated is called HUMANOID [Szekely90]. The primary focus of HUMANOID is on providing a clean software interface between its presentation methods and application-specific data structures, utilizing principles developed in previous work by [Szekely88; Szekely89]. In the approach represented by HUMANOID, mappings are maintained between (1) descriptions of presentation methods in a hierarchical taxonomy of such methods, and (2) descriptions of knowledge-base objects in their own hierarchical taxonomy. When it is time to present a particular object, HUMANOID can use these mappings to determine the set of presentation methods that most specifically fit that object.

These features of HUMANOID, coupled to BACKBORD, provide the ability to tailor the interface to application-specific objects. HUMANOID will choose the presentation based on the kind of data to be presented. This makes it possible to implement different instantiations of the specification by reformulation paradigm for different applications and to have interfaces tailored to the particular application. For instance, in the mail interface, the example mail message can be formatted as messages typically are in electronic mail handlers, rather than in a tabular form as is done in the default interface. The list of examples can be formatted to show the sender, date, and subject of the message, rather than the name of the knowledge-base instance as is done in the default interface.

Remaining Work

BACKBORD provides default handlers for the reformulation module, the query generation module, the retrieving module, and the example presentation module. We have also developed application-specific operation handlers and advice generation handlers for the mail interface and the notes interface. However, BACKBORD has not yet implemented the handler selector and the handler controller discussed in Section 18.5.2. The selection and the invocation of active handlers are done through hand-coded procedures in BACKBORD. Hence, the two major remaining tasks in developing the shell are (1) developing the handler controllers and (2) developing the handler selector. We will discuss some of the issues that are related to the development of these two components.

1. **The handler controller.** Two issues that the handler controller should address are the user interface and event tracking. The handler controller should serve as the interface between the handlers and the user interface component of the system. For example, a handler might want to present a piece of text on the screen, or a handler might need to be invoked by the user's input activities (e.g., clicking a mouse button). Having the controller as the standard communication channel between the user interface component and the handlers facilitates a clean separation between the application program and the UIMS, as advocated by [Szekely91]. Also, the handler controller should be able to monitor the status of the user's activities because the user might suspend one task (e.g., database browsing) and enter another (e.g., creating a message). The user expects to continue working on the suspended task later. To support this, the controller needs to record the status of the suspended task as well as the conditions for reactivating it.

2. **The handler selector.** The handler selector will be built using a production system that we have implemented on top of LOOM [Yen89]. The handler selector consists of a set of rules whose left-hand sides describe conditions about the user's task, results computed by previously executed handlers, and the classification of the current specification, and whose right-hand sides propose an addition or a deletion of active handlers. Since the rules triggered might propose multiple handlers for a functional module that is limited to one handler, the handler selector must also support control strategies for choosing rules (e.g., select the most specific one).

18.6 CONCLUSION

This paper has described specification by reformulation, an interaction paradigm that extends the retrieval by reformulation paradigm into activities beyond query-based retrieval. Examples of the use of the paradigm were shown through three applications built in BACKBORD: a database browser, a mail interface, and a notes interface. BACKBORD is an example of an integrated user-support environment—a modular set of tools that interact naturally with one another. Such an environment has two advantages:

1. *Integration and consistency.* The user is provided with one environment with the same interface conventions and with integrated capabilities.
2. *Reusability and ease of maintenance.* Modules that accomplish very different tasks can all be based on the specification by reformulation paradigm. Having a general, reusable module that captures this user interface paradigm significantly reduces the code size and maintenance problems for these application modules.

We have also described the architecture of a domain-independent shell for specification by reformulation systems. In essence, the shell is analogous to an expert system shell, in that it separates domain-independent components from domain-specific procedures and knowledge. Unlike an expert system shell, however, the specification by reformulation shell not only reduces the cost of developing and maintaining applications, it also facilitates cooperation between applications through a shared knowledge base. That is, it supports building a set of cooperating applications rather than building single applications. Moreover, the shell avoids undesirable interference between applications by explicitly modeling the user's task and by using the classification capabilities of LOOM to retrieve relevant modules based on the context of the system.

BACKBORD is the beginning of our effort to develop the shell. By building the appropriate knowledge base and adding domain-specific modules, system builders can extend BACKBORD to their own applications. The paradigm and the specification by reformulation shell described in this paper together represent an approach to building integrated user-support environments that benefits both the application builder and the end user.

Acknowledgments

We would like to thank John Granacki, Brian Harp, Paul Rosenbloom, and several anonymous reviewers for their comments on earlier drafts of this paper.

References

[Abrett87] Abrett, G., and Burstein, M. H. 1987. The KREME Knowledge Editing Environment. *International Journal of Man-Machine Studies, 27*, 103–126.

[Fischer89] Fischer, G., and Nieper-Lemke, H. 1989. HELGON: Extending the Retrieval by Reformulation Paradigm. *Proceedings of CHI '89, The Annual Conference on Human Factors in Computer Systems.*

[Harp88a] Harp, B., and DeBellis, M. 1988. Data Dependencies in LOOM. In *Proceedings of the IASTED Conference on Expert Systems Theory and Applications*, Los Angeles, CA.

[Harp88b] Harp, B., and Neches, R. A Knowledge-Based Notecard Environment. In *Proceedings of Workshop on Architectures for Intelligent Interfaces: Elements and Phototypes*, Monterey, CA, March.

[Harp90] Harp, B. 1990. Dealing with Understandability, Tools, and Memory Management in Knowledge Base Management Systems. In *Proceedings of the AAAI-90 Workshop on Knowledge-Base Management Systems*, Boston, MA, July.

[MacGregor87] MacGregor, R., and Bates, R. 1987. The LOOM Knowledge Representation Language Technical Report ISI/RS-87-188, USC/Information Sciences Institute.

[Moser83] Moser, M. G. 1983. An Overview of NIKL, the New Implementation of KL-ONE. In *Research in Natural Language Understanding.* Cambridge, MA: Bolt Breanek and Newman, Inc., BBN Technical Report 5421.

[Neches88] Neches, R. 1988. FAST Workstation Project Overview. Technical Report ISI/RS-88-203, USC/Information Sciences Institute.

[Neches90] Neches, R. 1990. Enabling Technology of Building Integrated User-Support Environments. In *Proceedings of the AAAI Spring Symposium Workshop on Intelligent Interfaces*, Stanford, CA.

[Patel-Scneider84] Petel-Scnieder, P. F., Brachman, R. J., and Levesque, H. J. 1984. ARGON: Knowledge Representation Meets Information Retrieval. In *Proceedings of the First Conference on Artificial Intelligence Applications*, Denver, CO, December.

[Robins87] Robins, G., 1987. The ISI Grapher: A Portable Tool for Displaying Graphs Pictorially. In *Symboliikka '87*, Helsinki, Finland, August. Reprints available through USC/ISI technical report ISI/RS-87-196.

[Schmolze83] Schmolze, J., and Lipkis, T. 1983. Classification in the KL-ONE Knowledge Representation System. In *Proceedings of the Eighth International Joint Conference on Artificial Intellegence*, 330–332.

[Stelzner86] Stelzner, M., and Williams, M. D. 1986. *Specification by Reformulation: An Approach to Knowledge Based Interface Design.* Mountain View, CA: Intellicorp.

[Szekely88] Szekely, P. 1988. Separating the User Interface from the Functionality of Application Programs. Ph.D. thesis CMU-CS-88-101, Carnegie-Mellon University.

[Szekely89] Szekely, P. 1989. Standarizing the Interface between Applications and UIMS's. In *Proceedings of the ACM SIGGRAPH Symposium on User Interface Software,* 34–42.

[Szekely90] Szekely, P. 1990. Template-based Mapping of Application Data to Interactive Displays. In *Proceedings of UIST '90, the Third Conference on User Interface Software Technology,* Snowbird, Utah, October.

[Szekely91] Szekely, P. 1990. Using Classification and Separation to Build Intelligent Interfaces. This volume, Chapter 19.

[Terveen90] Terveen, G. L., and Wroblewski, D. A. 1990. A Collaborative Interface for Editing Large Knowledge Bases. In *Proceedings of AAAI '90, The Eighth National Conference on Artificial Intelligence,* 491–496.

[Tou82] Tou, F. F., Williams, M. D., Fikes, R., Henderson, A., and Malone, T. 1982. RABBIT: An Intelligent Database Assistant. In *Proceedings AAAI-82,* 314–318.

[Williams84] Williams, M. D. 1984. What Makes RABBIT Run? *Int. J. Man-Machine Studies,* 21, 333–352.

[Williams81] Williams, M. D., and Hollan. J. D. 1981. The Process of Retrieval from Very Long Term Memory. *Cognitive Science,* 5, 87–119.

[Yen88] Yen, J., Neches, R., and MacGregor, R. M. 1988. Classification-based Programming: A Deep Integration of Rules and Frames. Technical Report ISI/RR-88-213, USC/Information Sciences Institute.

[Yen89] Yen, J., Neches, R., and MacGregor, R. 1989. Using Terminological Models to Enhance the Rule-based Paradigm. In *Proceedings of the Second International Symposium on Artificial Intelligence,* Monterrey, Mexico, October 25–27.

CHAPTER 19

STRUCTURING PROGRAMS TO SUPPORT INTELLIGENT INTERFACES*

PEDRO SZEKELY
University of Southern California

ABSTRACT

The ability to connect user interface building blocks with a wide variety of application programs is crucial in the construction of intelligent interfaces. This paper presents a language to specify the communication between building blocks and application programs. This language has two important features: first, the it is abstract enough to isolate the application program from the details of particular interface styles; second, the it is rich enough to support the communication of the information needed for the low level aspects of

*The initial research was supported by the Defense Advanced Research Projects Agency, ARPA Order No. 4976, Amendment 20, under Contract No. F33615-87-C-1499, monitored by the Avionics Laboratory, Air Force Wright Aeronautical Laboratories, Aeronautical Systems Division (AFSC), Wright-Patterson AFB. Further work has been supported in part by DARPA under Contract No. MDA903-86-C-0178 and in part by the Air Force Logistics Command under Contract No. F33600-87-C-7047. Views and conclusions contained in this report are the author's and should not be interpreted as representing the official policies, either expressed or implied, of DARPA, the Air Force Logistics Command, the U.S. Government, or any person or agency connected with them.

the user interface. The paper also describes a UIMS based on this language and discusses how the language supports tools to reason about the building blocks that the UIMS provides.

19.1 INTRODUCTION

Many user interface management systems (UIMSs) have a library of interface building blocks that can be used to assemble the interface for a program [Tanner83]. An *intelligent* UIMS has a reasoning component that uses a model of the program, the user, and the interface design to determine how to use this library. For instance, the Integrated Interfaces system [Arens88] uses a model of the objects and operations in the program and a model of interface building blocks such as icons, menus, and maps. The reasoning component employs a set of rules to decide what interface building blocks to use and then it connects them with the objects and operations of the application.

Connecting the interface building blocks with different applications requires that the building blocks use a standard language to communicate with the application objects and operations. Otherwise, it is necessary to write a program to translate between the separate languages used by the application and the building blocks, making it impossible to connect building blocks and applications automatically.

Suppose, for instance, that applications are programmed using an object-oriented programming language. The application objects would be defined as classes, and the application operations would be defined as methods for those classes. In such an environment, the standard language for user interface/application communication would consist of a list of methods that each application object must provide. If each application object provides these methods, then the interface building blocks could communicate with any application object because the building blocks would use only these methods to communicate with the application. Such a standard language would make the building blocks plug-compatible with a large number of application programs.

Defining such a standard language is difficult because the language must support a wide variety of interface styles and a wide variety of applications programs. This generality requirement produces two conflicting goals:

- The language must use abstract terms to define the communication with the application, without referring to any particular interface style. Otherwise, the application will not be independent of interface style, and hence cannot support a variety of interfaces.
- The language must support the communication of the information needed for each interface style, including the information needed to support application-dependent feedback (semantic feedback). Because different interaction styles provide different kinds of feedback (e.g., rub-

berbanding, gravity, highlighting), it appears that the language must be attuned to particular interface styles.

This paper describes a language that achieves a good compromise between these two conflicting goals. To achieve the generality goal, the language is based on an extension of the *language view* of programs [Foley82; Moran81; Newman79], a general model of interactive programs. The extensions mainly involve enriching the description of the semantics of a program. To ensure that the language supports a wide variety of interface styles, the language primitives were tested with a large number of interaction styles and refined to make sure that the appropriate information can be communicated. The resulting language primitives allow the communication of the application-specific information needed in many interface styles, but the information is described at a high enough level of abstraction that the details of the interface styles remain hidden.

The chapter is organized as follows: Section 19.2 presents the language view of programs. Section 19.3 introduces the primitives of the proposed language, and Section 19.4 shows how these primitives can explain the behavior of the interface to a chess program. Section 19.5 describes Nephew, a UIMS based on the proposed communication language, and shows how Nephew implements the interface to the chess program. Finally, Section 19.6 describes how the language can be used in the reasoning component of intelligent interfaces.

19.2 THE LANGUAGE VIEW OF PROGRAMS

Communication is "the exchange of meanings between individuals through a common system of symbols" [Encyclopae74]. To communicate a meaning, called a *concept* in this paper, the sender must encode the concept into a sequence of symbols with a concrete physical representation that can be perceived by the receiver. The receiver must decode the symbols it perceives and extract the corresponding concept.

A human and a program communicate concepts by encoding them as changes in the state of input and output devices attached to the computer. Users communicate concepts to programs by manipulating the input devices. Programs monitor the state of the devices to recover the concepts, process them, and produce new concepts. The program then encodes these new concepts in the state of the output devices to transmit them to the user.

The primitives of the proposed language were identified by classifying the concepts that users and programs communicate via graphical user interfaces. Each concept category corresponds to a primitive of the language. Put in object-oriented terms, each concept category corresponds to a method that computes the information embodied in the concept.

The classification of the concepts that users and programs communicate, called *communication concepts*, is based on the *language view* of programs

[Foley82; Moran81; Newman79]. According to the language view, the language to communicate with a program has four levels called the *conceptual, semantic, syntactic,* and *lexical* levels. The conceptual level describes the tasks the user is able to accomplish using the program. Complex tasks are specified by decomposing them into subtasks, and subtasks are decomposed further until they can be accomplished using a single operation provided by the program. The semantic level describes these operations and the objects that they operate on. The syntactic and lexical levels describe how the user employs the input and output devices to access the objects and operations.

These levels are consistent with the definition of communication given at the beginning of this section. The communication concepts are the meanings encoded in the lexical and syntactical levels. The user transmits them in order to use the facilities provided by the program, namely, the objects and operations.

Even though it seems intuitive to divide the language into these levels, no precise notation for describing the levels of an application program exists. Moran's CLG [Moran81] is perhaps the most complete notation, but it is not precise enough to be executable, and many aspects of graphics-based interfaces cannot be expressed in it. Most of the work on notations for describing programs according to the language model has concentrated on the syntactic and lexical levels. BNF, transition networks, and event based systems are the most popular methods [Green86].

The specification of the semantic level usually consists of a list of type and procedure declarations like those used in MIKE [Olsen86] and the ones used in Foley's user interface design environment [Foley88]. The idea behind such specifications is that the types specify the objects that the application provides, and the procedures specify actions that can be performed on those objects.

This kind of specification cannot express many attributes of a program that are conveyed to the user via graphical user interfaces. For insurance, the user interface for a chess program could highlight the pieces that can be legally moved at any given moment. To highlight the pieces the user interface needs to discover which pieces can be moved. The type/procedure method of specification would simply include in the specification a procedure that computes the relevant information. A better solution would be to record the purpose of the procedure, which is to test whether a given piece is a legal parameter for the move operation. Including in the specification a procedure that computes the relevant information would make it impossible to construct a generic user interface building block to highlight objects that are correct parameters to an operation. The building block would not know which procedure to call, and even if it knew, it would not know what parameters to provide and in what order. The specification language should capture more about the meaning of the types and procedures. The language should allow one to express that the "test-chess-piece" procedure tests whether an object is a legal candidate to become an operation input. Any interface building block can access this information by using the appropriate language construct.

Some UIMSs [Hayes85; Smith84] specify the semantics of programs using formalisms that specify more than types and procedures and capture the information needed to support the generation of menu-based interfaces. Unfortunately, they do not capture some of the aspects of the semantics of a program needed to support highly interactive graphical user interfaces.

The difficulties with levels specification in the language model might suggest that the model is inappropriate [Kamran83]. This paper shows that many of the difficulties of the language model can be overcome by enriching the semantic level description.

Finally, the classification of the concepts that users and programs communicate is also based on an analysis of the user interface of many Macintosh programs (e.g., MacDraw, Excel, and Finder). The communication concepts can explain the behavior of the interface features of these programs.

The communication concepts introduced in the next section capture the distinctions in semantics that are relevant to the construction of graphical user interfaces. Each class of communication concept captures a different semantic distinction.

19.3 COMMUNICATION CONCEPTS

The communication concepts are divided into *input* and *output*. The input communication concepts are the meanings encoded in the gestures produced with the input devices (syntactic and lexical levels). These concepts express what the user wants to do with the objects and operations (semantic level).

The set of concepts that a user might want to express about the objects and operations of a program are open-ended. The power of the set of communication concepts presented below is that the set is small, yet it is rich enough to explain the behavior of a large variety of graphical user interfaces. The set of interfaces includes mouse-based systems such as the Macintosh interface. The communication concepts can explain the effect of every input event, every mouse movement, for a large variety of interfaces. Section 19.4 illustrates this using a chess program.

The input communication concepts are used by the user to communicate to a program:

- **Activate** *operation*: expresses the user's intention to invoke an operation. After the operation has been activated, the user performs other activities, which are described below in the following entries, and then executes the operation.
- **Execute** *operation*: requests that an operation be executed. If the operation is ready to be executed (e.g., all required inputs have been specified), the appropriate procedure is called. Otherwise, a communication concept is transmitted to tell the user about the error.

- **Bind** *input* **of** *operation* **to** *value*: specifies a value for an input.

- **Preview** *operation*: computes an approximation of the effects that executing the operation would have, given the current setting of the input values. The rubberbanding effect in many graphical operations is an instance of the use of the **preview** concept.

- **Abort** *operation*: requests that the execution or activation of an operation be terminated.

These communication concepts can be qualified with the qualifiers **plan** and **not-plan**. Whereas the **bind** *input* **to** *value* concept specifies the value of an input to an operation, the **plan bind** *input* **to** *value* concept tells the program that the user has entered a state in which he or she can specify the given input. For instance, moving the mouse over a check box icon can be interpreted as a plan to set a value. Clicking the mouse will set the value, but moving the mouse away from the check box without clicking will not set the value, and can be interpreted as a **not-plan bind** *input* concept. Section 19.4 illustrates how these qualifiers are used in the interface for a chess program.

The output communication concepts are used by the program to communicate to the user:

- **Contents:** the state of an object.
- **Changes:** a change in the contents of an object.

The following set of output communication concepts refers only to operations:

- **Alternatives:** the set of values from which an input for an operation must be chosen.

- **Correct** *input* **of** *operation*: the value **true** if the input of an operation is bound to a valid value; otherwise, a description of why the binding is incorrect.

- **Using** *object* **as** *input* **of** *operation*: a concept that specifies that a given object is being used as an input value for an operation.

More details about the meaning of the communication concepts, and the role they play in user-program communication can be found in [Szekely88].

These communication concepts are the categories in a classification. To describe a program precisely, it is often necessary to define specializations of some of these concepts. For instance, the **changes** communication concept reports that an object has changed, but does not specify how. A specialization of the **changes** concept should be used when the need to specify how an object will change arises.

For example, a chess program could transmit the PIECE *changes* communication concept when PIECE is moved from one location to another, or when

PIECE is taken. The *changes* communication concept could be specialized for the chess program into, say, **changes-moved** and **changes-taken** to distinguish between the two kinds of changes. These two concepts would allow the chess program to transmit more accurate information about changes.

The most important point about the communication concepts is that they can express the communication between a user and a program using abstract terms, and they do not need to make reference to particular interaction techniques. The interpretation of every input event and all display updates can be viewed as the encoding of one of the communication concepts.

19.4 AN EXAMPLE

This section illustrates how the communication concepts can explain the input/output behavior of a program. The figures that follow show diagrams of a chess program display with the user using the mouse to drag a piece. The interface behaves as follows: when the user presses the mouse button over a piece that can be moved, the piece is highlighted, then an outline of the piece follows the mouse. The user can then drag the piece to its destination and release the mouse button to drop the piece there. During the dragging, the location under the mouse highlights if it is a legal destination for the piece.

The following screen snapshot shows the chess board after the user has moved the mouse over the knight, but has not pressed the mouse button.

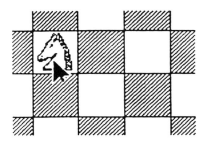

The following diagrams consist of two parts. The first part describes an input event and its related communication concepts, and the second one shows the new screen state after the communication concepts are processed. In what follows the *event* describes the input event received by the program, the *input CC* is the input communication concept encoded in the event, the *output CC* is the output communication concept produced as a result of processing the input CC, and the *display* is a description of how the program displays the output CC.

Event: the user presses the mouse button over the knight.
Input CC: **bind the** PIECE **input of the** MOVE **operation to** PIECE-UNDER-MOUSE.
Output CC: **the** PIECE **input of the** MOVE **operation is correct**.
Display: highlight the piece.

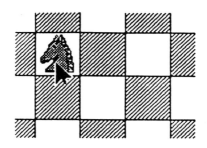

Event: user moves the mouse to adjacent square.
Input CC: **plan to bind the** LOCATION **input of the** MOVE **operation to** LOCATION-UNDER-MOUSE.
Output CC: **the** LOCATION **input of the** MOVE **operation is incorrect**.
Display: **nil**, only correct locations are highlighted.

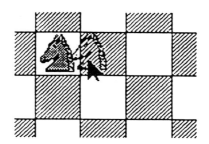

The program tells the user that if the piece is dropped in that location it is an illegal move. Should the user release the mouse button at this point the program would bind the location input to an incorrect value, beep to present the error, and de-activate the operation.

Event: user moves the mouse to adjacent square.
Input CC: **plan to bind the** LOCATION **input of the** MOVE **operation to** LOCATION-UNDER-MOUSE.
Output CC: **the** LOCATION **input of the** MOVE **operation is incorrect**.
Display: **nil**, only correct locations are highlighted.

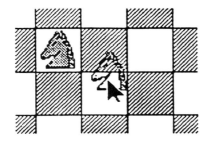

Event: user moves the mouse to adjacent square.
Input CC: **plan to bind the** LOCATION **input of the** MOVE **operation to** LOCATION-UNDER-MOUSE.
Output CC: **the** LOCATION **input of the** MOVE **operation is correct**.
Display: highlight the location.

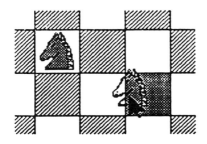

Event: user releases the mouse button.
Input CC: **bind the** LOCATION **input of the** MOVE **operation to** LOCATION-UNDER-MOUSE, **execute the** MOVE **operation**.
Output CC: **changed the** PIECE **input of the** MOVE **operation**.
Display: Erase the piece from the old location and display it at the new location.

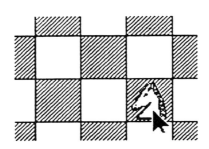

Should the user move the mouse to an adjacent location without releasing the mouse button, the program would interpret the event as a **not-plan to bind**, and would remove the highlighting from the location.

Note that even the low-level details of the interface, such as displaying feedback in response to individual mouse movements, can be expressed in terms of the communication concepts.

19.5 NEPHEW: A UIMS BASED ON COMMUNICATION CONCEPTS

The communication concepts described in the preceding text serve, not only to explain the behavior of graphical user interfaces, but also as the foundation of a UIMS. This section describes Nephew, a UIMS based on communication concepts [Szekely88]. Nephew is the successor to the COUSIN [Hayes85] UIMS.

Figure 19.1 shows the architecture of a typical Nephew application, in this case a chess program that behaves as described in Section 19.4. The program consists of four kinds of building blocks, called recognizers, commands, presenters, and the application objects (not shown in the figure).

FIGURE 19.1
THE ARCHITECTURE OF THE CHESS PROGRAM

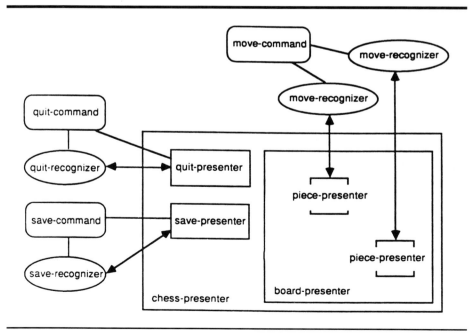

- **Recognizers.** A recognizer is a parser for a complete input gesture, such as a mouse click or a mouse drag. A recognizer produces communication concepts in response to input events in the gesture, and sends the concepts to a command for interpretation.

- **Commands.** A command is a communication concept interpreter for one specific operation. Each command receives communication concepts from recognizers and responds to them producing output communication concepts, which it sends to presenters to be displayed.

- **Presenters.** A presenter displays communication concepts.

As shown in Figure 19.1, an application implemented with Nephew consists of many recognizers, commands, and presenters. **Quit-command** and **save-command** are commands for the quit and save operations provided by the chess program. They are made accessible to the user through the presentation produced by **quit-presenter** and **save-presenter**. The **quit-recognizer** and **save-recognizer** are defined to activate their commands when they detect a click over their presentation. For instance, if the user clicks the mouse over the **quit-presenter**, then **quit-recognizer** sends an **activate** message to **quit-command**. Since the quit operation takes no parameters, **quit-command** responds to **activate** by sending itself an **execute** message, thus initiating the execution of the **quit** operation. The **move-recognizer**s and the **move-command** implement the behavior discussed in Section 19.4. Each piece presenter has a **move-recognizer** to handle drag gestures that start at the piece. While the mouse is dragging a piece, **move-recognizer** sends to **move-command** the sequence of communication concepts listed in Section 19.4. The output communication concepts are displayed by each **piece-presenter** and by **board-presenter**.

Nephew is implemented in Lisp on a Symbolics Lisp Machine using the Flavors object-oriented programming package. Nephew provides predefined building blocks of each kind, implemented as classes, and the job of the interface implementor is to assemble these building blocks to construct a program. The following subsections discuss the implementation in more detail.

19.5.1. Recognizers

A recognizer is a parser for a complete input gesture such as a mouse click or a mouse drag. Nephew implements recognizers as classes, one class for each kind of recognizer.

- **Recognizer-Basic** implements the behavior common to all recognizers. This includes methods to turn recognizers on and off, methods to connect recognizers to presenters, and methods to get the input events from a global event queue. The response to the input events is implemented by the subclasses listed below.

- **Click-Recognizer** implements the click gesture. The user interface implementor must supply the communication concepts that the recognizer transmits when the click starts and terminates.
- **Drag-Recognizer** implements the drag gesture. The default **Drag-Recognizer** is programmed to drag an outline of its presenter while the drag gesture is in progress. The implementor must provide the communication concepts that the recognizer transmits when the drag gesture begins, each time the mouse moves, and when the gesture terminates.
- **Dispatch-Recognizer** implements the standard dispatch behavior for distributing events to other recognizers. Instances of **Dispatch-Recognizer** are attached to presenters with sub-presenters to dispatch events to the presenters attached to the sub-presenters.
- **Window-Move-Mixin** is a subclass of **Drag-Recognizer** that allows windows to be moved by dragging them by their title bar.

For example, in the chess program implementation shown before in Figure 19.1, the **move-recognizers** are instances of **Drag-Recognizer**, and **quit-recognizer** and **save-recognizer** are instances of **Click-Recognizer**. Instances of **Dispatch-Recognizer**, not shown in the figure, are attached to **board-presenter** and **chess-presenter** to distribute the input events to the other recognizers.

19.5.2. Commands

A command is a communication concept interpreter for one specific operation. Nephew implements commands as classes, and implements input communication concepts as methods of command classes. The following are the methods that implement the communication concepts:

- **Execute:** executes the procedure that implements the operation
- **Preview:** invokes the procedure that implements the preview
- **Activate:** makes the command active
- **Deactivate:** makes the command inactive
- **Cancel:** cancels the execution of an operation

Newly defined command classes inherit default implementations for all of these methods. Implementors can override some of these methods to implement different interface styles.

In addition, a command must provide the following methods for each *input* of an operation. Nephew constructs default implementations for these methods from the operation declarations, but the developer can override them to provide non-standard behavior:

- *Input*: A command must provide a method called *input* corresponding to each operation input called *input*. These methods access the value of inputs or their plan component. For instance, the **move-command** used in the chess program provides methods called **piece** and **location**, corresponding to the piece and location parameters of the move operation.

- **Set-***input*: Likewise, a command must provide a method called **set-***input* corresponding to each operation input called *input*. These methods set the value of inputs or their plan component. For instance, **move-command** provides methods **set-piece** and **set-location** to set the command's piece and location inputs.

- **Test-***input*: Likewise, a command must provide a method called **test-***input* to test whether a value is a legal input.

- **Alternatives-***input*: Generates the set of valid inputs for input.

For instance, the **move-command** used in the chess program overrides the **test-piece** and **test-location** methods with predicates that define the rules of chess. **Move-command** also overrides the **alternatives-piece** method to return the set of pieces that can be moved at any given time, and the **alternatives-location** method to return the locations to which the selected piece can be moved. The alternatives methods are not used in the chess interface described above, but they could be used in an interface that highlights the pieces that can be moved, and the locations where a selected piece can be moved. No changes to the chess application would be needed to add this feature to the user interface.

Nephew also provides a library of command classes that implement common interface styles:

- **Command-Basic** provides the behavior common to all commands by defining default implementations for the methods listed above.

- **Input-Prompt-Mixin** provides facilities to associate a set of recognizers with each command input, and to switch on the appropriate recognizers when the application program requests input. Switching the recognizers on will allow them to receive input events and thus decode communication concepts that set the inputs.

- **Hour-Glass-Mixin** automatically runs the **hour-glass-recognizer** while an operation is executing. This recognizer displays an hour-glass cursor and intercepts all input events.

- **Confirmation-Mixin** overrides the **execute** method. Before invoking the application operation it switches on a recognizer to prompt the user for a confirmation to execute the operation.

For example, in the chess program the **quit-command** is an instance of a command class that includes **Confirmation-Mixin** so that the user is asked to confirm before exiting the chess program. The **save-Command** uses the **Input-Prompt-Mixin** to prompt for the file to save the state of the game.

19.5.3. Presenters

A presenter displays communication concepts. Nephew implements presenters as classes, one class for each particular way of displaying the communication concepts for each kind of object. Nephew provides presenter classes to display a variety of generic application classes such as lists, structures, and arrays, and also to display commands and even presenters themselves.

In Nephew, complex presentations are constructed by connecting several presenter instances to form a tree. Presenters with children are called *parent* presenters, and the children are called *sub-presenters*. For instance, in the chess example the board is a presenter, and the pieces are sub-presenters of the board presenter.

The following are the presenter classes in Nephew's library:

- **Presenter-Basic** provides the basic facilities to link presenters to the objects they present, and provides all the hooks into the graphics package. **Presenter-Basic** displays its object as a string identifying the type of object (e.g., a chess-piece). This is useful in the initial stages of the implementation of a user interface.

- **Borders-Mixin** provides the facilities to define the borders, background, and foreground of presenters.

- **Window-Mixin** provides the facilities to attach a presenter to a window.

- **Structured-Presenter** provides the facilities for a presenter to have sub-presenters.

- **Record-Presenter, List-Presenter** are sub-classes of **Structured-Presenter** that can present records and lists. They provide the methods that know how to construct and update sub-presenters for their respective data structures.

- **Homogeneous-Presenter** is a sub-class of **Structured-Presenter** for structured objects whose components are all of the same type. The sub-classes of **Homogeneous-Presenter** can use a single sub-presenter to display all the components of an homogeneous structured object, thus saving a large amount of storage. **Homogeneous-Array-Presenter** and **Homogeneous-List-Presenter** are sub-classes of **Homogeneous-Presenter** specialized to arrays and lists.

- **Rectangular-Alignment-Mixin** provides definitions to align sub-presenters in columns or rows.

- **String, Icon, Bitmap** and **Color-Presenter** provide commonly used presentations.

The chess program uses many of these classes. For example, the **piece-presenter**s are instances of **Icon-Presenter**, **board-presenter** is an instance of **Homogeneous-Array-Presenter**, and it uses the **Borders-Mixin** to define the borders of the board. The menu containing the save and quit commands is presented using a **List-Presenter** to present the list of **save-command** and **quit-command**, and uses the **Rectangular-Alignment-Mixin** to align the presentations in a column, left aligned, and with some space between the items.

Nephew presenters, commands, and recognizers are similar to Smalltalk's MVC views and controllers [Kasner88]. The main difference is that the role of the controllers is played by commands and recognizers in Nephew. By separating gesture handling (recognizers) from dialogue control (commands), Nephew simplifies the design of the controllers.

Presenters, controllers, and recognizers are also similar to MacApp's [Schmucker86] views and commands. The role of commands in both systems is very similar, serving to collect the inputs for the program operations. Nephew takes the idea one step further by using commands as an object representation of the program operations and allowing a command to be used anywhere that an object can be used. For example, the commands can be displayed with a presenter.

19.6 CLASSIFICATION AND SEPARATION IN INTELLIGENT INTERFACES

This section first gives a definition of *intelligent interface* and then shows how communication concepts and Nephew could be used to construct interfaces that are intelligent according to the definition given below.

19.6.1 Intelligent Interfaces

When a program communicates with the user it has to make certain decisions, called *communication decisions*, about the concepts it communicates. The program must decide *what* information to communicate to the user, *when* to communicate it, and *how* to encode it. Also, the program must *decode* the input from the user, and then *interpret* the decoded concept.

A user interface can be called *intelligent* in the measure to which communication decisions are conditioned on an analysis of the information listed below [Rissland82]:

- **Program model:** a model of the capabilities of the program, such as the objects it supports, and the operations it provides. Also included here is a description of the program's user interface design choices (e.g., whether the program uses a menu to display the operations).
- **User model:** a model of the characteristics of the user of the program, such as his or her expertise, preferences, and past history of interaction with the program.
- **Task model:** a model of the tasks the user wants to accomplish when using the program.

- **Workstation model:** a model of the characteristics of the workstation such as its operating system, speed, and input and output devices.
- **Knowledge about interface design:** knowledge about graphic design, wording of error messages, interaction styles, and so on.

For instance, an interface that decides whether to use a menu or a command line interface based on an analysis of the user model (e.g., to find out how familiar a user is with a program) is more intelligent than one that makes the decision irrespective of the information contained in the user model.

There are two major ways in which these models can be used. The difference comes from whether the knowledge is used only at the time the program is designed, or whether the program itself can reason with this knowledge at run time.

If the knowledge is used only at design time, it is used to make user interface design decisions, which are then hardwired into the specification of the program. Software tools that aid in incorporating intelligence into a user interface at design time can be called *designer's assistants*.

If the knowledge is used at run time, the program can make user interface design decisions tailored to the specific user and specific interaction problems that occur while the user is interacting with a program. These kind of interfaces can be called *adaptive*.

Figure 19.2 shows how interfaces are constructed using Nephew. The interface designer, represented by the box labeled **reasoning component** chooses presenters, commands, and recognizers from the **building block library**, and glues them together using **Nephew.**

In Nephew's current implementation, the reasoning component is a human acting at design time rather than at run time. A designer selects building blocks from the Nephew library, tailors them to a specific application, and

FIGURE 19.2
CONSTRUCTING INTERFACES WITH NEPHEW

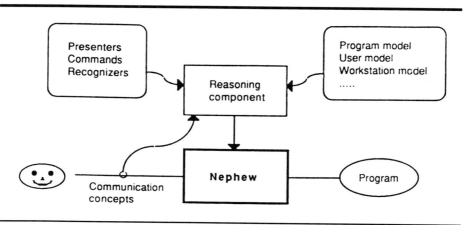

defines the connections between them. Given the architecture of Nephew, part of the reasoning component could be replaced by a designer's assistant and an adaptive interface. The designer's assistant would help the human designer choose and tailor the building blocks. The adaptive interface would be part of the Nephew run-time environment, and it could tailor and replace building blocks after reasoning about the state of the dialogue with the user. The following subsections discuss how communication concepts and the architecture of Nephew facilitates the automation of the reasoning component.

19.6.2. Revising Communication Decisions

Intelligent interfaces operate by generating or revising communication decisions. At design time, a designer's assistant generates communication decisions by suggesting different input techniques and different ways to display information. The human designer selects from the possibilities offered by the assistant and then iterates revising the decisions before settling on a design. The usefulness of such an automated assistant is hampered if the different designs cannot be quickly implemented and tested. Separation allows replacing the modules that implement the different designs without reprogramming, so separation facilitates testing different designs. An adaptive interface places even more stringent requirements on separation because the design decisions are changed at run time, and hence must be made without reprogramming.

For instance, consider the following alternative interface designs for an operation with a single parameter.

■ The parameter gets the value of the currently selected object, and the operation is chosen from a menu. The Macintosh interface has many examples of this design (e.g., cut and paste).

■ The operation is presented as an icon next or close to the presentation of the object that it acts upon. Clicking on the operation icon invokes the operation. For instance, in the Macintosh interface the *close-window* operation is presented as an icon, called the *close box*, in the top left corner of the window to which it applies. Each window has its own close box.

■ The operation is presented as an icon and the parameter is specified by dragging a presentation of the object into it. For example, the Macintosh Finder presents the *delete-file* operation as a trash-can icon. Files are deleted by dragging their presentation to the trash icon.

In Nephew, all these interfaces are defined in terms of the set of communication concepts discussed in Section 19.3. So, the modules that implement the different interface designs can be plugged into the functionality portion of the application without reprogramming. The revised communication decisions suggested by a designer's assistant could be implemented automatically and tested immediately by the human designer.

19.6.3. Reasoning About Building Blocks

A problem with many toolkits is that it is hard to find the appropriate building block for a given situation. Classification can be used to construct a designer's assistant to help user interface designers to find the right building block and to tailor it for a given situation.

Communication concepts can be used to describe building blocks, providing a powerful language for designer's assistants to index into a database of building blocks. A query by example browsing tool such as Rabbit [Tou82] or Backbord [Yen88] can then be used to find candidate building blocks given the specification of a few attributes of the building block.

For instance, suppose the drag-recognizer building block was described as follows:

> The dragger can be used to decode the **activate** communication concept.
>
> It is appropriate for operations that are presented as an icon.
>
> It is appropriate when the potential parameter objects are presented as icons.
>
> It can be used with operations that require at least one input.

Suppose the designer's problem is to design the input side of the interface for an operation with a single parameter. The designer first specifies a query for a recognizer to activate an operation with a single parameter. Given that many recognizers can activate operations, the browsing tool returns multiple choices (e.g., the designs for single parameter operations discussed above). The designer can then refine the query, say, by specifying that both the operation and the parameters will be displayed as icons, and narrow down the set of building blocks to find the above dragger.

Describing the building blocks in terms of the communication concepts also facilitates constructing consistent interfaces. For instance, if the designer specifies a command icon that presents the *command active* communication concept using reverse video, then the tool can easily detect an inconsistency if the designer specifies another command icon that also uses reverse video to present the *correct input* communication concept. The designer's assistant can point out the inconsistency and suggest ways to correct it.

19.7 FINAL REMARKS

The language of communication concepts described in this paper has two salient features:

- The communication concepts specify, in abstract terms, *what* information a program communicates with a user, without specifying *how* that information is communicated.

■ The communication concepts support the transmission of all the information needed to implement a wide variety of graphical interfaces.

The main consequence of these two features is that communication concepts can be used to define an application/user-interface interface, that is, the interface between the application and user interface modules of a program. The language specifies, not only *what* information must be supplied by the application module in order to support the user interface, but also *how* this information must be encoded.

This language is good from the modularity and code reusability point of views. The user interface can be changed without affecting the application portion of the program, and the interface building blocks can be reused because they are plug-compatible with the application portion of the program. Such a clean architecture is important for the construction of intelligent interfaces because it facilitates revising user interface design decisions. Also, communication concepts are concepts that intelligent interfaces can reason about when making design decisions.

Acknowledgments

I am grateful to the following people for their helpful comments: Richard Cohn, Mike DeBellis, John Granacki, Brian Harp, Phil Hayes, Richard Lerner, Brad Myers, Robert Neches, Barbara Staudt, Joseph Sullivan, Sherman Tyler, and John Yen. I also want to thank Kim Chau Luu for her help with the figures.

References

[Arens88] Arens, Y., Miller, L. Shapiro, S. C., and Sondheimer, N. K. 1988. Automatic Construction of User-Interface Displays. In *AAAI 88, The Seventh National Conference on Artificial Intelligence*, pp. 808–813.

[Encyclopae74] Encyclopaedia Britannica, Inc. 1974. *Micropaedia*, p. 45. Volume 3, Encyclopaedia Britannica, 15 edition.

[Foley82] Foley, J., and van Dam, A. 1982. *Fundamentals of Interactive Computer Graphics*. Addison-Wesley. pp. 218–243.

[Foley88] Foley, J., Gibbs, C., Kim, W. C., and Kovacevic, S. 1988. A Knowledge-Based User Interface Management System. In *CHI'88 Conference Proceedings*, ACM, pp. 67–72.

[Green86] Green, M. 1986. A Survey of Three Dialogue Models. *ACM Transactions on Graphics*, 5(3), 244–275.

[Hayes85] Hayes, P., Szekely, P., and Lerner, R. 1985. Design Alternatives for User Interface Management Systems Based on the Experience with COUSIN. In *CHI'85 Conference Proceedings*. New York: ACM, pp. 169–175.

[Kamran83] Kamran, A. 1983. Issues Pertaining to the Design of a User Interface Management System. In *Proceedings of the Workshop on User Interface Management Systems,* Springen-Verlag, pp. 43–48.

[Kasner88] Kasner, G., and Pope, S. 1988. A Cookbook for Using the Model-View Controller User Interface Paradigm in Smalltalk-80. *Journal of Object-Oriented Programming* 1(3), 26–41.

[Moran81] Moran, T. 1981. The command language grammar: a representation for the user interface of interactive computer systems. *International Journal of Man-Machine Studies,* 15, 3–50.

[Newman79] Newman, W., and Sproull, R. 1979. *Principles of Interactive Computer Graphics.* McGraw-Hill.

[Olsen86] Olsen, D. R. J. 1986. MIKE: The Menu Interaction Kontrol Environment. *ACM Transactions on Graphics,* 5(4), 318–344.

[Rissland82] Rissland, E. 1982. Ingredients of Intelligent User Interfaces. *International Journal of Man-Machine Studies,* 21, 377–388.

[Schmucker86] Schmucker, K. J. 1986. *Object-Oriented Programming for the Macintosh.* Hayden Book Company, pp. 84–164.

[Smith84] Smith, R., Lafue, G., and Vestal, S. 1984. Declarative Task Description as a User-Interface Structuring Mechanism. *Computer,* pp. 29–38.

[Szekely88] Szekely, P. 1988. *Separating the User Interface from the Functionality of Application Programs.* Ph.D. thesis CMU-CS-88-101, Carnegie-Mellon University.

[Tanner83] Tanner, P., and Buxton, W. 1983. Some Issues in Future User Interface Management System (UIMS) Development. *IFIP WG 5.2 Workshop on User Interface Management.*

[Tou82] Tou, F. F., Williams, M., Fikes, R., Henderson, A., and Malone, T. 1982. RABBIT: An Intelligent Database Assistant. In *AAAI 82, The National Conference on Artificial Intelligence,* William Kaufman, Inc., pp. 314–318.

[Yen88] Yen, J., Neches, R., and DeBellis, M. 1988. Specification by Reformulation: A Paradigm for Building Integrated User Support Environments. In *AAAI 88, The Seventh National Conference on Artificial Intelligence,* Morgan Kaufman, Inc., pp. 814–818.

INDEX

DATE DUE

DEMCO NO. 38-298